GLOBAL CREDIT REVIEW

Volume 4

NUS National University of Singapore | RMI Advancing Risk Management for Singapore and Beyond

World Scientific

Published by

World Scientific Publishing Co. Pte. Ltd.
5 Toh Tuck Link, Singapore 596224
USA office: 27 Warren Street, Suite 401-402, Hackensack, NJ 07601
UK office: 57 Shelton Street, Covent Garden, London WC2H 9HE

and

Risk Management Institute
National University of Singapore
21, Heng Mui Keng Terrace, Level 4
Singapore 119613

Library of Congress Control Number: 2013205296

British Library Cataloguing-in-Publication Data
A catalogue record for this book is available from the British Library.

GLOBAL CREDIT REVIEW
Volume 4

ISBN 978-981-4635-47-9 (pbk)

In-house Editor: Li Hongyan

Typeset by Stallion Press
Email: enquiries@stallionpress.com

Printed in Singapore

Message from the Editor

The Risk Management Institute (RMI), a university-level research institute at the National University of Singapore, strives to be a world class center in risk management where scholars, regulators and industry practitioners gather to advance cutting edge knowledge that has immediate relevance to the financial system. The Credit Research Initiative (CRI) launched in 2009 epitomizes the Institute's effort in advancing the knowledge frontier and raising the practice of financial risk management.

In line with this objective, this fourth annual volume of the Global Credit Review targets financial practitioners, policy makers and academics with an interest in credit markets. The Global Credit Review provides an overview of important developments in the global credit markets and the regulatory landscape. The GCR also covers theoretical and empirical research on credit ratings and credit risk, and reports on recent findings and evolutions of the RMI-CRI.

In the early part of 2014, financial markets have been driven by headline news such as the IMF-supported rescue package for Ukraine, the change of leadership in the US Federal Reserve and the continued concerns of China's economic growth. Overall, the global economy certainly has not taken off as many had hoped in Q4 2013. Growth in the US saw a sharp pullback in Q1 2014 from Q4 2013. The US economy barely grew and only expanded 0.1% (Y-o-Y), while the Japanese economy is still trying to gain a foothold despite aggressive stimulus under Abenomics. However, things are a bit better in the Eurozone having seen their economy expanding further in March. But overall, the growth in the European economic bloc is still anemic as the region remains plagued by high unemployment. On the other hand, Asia continues to grow at a low-6% growth rate. While strong by the standard of developed economies, it is just on par with Asia's performance in the past 2 years. Furthermore, the US Fed is poised to raise interest rates in 2015 as it continues tapering its bond purchases after over 5 years of loose monetary policy. Markets have to deal with the rebalancing of risk in an environment where global interest rates look to be on the uptrend in the longer term. Also, the increased policing by regulators to protect the global financial environment from excessive systemic shocks adds another challenge of balancing between risk and return.

To keep abreast with new developments in the credit markets, this edition of the Global Credit Review provides some critical analysis, reviews the introduction of new regulations and also offers new insights to address the challenges ahead in the new world.

This fourth volume of the Global Credit Review begins with *An Assessment of Systemic Risk in the Japanese Banking Sector* by Prof. Kanno Masayasu, which uses RMI PDs to measure the systemic risk in the Japanese banking sector. This is followed by the article *Evolving Global Capital Regulations and its Impact, Particularly on Asia* by Mr. Thomas Cho and Mr. Dexter Tan. In the third article *Actuarial Par Spread and Empirical Pricing of CDS by Decomposition* Prof. Jin-Chuan Duan proposes a measure similar to CDS spreads that summarizes the information embedded in the term structure of physical probabilities of default (PDs). This is followed by an article by Ms. Jenny Bai, Mr. Heikki Seppala and Prof. Ser-Huang Poon on *Fast Approximation of Loan Portfolio Loss: Concentration Risk and Multifactor Adjustments*. In the fifth article *Rejection and Partial Rejection of Consumer Credit Application*, Prof. Steven Plaut provides some new insights in the credit rationing and credit application process. Next is a joint article by IACMP and Oliver Wyman — *Perspectives on the Evolving Role of Enterprise-wide stress testing*. We conclude this fourth volume of the GCR with an updated *NUS-RMI Credit Research Initiative Technical Report* which offers technical details on the implementation of the current RMI-CRI corporate default prediction model and its performance. For a more elaborate discussion and update on our default predictions produced thus far, please refer to our *Quarterly Credit Report* for more details.

We hope you enjoy reading this fourth volume and welcome your feedback on the Global Credit Review and our Credit Research Initiative.

Prof. Jin-Chuan Duan
Project Lead, Credit Research Initiative
NUS-RMI
Cycle & Carriage Professor of Finance
NUS Business School

Contents

An Assessment of Systemic Risk in the Japanese Banking Sector

Masayasu Kanno
Faculty of Business Administration
Kanagawa University
2946, Tsuchiya, Hiratsuka
Kanagawa, Japan 259-1293
mkanno@kanagawa-u.ac.jp

Keywords: Systemic risk, distress insurance premium, deposit insurance system, dynamic conditional correlation, NUS–RMI–CRI's PDs.

INTRODUCTION

Recent financial crises such as the global financial crisis and the European debt crisis have happened in rapid succession. Compared to Western banks, Japanese banks suffered little from these crises, with the exception of Norinchukin bank, which suffered a loss of 190 billion yen in fiscal year 2009, by investing in securitized products. Norinchukin bank is a cooperative bank in the agriculture, forestry, and fisheries industry and a major institutional investor. Also, other major Japanese banks suffered from the crises, although their losses in absolute amounts were smaller.

Some large Japanese financial institutions declared bankruptcy during the Heisei great recession of 1997–1998 prior to the global financial crisis. Hokkaido Takushoku Bank, Yamaichi Securities Company, Sanyo Securities Company, Long-Term Credit Bank of Japan, and Nippon Credit Bank all defaulted before the appearance of material systemic risk.

Given this history, there is indeed a need in Japan for a system for monitoring and measuring systemic risk. It is mainly recently that banks have begun to contribute to systemic risk by holding securitized products or credit derivatives.

In the past several years, triggered by the global financial crisis, the banking supervisory authorities have been focusing not only on the micro level prudential policy emphasizing traditional consumer protection, but also on macro level prudence focused on the soundness of the financial system as a whole. This latter approach must take into account the interconnectedness between the financial system and the world economy.

In 2009, the Financial Stability Board (FSB) was established as a successor to the Financial Stability Forum. As an international body representing central bankers and international financial bodies such as the Basel Committee for Banking Supervision (BCBS), it intends to promote financial stability.

In September 2009, the G20 leaders requested the FSB to designate "Global Systemically Important Financial Institutions" (G-SIFIs). As a result, the FSB, IMF, and BIS cooperatively adopted the three valuation points — size, interconnectedness, and substitutability — as the evaluation criterion for G-SIFIs (see IMF, BIS and FSB (2009)).

The BCBS issued a consultative paper for the evaluation method of Global Systemically Important Banks (BCBS, 2011). The BCBS adopted a scoring-based valuation approach, and picked five evaluation criteria of wide-ranging categories such as size, interconnectedness, lack of readily available substitutes, global (cross-jurisdictional) activity, and complexity. In November 2011, BCBS published 29 bank names as G-SIFIs and announced the policy to revise and publish the G-SIFIs list officially in the month of November every year. Three Japanese mega-bank groups and Bank of China were selected then in the Asia-Pacific region.

The finance and banking literature has of course been discussing systemic risk for decades. Fortunately, many papers helpfully define various aspects of systemic risk. For example, we can look to Allen and Wood (2006), Fender and McGuire (2010), or Giesecke and Kim (2011) for the definition and concept, Adrian and Brunnermeier (2011), Acharya *et al.* (2010), Huang *et al.* (2009; 2012a), or Lehar (2005) for the modeling, Acharya *et al.* (2010), Bartram *et al.* (2007), Huang *et al.* (2009; 2012a; 2012b), or Duan and Zhang (2013) for measuring systemic risk, and Davis and Karim (2008), Cocco *et al.* (2009), or Haldane (2009) for work on early warning indicators.

Supervisory authorities will benefit from appropriate systemic risk measures, because Value at Risk (VaR) or Expected Shortfall (ES) are the measures that can be used only in normal times. For the purpose of macro prudence, the supervisory authority in each country must monitor the change of systemic risk. We summarize three recently proposed systemic risk measures below.

Adrian and Brunnermeier (2011) proposed the risk measure CoVaR for quantifying the risk for the financial system as a whole. CoVaR of an institution is defined as the VaR of the whole financial system conditional on the institution being in distress. CoVaR only implicitly takes into account the size, the probability of default (PD), and the correlation of each institution. ΔCoVaR as the difference between the CoVaR conditional on the distress of an institution and the CoVaR conditional on the normal state of the institution captures the marginal contribution (MC) of a particular institution to the overall systemic risk. CoES is also the ES measure with properties similar to CoVaR. However, CoVaR does not have a sub-additivity property, which is a major disadvantage since one cannot aggregate the systemic risk contributions of each financial institution comprising the financial system. Additionally, CoES and CoVaR provide individual measures that do not sum up to the total risk measure.

Acharya *et al.* (2010) introduced systemic expected shortfall (SES) to measure listed financial institutions' contributions to systemic risk. It is defined as an institution's propensity to be undercapitalized when the financial system as a whole is undercapitalized. The SES measure is built on publicly available share prices and balance sheet values and is easy to compute. They also introduced marginal expected shortfall (MES) as a measure of an institution's losses in the tail of the system's loss distribution. MES only implicitly takes into account the size, the PD, and the correlation of each financial institution.

The methodology we follow most closely in this paper was first proposed in Huang *et al.* (2009), who formulated a framework to integrate economically the main characteristics of systemic risk — size, leverage, and interconnectedness. The systemic risk is measured by the hypothetical distress insurance premium (DIP) which is the price of insurance against the distress loss of the total liabilities in the entire banking sector, and is based on ex ante measures of probabilities of default for individual banks and forecasted equity return correlations. Huang *et al.* (2012a) focused on the time-series change of systemic risk of the banking sector in the Asia-Pacific region excluding Japan and China for the period from January 2005 to May 2009. They also adopted the Dynamic Conditional Correlation (DCC), which was proposed by Engle (2002) as the correlation factors. It is possible to incorporate any pair of correlations for the heterogeneous portfolio using DCC. Huang *et al.* (2012b) calculated the hypothetical insurance premium for 19 US bank holding companies and assessed their individual MCs to systemic risk. In general, they find that a bank's contribution to systemic risk is roughly linear in its PD but highly nonlinear with respect to its size and the asset correlation.

Huang *et al.* (2009; 2012a; 2012b) adopted the method for estimating a bank's PD from its single-name CDS spread. It is difficult to specify the PD from the CDS spreads during the crisis period, because they reflect not only the default risk premium but also the liquidity risk premium that tends to escalate during the crisis period. Finally, CDS spreads do not exist for most of the banks in the Japanese banking sector, making this method problematic for Japanese regulators. Additionally, they treated the liability size and calculated the equity return correlations as inputs.

Duan and Zhang (2013) studied the systemic risk of a banking system arising from cascading defaults due to "interbank linkages". They argue that any large negative external shock can in principle trigger "cascading defaults", but shocks to systematic risk factors, as opposed to banks' idiosyncratic elements, are more likely to drive cascading defaults and hence to cause higher systemic risk. This paper proposes a structural model for a banking system, in which bank assets are subject to both systematic and idiosyncratic risks and bank liabilities contain interbank exposures which may or may not be subject to netting. Their model proposes two useful measures: "systemic exposure" and "systemic fragility". The former characterizes the expected losses due to interbank linkages under some prescribed macro stress scenario, whereas the latter measures the pervasiveness of bank defaults under the same condition. However, the liability side of major Japanese banks is mostly composed of consumers' deposits, and the average deposits-to-liability ratio in FY2007, as to their interbank counterparties' deposits, was only approximately 3% for major Japanese banks including regional banks. Hence, it may not be useful to apply Duan and Zhang (2013)'s measures to the Japanese banking sector.

In summary, both MES and DIP are measures for each financial institution's loss conditional on the system being in distress, while CoVaR measures the systemic losses conditional on each financial institution being in distress. By contrast, Duan and Zhang (2013)'s measures are based on cascading defaults due to interbank linkages. For risk factors, both CoVaR and MES only implicitly take into account the size, the PD, and the correlation of each financial institution, while DIP treats these risk factors as direct inputs. The two advantages of DIP compared to CoVaR or MES are as follows: one is that the systemic risk indicator measures the risk for a portfolio of heterogeneous sized banks, and the other is that the measure offers an assessment of the contribution of each bank or each bank group to the systemic risk indicator.

The motivation of our research is the development of a practical and forward looking systemic risk indicator for banking supervisory authorities to use in measuring and monitoring the systemic risk based on available data. After considering the features of these four types of measures,[1] we extend the approach of the DIP and empirically analyze its applicability to the Japanese banking sector. Owing to the scarcity of data for Japanese banks in the single-name CDS market, we cannot derive one-year PDs from single-name CDS spreads in the same way as Huang *et al.* (2009; 2012a; 2012b). Nonetheless, we can use the forward-looking PDs published by NUS–RMI–CRI[2] as an alternative. It is worth noting that the PDs from CDS spreads are risk-neutral probabilities while the PDs from NUS–RMI–CRI are physical probabilities which are conceptually the right kind of likelihood of default relevant to the issue of systemic risk. We construct a measurement methodology which can be utilized even by supervisory authorities facing financial sectors without CDS data.

I. MEASUREMENT APPROACH AND DATA

This section explains the systemic risk measurement approach and the data utilized.

I.1. Measurement Approach

We employ a credit portfolio simulation approach to derive the DIP proposed by Huang *et al.* (2009) on the Japanese banking sector.

There are, however, three important differences between the two approaches. Firstly, we derive the DIP in the explicitly tractable manner using a standard simulation technique in financial risk management. In contrast, Huang *et al.* (2009) do not get into the technical aspects of each bank's default and the whole banking sector's default.

Secondly, we calculate the physical measure of systemic risk or the actual distress loss in accordance with usual credit portfolio risk management framework, whereas Huang *et al.* (2009) calculate a risk-neutral measure of systemic risk.

Thirdly, we focus on Japanese banks and consider the Japanese banking sector's safety net for protecting depositors by the deposit insurance system in Japan, to calculate the effective loss-given-default rate[3] for each bank. Doing so is important because the liability side of most Japanese banks is mainly composed of consumers' deposits and interbank counterparties' deposits. More specifically, the average deposits-to-liability ratio in FY2007 was approximately 78% for major Japanese banks[4] including regional banks and 95% for regional banks, in particular. As a matter of fact, none of Huang *et al.* (2009; 2012a; 2012b) treat the Japanese banking sector, and Huang *et al.* (2012a) indeed analyzes a portfolio of 22 major banks in Asia-Pacific region but excludes Japanese and Chinese banks.

We use the "structural model approach of credit risk" (Merton, 1974) for modeling the default risk of each bank included in the banking sector. This model approach is based on the theory that default happens when the bank's asset value is below a predefined default threshold at a fixed maturity.

We define a standard normally distributed random variable for the standardized asset value log-return at the maturity date of a bank i $(i = 1, 2, \ldots, N)$ as X_i, where X_i is latent. If X_i is below the default threshold γ_i, then the bank defaults. The relationship between the default indicator D_i and the random variable X_i is as follows:

$$D_i = 1 \Leftrightarrow X_i \in (-\infty, \gamma_i]. \tag{1}$$

The default threshold γ_i at the risk horizon can be expressed as follows:

$$\gamma_i = \Phi^{-1}(PD_i), \tag{2}$$

where PD_i is the constant for the bank i's empirical PD for one year's risk horizon, and $\Phi^{-1}(\cdot)$ is the inverse of the standard normal cumulative distribution function $\Phi(\cdot)$.

The DIP can be calculated by Monte Carlo simulation hereinafter prescribed (see Fig. 1 for reference). The bank i's liability loss variable L_i is expressed in terms of i-specific parameters such as PD_i, LGD_i and EAD_i as follows:

$$L_i = D_i \cdot LGD_i \cdot EAD_i, \tag{3}$$

where D_i is the default indicator function associated with PD_i, expressed in Eqs. (1) and (2). LGD_i is the random variable for bank i's loss-given-default on its liability side and is independent of D_i. EAD_i is the constant for bank i's exposure-at-default on the liability side which is fixed each fiscal year.

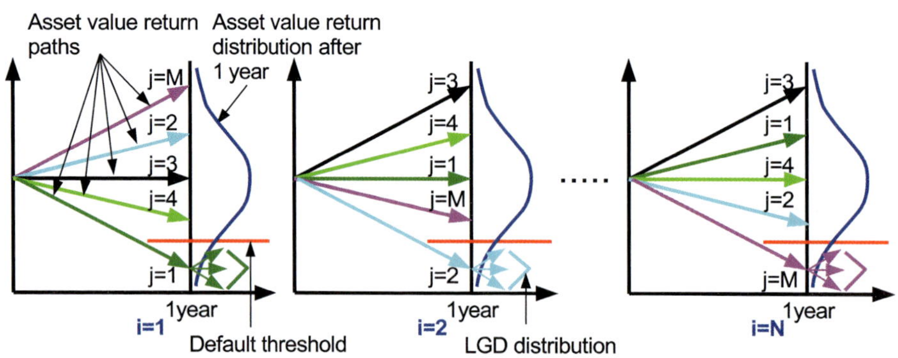

	i=1	i=2	i=3	·····	i=N	L vs L_{min}	Systemic default?
j=1	$L_{1,1}$	$L_{2,1}$=0	$L_{3,1}$	·····	$L_{N,1}$=0	$SL_1 \geq L_{min}$	○
j=2	$L_{1,2}$=0	$L_{2,2}$	$L_{3,2}$=0	·····	$L_{N,2}$=0	$SL_2 < L_{min}$	×
···	·	·	·	·····	·	·····	··
j=M	$L_{1,M}$=0	$L_{2,M}$=0	$L_{3,M}$	·····	$L_{N,M}$	$SL_M \geq L_{min}$	○

Figure 1. Systemic default mechanism.

Next, we set the total banking sector's liability loss variable as

$$SL = \sum_{i=1}^{N} L_i. \qquad (4)$$

If the SL at a scenario exceeds the minimum loss threshold $L_{\min}$ with relation to the total liabilities of the entire banking sector,[5] then we suppose the whole sector suffers from "systemic default" (namely, the default of the banking sector).

Hence, the DIP is expressed as the conditional expectation of SL under the physical measure P as follows:

$$DIP = E^P[SL \mid SL \geq L_{\min}], \qquad (5)$$

where DIP is the insurance premium that protects against distressed loss. $L_{\min}$ is the optimal level of which must be calibrated from the empirical data during the occurrence period of the systemic risk. Of course, no such data exist for the Japanese banking sector, so we use 15% of the sector's debt total as the figure in accordance with Huang *et al.* (2009).[6]

I.2. Bank's MC

We define each bank's MC[7] to the whole sector's DIP as follows:

$$MDIP \equiv E^P[L_i \mid SL \geq L_{\min}]. \qquad (6)$$

Owing to this property, the additivity of each individual bank's systemic risk measure DIP is maintained and we can decompose the portfolio's systemic loss into the individual bank's systemic loss.

Hence, from the macro-prudential view of a financial supervisory authority, the change in systemic risk can be monitored for each individual bank, owing to the MC calculated in Eq. (6). DIP's MC will be utilized as the judgment criteria to update G-SIFIs.

I.3. DIP Calculation by Monte Carlo Simulation

As shown in Fig. 1, we set a random number for a bank i's asset log-return X_i at each simulation scenario j ($j = 1, 2, \ldots, M$) as $x_{i,j}$. We set the simulation scenario number M to 500,000. Then, we decompose the correlations calculated by the three-month moving window into the lower triangular matrix by Cholescky Factorization, and generate the correlated random number series for the asset return path $x_{i,j}$ from the independent random number series and this lower triangular matrix.

In turn, we create new random numbers for LGDs for each defaulted asset value return path and calculate LGD distribution. It should be noted that the random numbers are for the loss to the bank's liability and are independent of the random number series for the asset value return paths.

I.4. Data

As the model's risk parameters, we need PD, LGD, and EAD for each bank, as well as the correlation matrix. We obtained the PDs from the above-mentioned web site of NUS–RMI–CRI[8] as of the end of July 2012.

Huang *et al.* (2009; 2012a; 2012b) chose to use 0.55 as LGD, which is typically assumed by researchers. However, the figure is the loss-given-default on a bank's asset side. By contrast, we need the figure on banks' liability sides. The liability sides of banks are mostly composed of consumers' deposits, which are protected under the deposit insurance system in Japan.[9] According to DICJ (2005), the average of loss-given-defaults as the ratio of a financial assistance amount by the Deposit Insurance Corporation of Japan to a bank's total liability amount related to 42 Japanese financial institutions with assets over 200 billions yen is 26.8%. These 42 institutions defaulted in the period from the end of March 1991 to the end of March 2004. Again, according to DICJ (2010), the average loss-given-default as the ratio of failed financial institutions' estimated loss amounts to their total deposit amounts for the US in 2009 is 21.3%, which is not too far from the Japanese figure.

Hence, we simulate the random numbers for the LGDs, following the symmetric triangular distribution with mean $LGD_t = 0.268$ at each time t and having the domain of definition $[0, 2 \times LGD_t]$ for each liability value return path.

We populate the figures on the liability side of each bank's financial statement with the bank's EADs, and the correlations between each bank's equity returns as correlation coefficients.

I.5. Correlation

We calculate the correlation between the asset returns of different banks. As the correlations between asset returns are latent and unobservable variables, we use the correlations between equity returns as a proxy for correlations between asset returns. This assumption is imposed in the CreditMetrics model, which is one of the most famous commercial-based portfolio credit risk models. In addition, Hull and White (2004) also measured the asset return correlation by the equity return correlation, as the equity market is the most liquid financial market and can incorporate new information on an institution's default risk in a timely way.

The idea of using the equity return correlation as a proxy for the asset return lies in the fact that when the firm leverage is constant, the asset return correlation equals the equity return correlation. When the leverage ratio is time-varying, this relationship breaks down and the level of the discrepancy depends on the comovements between asset returns and leverages and the comovements between changes in the leverages as well. As this fact is more likely to hold approximately true in the short window, we compute equity return correlations over one-quarter time horizons. Additionally, we apply the historical equity return correlations for the one-quarter window, calculated one month before the start date of the risk horizon, to the correlations for the forward-looking one-year risk horizon.

We use daily data in accordance with Huang *et al.* (2012a). In addition, we define the pre-crisis period as June 1, 2006 to June 30, 2007 and the during-crisis period as July 1, 2007 to March 31, 2009.

Since we use equity data, analyzed banks are limited to listed companies. We select Japanese major banks or banking groups for which equity data are available[10] and nine regional banks with available equity data and suitable for the BIS uniform international standard (Refer to Table 1). According to their Basel capital

Table 1. Japanese major banks (mega-banks and regional banks in accordance with the BIS Uniform International Standard).

Bank Name	BIS Std.	Equity Cap.	Net Assets	Total Assets	BIS Ratio	ROE
Shinsei Bank	DOM	749,823	965,261	11,525,762	11.74	6.51
Aozora Bank	DOM	800,348	768,060	7,259,076	14.29	11.03
Mitsubishi UFJ Bank	ITN	5,803,166	7,985,225	155,801,981	11.20	3.72
Mitsubishi UFJ T&B	ITN	1,283,191	1,394,324	20,701,464	13.13	6.20
Resona Bank	DOM	891,595	1,200,783	26,401,292	9.81	3.38
Chuo Mitsui T&B	DOM	697,963	743,245	14,233,141	11.20	4.90
Sumitomo Trust	ITN	1,013,338	1,280,954	22,180,734	11.84	4.57
SMBC	ITN	3,130,008	5,080,747	108,637,791	12.19	2.88
Mizuho Bank	DOM	1,831,262	2,370,250	69,698,828	11.97	2.63
Mizuho CB	ITN	2,143,528	3,648,383	88,098,142	12.17	2.43
Mizuho T&B	ITN	389,946	464,293	6,332,381	15.87	6.16
Gunma Bank	ITN	292,674	357,313	5,960,025	11.89	4.91
Chiba Bank	ITN	550,839	580,168	9,835,939	12.20	5.60
Yokohama Bank	DOM	653,625	748,348	11,989,520	10.80	5.45
82 Bank	ITN	370,740	462,849	6,090,385	13.00	6.09
Shizuoka Bank	ITN	592,095	717,391	9,098,425	14.70	6.51
Shiga Bank	ITN	194,915	256,868	4,115,109	11.16	4.74
Chugoku Bank	ITN	349,469	377,558	5,791,039	13.03	6.03
Yamaguchi Bank	ITN	285,815	336,005	4,900,810	10.66	5.83
Iyo Bank	ITN	260,458	378,047	4,824,111	11.64	5.40

Notes: 1. Equity Cap.: Equity Capital, DOM: Domestic Standard, ITN: BIS Uniform International Standard.
2. Use of FY2007 data. Units — amount: million yen, ratio: %.
3. BIS Standard dated March end, 2012. For Yokohama Bank, BIS Uniform International Standard has been applied since FY2010.
4. BIS ratio is the capital adequacy ratio (consolidated base).
5. Aozora Bank and Yamaguchi Bank are respectively analyzed after November 15, 2006 and October 2, 2006, since their equity data exists after those dates.
Source: Japanese Bankers Association.

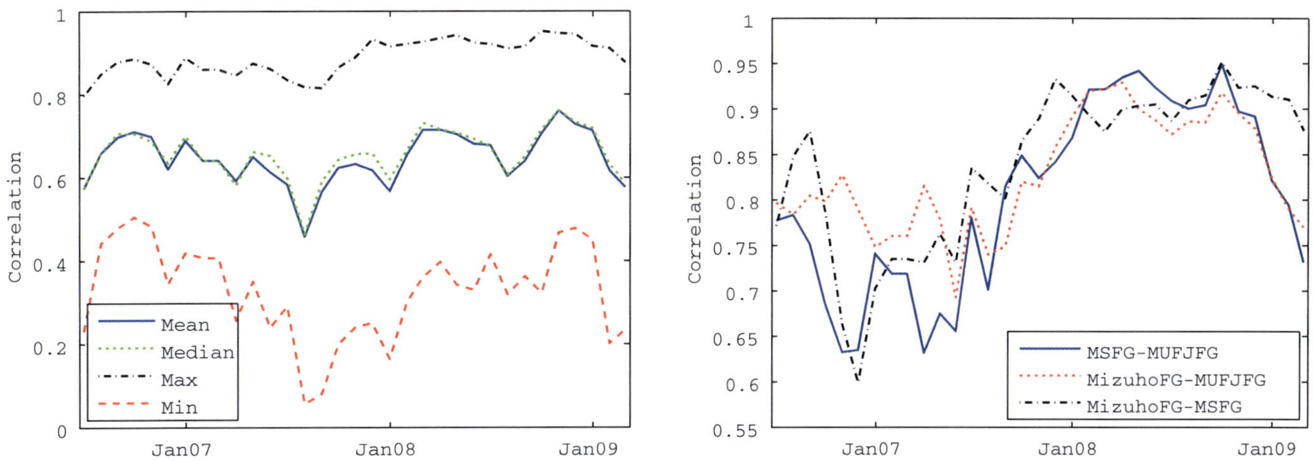

Figure 2. Correlation changes (left panel: pairs from whole sector; right panel: pairs from among Mitsubishi UFJ FG, Sumitomo Mitsui FG and Mizuho FG).

adequacy ratios (consolidated), all of the banks excluding Resona Bank have capital ratios higher than 10% at the end of March 2008.

If we calculate banks' equity capital ratios from their financial statements, the ratios of some Japanese mega-banks (Sumitomo Mitsui Banking Corporation, Mizuho Bank, and Mizuho Corporate Bank) are all low at about 2%.

In banking risk management, the portfolio risk amount is heavily affected by the variation of correlations between the assets or liabilities. Hence, if the variance of the correlation itself increases, the time-variation of the risk amount increases, affecting the banking sector as a whole.

II. RESULTS

II.1. Correlation

We calculated the correlations for any two banks' stock returns as risk parameters. The number of pairwise correlations we calculated was 91 prior to the crisis and 120 during the crisis. As the pairwise number is large, we first calculated the time series of descriptive statistics such as mean, median, maximum, and minimum for correlations.

The result for the whole sector and three mega-bank groups (Mitsubishi UFJ FG, Sumitomo Mitsui FG, and Mizuho FG) is shown respectively in the left and right panels of Fig. 2. The mean and standard deviation in the time series direction for these four descriptive statistics of the whole sector and the pairs from the three mega-bank groups are shown respectively in the upper and lower tables of Table 2.

For the whole sector, the means in time series directions for the Mean and the Median are both about 0.65. In contrast, for the three mega-bank groups, the means in time series directions are all in the 0.8 level and we can see that these three pairs' correlations are much higher than the sector's Mean and Median. This implies a strong interconnectedness among the three mega-bank groups.

II.2. DIP

We show four histograms of loss distributions for the sector as a whole by simulation in Fig. 3 and show the change of both DIP amount (unit: trillions of Japanese yen) and DIP ratio in Fig. 4. Here, DIP ratio is the figure obtained by dividing the DIP at each time point by the

Table 2. Correlation descriptive statistics.

Total Sector	Mean	Median	Max	Min
Mean	0.646	0.656	0.888	0.328
Std	0.063	0.060	0.043	0.115
Mega-Banks	**SM/MU**	**MZ/MU**	**MZ/SM**	
Mean	0.804	0.827	0.839	
Std	0.102	0.063	0.089	

Note: Each symbol is as follows: MU: Mitsubishi UFJ FG, SM: Sumitomo Mitsui FG, MZ: Mizuho FG.

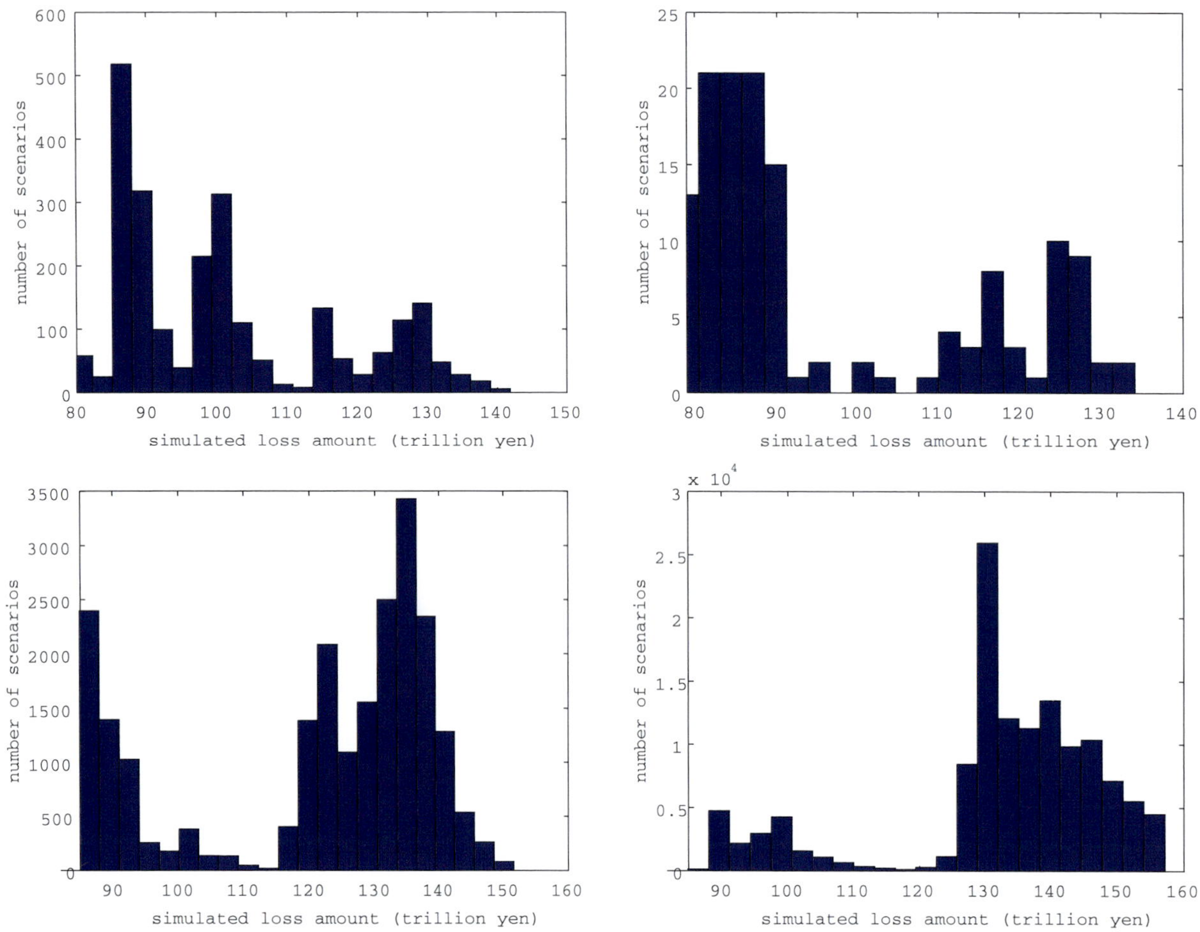

Figure 3. Histograms of simulated loss amount distributions.
Note: The left upper panel is as of the end of June 2006, with the minimum loss threshold $L_{\min} = 80$ trillion yen, the right upper panel is as of the end of March 2007, with the $L_{\min} = 79$ trillion yen, the left lower panel is as of the end of March 2008, with the $L_{\min} = 85$ trillion yen, and the right lower panel is as of the end of March 2009, with the $L_{\min} = 88$ trillion yen.

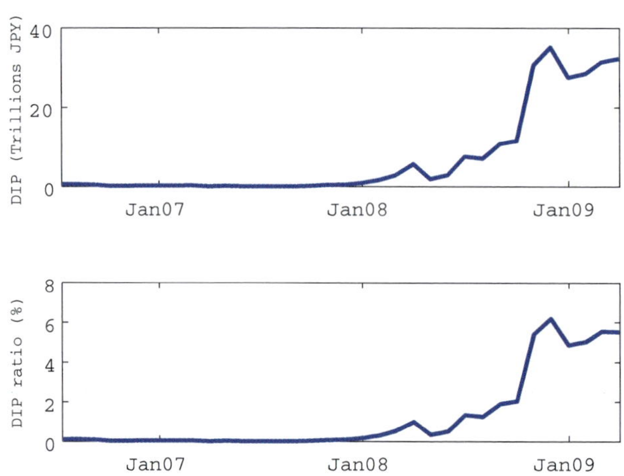

Figure 4. DIP amount and DIP ratio.
Note: The upper panel plots the systemic risk measure DIP amount in Japanese yen and the lower panel plots the DIP ratio as a percentage of total liabilities at the time.

Table 3. DIP and MC.

Date	MC by Bank																DIPs	DIP	DIP
	Shinsei	Aozora	MUFG	Resona	STB	SMFG	MHFG	Chiba	Yoko	Gunma	Shizu	82	Shiga	Chugo	Iyo	Yama		Ratio 1	Ratio 2
2006/6/30	0.008	—	0.256	0.033	0.003	0.075	0.156	0.001	0.000	0.000	0.000	0.000	0.001	0.002	0.001	—	0.54	0.10	17.1
2006/7/31	0.009	—	0.283	0.036	0.004	0.083	0.171	0.001	0.001	0.000	0.000	0.000	0.001	0.002	0.001	—	0.59	0.11	18.9
2006/8/31	0.007	—	0.233	0.030	0.005	0.052	0.167	0.002	0.001	0.001	0.000	0.000	0.001	0.002	0.000	—	0.50	0.09	15.9
2006/9/30	0.000	—	0.059	0.012	0.002	0.024	0.022	0.001	0.000	0.000	0.000	0.000	0.000	0.000	0.000	—	0.12	0.02	3.9
2006/10/31	0.003	—	0.088	0.017	0.003	0.046	0.011	0.001	0.000	0.000	0.000	0.000	0.000	0.001	0.000	—	0.17	0.03	5.5
2006/11/30	0.003	—	0.105	0.019	0.003	0.051	0.019	0.001	0.000	0.000	0.000	0.000	0.000	0.002	0.000	—	0.20	0.04	6.4
2006/12/31	0.004	—	0.124	0.027	0.003	0.070	0.003	0.001	0.000	0.000	0.000	0.000	0.000	0.001	0.000	—	0.23	0.04	7.5
2007/1/31	0.005	—	0.131	0.018	0.007	0.073	0.001	0.000	0.000	0.000	0.000	0.000	0.000	0.001	0.000	—	0.24	0.04	7.5
2007/2/28	0.006	—	0.145	0.015	0.008	0.080	0.002	0.000	0.000	0.000	0.000	0.000	0.000	0.001	0.000	—	0.26	0.05	8.2
2007/3/31	0.001	—	0.014	0.002	0.001	0.007	0.005	0.000	0.000	0.000	0.000	0.000	0.000	0.000	0.000	—	0.03	0.01	1.0
2007/4/30	0.003	—	0.057	0.010	0.004	0.032	0.013	0.000	0.000	0.000	0.000	0.000	0.000	0.001	0.000	—	0.12	0.02	3.8
2007/5/31	0.001	—	0.014	0.002	0.001	0.007	0.001	0.000	0.000	0.000	0.000	0.000	0.000	0.000	0.000	—	0.03	0.00	0.8
2007/6/30	0.000	—	0.007	0.001	0.000	0.004	0.000	0.000	0.000	0.000	0.000	0.000	0.000	0.000	0.000	—	0.01	0.00	0.4
2007/7/31	0.000	0.000	0.002	0.001	0.000	0.002	0.002	0.000	0.000	0.000	0.000	0.000	0.000	0.000	0.000	0.000	0.01	0.00	0.2
2007/8/31	0.001	0.000	0.020	0.003	0.001	0.012	0.016	0.000	0.000	0.000	0.000	0.000	0.000	0.000	0.000	0.000	0.05	0.01	1.7
2007/9/30	0.003	0.002	0.052	0.013	0.004	0.026	0.050	0.001	0.000	0.000	0.000	0.000	0.000	0.000	0.000	0.000	0.15	0.03	4.7
2007/10/31	0.008	0.005	0.064	0.036	0.013	0.088	0.146	0.003	0.001	0.000	0.000	0.000	0.000	0.000	0.000	0.000	0.36	0.07	11.4
2007/11/30	0.009	0.006	0.129	0.043	0.016	0.101	0.189	0.004	0.001	0.000	0.000	0.000	0.000	0.000	0.000	0.000	0.50	0.09	15.6
2007/12/31	0.007	0.008	0.308	0.049	0.017	0.172	0.338	0.005	0.002	0.000	0.000	0.001	0.000	0.000	0.000	0.001	0.91	0.17	28.5
2008/1/31	0.018	0.016	0.536	0.104	0.033	0.321	0.576	0.010	0.006	0.001	0.000	0.001	0.001	0.000	0.000	0.001	1.62	0.30	51.0
2008/2/29	0.034	0.034	0.969	0.179	0.046	0.608	0.984	0.026	0.008	0.001	0.001	0.003	0.002	0.001	0.000	0.007	2.90	0.54	91.1
2008/3/31	0.100	0.073	1.895	0.340	0.082	1.242	1.823	0.042	0.020	0.003	0.001	0.008	0.003	0.003	0.000	0.010	5.64	0.99	168.9
2008/4/30	0.033	0.025	0.633	0.126	0.023	0.415	0.608	0.017	0.009	0.001	0.001	0.004	0.002	0.001	0.000	0.003	1.90	0.33	56.9
2008/5/31	0.059	0.034	1.038	0.180	0.037	0.578	0.956	0.022	0.010	0.002	0.001	0.003	0.002	0.001	0.000	0.002	2.93	0.52	87.6
2008/6/30	0.143	0.088	2.746	0.406	0.128	1.533	2.410	0.022	0.029	0.007	0.004	0.005	0.004	0.003	0.000	0.005	7.53	1.33	225.4
2008/7/31	0.142	0.091	2.482	0.447	0.125	1.386	2.306	0.026	0.032	0.009	0.002	0.005	0.003	0.005	0.000	0.005	7.07	1.24	211.4
2008/8/31	0.174	0.141	3.825	0.690	0.155	2.250	3.448	0.050	0.058	0.011	0.003	0.005	0.002	0.002	0.000	0.008	10.82	1.91	323.8
2008/9/30	0.247	0.161	3.560	0.770	0.274	2.531	3.737	0.100	0.114	0.019	0.008	0.016	0.007	0.006	0.001	0.011	11.56	2.04	345.9
2008/10/31	0.627	0.409	10.282	1.657	0.770	6.573	9.391	0.298	0.317	0.094	0.078	0.063	0.027	0.024	0.010	0.103	30.72	5.41	919.2
2008/11/30	0.729	0.456	12.664	1.348	0.892	7.263	10.747	0.315	0.286	0.081	0.065	0.067	0.056	0.031	0.012	0.133	35.15	6.19	1, 051.5
2008/12/31	0.575	0.361	9.833	1.061	0.662	5.659	8.695	0.198	0.227	0.068	0.046	0.052	0.030	0.022	0.009	0.087	27.58	4.86	825.3
2009/1/31	0.616	0.366	10.491	0.850	0.689	5.556	9.137	0.228	0.243	0.096	0.060	0.046	0.047	0.026	0.011	0.081	28.54	5.03	854.0
2009/2/28	0.706	0.384	11.870	0.436	0.796	6.143	10.214	0.251	0.279	0.075	0.078	0.028	0.049	0.029	0.012	0.110	31.46	5.54	941.2
2009/3/31	0.656	0.345	11.949	0.914	0.898	6.471	10.152	0.266	0.274	0.085	0.073	0.028	0.048	0.031	0.018	0.092	32.30	5.53	938.5

Notes: 1. DIP and MC are expressed in units of trillions of Japanese yen. Each date corresponds to the month end. DIP ratio 1 is expressed in units of percents. And DIP ratio 2 indicates the DIP ratio 1 compared to the one on March 31, 2007.

2. Shinsei: Shinsei Bank, Aozora: Aozora Bank, MUFG: Mitsubishi UFJ FG, Resona: Resona Holdings, STB: Sumitomo Trust & Banking, SMFG: Sumitomo Mitsui FG, MHFG: Mizuho FG, Chiba: Chiba Bank, Yoko: Yokohama Bank, Gunma: Gunma Bank, Shizu: Shizuoka Bank, 82: 82 Bank, Shiga: Shiga Bank, Chugo: Chugoku Bank, Iyo: Iyo Bank, Yama: Yamaguchi FG.

total liability amount in the entire sector to adjust the differences among banks included in the calculation cohort.

We also calculate MCs using monthly data from the end of June 2006 to the end of March 2009. The calculations of DIPs and MCs are based on Eqs. (5) and (6) respectively. The results are shown in Table 3.

II.2.1. DIP

First, looking at the four panels of Fig. 3, while we can see some peaks around the threshold on the upper left panel prior to the crisis, there are two peaks on the other three panels during the crisis from the end of March 2007 through March 2009, the highest peak of which is related to Japanese mega-bank groups such as Mitsubishi UFJ FG, Sumitomo Mitsui FG, and Mizuho FG, which can be seen in Table 3. In addition, many scenarios passed beyond the threshold, especially from March 2008 through March 2009.

Next, Fig. 4 shows that both the DIP amount and the DIP ratio grew with time while the loss amount for the banking sector as a whole greatly increased. Looking back at Table 3, we see that the DIP ratio increased by a factor of about 169 from March 2007 to March 2008 and by a factor of up to about 1,052 by March 2009. This striking increase was caused not by correlations but mainly by PDs; because correlations' trend for the whole sector was almost flat during the crisis period, while it is shown in Fig. 5 that PDs greatly increased during the crisis period.

II.2.2. MC

Three mega-bank groups, namely Mitsubishi UFJ FG, Sumitomo Mitsui FG, and Mizuho FG, overwhelmed all the others' MC at almost every point in time. Their total share amounted to about 81–90% during the crisis period. This result is acceptable given that the three mega-bank groups have already been designated as G-SIFIs. It is understood respectively from Table 1 and the right panel of Fig. 2 that the determinants of the MC to the systemic risk indicator for each bank are primarily size and correlation too. For the PD, it is understood from Fig. 6 that the PDs for three mega-bank groups are smaller than the PDs for both Aozora bank and Shinsei

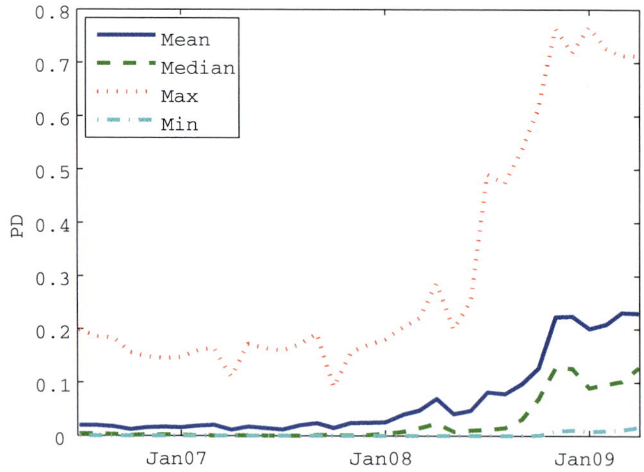

Figure 5. PD by descriptive statistics.
Note: Banks in data sample are as follows: Shinsei Bank, Aozora Bank, Mitsubishi UFJ FG, Resona Holdings, Sumitomo Trust & Banking, Sumitomo Mitsui FG, Mizuho FG, Chiba Bank, Yokohama Bank, Gunma Bank, Shizuoka Bank, 82 Bank, Shiga Bank, Chugoku Bank, Iyo Bank, Yamaguchi FG.

bank mostly during the crisis period and the PD does not have a big effect on the MC.

II.3. Determinants of DIP

As mentioned in Sec. II.2.2, during the crisis period, the MCs for three mega-bank groups carried considerable weight in DIP as the systemic risk premium of the whole banking sector.

However, during the crisis period, the available CDS spreads data were restricted to three mega-bank groups out of the 16 Japanese banks or bank groups listed in Table 3. Therefore, we adopted the physical probabilities of default (PDs) of NUS–RMI–CRI instead of risk-neutral ones. CDS spreads include information on not only the expected actual default losses of the banking sector but also the default risk premium in the global financial market and liquidity risk premium components.

While the systemic risk premium DIP is based on the physical measure, an interesting question is how much of the variation is attributable to the change in the expected default rate of the banking sector and how much is driven by market sentiments or a liquidity shortage.

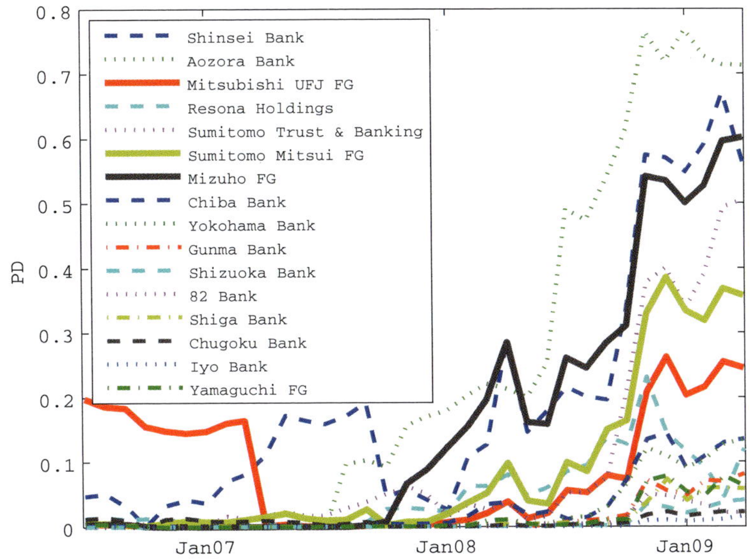

Figure 6. PDs by bank.

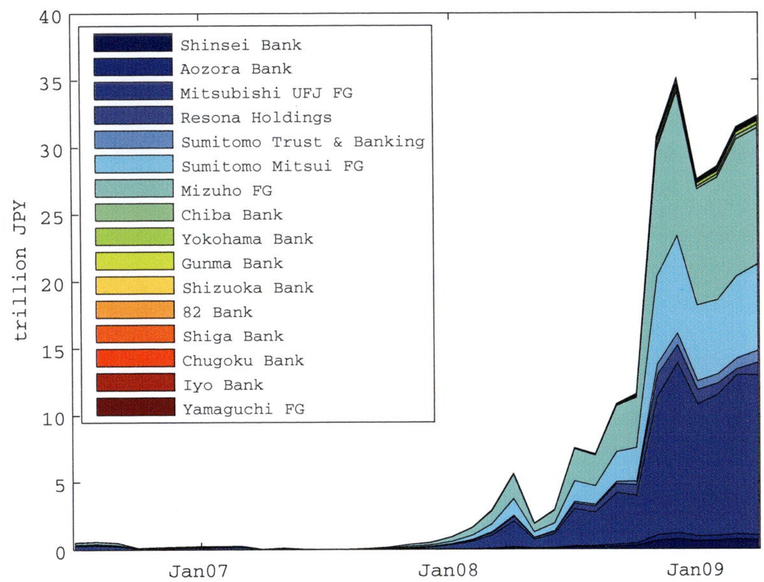

Figure 7. MCs by bank.

Hence, we examine the impact of single-name CDS spreads of mega-banks and the volatility index on the systemic risk premium. The volatility index used is the Nikkei Stock Average Volatility Index (Nikkei 225 VI)[11] in the Japanese financial market, a measure of market sentiment.

In addition, the proxy for the default risk premium in the global financial market is the difference between spreads on corporate bonds rated BBB and AAA (see Chen *et al.*, 2009); the liquidity risk premium is proxied by the difference between 3M–LIBOR and the past three months' average of overnight index swap rates at each date.

To examine the effect of four risk factors on the systemic risk premium, we run linear regression analyses. In multiple regression analysis, variance inflation factors (VIFs)[12] are used to check the serial correlations between the variables, and the signs of

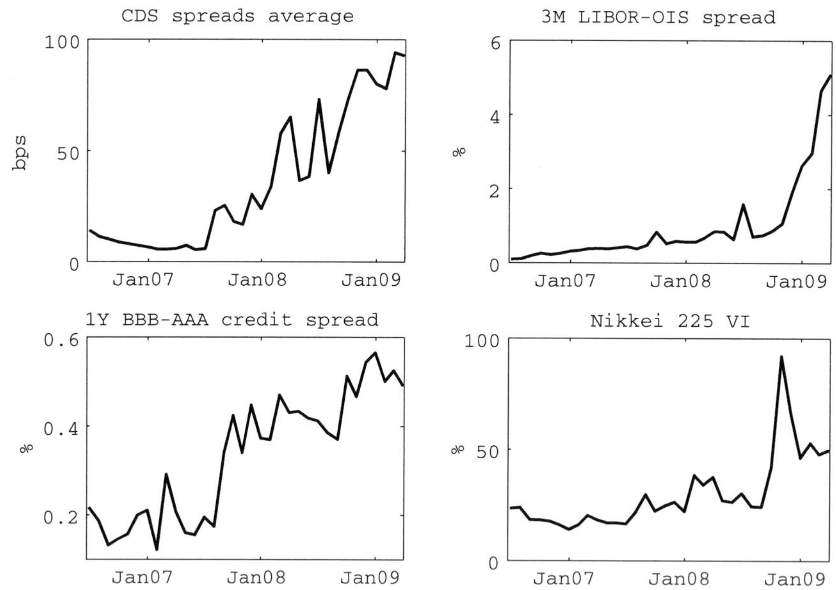

Figure 8. Time-series of risk factors.

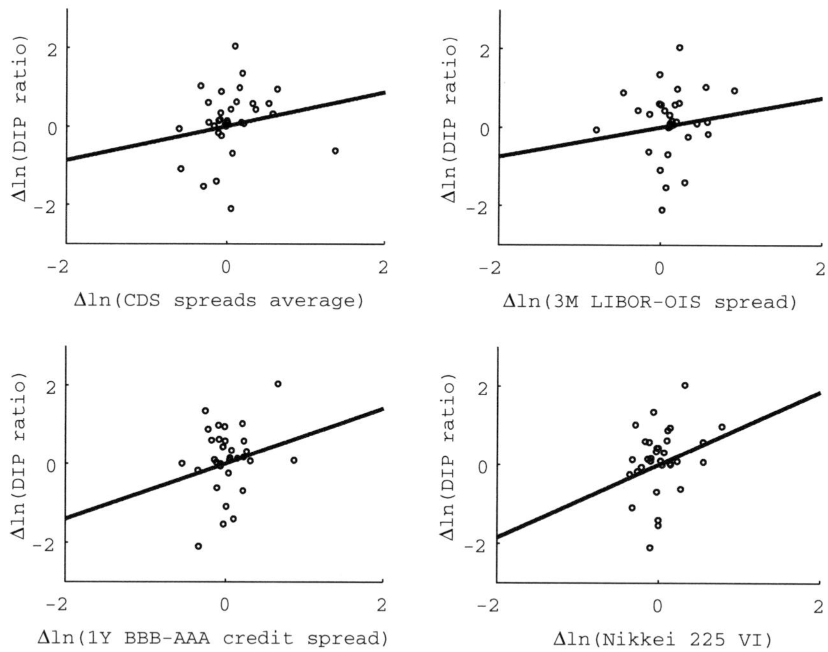

Figure 9. Regressions of risk factors on the logarithm change of systemic risk premium.

the variables are checked during successive steps of the selection. In these analyses, the dependent variable is the systemic risk premium–DIP ratio, and we select four variables as candidates of explanatory variables, namely, CDS spreads' average over the three mega-bank groups (four mega-banks), 3M–LIBOR–OIS spread, 1Y–BBB–AAA credit spread, and Nikkei 225 VI (see Fig. 8). We take the changes of logarithms of both the DIP ratio and four risk factors. Each of the four panels in Fig. 9 draws a scatter diagram and a regression line with zero intercept, based on the monthly data for the changes of the logarithms of both the DIP ratio and each financial market variable.

Table 4. Determinants of the systemic risk.

Dependent Variables	Regression-1	Regression-2	Regression-3	Regression-4
CDS spreads' average	0.433 (1.113)			
BBB-AAA spread		0.373 (0.844)		
LIBOR-OIS spread			0.704 (1.342)	
Nikkei 225 VI				0.928* (1.695)
R^2	0.037	0.022	0.053	0.082

Notes: 1. Regression-1 to Regression-4 are single regression analyses. A stepwise multiple regression analysis is also run, and the result corresponds to one of Regression-4.
2. The dependent variable is the logarithm change of the systemic risk premium for 16 Japanese banks listed in Table 3, defined as the DIP. The figures in the parenthesis are *t*-statistics.
"*" denotes the significance at the two-sided 90% confidence interval.

The result for the regression analyses are shown in Table 4. Looking at Regression-1 to Regression-4, only a change of Nikkei 225 VI out of the four factors has a significant effect on a change of the systemic risk premium, with the expected positive sign. A 1% point increase in a change of the market risk premium will result in an increase of 0.925% in the systemic risk premium.

Finally, excluding multicollinearity between factors by VIFs, based on stepwise multiple regression analysis confirms that only one factor — Nikkei 225 VI — is statistically significant at the two-sided 90% confidence interval, with the expected positive sign. We recognize that a change of the market risk contributes to most of a change of the systemic risk premium during the crisis period.

III. CONCLUSIONS

First, this paper contributes to the literature by proposing a systemic risk measure to dynamically capture the increase in systemic risk for the banking sector as a whole in consideration of the protection under the deposit insurance system in Japan. Second, we validated the consistency with BCBS's selections that three mega-bank groups have been designated as G-SIFIs every year since November 2011. Third, we denoted that a change in market risk contributed the most to the change of the systemic risk premium during the crisis period.

Our results show that our extended DIP is a hopeful measure but there is room to improve with future model validations. Finally, from the point of view of a banking supervisory authority, we expect this measure to be valued as one of the tools for monitoring systemic risk.

ACKNOWLEDGMENT

This work was supported by KAKENHI Grant Number 26380408.

NOTES

1 We count Duan and Zhang (2013)'s measures — systemic exposure and systemic fragility as one type.

2 The Credit Research Initiative (CRI) is a non-profit undertaking by the Risk Management Institute at National University of Singapore (NUS), which seeks to promote research and development in the critical area of credit risk. The foundation of the CRI is the PD model, which has been developed using a database of about 60,400 listed firms in the Asia Pacific, North America, Europe, Latin America, the Middle East, and Africa. They present PDs from this model at the web portal http://www.rmicri.org/. Refer to Duan *et al.* (2012) and RMI (2013) for the model's details.

3 For details, see the following paragraph "Data" in this section.

4 See Table 1 for the list of banks.

5 For reference, a percentage of the total liabilities of sample bank groups to the total liabilities of the entire banking sector including Japanese mega-bank groups and other major banks, regional banks, second-tier regional banks, Norinchukin bank is 68.3% as of the end of March 2008.

6 Huang *et al.* (2009) set the thresholds at 10%, 20% and 30%, and they reported similar results. Additionally, we calculated the insurance premium at some different threshold levels, and confirmed there are no substantial differences among the levels.

7 This is a kind of risk contribution. For details, refer to Kanno (2010, pp. 174–176).

8 *Source*: National University of Singapore, Risk Management Institute, CRI database. Available at http://rmicri.org [Accessed 10 August 2012].

9 The deposit insurance system provided a blanket guarantee on all deposits in 1996. Subsequently in April 2002, some types of deposits, such as time deposits, were shifted to the limited coverage. From April 2005, the scope of deposits under the limited coverage has been extended and the deposits under full coverage has been only limited to "deposits for payment and settlement purposes" which satisfy all of the following three conditions — "bearing no interest", "being redeemable on demand" and "providing normally required payment and settlement services". Excluding those "deposits for payment and settlement purposes", the protection of current deposits, ordinary deposits and specified deposits, which formally had been under the blanket guarantee, is total up to a maximum principal of 10 million yen plus accrued interest thereon per depositor per financial institution.

10 Norinchukin bank is excluded from the data sample because it neither issues shares nor deals with individual deposits.

11 This index, calculated and published by a Japanese newspaper company, Nikkei Inc., is the degree of expected fluctuation of the Nikkei Average Stock Price for one month forward and is similar to the VIX published by CBOE which is regarded as the "market gauge of fear" by practitioners. In the existing research of systemic risk, Huang *et al.* (2009) used the VIX as one candidate for the determinants of PDs connected with individual banks.

12 If the VIF is less than or equal to 5, then this indicates mutlicollinearity in the explanatory variable, and the variable is excluded from the list of candidate variables.

REFERENCES

Acharya, V. V., L. H. Pedersen, T. Philippon and M. P. Richardson (2010), Measuring Systemic Risk. New York University Stern School of Business, AFA 2011 Denver Meetings Paper.

Adrian, T. and M. Brunnermeier (2011), CoVaR. NBER, Working Paper, No. 17454.

Allen, W. and G. Wood (2006), Defining and Achieving Financial Stability. *Journal of Financial Stability*, 2(2), pp. 152–172.

Bartram, S., G. Brown and J. Hund (2007), Estimating Systemic Risk in the International Financial System. *Journal of Financial Economics*, 86(3), pp. 835–869.

BCBS (2011), Global Systemically Important Banks: Assessment Methodology and the Additional Loss Absorbency Requirement. Rules Text.

Chen, L., P. Collin-Dufresne and R. S. Goldstein (2009), On the Relation Between the Credit Spread Puzzle and the Equity Premium Puzzle. *Review of Financial Studies*, 22(9), pp. 3367–3409.

Cocco, J., F. Gomes and N. Martins (2009), Lending Relationships in the Interbank Market. *Journal of Financial Intermediation*, 18(1), pp. 24–48.

Davis, E. and D. Karim (2008), Comparing Early Warning Systems for Banking Crises. *Journal of Financial Stability*, 4(2), pp. 89–120.

Deposit Insurance Corporation of Japan (2005), Quantitative Analysis of Financial Institution Bankruptcies (in Japanese). *Deposit Insurance Research*, 4, pp. 1–240.

Deposit Insurance Corporation of Japan (2010), Latest Trend of the Resolution of Failed Financial Institutions in the United States of America (in Japanese). *Deposit Insurance Research*, 12, pp. 1–28.

Duan, J.-C., J. Sun and T. Wang (2012), Multiperiod Corporate Default Prediction — A Forward Intensity Approach. *Journal of Econometrics*, 1, pp. 191–209.

Duan, J.-C. and C. Zhang (2013), Cascading Defaults and Systemic Risk of a Banking Network. NUS Working Paper.

Engle, R. (2002), Dynamic Conditional Correlation: A Simple Class of Multivariate Generalized Autoregressive Conditional Heteroskedasticity Models. *Journal of Business and Economic Statistics*, 20(3), pp. 339–350.

Fender, I. and P. McGuire (2010), Bank structure, Funding Risk and the Transmission of Shocks across Countries: Concepts and Measurement. *BIS Quarterly Review*, September, pp. 63–79.

Giesecke, K. and B. Kim (2011), Systemic Risk: What Defaults Are Telling Us. *Journal of Management Science*, 57(8), pp. 1387–1405.

Haldane, A. (2009), Rethinking the Financial Network. Speech at the Financial Student Association, Amsterdam.

Huang, X., H. Zhou and H. Zhu (2009), A Framework for Assessing the Systemic Risk of Major Financial Institutions. *Journal of Banking and Finance*, 33, pp. 2036–2049.

Huang, X., H. Zhou and H. Zhu (2012a), Assessing the Systemic Risk of a Heterogeneous Portfolio of Banks during the Recent Financial Crisis. *Journal of Financial Stability*, 8, pp. 193–205.

Huang, X., H. Zhou and H. Zhu (2012b), Systemic Risk Contributions. *Journal of Financial Services Research*, 42, pp. 55–83.

Hull, J. and A. White (2004), Valuation of a CDO and an N-th to Default CDS without Monte Carlo Simulation. *Journal of Derivatives*, 12, pp. 8–23.

IMF, BIS and FSB (2009), Guidance to Assess the Systemic Importance of Financial Institutions, Markets and Instruments: Initial Considerations. Report to the G-20 Finance Ministers and Central Bank Governors.

Kanno, M. (2010), *Financial Risk Capital and Integrated Risk Management (in Japanese)*, Kinzai Institute for Financial Affairs Inc.

Lehar, A. (2005), Measuring Systemic Risk: A Risk Management Approach. *Journal of Banking and Finance*, 29(10), pp. 2577–2603.

Merton, R. C. (1974), On the Pricing of Corporate Debt: The Risk Structure of Interest Rates. *Journal of Finance*, 29(2), pp. 449–470.

NUS — Risk Management Institute (2012), CRI database, Available at http://rmicri.org [Accessed 10 August 2012].

NUS — Risk Management Institute (2013), NUS–RMI Credit Research Initiative Technical Report Version: 2013 update 1. *Global Credit Review*, pp. 77–167.

Evolving Global Capital Regulations and Its Impact Particularly on Asia

Dexter Tan
Risk Management Institute
National University of Singapore
rmidtkb@nus.edu.sg

Thomas Cho
Risk Management Institute
National University of Singapore
thomascho@nus.edu.sg

Keywords: Bank regulation, Basel III, capital requirements, capital adequacy ratio, Asian banks.

INTRODUCTION

Banks globally increasingly face demanding supervisory oversight requiring them to have higher levels of better quality capital and increased liquidity levels in a more rigorous tax and regulatory landscape.[1] However, with so many regulations imposed, it will not be straightforward for banks doing business worldwide to fulfill all the new requirements. This is especially difficult as regulatory authorities in certain countries are still in the developing stages of their regulatory frameworks.

The 2008 Global Financial Crisis pushed the preparation of the third Basel Accord, or Basel III, to a top priority on the global regulatory agenda. In September 2010, regulators from major countries around the world approved and released the guidelines and implementation timeline for Basel III. At the November 2010 Seoul Summit, the G20 discussed collaborative risk management and agreed, in principle, on the Basel III regime.

Even though the Basel accord is not legally binding, different jurisdictions are keen to follow Basel principles and criteria in achieving a sound banking system. But, policy makers still have discretion in implementing the final regulations. With the onset of Basel III, banks would have to enhance their level of risk management, compliance and corporate governance standards to follow the tighter requirements.

The Basel III framework sets out:

- Higher risk-adjusted capital ratio requirements, along with stricter rules on the types of loss-absorbing capital[2];
- More targeted guidelines for the risk-weighting of assets, especially with regards to capital market activities;
- The introduction of a leverage ratio[3] as a new monitoring tool for banks;
- The introduction of two new global liquidity standards: the Liquidity Coverage Ratio (LCR) and the Net Stable Funding Ratio (NSFR).[4,5]

The latest monitoring exercise by the Basel international group provides a glimpse of the present state of the global banking industry.[6] A survey of 227 banks showed that the total capital shortfall for the sector was EUR 3.3 bn in meeting a common equity

Tier 1 (CET1) minimum of 4.5%, and a capital shortfall of EUR 57.5 bn for a CET1 of 7.0%, which includes the capital conservation buffer in "good times". The average CET1 ratio for internationally active banks with Tier 1 capital in excess of EUR 3 bn (Group 1 banks), would fall from 11.0% to 9.5% if they implemented the new Basel III framework, partly due to a tightened definition of Tier 1 capital. Additionally, the weighted average Basel III Tier 1 leverage ratio for banks would be between 20 and 40 basis points lower under the new leverage ratio framework introduced in January 2014.[7] Weighted Tier 1 leverage ratios for Group 1 institutions would fall from the current 4.3% to 3.7% while the leverage ratio for Group 2 banks (all other banks outside Group 1) would fall from 4.8% to 4.4% following the new leverage ratio framework. The weighted average LCR for Group 1 and Group 2 banks were 114% and 132% respectively.

Figure 1 gives an overview of average Tier 1 capital ratios of all listed banks in leading Asian economies.

Currently, regulatory developments within different jurisdictions are progressing at a different pace with respect to capital reform, liquidity standards and disclosure requirements. Divergences do exist among the different jurisdictions, which makes adhering to capital legislation a complex task for lenders.

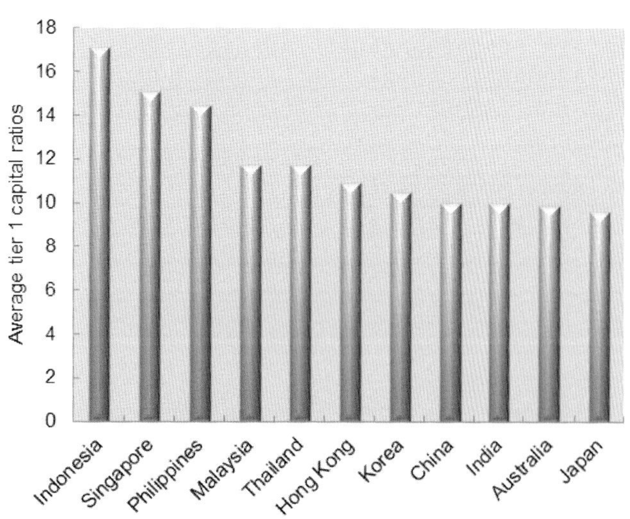

Figure 1. Tier 1 capital to risk weighted assets for listed banks domiciled in leading Asian economies, based on December 2012 annual financial statements.

Source: Bloomberg.

The article first introduces major capital regulatory developments in the United States, European Union and Asia. The next section lists the challenges of adhering to Basel III guided capital regulations in Asia and discusses the impact on Asian banks. Then it concludes with a discussion on what the future of banking regulation might be going forward.

I. REGULATORY DEVELOPMENTS

I.1. United States

The Federal Deposit Insurance Corporation (FDIC), the Office of the Comptroller of the Currency (OCC) and the Federal Reserve Board (Fed) issued final rules revising the regulatory capital framework for US banks in July 2013. The rules will be used to implement the Basel III framework, but also incorporate changes that are required by the Dodd–Frank Act.[8] In mid-March 2014, the Fed passed 29 of the 30 big banks that underwent the Dodd–Frank Act stress test, which sets out to determine if US banks have enough capital on hands to endure a major economic downturn. Another health check — the CCAR 2014 — at the end of March, however, saw more failures with the Fed only approving the capital plans of 25 out of the 30 banks. Plans of the five participating banks failed to make the cut with four being rejected based on qualitative concerns (Citigroup, HSBC North America, RBS Citizens and Santander USA). But Zions Bancorporation's plan was objected because it did not meet the minimum, post-stress Tier 1 common ratio of 5%. However, Bank of America was forced to re-submit a new capital plan to the Fed after discovering a USD4 billion accounting blunder that arrested its dividend and repurchase plans.

US Basel capital regulations do not apply to some small banks and non-qualified savings and loan holding companies. It is generally applicable to large US banks.[9,10] These so-called 'advanced approaches' rules would apply to national banks and financial institutions with USD 250 bn or more in consolidated assets or USD 10 bn or more in foreign exposure.[11] In short, that means large banks will have to introduce regulatory capital requirements for counterparty credit risk (CCR), credit valuation adjustments (CVA), wrong-way risk, as well as a more risk-sensitive approach for capitalization of exposures to central counterparties on risk weighted assets.

To comply with the market risk capital rule, any bank with significant trading activity has to use customized methods to determine their standardized measure and advanced measure (if applicable) for market risk.[12] The rule was modified in December 2013 to reflect modifications by the Organization for Economic Cooperation and Development regarding country risk classifications and conform to the Basel III revised capital framework.

As shown in Tables 1 and 2, lenders who are not using advanced measurement approaches are not required to comply with the minimum capital requirements until January 1, 2015. The Fed thinks that this would give smaller banks ample time to upgrade existing banking infrastructure and raise any additional capital needed to meet the new minimum capital

Table 1. Capital adequacy ratios for small US banks (non-advanced approaches banking organizations) and Basel III qualified savings and loan holding companies.

	January 1, 2015	**January 1, 2016**	**January 1, 2017**	**January 1, 2018**	**January 1, 2019**	**January 1, 2020**	**January 1, 2021**	**January 1, 2022**
Minimum CET1 ratio	4.5%	4.5%	4.5%	4.5%	4.5%	4.5%	4.5%	4.5%
Minimum Tier 1 capital ratio	6.0%	6.0%	6.0%	6.0%	6.0%	6.0%	6.0%	6.0%
Minimum total capital ratio	8.0%	8.0%	8.0%	8.0%	8.0%	8.0%	8.0%	8.0%
Capital conservation buffer		0.625%	1.25%	1.875%	2.5%	2.5%	2.5%	2.5%
Phase in of deductions from CET1	40%	60%	80%	100%	100%	100%	100%	100%
Percentage of unqualified instruments issued before September 12, 2010 includable in Tier 1 or Tier 2 capital	70%	60%	50%	40%	30%	20%	10%	0%

Source: Board of Governors of the Federal Reserve System, as of October 11, 2013.

Table 2. Capital adequacy ratios for large US banks (advanced approaches banking organizations).

	January 1, 2014[14]	**January 1, 2015**	**January 1, 2016**	**January 1, 2017**	**January 1, 2018**	**January 1, 2019**	**January 1, 2020**	**January 1, 2021**	**January 1, 2022**
Minimum CET1 ratio	4.0%	4.5%	4.5%	4.5%	4.5%	4.5%	4.5%	4.5%	4.5%
Minimum Tier 1 capital ratio	5.5%	6.0%	6.0%	6.0%	6.0%	6.0%	6.0%	6.0%	6.0%
Minimum total capital ratio	8.0%	8.0%	8.0%	8.0%	8.0%	8.0%	8.0%	8.0%	8.0%
Capital conservation buffer			0.625%	1.25%	1.875%	2.5%	2.5%	2.5%	2.5%
Phase in of deductions from CET1	20%	40%	60%	80%	100%	100%	100%	100%	100%
Percentage of unqualified instruments issued before September 12, 2010, or TruPS includable in Tier 1 or Tier 2 capital	80%	70%	60%	50%	40%	30%	20%	10%	0%
Percentage of unqualified instruments issued before May 19, 2010 includable in additional Tier 1 or Tier 2 capital.[15]	50%	25%	0%	0%	0%	0%	0%	0%	0%

Source: Board of Governors of the Federal Reserve System, as of October 11, 2013.

Table 3. Current supplementary leverage ratios for 8 largest US banks.

Bank	Leverage Ratio
Bank of America Corporation	5.00%
The Bank of New York Mellon	4.30%
Citigroup Inc.	5.40%
The Goldman Sachs Group, Inc.	5.00%
JPMorgan Chase & Co.	4.70%
Morgan Stanley	4.20%
State Street Corporation	5.20%
Wells Fargo & Co.	Not available

Source: Bloomberg, following company statements ending December 2013.

requirements without affecting their lending capacity. On the contrary, the transition provisions for large US banks are consistent with Basel III recommendations for internationally active banks. Under the final rule for capital adequacy ratios starting January 1, 2015, an advanced approaches banking organization would have to keep a minimum CET1, Tier 1 and total capital ratio of 4.0%, 5.5% and 8% respectively during 2014 and 4.5%, 6% and 8% for the small banks from 2015. Advanced approaches banking organizations will have to phase out trust preferred securities (TruPS) in Tier 1 and Tier 2 capital from 2016. While small US banks, are exempted if they have less than USD 15 bn in total consolidated assets as of December 31, 2009, or organized in mutual form as of May 19, 2010, from this requirement.

As an extra challenge for the big banks, the regulators proposed in April 2014 to implement a portion of the Basel III agreement, known as the leverage ratio, by January 2018.[13] The rule would require the eight biggest BHCs in US to maintain top-tier capital equal to 5% of total assets. That's higher than the 3% ratio included in the Basel agreement. If implemented, the eight biggest US banks will have to boost capital levels by a total of approximately USD 68 bn. The rules would limit banks' reliance on debt as part of efforts to prevent another financial crisis. The banks have until June to comment on the proposed changes.

I.1.1. *Counterparty credit risk*

The CCR sections of Basel III involve the recognition of financial collateral; holding periods and the margin period of risk; use of stressed inputs within the internal model methodology (IMM); incorporation of CVA; treatment of centrally cleared transactions; and inclusion of stressed periods within internal estimates.

Among the important changes in the new capital requirements is the implementation of CVA in the US and Europe. The change materially increases the required capital for over-the-counter (OTC) derivative trading activities and is driving significant changes in that sector. CVA applies to non-cleared trades as exposures towards central counterparties are exempt from the charge. In the US, the regulators are sticking to the Basel III script by implementing the new prudential framework with no exemptions to the CVA charge for derivatives counterparty risk. The US agencies require CVA charge to apply to entities including US public sector entities (PSE), pension funds and corporate end-users. Only central bank-type entities like central banks, multilateral development banks, the Bank for International Settlements and the European Central Bank, are exempted from the 0.03% probability of default floor in rules and qualify for a zero risk weighting.

The US version addresses a long-standing complaint relating to the treatment of market risk hedges used to mitigate market risk exposures. Non-credit risk hedges of CVA, whether they are market risk hedges or exposure hedges, are not subject to market risk capital requirements.

I.1.2. *Volcker rule*

In a separate regulatory development, the Fed, OCC, FDIC and the Securities and Exchange Commission (SEC) finalized the Volcker Rule for banks. Regulated firms have until July 21, 2015 to comply with the new legislation. The revised Volcker Rule has appeared to be less demanding than what was originally planned. The agencies have reduced the compliance burden for banking entities with total assets of less than USD 10 bn, and eliminated the compliance requirement for firms that do not engage in investments or covered activities apart from investing in US government obligations, agency guaranteed obligations or municipal obligations. Furthermore, firms engaging in loans, spot foreign exchange or spot physical commodities do not need to comply with the proprietary trading ban.

The finalized Volcker Rule also allows proprietary trading in the following circumstances:

(1) purchase or sale of a financial instrument under certain repurchase and reverse purchase agreements and securities lending agreements[16];
(2) bona fide liquidity management[17];
(3) certain clearing agencies, derivatives clearing organizations in connection with clearing activities;
(4) a member of a clearing agency, derivatives clearing organization, or designated clearing organization, or designated financial market utility engaged in excluded clearing activities;
(5) to satisfy existing delivery obligations;
(6) to satisfy an obligation of the banking entity in connection with a judicial, administrative, or arbitration proceeding;
(7) to satisfy a debt previously contracted;
(8) solely as broker, agent, custodian.

I.1.3. *Comprehensive capital analysis and review (CCAR) and CCAR 2014 results*

CCAR is an annual exercise carried out by the US Federal Reserve for an intensive assessment of the capital adequacy and capital spending at large US BHCs under stressed macroeconomic conditions.

The CCAR tests banks for a minimum 5% CET1 ratio and other required minimum regulatory capital levels (Tier 1 common ratio, CET1, Tier 1 risk-based capital ratio, Total risk-based capital ratio, and Tier 1 leverage ratio).[18] Regulators then evaluate the firms' planned capital actions for the next nine-quarters to better understand each bank's longer-term capital management strategy and to assess post-stress capital levels over the full planning horizon. Additionally, the Fed evaluates the following qualitative factors: reasonableness of the assumptions and analyses underlying the capital plan, robustness of the capital adequacy process, risk-management practices, corporate governance and controls in the capital planning process.

Table 4. Summary of the Federal Reserve's actions on capital plans in CCAR. 2014.

Non-Objection to Capital Plan	Objection to Capital Plan
American Express Company	Citigroup
The Goldman Sachs Group, Inc.	HSBC North America
JPMorgan Chase & Co.	RBS Citizen's Financial
Morgan Stanley	Santander Holdings USA
Northern Trust Corp.	Zions Bancorporation
State Street Corporation	Bank of America Corporation (Re-submission of Capital Plan)
Wells Fargo & Co.	

Source: Board of Governors of the Federal System.

The CCAR 2014 covered 30 BHCs, including 12 new BHCs that did not feature in the earlier reviews. Results show that most of the large BHCs have continued to bolster their capital position since the crisis. Only 2 of the 30 participating BHCs will need to raise additional capital through Q2 2014 and Q1 2015, while 25 out of 30 participating US banks have the ability to lend to households and businesses and continue to meet financial obligations even in times of economic difficulty.

Unlike CCAR 2013, the 2014 review included a counterparty default component required to be modelled by the eight largest BHCs with large trading and custodial operations.

In the 2014 review, the Federal Reserve cleared the capital plans of all but five BHCs — Citigroup, HSBC North America Holdings, RBS Citizen's Financial Group, Santander Holdings and Zions Bancorporation. The Fed objected to Citigroup's proposed USD 6.4 bn common stock repurchase program up until Q1 2015 and an increase of Citi's quarterly common stock dividend to USD 0.05. The objections on other banks (all new to the CCAR assessment) were qualitative and mostly to do with the capital planning processes at these banks. These banks are now required to re-submit new capital plans subject to the required minimum capital levels for five capital ratios: as per the CCAR guidelines. Displays 1–3 (in Annex A) report minimum capital ratios based on both the original planned capital actions for large BHCs. Meanwhile, Bank of America had to re-submit its capital plan after discovering a USD4 bn accounting blunder and the Fed

Table 5. Summary of the Federal Reserve's actions on capital plans in CCAR 2013 for major US banks.

Non-Objection to Capital Plan	Conditional Non-Objection to Capital Plan	Objection to Capital Plan
Bank of America Corporation	The Goldman Sachs Group Inc.	Ally Financial Inc.
Citigroup Inc.	JPMorgan Chase & Co.	BB&T Corporation
Morgan Stanley		
State Street Corporation		
Wells Fargo & Co.		

Source: Board of Governors of the Federal System.

has 75 days from 26 May to respond to BOA's new submission.

Last year (CCAR 2013), 2 US banks — Ally Financial Inc. and BB&T Corporation had received objections to their capital action plans.[19] Ally Financial did not meet the minimum 5% capital requirement for CCAR, because the results incorporated a scenario where Ally Financial remained subject to contingent liabilities associated with Residential Capital, LLC.

I.2. Europe

Just like the US, Europe has adopted the Basel III standards through two legislative acts, the Capital Requirements Regulation (CRR) and the Capital Requirements Directive (CRD) (together CRD IV). Credit institutions and other investment firms within the member states of the European Union and the European Economic Area were subjected to the new rules starting from January 1, 2014.

Besides defining the scope of regulations to cope with capital requirements, liquidity and leverage ratios, CRD IV also issues rules on supervision, corporate governance, remuneration, sanctions, counterparty risk for derivatives and reliance on credit ratings.

CRD IV gives EU member states an option to introduce a systemic risk buffer consisting of additional Tier 1 capital for its financial sector. Each member state shall designate a local authority in charge of setting the systemic risk buffer and identifying the important institutions to which it applies. Systemic risk buffers may be set between 1% and 5%, but the designated authority has to notify the European Commission and other relevant supervisors before applying the charge on banks.

Similarly, most Asian nations have their own way of buffering systemic risk. They have imposed higher capital requirements for their banks to weather external shocks. However, in developing Asia except China, most of the countries are still in the early phases of the Basel III implementation and have yet to impose additional capital buffers onto their systemically important banks. Further details are provided in specific geographical sections.

Table 6 highlights the schedule for the implementation of CRD IV for European banks. As shown in the table, capital requirements for global systemically important banks (G-SIBs) and other (i.e., EU or domestic) systemically important banks (O-SIBS) have been agreed upon. Capital surcharges for O-SIBs will be capped at 2%. G-SIBs will be assigned to 1 of 5 categories, depending on their systemic importance. They will be subjected to progressive additional CET1 capital requirements, ranging from 1% to 2.5% for the first 4 groups of G-SIBs. Although, technically banks in the highest category would require a buffer of 3.5% capital surcharge but so far, none of the G-SIBs falls in that category. Figure 2 gives a view of systemically important banks in Europe as compared to their peers in the US and Asia in terms of capital buffers they are required to hold.

I.2.1. *Additional capital charges*

CRD IV requires financial institutions to calculate a CVA capital charge for all OTC derivative instruments in respect of all their business activities, except for credit derivatives that are used to reduce risk weighted exposure for credit risk mitigation purposes.

However, unlike the US, Europe has diverged from the Basel III by exempting transactions from the capital calculation for CVA risk where such transactions are between EU-based banks and non-financial corporates, sovereigns or for a limited period, pension funds.

The exemptions will give EU-based banks a boost in their treatment of the bank's capital adequacy ratio. Take for example, RBS who revised its 2012 annual RWA in June 2013 from GBP567.9 bn to GBP495 bn as a result of the CVA exemption.

Table 6. CRD IV capital requirements timeline.

	January 1, 2014	January 1, 2015	January 1, 2016	January 1, 2017	January 1, 2018	January 1, 2019	January 1, 2020	January 1, 2021	January 1, 2022
Minimum CET1 ratio	4.0%	4.5%	4.5%	4.5%	4.5%	4.5%	4.5%	4.5%	4.5%
Minimum Tier 1 capital ratio	5.5%	6.0%	6.0%	6.0%	6.0%	6.0%	6.0%	6.0%	6.0%
Minimum total capital ratio	8.0%	8.0%	8.0%	8.0%	8.0%	8.0%	8.0%	8.0%	8.0%
Capital conservation buffer			0.625%	1.25%	1.875%	2.5%	2.5%	2.5%	2.5%
Phase in of deductions from CET1	20%	40%	60%	80%	100%	100%	100%	100%	100%
Phase out of unqualified instruments issued before September 12, 2010	80%	70%	60%	50%	40%	30%	20%	10%	0%
Countercyclical buffer			0.625%	1.25%	1.875%	2.5%	2.5%	2.5%	2.5%
Global systemic institution buffer					Surcharge between 1% and 3.5% of CET1				
Other systemic institution buffer					Option surcharge with an upper limit of 2% CET1				
Systemic risk buffer	0–3%				3–5%				

Source: European Commission, as of June 2013.

Figure 2. Comparison of systemically important European banks with US and Asia.

Source: Financial Stability Board, as of November 11, 2013.

But many US banks fear that the difference in treatment of counterparties may make them less competitive than European banks as US lenders need to set aside capital buffers when trading with non-financial corporates.

I.2.2. *EBA stress tests*

This year, European banks will be undergoing an annual stress test as part of efforts to monitor and assess market developments and identify trends, potential risks and vulnerabilities in the industry. The European Banking Authority (EBA) announced the key components of the 2014 EU wide stress test on January 31, 2014. It will be conducted on a sample of banks to help authorities determine the resilience of the financial sector in adverse market scenarios. The EBA might examine the banks' CET1 ratios as well as stress test the banks' credit risk, market risk, sovereign risk, securitization and cost of funding in varied situations. The methodology and final scenarios for the test will be released in April 2014 while exact treatments such as sovereign bond haircuts and marking the banks' trading books to market would be disclosed in October 2014. The stress test covers most European banks in the European Economic Area on a consolidated level, including a bank in Norway.

In the lead up to the ECB's assuming the full supervisory role of the entire Euro-area banks in November 2014, a comprehensive risk and asset quality assessment of the Euro region banks will be conducted.

The assessment will consist of three elements: (1) a supervisory risk assessment to review key risks, including liquidity, leverage and funding; (2) Asset Quality Review (AQR) to enhance the transparency of bank assets and (3) a stress test to examine the resilience of banks to stress scenarios.

The assessment will be based on a capital benchmark of 8% CET1 ratio, including transitional arrangements, for both the AQR and the baseline stress test scenario. The result of the exercise will be an aggregated disclosure of the outcomes, at country and bank level, together with any recommendations for supervisory measures. This comprehensive outcome will be published prior to the ECB assuming its supervisory role in November 2014.

I.2.3. *AQR*

An AQR of all banks in the 27 Euro member states will need to be performed before ECB assumes full regulatory responsibility this year and before the stress testing of 140 banks is carried out. From November 2013, an AQR of 128 of the EU's largest banks will be conducted and the results of the Review are expected by Q2 2014.

The methodology for the AQR is risk based and will concentrate on the individual banks' balance sheets that are believed to be the most risky. This assessment will be broad and extensive, comprising credit and market exposures (including a quantitative and qualitative review of hard-to-value assets, particularly those qualifying as level-3 assets, on and off-balance sheet positions and domestic and non-domestic exposures). All asset classes, including non-performing loans and restructured loans will be covered. The Review will scrutinize portfolios that faced the greatest credit deterioration during the crisis i.e., largely

Table 7. AQR.

Objective	Review of European Banks' Balance Sheets		
Supervisor in charge and target markets	ECB	17 Euro countries joining the Banking Union (~140 banks)	Austria, Belgium, Cyprus, Estonia, Finland, France, Germany, Greece, Ireland, Italy, Luxembourg, Malta, Netherlands, Portugal, Slovakia, Slovenia, Spain
	National banking regulators	10 Remaining EU members	Bulgaria, Czech Republic, Denmark, Hungary, Latvia, Lithuania, Poland, Romania, Sweden, United Kingdom
Timeline	Expected between Q3 2013 and Q1 2014		

Source: EBA, centralbanking.com, Moody's Analytics.

corporate commercial real estate, mortgages, consumer loans, and small and medium enterprises (SMEs).

The AQR consists of three phases. The first phase, portfolio selection, helps to ensure that the banks' exposures with the highest risk are subjected to an in-depth review. The second phase, execution, will involve verifying the data integrity, validation, sampling and on site reviews of files, collateral valuation and recalculation of provisions and risk weighted assets. The last phase, collation, is an exercise to ensure the comparability of results across all bank portfolios, with an objective to ensure quality assurance and harmonized definitions for consistency. The AQR is a prerequisite for the EBA's stress tests as the results will be used as one of the starting points for the stress tests.

However, the execution of the AQR within the bank will be challenging. The first challenge with onboarding will be having all stake-holders (accountants, bankers and regulators) agree on common requirements and processes. Moreover, banks are bound to value their own assets in accordance with international accounting rules and cannot simply use the ECB's valuations directly into their balance sheets.

For instance, IFRS reporting standards have a guiding principle that provisions can only be taken for losses actually incurred, and not for expected losses. Furthermore, while some regulators may favor greater disclosure, consensus building could be a hurdle as it requires a long and painful process.

Importantly, the Review is expected to highlight capital inadequacies in bank balance sheets; however, politicians have yet to agree on how to address these inadequacies.

I.3. Asia Pacific

I.3.1. *Australia*

The Australian Prudential Regulation Authority (APRA) introduced ARS 111 Fair Values — a new reporting standard — and made changes to many existing prudential standards to comply with the new Basel framework for banks. Capital adequacy ratios for lenders were raised with effect from January 1, 2013; regulators also introduced additional capital requirements like the countercyclical buffer, the capital conservation buffer and the credit value adjustment capital risk charge.

The APRA does not recognize the threshold treatment when calculating CET1 assets for capital requirements.[20] Instead, it requires banks to deduct the items fully from their common equity. In their view, the threshold treatment could allow banks to double count capital in the financial system if implemented.

Early last year, lawmakers enhanced the Prudential Standard 330: Public Disclosure of Prudential Information to help banks revise disclosure requirements. The changes mandated institutions to report data in a standard format and frequency which facilitates comparisons between banks in Australia and across jurisdictions. Banks have complied with the new formats starting on June 30, 2013.

Domestic systemically important banks face an additional capital buffer charge of 1%. In December 2013, APRA released an information paper which outlined the approach the Authority intends to take in implementing the D-SIB framework in Australia.[21] Taking various considerations into account, APRA has required an additional 1% higher loss absorbency requirement from the nation's largest lenders. As a result, Australian banks including Commonwealth Bank, ANZ, Westpac, and the National Australia Bank will have to raise their capital buffers to 8% from 7% beginning 2016.[22] The increase must be met by the banks' CET1 capital, which primarily consists of common stock and disclosed reserves.

APRA also clarified its approach to the implementation of the Basel III liquidity framework especially regarding the operation of the committed liquidity facility (CLF) in August 2013. The Authority requires setting aside the size of CLF for banks to the lender's target Australian dollar net cash outflows. Australian banks would have to hold significant high quality liquid assets equivalent to level 1 in Basel III liquidity framework (HQLA1) to reduce the size of these buffers to a level in line with its peers. This means reducing HQLA1 assets with CLF eligible securities. The Reserve Bank of Australia has undertaken to supply, on an annual basis, an estimate of the aggregate amount of Australian dollar HQLA that could reasonably be held by a locally incorporated banks.

On January 30, 2014, APRA asked participating banks to notify the Reserve Bank of Australia about the size of their CLF. Additionally, banks have to show that they have taken measures towards fulfilling their LCR requirements through balance sheet management, and prove that banks have implemented steps to reduce their liquidity risk. Assets will get a liquidity based weight. APRA proposes that depository institutions be required to maintain an LCR of no lower than 100%.

I.3.2. *China*

The Chinese Banking and Regulatory Commission (CBRC) drafted Basel III capital regulations and implemented *Capital Rules* for banks which became effective from January 1, 2013.

The Capital Rules have been enforced on 511 Chinese commercial banks, which include unlisted small and medium sized lenders. Policy banks, or state guaranteed investment institutions that do not receive deposits from the public are exempted from the Capital Rules.

The rules provide detailed guidance for commercial banks to improve the risk management capabilities of domestic lenders. The Capital Rules were found to be close to the Basel guidelines by the Basel Committee Regulatory Consistency Assessment Programme (RCAP) during their recent audit in 2013. After gathering feedback from industry participants in July 2013, regulators disclosed capital requirements for exposures to central counterparties, capital composition as well as rules on adopting the internal ratings based (IRB) approach for regulatory capital.

During 2013, the CBRC also released supervisory guidance on capital instruments for Chinese commercial banks. In addition to keeping capital requirements, Tier 1 and Tier 2 securities issued by lenders should contain provisions that require contingent convertible capital instruments (CoCos) to be written off or converted into common equity when a trigger event occurs. The CBRC is working with the People's Bank of China (PBOC) in preparing a formal framework for the countercyclical capital buffer which would form a section of the Chinese macro-prudential framework. The details for the regulations would be finalized before January 2016 (see Table 8 on how the capital ratios would be scheduled).

I.3.3. *Hong Kong*

The Legislative Council updated the Banking (Amendment) Ordinance for the compliance with Basel III liquidity, capital and disclosure standards. The Banking (Capital) Rules were updated in June 2013 after the Basel Committee clarified on capital treatments for counterparty risk in December 2012.[23] The updates

Table 8. Implementation of capital adequacy ratios in China.

Banks	Capital Ratio (Including the Capital Conservation Buffer)	January 1, 2014	January 1, 2015	January 1, 2016	January 1, 2017	January 1, 2018	January 1, 2019
Domestic systemically important banks	Minimum CET1 capital adequacy ratio	6.5%	6.9%	7.3%	7.7%	8.1%	8.5%
	Minimum Tier 1 capital adequacy ratio	7.5%	7.9%	8.3%	8.7%	9.1%	9.5%
	Minimum total capital adequacy ratio	9.5%	9.9%	10.3%	10.7%	11.1%	11.5%
Other banks	Minimum CET1 capital adequacy ratio	5.5%	5.9%	6.3%	6.7%	7.1%	7.5%
	Minimum Tier 1 capital adequacy ratio	6.5%	6.9%	7.3%	7.7%	8.1%	8.5%
	Minimum total capital adequacy ratio	8.5%	8.9%	9.3%	9.7%	10.1%	10.5%

Source: China Banking Regulatory Commission, as of July 2013.

Table 9. Capital adequacy ratios for Hong Kong banks.

	January 1, 2014	January 1, 2015	January 1, 2016	January 1, 2017	January 1, 2018	January 1, 2019	January 1, 2020	January 1, 2021	January 1, 2022
Minimum CET1 capital ratio	4.0%	4.5%	4.5%	4.5%	4.5%	4.5%	4.5%	4.5%	4.5%
Minimum Tier 1 capital CAR	5.5%	6.0%	6.0%	6.0%	6.0%	6.0%	6.0%	6.0%	6.0%
Minimum total capital CAR	8.0%	8.0%	8.0%	8.0%	8.0%	8.0%	8.0%	8.0%	8.0%
Capital conservation buffer			0.625%	1.25%	1.875%	2.5%	2.5%	2.5%	2.5%
Phase out of unqualified instruments	80%	70%	60%	50%	40%	30%	20%	10%	0%
Phase in of deductions from CET1	20%	40%	60%	80%	100%	100%	100%	100%	100%

Source: HKMA, as of July 2013.

included the transitional arrangements for the treatment of certain capital deductions and capital instruments and details about how a bank should recognize credit risk mitigation under the standardized CVA method and framework for calculating regulatory capital for exposures to central counterparties.

At the same time in June 2013, the Hong Kong Monetary Authority (HKMA) amended the Banking (Disclosure) Rules to comply with capital disclosure requirements by the Basel Committee and to incorporate Basel III Pillar 3 disclosure principals, specifically for banks using the internal models approach to determine capital requirements for counterparty credit risk exposures.

Moreover, Hong Kong regulators have asked the banks to provide feedback on the proposed Basel III liquidity standards which is due to take effect from 2015. Under the draft rules, Category 1 banks (or licensed banks) would have to follow the Basel LCR and NSFR, while category 2 (i.e., banks with restricted licenses and deposit taking companies) would be subject to a modified liquidity ratio. Banks have also been invited to comment on a draft framework to identify domestic systematically important banks (D-SIBs) and specify additional capital requirements. Policy makers proposed a higher loss absorbency requirement ranging from 1% to 3.5% for D-SIBs, similar to the "bucketing" approach proposed for G-SIBs, where banks are ranked based on their systemic importance and classified into various buckets.

In October 2013, the HKMA asked banks to submit information on their leverage ratios on a quarterly basis before the Leverage Ratio is ultimately adopted as a minimum Pillar 1 requirement in 2018. Lawmakers will consider if the 3% minimum leverage ratio recommended by the Basel Committee would be appropriate for Hong Kong banks (see Table 8 for a timeline). The Basel Committee on Banking Supervision (BCBS), of which HKMA is a member, expects full implementation of Basel III regulations by 1 January 2019.

Recently, the HKMA made the calls in the first public consultation from an Asian regulator for far-reaching powers to prop up or shut failing banks including the ability to suspend creditor rights. In short, it will give the HKMA the power to make financial institutions easier to break up and sell in a crisis.

LCR

In 2013, the BCBS has made some revisions to the LCR namely in four major areas:

- Expansion of the range of assets eligible for HQLA;
- Recalibration of the stress assumptions for some cash-flow items including retail and non-financial corporate deposits and undrawn committed facilities;
- Affirmation of usability of stock of HQLA by banks in times of stress;

- Adoption of a phase-in arrangement that introduces the LCR as planned on 1 January 2015, but with the minimum requirement set at 60%.

BCBS also proposed further refinements to the Banking (Capital) rules and amendments to it with further consultation on Basel III implementation towards disclosure requirements and liquidity standards.

I.3.4. *India*

The Reserve Bank of India (RBI) issued guidelines on Basel III reforms two years ago, which would become effective in a few phases until 2018. The central bank was receptive to the new Basel recommendations but the implementation deadlines for the elements have been extended to reflect the Indian Financial Year which begins on April 1 every year. Capital based ratios became effective from April 1, 2013, which is 3 months later than the Basel timeline (see Table 10) and banks now have until March 2019 to comply with the complete Basel III demands. The latest announcement came in March 2014, after lenders' ability to tap capital markets was affected by deteriorating asset quality. The new move will give banks another year to conform to Basel III Capital Conservation Buffer requirement. Additionally, Basel III compliant Additional Tier 1 (AT1) instruments issued up till March 31, 2019 will have two pre-specified trigger points. The point of write-down or conversion into common shares will be a CET1 ratio of 5.5% before March 31, 2019 and will be raised to CET1 of 6.125% thereafter.

The effective deadline for banks to adopt CVA risk capital charges on OTC derivatives that would have become effective from January 1, 2014 was subsequently extended to April 1, 2014. The postponement was done in view that the introduction of mandatory inter-bank forex forward guaranteed settlement would take some time to finalize.

In December 2013, RBI issued a draft regulation clarifying how the countercyclical capital buffer would apply to banks. The committee suggested that other indicators such as the growth rate of gross nonperforming assets should be used in conjunction with the credit to GDP gap to determine the countercyclical capital buffer. Other supplementary indicators like the industry outlook assessment index and the interest coverage ratio must be factored into deciding the countercyclical capital buffer for banks.

From January 1, 2013 to January 1, 2017, the RBI requires banks to maintain a minimum leverage ratio of 4.5%. Depending on the performance of the banks, the final leverage ratio will be decided by the central bank in 2018. The RBI has been monitoring Indian banks on a quarterly basis since June 2013. Lenders were required to disclose information on Tier 1 leverage ratios together with detailed calculations on capital and exposure measures to the RBI (Department of Banking Operations and Development). Banks will publicly disclose their leverage ratio and its components starting April 1, 2015.

While on an ongoing consultation, RBI asked the industry to comment on its draft framework to regulate domestic systemically important banks. The document delivered a methodology for identifying global and domestic systemically important banks, as well as proposals for additional capital surcharges for the

Table 10. Capital ratio timeline for Indian banks.

	April 1, 2013	March 31, 2014	March 31, 2015	March 31, 2016	March 31, 2017	March 31, 2018	March 31, 2019
Minimum CET1 capital ratio	4.5%	5.0%	5.5%	5.5%	5.5%	5.5%	5.5%
Minimum Tier 1 capital ratio	6.0%	6.5%	7.0%	7.0%	7.0%	7.0%	7.0%
Minimum total capital CAR	9.0%	9.0%	9.0%	9.0%	9.0%	9.0%	9.0%
Capital conservation buffer				0.625%	1.25%	1.875%	2.5%
Phase out of unqualified instruments[24]	80%	80%	70%	60%	50%	40%	30%
Phase in of deductions from CET1	20%	40%	60%	80%	100%	100%	100%

Source: RBI, as of March 27, 2014.

banks. Based on their systemic importance scores, systemically important banks would need additional CET1 capital on top of existing capital requirements (i.e., capital adequacy ratios plus capital conservation buffer) ranging from 0.2% to 0.8% of risk weighted assets starting from April 1, 2016. The RBI will then publish a list of banks classified as D-SIBs in August every year starting from 2015.

I.3.5. *Indonesia*

From December 31, 2013, Bank Indonesia (BI) delegated micro prudential supervision duties to the Indonesia Financial Service Authority.[25] BI will continue to supervise macro prudential areas in the banking system. The Financial Services Authority and BI are collaborating to construct a framework to identify D-SIBs.[26] Regulators will use the methodology by the BCBS to decide which banks are systemically important to the financial system.

Indonesia has just implemented Basel III risk based capital ratios for its banks in January 2014. BI requires banks to maintain a range of capital requirements according to their risk profiles. The central bank groups the 120 banks into 5 risk profiles every 6 months:

(i) 8% of the Risk Weighted Assets (*aset tertimbang menurut risiko*, or ATMR) for banks with a rating 1 risk profile;
(ii) 9% to less than 10% of the ATMR for banks with rating 2 risk profile;
(iii) 10% to less than 11% of ATMR for Banks with a rating 3 risk profile;
(iv) 11% to 14% of ATMR for Banks with a rating 4 or rating 5 risk profile.

For banks with subsidiaries, the above minimum capital adequacy requirements apply to the banks individually as well as to the consolidated entities. To further ensure compliance with the requirement, BI Regulation 14/18 prohibits a bank from distributing its profit if the profit distribution results in the bank's capital requirement inadequacy.

According to statistics released by the central bank, the average CAR amongst banks was 18.1% in July 2013, up from 17.3% in July 2012 and well above Basel III standards.

I.3.6. *Japan*

During the transitional period from January 1, 2013 up to and including 2019, the minimum capital requirements expressed in risk weighted assets will gradually be stepped up. Equity capital ratio will rise from 3.5% to 4.5%, Tier-1 capital from 4.5% to 6% while, total capital ratio stays at 8%.

As for the conservation buffer, it will be built up along gradual lines to a percentage of 2.5% from January 1, 2016 to January 1, 2019. Thus, banks will ultimately have to hold 10.5% of their total capital expressed in risk-weighted asset.

National supervisors will gradually introduce additional allowable deductions from bank capital such as deferred tax assets and investments in financial institutions from January 1, 2014 to January 1, 2018.

The Japanese Financial Services Agency (JFSA) issued the FSA Administrative Notice on capital adequacy rules for internationally active banks pursuant to Article 14-2 of the Banking Act to follow Basel III guidelines. Additional secondary legislations, including a set of FAQs, were published in June and August 2012 for public clarification.[27] In March 2013, the JFSA released comprehensive details regarding the regulatory supervision of financial instruments, stating that lenders have to monitor and maintain an acceptable capital adequacy ratio.[28]

Table 11. Capital adequacy ratios for Japan's largest banks by assets.

	CET1 Ratio	Tier 1 Capital Ratio	Total Capital Risk Based Ratio
Mitsubishi UFJ Financial Group	11.16%	12.11%	15.50%
Mizuho Financial Group	8.75%	11.58%	14.87%
Sumitomo Mitsui Financial Group	9.98%	11.61%	15.43%

Source: Bloomberg estimates, based on Q4 2013 company filings.

Japanese banks continue their hunt for capital to replenish capital lost under regulation's grandfathering arrangements, which is the phasing-out process of ineligible capital instruments. Morgan Stanley estimated that in Japan, at least USD 12 bn of legacy capital is lost each year under Basel III's grandfathering arrangement.

Big Japanese lenders like Sumitomo Mitsui Financial and Mizuho Financial have turned to capital markets to raise funds with Basel III compliant note. Historically, Japanese banks have enjoyed very strong support from the government despite the industry has a low-level government ownership. Tokyo has allocated USD 283.5 bn for capital injections in a point of non-viability trigger event, when investors could lose all their money if a bank is deemed to be insolvent.

I.3.7. *Malaysia*

Bank Negara updated its capital adequacy framework for both commercial and Islamic banks at the start of 2013 to follow the Basel Committee's recommendations in implementing capital and liquidity standards for banks. A final decision to formally adopt the Leverage Ratio, as a binding measure, will be made by the central bank closer to the targeted 2018 deadline set under Basel III and after an assessment has been made on whether the leverage ratio would work as intended.

Bank Negara will implement Basel III Liquidity standards in Malaysia through enhancements to the existing Liquidity Framework. The Basel III LCR will be adopted as the standard for ensuring that banking institutions hold sufficient high quality liquid resources to survive an acute stress scenario lasting a month. Amendments to the existing measurement standard underpinning the Liquidity Framework will be made.

The Bank will also consider implementing the Net Stable Funding Ratio, which aims to create incentives for banking institutions to fund activities with more stable sources of funding over a one-year horizon. The new standard will act as a supplemental measure to the LCR under the Liquidity Framework.

Before enforcing the rules, Bank Negara will use an observation period to comprehensively assess the impact of the standards and consider appropriate transitioning arrangements. Therefore, banking institutions have begun to calculate, and report the LCR and NSFR to the central bank from June 2012 (see Table 12 for capital regulation developments in Malaysia).

I.3.8. *The Philippines*

Bangko Sentral ng Pilipinas laid down the groundwork for the implementation of Basel III through the issuance of a series of circulars, which amends the existing risk based capital adequacy framework by including non-common equity regulatory capital instruments as qualifying capital.

Commercial banks will be required to adopt the capital adequacy standards at the start of 2014. The

Table 12. Implementation timeline for Malaysian banks.

	January 1, 2014	January 1, 2015	January 1, 2016	January 1, 2017	January 1, 2018	January 1, 2019	January 1, 2020	January 1, 2021	January 1, 2022
Minimum CET1 capital ratio	4.0%	4.5%	4.5%	4.5%	4.5%	4.5%	4.5%	4.5%	4.5%
Minimum Tier 1 capital CAR	5.5%	6.0%	6.0%	6.0%	6.0%	6.0%	6.0%	6.0%	6.0%
Minimum total capital CAR	8.0%	8.0%	8.0%	8.0%	8.0%	8.0%	8.0%	8.0%	8.0%
Capital conservation buffer			0.625%	1.25%	1.875%	2.5%	2.5%	2.5%	2.5%
Phase out of unqualified instruments	Phased out over a 10 year horizon beginning 2013								

Source: Bank Negara Malaysia, as of March 2013.

minimum capital adequacy ratio that banks have to maintain is 10%, higher than the 8% required by the Basel Committee. Banks are required to have a minimum Tier 1 ratio of 7.5%, also higher than the Basel recommendation of 6.0%. Banks have to keep a CET1 ratio of 6.0%, which is greater than the 4.5% required under Basel guidelines.

The new guidelines introduced a capital conservation buffer of 2.5%, which shall be made up of CET1 capital. In addition, banks which issued capital instruments from 2011 will be allowed to count these instruments towards capital requirements under Basel III until end 2015. These instruments can qualify as hybrid Tier 1 or lower Tier 2 capital defined in Circular Nos. 709 and 716. Circular No. 709 deals with the definition of Qualifying Capital Instruments but was subsequently amended to remove the requirement of an external legal opinion on the compliance of lower Tier 2 capital. The new provision, or Circular No. 716 which is in place as of March 2010 now applies a subordination feature to lower Tier 2 instruments, while a loss absorption feature applies only to hybrid Tier 1 instruments. The central bank no longer allows new issuances of capital instruments as upper Tier 2 capital. But, the minimum capital ratios as well as the limits on the amounts that could be included as hybrid Tier 1 and upper or lower Tier 2 capital were being retained.

Regulatory capital instruments that do not qualify for Basel calculations were immediately phased out from January 1, 2014. This is stricter than the timeline issued under the Basel Committee's guidance, which allows jurisdictions to phase out ineligible capital instruments gradually according to the staggered timeline. Regulators have yet to formalize regulations relating to the liquidity coverage and leverage ratios.

So far, most of the major banks in the Philippines have already complied with the Basel III capital requirements, but some relatively smaller banks have yet to increase their capital base to meet the deadline set by the BSP.

I.3.9. *Singapore*

Notice 637 was recently updated by the Monetary Authority of Singapore (MAS) to reflect the latest capital requirements for locally incorporated Singapore banks. Banks were given a deadline of July 1, 2013 to comply with the implementation standards for capitalization of banks' exposures to central counterparties. MAS consulted with the public in October 2013 to amend Notice 637 after receiving their assessment results from the Basel Committee RCAP. MAS proposed to make improvements to Pillar 3 disclosures, so that banks regularly (i) disclose information on the 12 indicators used in the Basel framework which identify G-SIBs, and (ii) submit information to the BCBS to assess their global systemic importance. MAS also amended Annex 6B of Notice 637.

MAS Notice 637 is stricter than the Basel III guidelines by requiring the locally incorporated banks to meet CET1 ratio of 5.5% by January 1, 2014 and 6.5% by 1 January 2015, more than the Basel III recommendation of 4.5% by January 1, 2015. The minimum CAR is 10% — higher than the Basel III requirement that the CAR must be no lower than 8%. MAS will also require banks to hold a counter-cyclical buffer of 2.5% of risk-weighted assets by January 1, 2019.

During the course of 2013, Singapore incorporated banks were required under Notice 637 to meet risk based capital adequacy requirements, meeting guidelines on risk management and most importantly Notice 643 which requires reporting of transactions with related parties. MAS 643 seeks to address and reduce the risk of abuses arising from related party transactions and align industry practices with the Basel Core Principles for Effective Banking Supervision.

Notice 637 applies to the 8 locally incorporated banks. Six of the eight banks operate as part of the three main banking groups namely, DBS Bank (DBS), Overseas-Chinese Banking Corporation (OCBC) and United Overseas Bank (UOB). Citibank Singapore Limited and Standard Chartered Bank are the only locally incorporated banks which are subsidiaries of foreign banks[29] (see Table 13 for an implementation timeline of Basel III elements).

I.3.10. *South Korea*

The Financial Services Commission (FSC) was late in adopting Basel III capital guidelines for its lenders as compared to its Asian peers. The Korean authorities postponed the initially scheduled date for

Table 13. Singapore bank capital regulation timeline in Notice 637.

	January 1, 2014	January 1, 2015	January 1, 2016	January 1, 2017	January 1, 2018	January 1, 2019	January 1, 2020	January 1, 2021	January 1, 2022
Minimum CET1 CAR	5.5%	6.5%	6.5%	6.5%	6.5%	6.5%	6.5%	6.5%	6.5%
Minimum Tier 1 capital CAR	7.0%	8.0%	8.0%	8.0%	8.0%	8.0%	8.0%	8.0%	8.0%
Minimum total capital CAR	10.0%	10.0%	10.0%	10.0%	10.0%	10.0%	10.0%	10.0%	10.0%
Capital conservation buffer			0.625%	1.25%	1.875%	2.5%	2.5%	2.5%	2.5%
Phase in of deductions from CET1	20%	40%	60%	80%	100%	100%	100%	100%	100%
Phase out of unqualified instruments	80%	70%	60%	50%	40%	30%	20%	10%	0%
Countercyclical buffer			0.625%	1.25%	1.875%	2.5%	2.5%	2.5%	2.5%

Source: MAS, as of December 2013.

Table 14. Capital adequacy ratios for Korean banks.

	December 1, 2013	January 1, 2014	January 1, 2015	January 1, 2016	January 1, 2017	January 1, 2018	January 1, 2019	January 1, 2020	January 1, 2021
Minimum CET1 capital ratio	3.5%	4.0%	4.5%	4.5%	4.5%	4.5%	4.5%	4.5%	4.5%
Minimum Tier 1 capital ratio	4.5%	5.5%	6.0%	6.0%	6.0%	6.0%	6.0%	6.0%	6.0%
Minimum total capital ratio	8.0%	8.0%	8.0%	8.0%	8.0%	8.0%	8.0%	8.0%	8.0%
Capital conservation buffer				0.625%	1.25%	1.875%	2.5%	2.5%	2.5%
Phase out of unqualified instruments	90%	80%	70%	60%	50%	40%	30%	20%	10%

Source: Korea FSC, as of December 2013.

implementation (January 1, 2013) considering the uncertainty of adoption status of other member countries and decided to adjust its Basel III implementation schedule after closely monitoring the progress of other member countries. The FSC only came to a decision to implement Basel III on December 1, 2013 (see Table 14) after major Asian economies had already implemented Basel III capital regulations in 2013. Banks are required to meet detailed adequacy ratios and minimum requirements for each category of capital. Moreover, qualifying conditions for each capital class will be modified to enhance quality of banks' capital.

In line with the Basel III framework and according to Table 15, capital distribution constraints will be imposed on a bank when capital levels fall within a minimum threshold. Elements which are subjected to restrictions include share buybacks, dividend payments

Table 15. Capital distribution constraints for Korean banks.

Percentage of Earnings Permitted to Withdraw	0%	20%	40%	60%	100%
Common Equity Capital Ratio, or	Below 5.125%	Below 5.75%	Below 6.375%	Below 7.0%	7% or above
Tier 1 Capital Ratio, or	Below 6.625%	Below 7.25%	Below 7.875%	Below 8.5%	8.5% or above
Total Capital Ratio	Below 8.625%	Below 9.25%	Below 9.875%	Below 10.5%	10.5% or above

Source: Korea FSC, as of December 2013.

and discretionary bonus payments to staff. The restrictions imposed on banks ease as their capital levels improve. Similarly, if a bank experiences losses and its capital levels fall, the percentage of earnings allowed for distribution or withdrawal decreases.

Upon implementation, the FSC will continue to monitor progress in order to ensure that Basel III will not cause banks to reduce their lending to SMEs and low-income households, while strengthening banks' soundness.

I.3.11. *Thailand*

The Bank of Thailand posted several notifications concerning Basel III capital requirements together with 2 circulated letters on (1) guidelines for the calculation of the leverage ratio, and (2) reporting requirements for liquidity risk.

The Bank of Thailand issued 7 notifications on Basel III regulatory capital requirements.[30] With effect from January 1, 2013, banks have to maintain a CET1 ratio of 4.5%, Tier 1 ratio of 6% and total capital ratio of 8.5%. Lenders have to maintain an additional conservation buffer of 2.5% from January 2016, with gradual increments of 0.625% per year till January 2019. Additionally, banks have to set aside capital to meet the countercyclical buffer to cushion losses during a crisis. The Bank of Thailand shall consider economic indicators and evaluate credit conditions when formulating an appropriate level of countercyclical buffer.

In December 2012, the Bank of Thailand issued 2 draft regulations on the calculation of the Leverage Ratio, and the reporting requirement for the LCR and the NSFR. Banks will have to report their liquidity risk and leverage ratios on a regular basis to the central bank.

II. CHALLENGES FOR REGULATORS

Basel III could hit banks hard through its range of new and stricter regulations, from higher capital requirements, liquidity and disclosure standards, and right down to tighter risk management. However, the combined effect of the requirements will vary from bank to bank, and among large banks almost all will have to deal with its far reaching implications of harsher capital definition and significantly increased risk weighted assets for securitizations, trading book positions and certain counterparty credit risk exposures. Although most of Asia like Hong Kong, India, China, Japan and Singapore have completed adopting the Basel risk based capital requirements at the start of 2014, there are still challenges for the regulatory authorities to implement them on a level playing field.

Table 16 highlights the progress on the adoption of Basel III regulatory elements in various Asian economies. Although it appears that most of the jurisdictions have established capital adequacy ratios for lenders, the measure of risk weighted assets differs across economies. Thailand for one, has not endorsed the CVA capital charge for OTC derivative transactions, which is meant to enhance banks' resilience to deterioration in the credit quality of their counterparties in respect to their OTC derivative transactions.

In Hong Kong, the HKMA highlighted some of the challenges in establishing Basel III.[48] There was a lack of HKD denominated high quality assets such as highly rated non-financial corporate, sovereign and central bank debt to satisfy the Basel III LCR requirements. The HKMA had discussed with banks about the capital shortfall and potential demand for such instruments and the options available to banks.

II.1. China

After enforcing the Basel compliant rules in China, there are still some areas in which the Capital Rules differ from Basel III. An example is in the treatment

Table 16. Implementation of Basel III rules across Asia.

	China	Singapore	Malaysia	Thailand	Hong Kong	Indonesia	Japan	Korea	Philippines	Australia	India
Risk based capital[31]	4	4	4	4[32]	4	4	4	4	4	4	4
Countercyclical capital buffer	1	3[33]	1	1[34]	2[35]	1	1	1	1	1	2[36]
Leverage ratio	1[37]	2[38]	2[39]	2	3	1	1	1	1	1	2
Domestic/Globally SIBs	1[40]	1[41]	1	1	1	1	1	1	1	2	2[42]
LCR	2[43]	2[44]	1[45]	2	2[46]	1	1	1	1	2	1[47]

Source: Various central banks, progress reports by the Bank of International Settlements and the Financial Stability Board. Information correct as of January 31, 2014. The following abbreviations for legislature status are used in the table: 1 = Draft regulation not published, 2 = Draft regulation published, 3 = Final rule published, 4 = Final rule in force.

of loans past due for more than 90 days. Such loans issued to PSEs and banks have a risk weight lower than indicated in the new Basel guidelines.[49]

Eligible collateral is also treated differently under the Capital Rules set by the CBRC. Debt securities issued by foreign banks and PSEs have a different regulatory treatment unlike debt securities issued by domestic banks. The eligibility criteria used in assessing bonds sold by foreign banks and PSEs takes into account the jurisdiction's sovereign rating but does not consider the credit quality of individual foreign bank and PSE.

There was a general lack of requirements regarding liquidity facilities and asset backed commercial paper programmes (ABCP). This is because the size of such programs and related instruments is very small in China. The securitization program in China was initially launched in 2005 but was disbanded during the financial crisis.[50] The program came back online in 2011 as policy makers wanted alternative sources of funding for small and medium sized enterprises. In Basel III, banks have to fully consider the potential liquidity risk arising from loss of funding on any asset-backed investments and financing facilities within 30 days.

The Capital Rules also do not cover all of the approaches mentioned in the Basel market risk framework. The Basel standards call for sophisticated risk measures to scrutinize derivatives risk, but this was not adopted by most Chinese banks as most of the business is focused on traditional banking. Chinese banks are however growing their trading divisions but will not be required under the Capital Rules to use more advanced approaches in assessing risk. The CBRC says that trading assets constitutes only less than 1% of total risk weighted assets at the end of 2012.

Additionally, certain sections of the Capital Rules have not addressed the core Pillar 3 requirements set forth in the Basel III requirements. For example, disclosure about credit quality is missing as a detailed revelation of the impaired loans and loan loss allowances by industry are not explicitly required by the CBRC. Disclosure about securitization in the banking industry is also limited which the CBRC attributes to the narrow size of the industry.

II.1.1. *Stricter rules*

CBRC rules for banks are stricter than Basel III requirements. Even though the Basel guidelines are for internationally active banks, the Capital Rules are equally strict on small banks which have little presence overseas. When calculating capital requirements, equity investments in commercial entities have to use a risk weight of 1250%, which is much larger than the 100% risk weight mentioned in the Basel references, provided the investment is immaterial to the bank.[51,52]

When measuring credit risk for claims secured by residential property under the standardized approach, the Capital Rules only recognize high quality fixed income bonds as collateral. Under Basel guidelines, equities (including convertible bonds) that are included in a main index and UCITS compliant funds are also allowed as collateral. Moreover, such claims are risk weighted at 50% instead of the Basel's standard of 35%. In the Basel IRB approach for calculating corporate risk, banks are allowed to distinguish exposures to SME borrowers by allowing a firm size adjustment to be made to the risk weight formula.[53]

II.2. Singapore

Meanwhile in Singapore, Notice 637 is more demanding than Basel III risk based capital standards but there are a few differences. In the Standardized Approach for credit risk, banks are able to use structured deposits as eligible financial collateral but this is not allowed under Basel as they are not considered cash equivalents and carry a higher risk. For example, dual currency investments carry a risk of change in liquidation value and are not eligible for insurance cover under the Deposit Insurance and Policy Owner's Protection Schemes Act.

During the 2013 RCAP assessment, examiners said that MAS Notice 637 did not address the banks' motivation to adopt the IRB approach when calculating capital charges. Basel recommendations state that the migration to IRB approaches should not be driven by the desire to minimize its capital charge but by the practicality of changing to a more advanced approach. In the Basel document, residential mortgage loans to individuals who are owner-occupiers of the property can qualify for retail treatment. The definition of retail residential mortgages in Notice 637 does not mention owner occupancy, except that such loans "must be originated and managed on a pooled basis by reference to standards that would be applied by the reporting bank to an individual that is an owner-occupier of the property.[54]"

II.2.1 *Notice* 637 *more stringent than Basel rules*

Notice 637 is stricter than the Basel recommendations in a number of sections. One of them relates to the disparity on the regulatory treatment of exposures to individuals managed as a pool under the IRB approach to calculating credit risk. Under the Basel framework, loans to individuals do not need to be always classified as retail and the framework includes examples in which they should be classified as corporate exposure. It is suggested that regulators prescribe corporate rather than retail treatment for bank assets that are managed as a pool, such as residential retail properties that are not occupied by the owners. Under the MAS rules, such loans are treated as an "other asset", which would be assigned a 100% risk weight, rather than as a corporate exposure. Second, the scope of instruments that banks may use as financial collateral is more stringent than Basel as it does not include unrated debt securities issued by banks.

II.3. Other Countries

In Japan, regulations are often seen as less strict compared to the Basel conventions. Firstly, a number of the Japanese standards were implemented through secondary legislation, rather than primary legislation. This means that some of the JFSA capital rules are not binding in legal terms.

Japanese regulations differ from Basel requirements with respect to the definition of an 'internationally active bank'. Japanese regulators define an internationally active bank as one that has one or more overseas business locations. But a bank with no overseas offices may still compete with foreign banks in markets abroad. Therefore, a Japanese bank with no establishment overseas but having international dealings with foreign banks through electronic networks may not be classified as an internationally active bank, implying that the bank has the option of maintaining a minimum capital adequacy ratio of 4%. Until now, Japanese banks have not violated Basel requirements because lenders with significant foreign presence are also the internationally active banks, which have at least one subsidiary or branch operating overseas.

According to Japanese supervisory guidelines regarding loss absorption methods of Tier 1 instruments, banks are able to avoid writing down or converting the instrument, if the bank submits a contingency plan to the JFSA about the remedial actions the bank would take to ensure that the CET1 ratio for the bank will surpass the trigger level of the instrument moving forward. Once the JFSA approves the plan, the bank can choose not to convert or write down the assets. Such an option with remedial actions is not included in the Basel III guidelines.

In the standardized approach to calculating credit risk, the JFSA classifies the risk weight applied to exposures to an individually supervised securities firm to be treated as exposures to deposit taking financial institution. Under the Basel framework, such an exposure would be classified as a corporate exposure. Moreover, when considering whether a credit derivative contract should be recognized under the standardized approach, the Japanese Basel rules leave out the condition which states that credit derivatives for cash settlement are recognized for capital purposes so that loss can be reliably estimated.

According to the Japan FSA Administrative Notice, banks may not need to disclose their capital requirements for market risk if the size of their trading books is smaller than JPY100 bn and less than 10% of the bank's total assets. Only the credit risk of the positions in the trading book is considered. This exemption is not highlighted in the Basel framework. Likewise, the JFSA requires banks to use the simplified or internal model approach when calculating capital requirements for commodities risk. More sophisticated methods such as the maturity ladder approach are not allowed. Under the Basel Accord, the simplified approach is only allowed if the lender has a small portfolio in the commodity business.

III. IMPACT ON ASIAN BANKS

Basel III implementation across Asia has impacted the risk taking behavior of banks. The rules were designed to strengthen the capital and liquidity standards of banks, but not to affect the individual economy's lending activities. According to Piyush Gupta, the CEO of Singapore-based DBS, the impact is most significant through the issuance of contingent capital, or "bail-inable" bonds in Asia as the requirements of Basel III could force Asian banks to raise USD 1 tn capital within 5 years. Alongside with decreased merger and acquisition activities in the banking sector either due to restrictions on foreign ownership like DBS' failed courtship of Bank Danamon in Indonesia or reluctance from regulators to let "too big to fail" banks get any bigger, capital raising has become more challenging. Ultimately, small banks that need the necessary capital injections may have to turn to the debt market. In fact, at the beginning of 2014, Ayala-led Bank of Philippine Island (BPI) and Malaysia's CIMB Group embarked on their respective capital-raising exercises to keep themselves in shape.

The stricter definition of capital has also compelled lenders to restructure their balance sheets. For example, banks operating in Indonesia have had to rethink their strategic stakes in banks. The ANZ Group considered selling its 39% stake in Bank Panin to Japanese Bank Mizuho Group for USD 570 mn.[55] ANZ CEO Mike Smith said in April 2013 that the benefits of its non-majority investment in foreign banks might outweigh the costs. Under Basel III international capital adequacy rules, ANZ has to consider Panin's retained earnings and common equity (which increases the CET1's numerator) against its liabilities (contributing to the denominator).

As another example, DBS walked away from its Bank Danamon bid in August 2013, after failing to gain regulatory approval to take over the Indonesian lender as a non-majority stake under Basel requirements.[56] Without such approval, the costs would become quite prohibitive because DBS might have to allocate more Tier 1 capital in its balance sheet to satisfy regulatory capital requirements.

III.1. Falling Merger and Acquisition Transactions

Merger and acquisition activities amongst banks have fallen significantly since the introduction of Basel III capital requirements in 2010. The amount of completed deals involving Asian banks has dropped significantly from USD 38.7 bn in 2010 to USD 29.3 bn in 2013, representing a decrease of 24.2%[57] (see Table 17). The number of deals amongst Asian lenders has also fallen considerably. The number of completed deals had been decreasing since its peak in 2007. After the Basel III rules were announced in 2010, the number of deals immediately dropped to 199 in 2012 from 218 in 2011. 2013 saw the lowest number of completed deals in more than a decade, a year which bankers managed to complete 172 deals.

The latest version of Basel regulations requires minority holdings to be fully deducted against capital. Thus, penalizing firms that try to acquire banks in

Table 17. Total M&A activity for Asian banks between 2002 and 2013.

Year	Volume (USD bn)	Deal Count
2002	13.03	214
2003	15.47	179
2004	31.12	182
2005	68.28	232
2006	45.43	220
2007	59.39	331
2008	75.63	286
2009	34.21	275
2010	38.66	230
2011	19.89	218
2012	19.37	199
2013	29.34	172

Source: Bloomberg, as of February 5, 2014.

Table 18. Number of Asian banks increasing stakes or seeking minority purchases in other lenders between 2002 and 2013.

Year	Number of Deals Involving Additional Stake Purchases	Minority Purchase Deals
2002	24	54
2003	24	32
2004	24	50
2005	45	52
2006	47	50
2007	71	95
2008	64	78
2009	70	55
2010	41	50
2011	40	48
2012	27	47
2013	33	34

Source: Bloomberg, as of February 5, 2014.

Asia because foreign ownership restrictions automatically make these transactions capitally onerous. Under Basel III, a bank which holds a minority stake of more than 10% in another financial institution is required to be fully deducted against Tier 1 capital. With the introduction of limiting foreign ownership in most Asian banks, banks will find it more difficult to make cross border acquisitions.

Lenders have little regulatory incentive to keep existing minority interests on their balance sheets for too long. They could either dispose their investments or increase their stakes to become controlling shareholders of the companies. Naturally, banks would have to consider carefully if the benefit of any capital investment in another financial institution would outweigh the cost of a lower capital adequacy ratio.

Not many Asian financial institutions have increased their stakes in other Asian lenders in recent years. According to Table 18, there were 33 deals involving additional stake purchases in 2013. In 2012, only 27 banks were interested in increasing their stakes in other banks. Deals involving minority purchase among banks also decreased to 34 in 2013 from 47 in 2012 and 48 in 2011.

Restrictions on foreign ownership could be a reason limiting buyer's investments in other Asian banks. In June 2013, the Dutch bank Rabobank failed to find a buyer for its Indonesian operations due to the laws that restrain foreign ownership to 40%.[58] The bank received bids from Japanese financial firms but the sale process was stopped after Indonesian authorities imposed ownership thresholds.[59]

III.2. More Basel Compliant Bonds

After January 1, 2013, new non-equity bank instruments issued by Asian internationally active banks should include a point of non-viability loss absorption feature to comply with the new Basel framework's requirements, in order to be included as AT1 or Tier 2 capital. All non-equity capital issued by these banks therefore could have a new contingent capital clause.[60]

The BCBS recently finalized minimum requirements for regulatory capital instruments under Basel III. They include a requirement that Tier 1 instruments other than common stock as well as all Tier 2 instruments contain a feature requiring a "write-off" or conversion into common stock. The requirement is one of several important international developments that have broadened interest in bank-issued contingent capital securities.

Under the Basel III contingent capital requirement, the country supervisor of an international bank would have the authority to trigger a write-off or a conversion of non-common Tier 1 or Tier 2 instruments issued by the bank. A trigger event may be declared to avoid a systemic failure and prevent the issuer from becoming insolvent. The instrument may also be triggered by a going-concern contingent capital requirement, which applies only to non-common Tier 1 instruments classified as liabilities. Non-common equity securities do not have to meet the going-concern contingent capital requirements.

According to Bloomberg data, global banks have issued 119 contingent capital bonds since 2009, amounting to more than USD 109 bn. Issuances have increased through the years, from USD 17 bn in 2009 to USD 41.5 bn in 2013 (See Table 19), the highest on record. The amount of issuances in January 2014 nearly matched total bond issuances for 2010. Europe accounted for the bulk of CoCo issuances, while not many Asian and Latin American banks issued contingent capital bonds.

UK banks have been the most active issuers of contingent capital securities having issued USD 24 bn worth of bonds between 2009 and January 2014. The lenders have been primarily motivated by their need to satisfy the loss-absorbing capital requirements of UK regulators. Swiss banks are ranked second among issuers, with USD 17 bn of recorded bond sales. Investors could be attracted by the higher yields from the securities, as they are subordinated to other debt instruments in the bank's capital structure. The average yield to maturity (YTM) at issuance tends to be greater than other subordinated debt and unsecured debts.[61] YTMs of newly issued contingent capital bonds is on average 2.8% higher than that of non-contingent capital debt and 4.7% higher than that of senior unsecured debt of the same issuer.

One major difference about Asian bonds in the data set is that many bonds that were issued by Asian banks had a bail-inable (gone-concern contingent capital) clause but without a clear balance sheet-based trigger.

Table 19. Amount of contingent capital bonds issued worldwide (in US$ billions).

Year	Asia	Europe	Latin America	Global
2009		17.0		17.0
2010		4.3		4.3
2011	2.4	10.0		12.4
2012	0.3	27.1	3.5	30.8
2013	2.6	32.3	6.6	41.5
Jan 14 YTD	0.3	3.5		3.8

Source: Bloomberg, as of February 5, 2014.

This would mean that the bonds would be written down or converted into equity only when the firm is near insolvency. Most fixed income securities issued in Europe and to a lesser extent in Latin America were issued with a going-concern contingent capital clause, which operates well before resolution mechanisms come into play. Other securities in the data sample carried clauses which state that the trigger points for conversion or write down would be the earlier of a book value or market value based event.

Asian banks issued 11 contingent capital bonds since 2011, probably to satisfy domestic local capital requirements. However, not all issued securities could qualify as Tier 1 Basel III compliant capital. Three of the issuances qualify as Tier 1 capital while the remaining bonds could be classified as Tier 2 instruments. Under Basel III, AT1 capital must be perpetual. Only the bonds issued by United Overseas Bank and DBS Group had no maturity dates.

The Asian contingent capital bond market remains small and there is no indication of strong demand for the instruments, as shown by the whipsaw pattern of issuances between 2011 and 2014. The reason for the lukewarm response is that many Asian policy makers and the Basel Committee appear to favor bonds that allow regulators to decide the reason, time and amount for conversion/write down. This sort of trigger typically would function at the point of non-viability or just before either bankruptcy or what would otherwise be an injection of public sector funds. While regulatory preferences may vary, investors across the board strongly prefer an objective, capital based trigger that is enhanced by greater, standardized disclosures. Investors cannot properly assess the likelihood of whether and when a discretionary trigger could be breached, or how much of the debt might be converted once triggered. This uncertainty prevents them from assessing the risk associated with a contingent capital security, and therefore they are not able to decide on the intrinsic value of the bond.

Issuers on the other hand face no simple task in valuation either. Banks cannot simply take the difference between the issue price and the theoretical price of a straight bond with the same maturity. Instead, the issuer needs to value the embedded option and then take the difference between it and the issue price as the bond component. However, the strike price for the point of

Issue Date	Issuer	Issuance Amount (USD mn)	Issuer rating	Pricing	Non viability conversion trigger
Jul-13	United Overseas Bank	672.5	Baa1	4.90%	Determined by regulator
Dec-13	DBS Group Holdings	642.32	Baa1	4.70%	Determined by regulator
Nov-13	China CITIC Bank International Ltd	300	NR	6.00%	Determined by regulator
Oct-13	Industrial & Commercial Bank of China Asia Ltd	500	NR	4.50%	Determined by regulator
Nov-13	United Overseas Bank	401.97	Baa1	4.75%	Determined by regulator
Jan-14	Bendigo and Adelaide Bank Ltd	262.98	Baa2	5.42%	Determined by regulator
Mar-12	Macquarie Bank Ltd	250	NR	10.25%	CET1 ratio < 5.125%
Nov-11	Industrial & Commercial Bank of China Asia Ltd	236.52	NR	6.00%	Determined by regulator
May-13	Suncorp Group	746.82	BBB+ (S&P)	5.48%	Determined by regulator
Dec-11	Nomura Holdings Inc.	1.98	NR	2.24%	Tier 2 ratio < limit set by regulator
Dec-11	Nomura Holdings Inc.	201.49	NR	2.24%	Tier 2 ratio < limit set by regulator
Sep-13	Bank of India	79.8	NR	9.80%	RBI has set a CET1 trigger of 6.125%

Figure 3. Asia Pacific CoCo bond issuances.

Source: Bloomberg, February 21, 2014.

conversion/write down is unknown as the bail-in terms may vary — different bonds may have various write down or write off conversions.

Issuers may also be influenced by country tax treatments and non-viability trigger points when deciding a destination to issue CoCos. India, for instance has set a pre-specified CET1 loss absorption/write down trigger level of 6.125% (higher than the Basel guideline of 5.125%) to ensure that banks would always operate above the minimum CET1 level.[63] Due to the conversion feature and perpetual requirement for AT1 instruments, many jurisdictions have yet to clarify whether to treat the securities as debt. If fiscal authorities treat contingent capital bonds as debt, then the interest expense associated with them is typically tax-deductible for the issuing bank. Singapore clarified the treatment of Basel III AT1 securities during the Budget in February 2014. The government's position is that the instruments will be treated as debt for tax purposes.

III.3. Relationship Between ROE/RMI PD and CAR

Basel III regulations require banks to follow the timetable to maintain their CAR by the required deadline. But questions are often asked about the implications of building a strong and better capital buffer for banks. Bankers often complain that setting aside more capital to buffer shocks may instead diminish the return to common equity for shareholders. Looking at Figs. 4(a), 4(c), 4(e), 4(g) and 4(i), the inverse relationship between change in CAR and the change in ROE seems to be true in all regions even though the relationship may not be too sharp in a statistical sense.

Data from a total of 225 banks in the US was used to measure the difference in CAR from FY 2011 to FY 2012 against the difference on the return in common equity from FY 2012 to FY 2013. The rationale is that any impact from the change in CAR will likely be reflected in the ROE the following year. On average, banks in the US would see their ROEs dipping some 0.59% over FY2012–FY2013 as CAR increased by 1% (Fig. 4(c)). For example, First Financial Corp had its CAR increase from 14.21% in FY 2011 to 15.38% in FY 2012, while its ROE dropped 0.81% from FY 2013 versus FY 2012. This is also reflected in Fig. 4(a), which shows that ROEs were declining with improving CARs based on data from 39 banks from 14 countries within the European Union based on the same financial year's comparison. However, data were not available for some of the countries like Greece, which is on a bailout from the EU. For European banks, an increase of 1% in the CAR would on average see a 0.7% drop in ROE.

As shown by the trend lines in Figs. 4(e) and 4(g), the inverse relationship between CAR and ROE also exists in developing and developed Asian economies where data from 172 banks including China and India were collected. The impact of an increase in CAR affects developed Asia lenders more than the other groups studied. As per the change between FY 2011 and FY 2012 CARs, lenders in developed Asia see an average change of negative 1.21% in ROEs for every increase of 1% in their CARs within the periods studied. While, the general observation of banks in developing countries showed a contraction of 0.16% in ROE for a 1% increase in CAR.

On the issue of whether having a higher capital buffer will help to offset risks, most economies showed an improvement in the change in 1-year Risk Management Institute probabilities of default (RMI PD) and the change in CAR between FY 2011 and FY 2012, which is evident in Figs. 4(b), 4(d), 4(f), 4(h), and 4(j). Figure 4(d) revealed that a 1% increase in CAR on average led to a 10 bps decrease in RMI PDs for US banks. The correlation of an improving CAR to lower PDs is also observable in banks in developed Asia but the relationship is less significant (just 1 bps) when examining lenders in Europe and developing Asia.

Only India and China showed a different set of results from the regression analysis, as displayed in

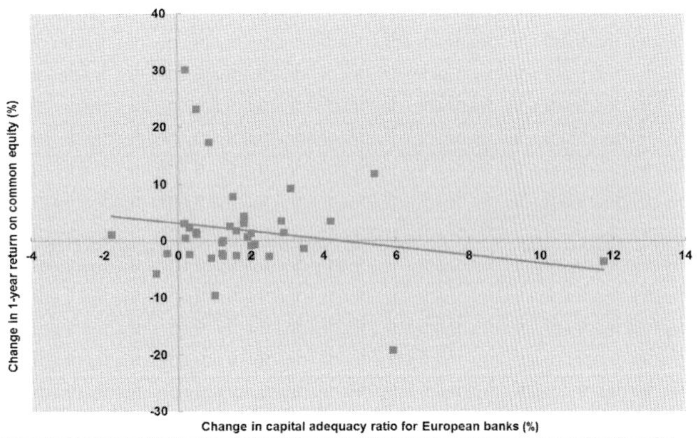

Data notes: Graphs are plotted based on the latest Bloomberg estimate for 1 year return on common equity while capital adequacy ratios follow 2012 and 2011 tier 1 capital to risk-weighted assets. Information includes 39 banks reporting FY2012 figures in 14 countries in Austria, Belgium, Switzerland, Czech Republic, Germany, Denmark, Spain, Finland, France, England, Italy, Poland, Portugal and Sweden.

(a)

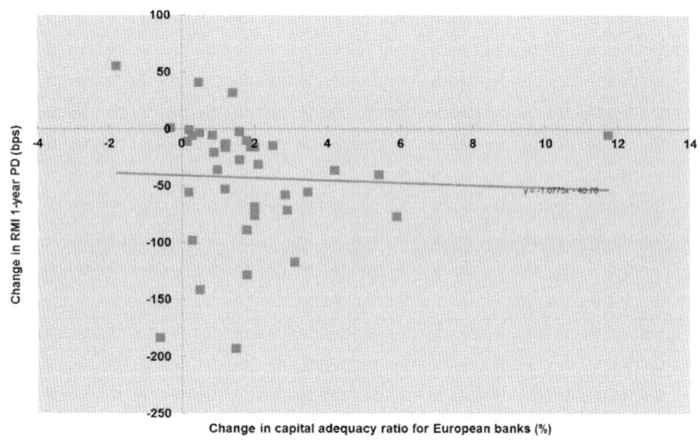

Data notes: Graphs are plotted based on the latest Bloomberg estimate for tier 1 capital adequacy ratios follow 2012 and 2011 tier 1 capital to risk-weighted assets. RMI PDs are calibrated in February 2014. Information includes 39 banks reporting FY2012 figures in 14 countries in Austria, Belgium, Switzerland, Czech Republic, Germany, Denmark, Spain, Finland, France, England, Italy, Poland, Portugal and Sweden.

(b)

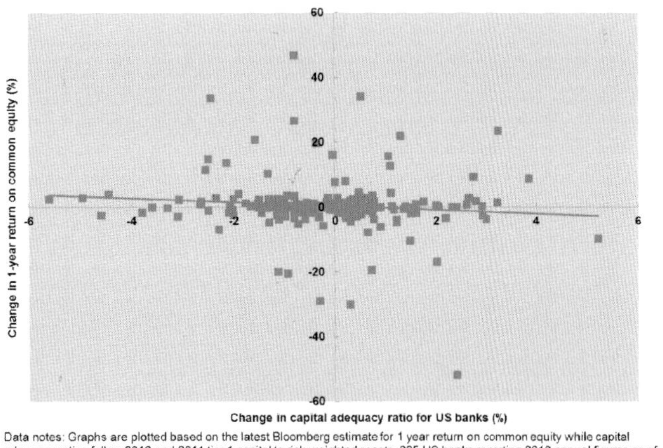

Data notes: Graphs are plotted based on the latest Bloomberg estimate for 1 year return on common equity while capital adequacy ratios follow 2012 and 2011 tier 1 capital to risk-weighted assets. 225 US banks reporting 2013 annual figures as of Mar 5, 2014 are displayed. Old Second Bancorp is excluded from the plot due to an unusual large gain in ROE in 2013 from a sharp increase in net income.

(c)

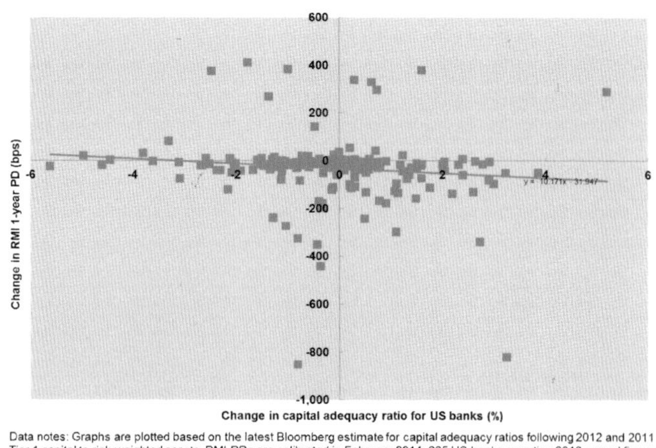

Data notes: Graphs are plotted based on the latest Bloomberg estimate for capital adequacy ratios following 2012 and 2011 Tier 1 capital to risk-weighted assets. RMI PDs are calibrated in February 2014. 225 US banks reporting 2013 annual figures as of Mar 5, 2014 are displayed. Old Second Bancorp is excluded from the plot due to an unusual large gain in ROE in 2013 from a sharp increase in net income.

(d)

Figure 4. (a) Change in Return on equity with CAR ratios for European banks. (b) Change in RMI PDs with CAR ratios for European banks. (c) Change in Return on equity with CAR ratios for US banks. (d) Change in RMI PD with CAR ratios for US banks. (e) Change in Return on equity with CAR ratios for banks in Developed Asia. (f) Change in RMI PD with CAR ratios for banks in Developed Asia. (g) Change in Return on equity with CAR ratios for banks in Developing Asia. (h) Change in RMI PD with CAR ratios for banks in Developing Asia. (i) Change in Return on equity with CAR ratios for Indian and Chinese banks. (j) Change in RMI PD with CAR ratios for Indian and Chinese banks.

Source: Parts (a), (c), (e), (g) and (j) are taken from RMI, ROE and CAR ratios taken from Bloomberg, March 5, 2014. Part (b), (d), (f) and (h) taken from RMI, CAR ratios taken from Bloomberg, March 5, 2014. Part (d) taken from RMI, CAR ratios taken from Bloomberg, March 5, 2014.

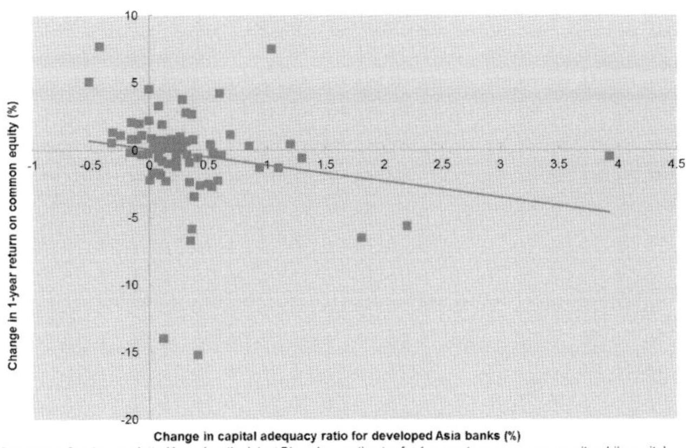

Data notes: Graphs are plotted based on the latest Bloomberg estimates for 1 year return on common equity while capital adequacy ratios follow 2012 and 2011 Tier 1 capital to risk-weighted assets. Developed Asian banks include 75 banks in Japan 4 banks in Hong Kong, 3 banks in Singapore and 2 banks in Korea. Tsukuba Bank is excluded from the graph due to an exceptional gain in Tier 1 ratio between 2011 and 2012. Fiscal year for Japanese banks end in March.

(e)

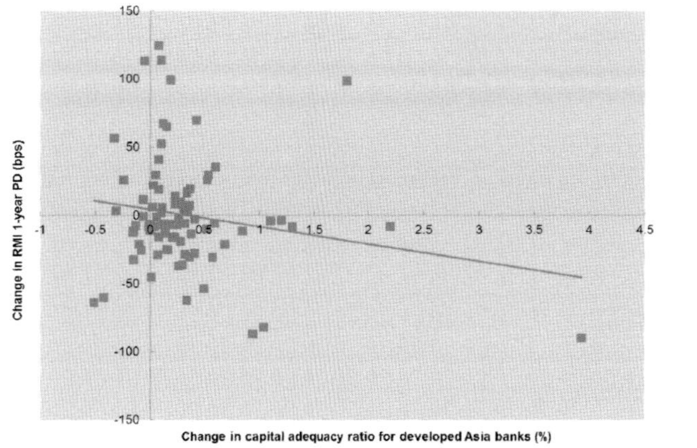

Data notes: Graphs are plotted based on the latest Bloomberg estimates for capital adequacy ratios following 2012 and 2011 Tier 1 capital to risk-weighted assets. RMI PDs are calibrated on February 2014. Developed Asian banks include 75 banks in Japan, 4 banks in Hong Kong, 3 banks in Singapore and 2 banks in Korea. Tsukuba Bank is excluded from the graph due to an exceptional gain in Tier 1 ratio between 2011 and 2012. Fiscal year for Japanese banks end in March.

(f)

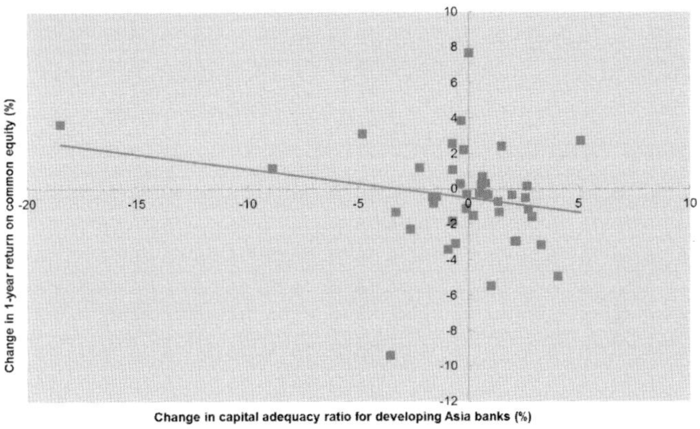

Data notes: Graphs are plotted based on the latest Bloomberg estimate for 1 year return on common equity while capital adequacy ratios follow 2012 and 2011 Tier 1 capital to risk-weighted assets. Developing Asian banks include 19 banks in Indonesia, 5 banks in the Philippines, 9 Malaysian banks and 9 Thai banks.

(g)

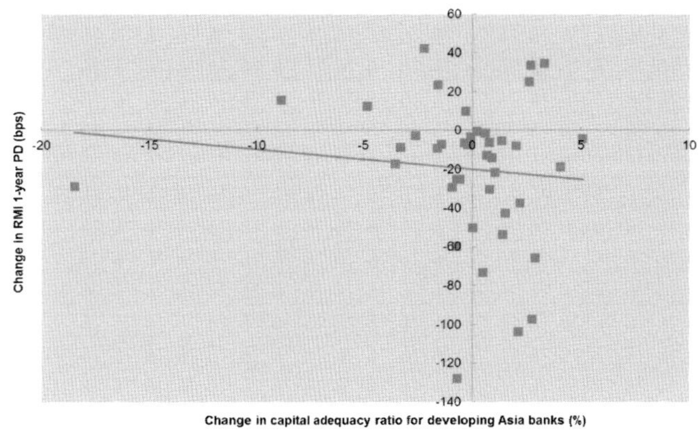

Data notes: Graphs are plotted based on the latest Bloomberg estimate for capital adequacy ratios following 2012 and 2011 Tier 1 capital to risk-weighted assets. 2012 RMI PDs are calibrated in February 2014. Developing Asian banks include 19 banks in Indonesia, 5 banks in the Philippines, 9 Malaysian banks and 9 Thai banks.

(h)

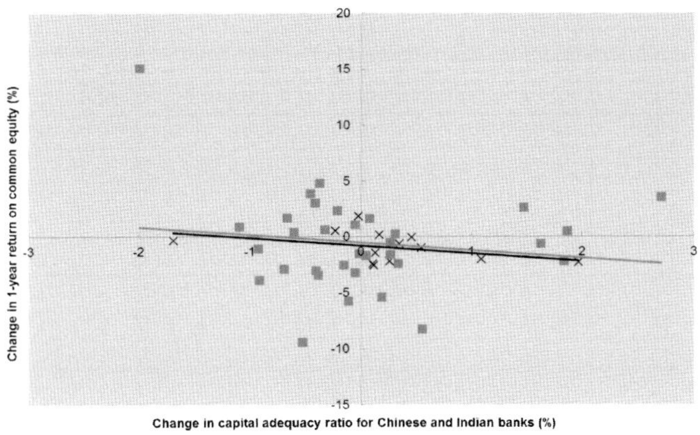

Data notes: Graphs are plotted based on the latest Bloomberg estimate for capital adequacy ratios following 2012 and 2011 Tier 1 capital to risk-weighted assets. RMI PDs are calibrated in February 2014. Fiscal year for Indian banks end in March.

× ROE_China ■ ROE_India

(i)

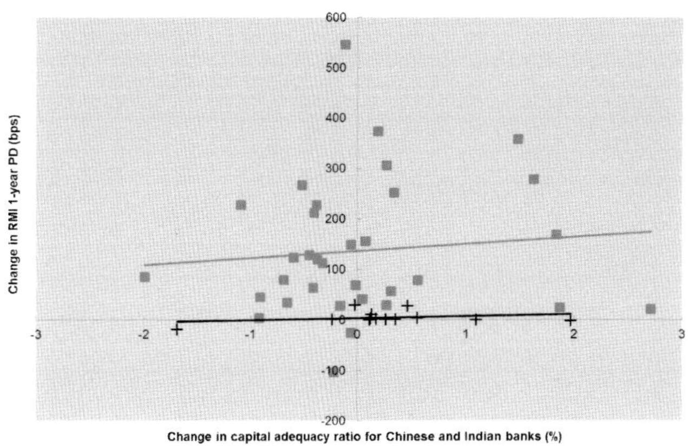

Data notes: Graphs are plotted based on the latest Bloomberg estimate for capital adequacy ratios following 2012 and 2011 Tier 1 capital to risk-weighted assets. RMI PDs are calibrated in February 2014. Fiscal year for Indian banks end in March.

+ PD_China ■ PD_India

(j)

Figure 4. *(Continued)*

Fig. 4(j). The Chinese banks showed an increase of +3.8 bps in RMI PDs as CAR increases. Even though CAR (the proportion of Tier 1 capital to risk weighted assets) increased an average of 0.25%, financial leverage measured as total liabilities over total assets for Chinese banks grew by an average of 2.97% in 2012. This is because Chinese banks were recommended by the CBRC since 2011 to maintain a minimum provision coverage ratio of 150% as a precautionary amount of reserves ahead of the likelihood that an increasing proportion of their loans should turn bad. CBRC's recommendation prompted Chinese banks to set aside more provisions as non-performing loan levels were rising due to an economic slowdown and faltering property market. This added the pressure of capital supplementation through increasing bond issues to continue their credit expansion during FY 2011 and 2012. Likewise, Indian banks suffered from an increase in financial leverage during the period of study of the 33 lenders, which showed an increase in their RMI PDs. CARs for Indian banks increased by an average of 0.04% in FY 2012, but financial leverage climbed by 1.51%.

IV. FUTURE IMPLICATIONS

With the new capital rules in place, banks could also be impacted by Basel III regulations in other ways. First, the framework creates heavy reliance on core capital (common equity and retained earnings). At the same time, financial firms might face difficulty in raising capital as investors may take the opportunity to discount minority interest, Tier 2 capital and hybrid instrument issuances when fellow financial institutions have to face a capital charge under Basel III for minority investments. Furthermore, banks may not have the incentive to redeem existing securities as they are able to include them as eligible Basel III capital. The guidelines allow banks to phase out their existing pool of non-qualified instruments through 2022. The largest US lenders, for example were reported to be moving assets into the "held-to-maturity" classification instead of designating them as "available for sale".[64] The top 50 banks increasingly held to maturity securities up to USD 38.4 bn in Q4 2013 while reducing the available for sale investments by USD 23.3 bn.

Lenders who are unable to meet capital requirements would have to raise additional capital to prepare for future economic stress conditions, as well as face constraints on their capital distribution. These banks could face restrictions in their treatment of retained earnings, dividend distributions, bonuses to executives and directors. State run United Bank of India was instructed by the RBI in February 2014 to limit its risk weighted asset expansion and eliminate its dividends to shareholders after the bank's capital adequacy ratio dropped below regulatory requirements following large losses during Q4 2013.[65]

Under the Basel guidelines for countercyclical buffers, internationally active banks would have to look at the geographic location of their private sector credit exposures and calculate their bank specific countercyclical capital buffer requirement as a weighted average of the buffers deployed across all the jurisdictions to which it has credit exposures. This could affect the bank's overseas expansion into a weaker economic zone as it comes at a higher cost. This is reflected in the falling number of cross border deals across Asian lenders between 2011 and 2013 (see Fig. 5).

Moreover, systemically important banks would have to keep strong balance sheets and avoid taking too much risk as they will be subjected to capital surcharges on top of normal Basel capital requirements.

Although leverage ratios will be calculated in a comparable manner across countries, adjustments

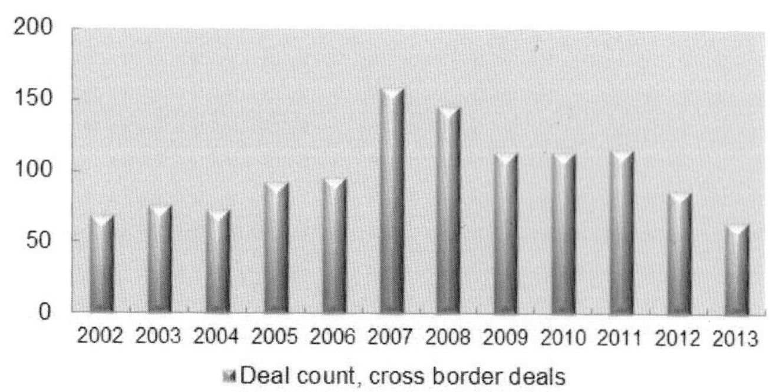

Figure 5. Number of Asian cross border deals between 2002 and 2013.

Source: Bloomberg, February 5, 2014.

would have to be made to the differences in accounting standards adopted in various countries. This means that the leverage ratio could be applied differently in nations. With a leverage ratio constraint of 3%, banks might be challenged to achieve return on equity improvements through leverage. Banks with businesses focused on direct lending and less on capital markets, like many in Asia, could continue to maintain high returns on equity. Therefore, the return on equity disparity could be enlarged between Western and Asian banks after 2016.

The LCR, soon to be implemented in 2015, would require global banks to hold high quality, cash convertible liquid assets in excess of expected cash outflows over a 30-day period of severe stress scenarios. This would mean that banks would have to hold more liquid assets to meet the LCR requirement which could lead to a negative impact on net interest margins.

Financial institutions need to support their business activities with more stable funding over longer term time horizons. Banks need to examine the liquidity profile of their on- and off-balance sheet assets, keep them funded on a regular basis, and also need to forecast the potential contingent calls on its funding profile. Banks have to invest in monitoring mechanisms over their assets and have to understand any likely mismatch and implement further actions to ensure a balanced NSFR. Some financial firms might have to invest considerable time in changing their infrastructure to execute their Basel implementation programs. These include setting up key middle office functions like technology support departments to handle consolidation of risk weighted assets, disclosures and reporting.

With the new capital rules in place, banks have to estimate the overall required Tier 1 or total capital with a fair amount of precision. To monitor their risk weighted assets, banks need to be familiar with their individual trading positions, its correlations with other instruments, and use of VaR, stressed VaR and the loan portfolio's internal ratings. Under Basel III, banks will likely see higher market risk requirement and more stringent calibration on counterparty credit risk exposures arising from derivatives, repos and security financing activities.[66]

V. CONCLUSION

To meet the new regulatory obligations, banks will require significant investments in people, systems and processes. They also need to increase senior management supervision and maintain its returns to its shareholders. International banks operating in Asia could face more challenges as they juggle between home and host country requirements and face issues on funding and pressure to embrace Basel regulations in different jurisdictions. Already, there are increasing calls from different regulators towards international banks operating in their jurisdiction to 'localize' their operations. Although, being a locally incorporated subsidiary rather than operating as branches will bring in some carrots for the banks to increase ability to expand and grow the business but they need to balance against greater regulatory scrutiny, higher capital requirements and need for more sophisticated operations so as to be less systemic to any turmoil at the parent level. More stringent regulatory requirements will reduce the risk of banks failing but questions do arise on the ability of Asian banks to supplement their equity capital with new-style subordinated debt under Basel III, such as CoCos, which are largely untested in the Asian context. In fact, banks like India's IDBI bank are already pushing investors in its USD 140 mn bonds to accept a controversial change in terms that grant the state-run lender the right to write down the debt or convert them into shares. So, with more banks seeking to be compliant with newer Basel III capital norms, investors may see more offerings of Basel III-compliant bond sales with low compensation, but are not fully aware of the conversion or write-down risk.

A number of Asia-Pacific jurisdictions are at present ahead of the US and Europe in formalizing their regulatory reforms, but there are still areas that are more contentious and less easily implementable such as the liquidity and OTC derivative reforms. The Group of Twenty governments responded to the crisis by committing that all standardized derivatives would be moved to central clearing and derivatives that are not centrally cleared would be subject to margin requirements. The consequences to the world economy are still unclear. The challenge of global consistency in regulations also remains. Regulators worldwide are wrestling with the rule-making process by tailoring policies to suit their own economies, resulting in a situation in which some countries are far ahead in their implementation process and even begin to impose requirements that are beyond Basel III. As we progress toward the full implementation of Basel III guidelines in 2019, the banking industry may witness an even more restrictive calculation of capital requirements, higher minimum leverage ratio and greater disclosure, which later forms the basis for a future Basel IV.

NOTES

1 Other international directives for banks include (1) tax regulation like the US Foreign Account Tax Compliance Act (FATCA); (2) requirements of the US Commodity Futures Trading Commission (CFTC) related to the registration of counterparties among others, and requirements contained in the newly approved Dodd–Frank Act.

2 Regulatory capital consists of Tier 1 capital, (CET1 and additional Tier 1 capital, AT1) and Tier 2 capital. CET1 includes the bank's common shares, retained earnings, accumulated other comprehensive income, other disclosed reserves, and regulatory adjustments.

3 The leverage ratio is defined as Tier 1 capital divided by the bank's total exposure. Total exposure is made up of (1) on balance sheet exposure, (2) derivative exposure, (3) securities financing transaction exposure, and (4) off balance sheet items. Netting of loans and deposits is not allowed.

4 The LCR is defined as the ratio of HQLA over the total net cash outflows over the following 30 calendar days. HQLAs are level 1 and level 2 (2A and 2B) assets; level 1 assets include cash, central bank reserves, and certain marketable securities backed by sovereign and central banks. Level 2A assets include certain government securities, covered bonds and corporate debt securities. Level 2B assets comprise of lower rated corporate bonds, residential mortgage backed securities and equities that meet certain conditions. Level 2A/2B assets may not account for more than 40%/15% of the bank's HQLA. The denominator is the total expected cash outflows minus total expected cash inflows in a specified stress scenario.

5 NSFR is the amount of available stable funding ratio relative to the required stable funding. The numerator would be the amount of supplied capital expected to be reliable over an appropriate time horizon, which could include Tiers 1 & 2 capital and term deposits. The denominator would be the amount of liabilities which would be a function of liquidity characteristics and residual maturities of various assets and off balance sheet items. Some elements of the NSFR remain subject to national supervisors due to special jurisdiction conditions.

6 Bank of International Settlements (2014).

7 BCBS. Basel III leverage ratio framework and disclosure requirements. January 2014. Bank for international settlements.

8 The Dodd–Frank Wall Street Reform Act is the most comprehensive financial reform since the Glass–Steagall Act. Similar to Glass–Steagall, it aims to regulate the financial markets and make another economic crisis less likely. Signed by President Barack Obama on July 21, 2010, Dodd–Frank is designed to help prevent the excessive risk-taking behavior of banks that led to the financial crisis. The Act also provides common-sense protections for American households, creating a new consumer watchdog to prevent lenders and mortgage companies from exploiting consumers. These new rules are the solid ground for a safer, more stable financial system—one that provides a robust foundation for lasting economic development and job creation.

9 Small banks with less than USD 500 mn in total consolidated assets that (1) are not engaged in significant nonbanking activities, (2) do not conduct significant off balance sheet activities and (3) do not have a material amount of SEC registered debt or equity securities. Savings and loan holding companies who are either (1) grandfathered units substantially engaged in commercial activities (more than 50% assets or revenues in commercial activities), (2) an insurance underwriting company and (3) substantially engages in insurance underwriting activities (more than 25% assets held in insurance underwriting subsidiaries).

10 Banks which have more than USD 250 bn in total consolidated assets and more than USD 10 bn on balance sheet foreign exposure or those seeking approval to use advanced approaches.

11 Banks who have been given permission by regulators may also use advanced approaches to calculate risk based capital requirements.

12 US banks with aggregate trading assets and trading liabilities of more than 10% of total assets or more than USD 1 bn of aggregate trading assets and trading liabilities.

13 Board of Governors of the Federal Reserve (2014).

14 Large banks must calculate risk weighted assets using existing Basel I based rules between January 1, 2014 and December 31, 2014 for compliance with capital requirements in Basel III rules.

15 This only applies to large depository institutions with USD 15 bn or more in total consolidated assets as of December 2009 that are not 2010 mutual holding companies.

16 Proprietary trading is allowed when the account is used to acquire or cover one or more covered financial positions that arise under (1) a repurchase or reverse purchase agreement which the bank had agreed in writing at the start of the transaction or (2) a transaction in which the bank lends or borrows a security temporarily to or from another party under which the lender owns the security and has the right to terminate the transaction and recall the loaned security on terms agreed by all parties.

17 Proprietary trading is allowed for accounts taking a position for the purpose of bona fide liquidity management, subject to certain requirements. For more information, refer to *Prohibitions and restrictions on proprietary trading and certain interests in, and relationships with, hedge funds and private equity funds.* SEC File No. S7-41-11, p. 65. December 10, 2013.

18 The primary difference between the Dodd–Frank Act Supervisory Stress Test (DFAST) and the CCAR post stress capital analysis is the capital action assumptions that are combined with the projections of pre-tax net income to estimate post stress capital levels and ratios. DFAST tests whether banks have sufficient capital to absorb losses and support operations during adverse economic conditions while using a standardized set of capital action assumptions that are specified in the Dodd–Frank Act stress test rules. On the other hand, CCAR uses BHCs planned capital actions like dividend payments and share repurchase to assess whether a BHC would be capable of meeting supervisory expectations for minimum capital ratios even if stressful conditions persist.

19 In the wake of the Global Financial Crisis (2007–2012), the Federal Reserve Bank of US started the annual CCAR exercise in late 2010. CCAR assesses large, complex BHCs and tests their soundness not just in terms of their capital adequacy and internal capital adequacy assessment processes, but also their capital distribution plans, such as dividends or stock repurchases. CCAR applies to all US banks with assets greater than USD 50 bn.

20 Instead of a full deduction, the threshold treatment allows the following items to receive limited recognition when calculating CET1, with recognition capped at 10% of the bank's common equity: (1) significant investments in common shares of unconsolidated financial institutions, (2) mortgage servicing rights, and (3) deferred tax assets that arise from temporary differences.

21 Australia Prudential Regulation Authority (2013)

22 Kelly (2013).

23 BCBS (2012).

24 The phasing out of instruments which do not qualify as non-CET1 or Tier 2 will start in January every year, unlike the schedule for other regulatory elements which starts in April.

25 Bank Sentral Republik Indonesia (2013).

26 Sipahutar (2014).

27 http://www.fsa.go.jp/news/24/ginkou/20120807-3/08.pdf.

28 Securities Business Division (March 2013).

29 Yahya (2013).

30 Bank of Thailand (2012).

31 Includes rules defined for capital, risk coverage and the capital conservation buffer under the Basel III framework.

32 The Bank of Thailand has not updated local rules to reflect CVA charges when calculating capital requirements.

33 Countercyclical buffers will take effect from January 1, 2016.

34 Some Thai banks have set aside countercyclical capital buffers, but it is not clear if they are within the 2.5% of its risk weighted assets, or reflective of its geographic composition of its portfolio of credit exposures.

35 The HKMA is asking to hold up to 3.5% of capital as a countercyclical reserve, higher than the 2.5% required by Basel III.

36 RBI (2013a).

37 The definition of the leverage ratio for Chinese banks is different from those defined in the Basel rules. The consolidated and non-consolidated leverage ratio of a commercial bank shall not fall below 4%. Refer to the decree of China Banking Regulatory Commission, No 3, 2011.

38 Banks will report their leverage ratios to authorities on a quarterly basis from January 1, 2013.

39 In Malaysia, leverage levels of individual banks are monitored and assessed by the central bank as part of the supervisory process. A final decision to adopt the Leverage Ratio as a binding measure will be made closer to 2018. In the meantime, banks have been reporting to Bank Negara their leverage ratio positions calculated according to Basel III rules.

40 The domestic systemically important bank shall be subjected to a capital surcharge of 1% of risk weighted assets and shall be comprised of Tier 1 common equity capital. Details about the rule will be released in future.

41 Notice 637 only specified the data submission and disclosure requirements for assessing globally systemically important banks.

42 RBI (2013b).

43 China's banking regulator proposed that banks meet the required minimum LCR by end 2018. Banks could first meet a more lenient LCR of 60% by the end of 2014.

44 Singapore is proposing to change the existing Minimum Liquid Assets requirement for banks, under MAS Notice 613 to adopt the recommendations by the Basel Committee.

45 Malaysia has their own liquidity framework for its banks, which will be changed to reflect Basel III recommendations in future.

46 Under the 2-tiered approach, the LCR will be applied to category 1 banks, while the modified liquidity ratio will be applied to category 2 banks.

47 The RBI introduced draft guidelines on liquidity risk management and Basel III framework on liquidity standards on February 21, 2012. The central bank asked the banking industry for their feedback but they were in response to the Basel rules introduced in December 2010, and not the standards announced in January 2013 regarding the LCR and market monitoring tools.

48 Kemp (2011).

49 Under Basel, the unsecured portion of any loan that is past 90 days will be risk weighted as follows: (1) 150% risk weight when provisions are less than 20% of outstanding loans, (2) 100% risk weight when provisions are no less than 20% of outstanding loans, (3) 100% risk weight when provisions are no less than 50% of total loans but with supervisory discretion reduce the risk weight to 50%. The CBRC also does not require a higher risk weighting for unsecured sections of the loans when the provisions set by the bank are less than a certain percentage of the outstanding amount. This is because Chinese banks already have to keep the higher of (1) ratio of total loan loss provisions to total loans of at least 2.5% and (2) a proportion of total loan loss provisions to non-performing loans higher than 150%.

50 Chitkara (2013).

51 This reduces to 400% in two situations. First, the equity investment is in a commercial entity passively held by the bank within the legally prescribed period. Second, the bank has invested in a commercial entity due to policy reasons and with special approval from the State Council.

52 An investment is considered to be material if it exceeds 15% of the bank's capital on an individual basis and 60% of the bank's capital for the aggregate of such investments.

53 China's Capital Rules are harsher than Basel III in other areas. In the Capital Rules, Chinese banks cannot apply the firm size adjustment for claims on certain financial institutions because they are classified under the bank exposures class and not in the corporate exposures class. Additionally, banks have to apply an asset value correlation multiplier on claims across all financial institutions. Under Basel III, this increase in capital requirement for the banks is only applicable to claims on large financial institutions (i.e., firms with more than or equal to USD 100 bn of assets). The Capital Rules do not offer the double default framework under the IRB exposures. As a result, the capital requirement for positions eligible for the double default framework — such as exposures hedged certain credit derivatives — would be higher than if the double default framework were applied.

According to Basel, the exposure at default (EAD) for unused committed credit lines (an off balance sheet item) under the IRB Foundation approach is based on the lower of the value of the unused committed credit line and the value that reflects any possible constraining availability of the facility, provided that certain requirements are met. The Capital Rules do not recognize any possible constraining availability and the resulting EAD will therefore be equal or higher than under Basel. Under the simple risk weight method for equities, Basel requires a 300% risk weight to be applied for equity holdings that are publicly traded and a 400% risk weigh to all other exposures.

The Capital Rules do not offer the simple risk weight method separately for the IRB approach; instead, the implementation of the Standardized Approach is required to be applied to all equity exposures. The risk weights applied are either 400% or 1250%. This method of implementation effectively results in the mandatory application of the simple risk weight method to all equity exposures, whereby the risk weight for certain equity exposures are higher than required by Basel. All publicly traded equity holdings receive a risk weight of 40% instead of 300%. Equity exposures that are neither passive holdings of equity investments in commercial entities nor investments due to policy reasons and with approval of the State Council receive a risk weight of 1250% instead of 400%.

Basel requires a 2% capital charge for the specific risk of OTC equity index futures and equity index options, whereas the Capital Rules apply an 8% capital charge. Of the three approaches for counterparty credit risk (CCR) available in the Basel framework, only the simplest one (current exposure method) has been adopted in the Capital Rules, but it disallows collateral received by banks as margin to reduce the exposure.

54 Notice on risk based capital adequacy requirements for banks incorporated in Singapore. MAS. September 14, 2012.

55 Kehoe (2013).

56 Raghuvanshi (2013).

57 Banks in Australia, China, Hong Kong, India, Indonesia, Japan, Malaysia, Philippines, Singapore, South Korea and Thailand.

58 Lee (2013).

59 The Jakarta Globe (2013).

60 The Basel Committee defines that the terms and conditions of all non-common Tier 1 and Tier 2 instruments issued by an internationally active bank must have a provision that requires such instruments, at the option of the relevant authority, to either be written off or converted into common equity upon the occurrence of the trigger event unless (1) the governing jurisdiction of the bank has in place laws that require such Tier 1 and Tier 2 instruments to be written off upon such events, or otherwise require such instruments to fully absorb losses before tax payers are exposed to loss (2) a peer group review confirms that the jurisdiction conforms with clause (1) and (3) it is disclosed by the relevant regulator and by the issuing bank, in issuance documents going forward, that such instruments are subject to loss under clause (1) in this paragraph.

61 Avdjiev *et al.* (2013).

62 This is only effective after March 31, 2019. Before that, instruments will have a trigger point of 5.5% CET1 ratio.

63 This is effective after March 31, 2010. Before that, bonds will have a trigger point of 5.5% CET1.

64 Shenn (2014).

65 Saha and Chakraborty (2014).

66 Basel III has set a harsher approach for calculating capital charges. Under the new IRB based approach, the assets value correlation multiplier has increased to 1.25. For firms adopting the Standardized approach, a new capital charge will be assessed on price fluctuation risk stemming from changes in counterparty credit risk in the OTC derivative trades. In addition, the interconnectedness/correlations between large financial institutions shall also be factored into the calculation for additional capital charges for counterparty risk exposures. Under existing rules, 3 years of market data are run through internal models to measure expected returns. In the revised proposal, banks must compare (1) a 3-year period that includes a 1 year stress period and (2) the most recent 3-year period and use whichever set of data produces the larger exposure.

ANNEX A

Severely Adverse Scenario — Actual Q3 2013 and projected minimum regulatory capital ratios and Tier 1 common ratios for advanced approaches BHCs (Q4 2013–Q4 2015)													
BHC	Capital actions	Tier 1 Common Ratio (%)		CET1(%)		Tier 1 Risk-based Capital Ratio (%)				Total Risk-based Capital Ratio (%)		Tier 1 Leverage Ratio (%)	
		Actual Q3 2013	Projected minimum	Projected 2014 minimum	Projected 2015 minimum	Actual Q3 2013	Projected Q4 2013	Projected 2014 minimum	Projected 2015 minimum	Actual Q3 2013	Projected minimum	Actual Q3 2013	Projected minimum
American Express	Original	12.80	8.40	10.60	8.90	12.80	12.30	11.20	10.20	14.70	12.00	10.70	8.50
	Adjusted												
Bank of America	Original	11.10	5.00	8.00	6.00	12.30	9.50	8.00	6.00	15.40	8.40	7.80	3.90
	Adjusted	11.10	5.30	8.00	6.30	12.30	9.50	8.00	6.30	15.40	8.70	7.80	4.10
Citigroup Inc.	Original	12.70	6.50	10.80	9.10	13.60	10.50	10.80	9.10	16.70	11.60	8.10	5.60
	Adjusted												
Goldman Sachs Group	Original	14.20	5.70	7.50	5.00	16.30	10.30	8.20	6.00	19.40	8.00	7.90	3.90
	Adjusted	14.20	6.10	7.80	5.60	16.30	10.30	8.60	6.40	19.40	8.40	7.90	4.20
HSBC	Original	14.70	6.60	12.60	9.40	17.10	15.60	12.60	9.40	26.50	18.20	7.80	4.40
	Adjusted												
JPMorgan Chase & Co.	Original	10.50	5.50	6.90	5.40	11.70	9.20	8.10	6.60	14.30	8.70	6.90	4.20
	Adjusted												
Morgan Stanley	Original	12.60	5.90	8.50	6.80	15.30	10.80	8.80	7.20	16.10	9.40	7.30	4.60
	Adjusted												
State Street Corp.	Original	15.50	11.40	13.90	9.40	17.30	15.00	16.10	11.50	19.80	13.50	7.20	6.30
	Adjusted												
Wells Fargo & Co.	Original	10.60	6.10	7.70	5.20	12.10	11.30	9.20	6.90	15.10	10.90	9.80	5.60
	Adjusted												

Figure A.1. Federal Reserve estimates in the severely adverse scenario — projected minimum regulatory capital ratios and Tier 1 common ratios, Q4 2013 to Q4 2015.

Note: These projections represent hypothetical estimates that involve an economic outcome that is more adverse than expected. These estimates are not forecasts of capital ratios. The tables include the minimum ratios assuming the capital actions originally submitted in January 2014 by the BHCs in their annual capital plans and the minimum ratios incorporating any adjustments to capital distributions made by BHCs after reviewing the Federal Reserve's stress test projections.

Required Minimum Capital ratios for advanced approaches BHCs in 2014			
Regulatory Ratios	**Q4 2013**	**2014**	**2015**
Tier 1 Common Ratio	5%	5%	5%
CET1 ratio	N/A	4%	4.5%
Tier 1 risk-based capital ratio	4%	5.5%	6%
Total risk-based capital ratio	8%	8%	8%
Tier 1 leverage ratio	3 or 4%	4%	4%

Figure A.2. Required minimum capital ratios for advanced approaches BHCs in CCAR 2014.

Note: For purposes of CCAR 2014, an advanced approaches BHC includes any BHC that has consolidated assets greater than or equal to USD 250 bn or total consolidated on-balance sheet foreign exposure of at least USD 10 bn as of December 31, 2013.

The projected Tier 1 common ratio is calculated using the definitions of Tier 1 capital and total risk-weighted assets in effect at the start of the capital planning cycle in 2013, without incorporating the new definitions from the revised capital framework issued in July 2013. All other ratios are calculated in accordance with the transition arrangements provided in the Board's revised capital framework.

Adverse Scenario - Actual Q3 2013 and projected minimum regulatory capital ratios and tier 1 common ratios for advanced approaches BHCs (Q4 2013 - Q4 2015)													
		Tier 1 Common Ratio (%)		CET1(%)		Tier 1 Risk-based Capital Ratio (%)				Total Risk-based Capital Ratio (%)		Tier 1 Leverage Ratio (%)	
BHC	Capital actions	Actual Q3 2013	Projected minimum	Projected 2014 minimum	Projected 2015 minimum	Actual Q3 2013	Projecte d Q4 2013	Projecte d 2014 minimum	Projecte d 2015 minimum	Actual Q3 2013	Projected minimum	Actual Q3 2013	Projected minimum
American Express	Original	12.80	10.60	11.80	10.70	12.80	12.60	12.20	11.90	14.70	13.80	10.70	9.90
	Adjusted												
Bank of America	Original	11.10	8.40	9.50	7.90	12.30	10.40	9.80	8.40	15.40	11.00	7.80	5.40
	Adjusted	11.10	8.40	9.50	8.00	12.30	10.40	9.80	8.40	15.40	11.10	7.80	5.50
Citigroup Inc.	Original	12.70	9.30	12.50	10.80	13.60	11.50	12.50	10.80	16.70	13.20	8.10	6.60
	Adjusted												
Goldman Sachs Group	Original	14.20	7.20	7.90	5.80	16.30	12.40	11.10	7.10	19.40	9.20	7.90	4.40
	Adjusted	14.20	8.00	10.10	6.50	16.30	12.40	11.50	7.80	19.40	9.90	7.90	4.80
HSBC	Original	14.70	11.10	13.60	11.60	17.10	16.30	14.20	12.20	26.50	20.70	7.80	5.60
	Adjusted												
JPMorgan Chase & Co.	Original	10.50	8.30	8.30	7.10	11.70	10.50	9.60	8.40	14.30	10.50	6.90	5.40
	Adjusted												
Morgan Stanley	Original	12.60	8.50	10.90	8.00	15.30	12.60	11.60	8.70	16.10	11.00	7.30	4.90
	Adjusted												
State Street Corp.	Original	15.50	13.40	14.00	9.70	17.30	15.70	15.60	11.20	19.80	13.20	7.20	6.10
	Adjusted												
Wells Fargo & Co.	Original	10.60	8.70	9.00	7.40	12.10	11.60	10.40	9.00	15.10	13.10	9.80	7.30
	Adjusted												

Figure A.3. Federal Reserve estimates in the adverse scenario — projected minimum regulatory capital ratios and Tier 1 common ratios, Q4 2013 to Q4 2015.

Note: These projections represent hypothetical estimates that involve an economic outcome that is more adverse than expected. These estimates are not forecasts of capital ratios. The tables include the minimum ratios assuming the capital actions originally submitted in January 2014 by the BHCs in their annual capital plans and the minimum ratios incorporating any adjustments to capital distributions made by BHCs after reviewing the Federal Reserve's stress test projections.

REFERENCES

Australia Prudential Regulation Authority (2013), Information Paper, Domestic Systemically Important Banks in Australia, December.

Avdjiev, S., A. Kartasheva and B. Bogdanova (2013), CoCos: A primer. *BIA Quarterly Review*, September.

Bank of International Settlements. Basel III Monitoring Report, March 6, 2014.

Bank Sentral Republik Indonesia (2013), BI Transferring Regulation and Supervision of Banks to Financial Services Authority, December 31.

Bank of Thailand (2012), Issuance of BOT Notifications on Capital Adequacy Framework Under Basel III. BOT Press Release, December 14.

BCBS (2012), Basel III Counterparty Credit Risk and Exposures to Central Counterparties — Frequently Asked Questions. Bank for International Settlements, December.

Board of Governors of the Federal Reserve (2014), Board Meeting Board Memo, April 8.

Chitkara, G. (2013), Chinese Securitization Market Risks Fragmentation Under Current Dual Framework. *Risk. Net.*, November 20.

Kehoe, J. (2013), ANZ in Talks to Sell Indonesian Stake. *The Australian Financial Review*, August 14.

Kelly, R. (2013), Australia Orders Banks to Raise Capital. *The Wall Street Journal*, December 23.

Kemp, K. (2011), Implementation of Basel III in Hong Kong. Banking Policy Department, HKMA, January 26.

Lee, J. (2013), Basel III Capital Charge to Dent Bank M&A Activity. *Asia Risk*, September 4.

RBI (2013a), Draft Report of the Internal Working Group on Implementation of Counter-Cyclical Capital Buffer, December 2.

RBI (2013b), RBI Seeks Comments on Draft Framework for Dealing with Domestic Systemically Important Banks (D-SIBs), December 2.

Raghuvanshi, G. (2013), DBS Still Bullish on Indonesia After Failed Danamon Deal. *The Wall Street Journal*, August 1.

Saha, M. and S. Chakraborty (2014), Reserve Bank to Enforce Strict Regime on UBI. *Business Standard News*, February 21.

Securities Business Division, Supervisory Bureau, Japan Financial Services Agency (2013), Comprehensive Guidelines for Supervision of Financial Instruments Business Operators, March.

Sipahutar, T. (2014), OJK, BI to Identify "Too Big to Fail" Domestic Banks. *The Jakarta Post*, January 6.

Shenn, J. (2014), Banks Averting Bond Losses with Accounting Twist. *Bloomberg News*, February 26.

The Jakarta Globe (2013), Rabobank to Stay in Indonesia, June 28.

Yahya, Y. (2013), Standard Chartered Completes Local Incorporation of Subsidiary. *The Straits Times*, October 7.

Actuarial Par Spread and Empirical Pricing of CDS by Decomposition

Jin-Chuan Duan
Risk Management Institute
Business School and Department of Economics
National University of Singapore
bizdjc@nus.edu.sg

Keywords: Actuarial value, par spread, CDS, default, recovery rate, forward intensity.

INTRODUCTION

A credit default swap (CDS) is a financial contract that works much like typical insurance. The contract defines a reference instrument (a bond) issued by some reference entity (the obligor). The buyer of a CDS pays periodic premiums in exchange for protection against potential losses incurred on the reference instrument when the obligor defaults. Buyers may or may not hold the reference instrument because CDS are often used as a cross hedge for credit exposures arising from other business dealings with the obligor; for example, a supply chain relationship. Of course, CDS can also be used for speculative purposes just like other financial instruments. CDS were invented in the 1990s and steadily gained popularity to reach a peak in 2007 with over 60 trillion USD notional outstanding. The onset of the global financial crisis in 2008 put a dent in its popularity, and CDS were blamed as a main contributor to the global financial crisis. Even so, CDS are still a multi-trillion market these days because they play a vital risk management function.

In earlier years of CDS trading, the spread was generally set without involving an upfront fee. We will refer to such a spread as CDS par spread. Since the introduction of the CDS Big Bang Protocol in April 2009, CDS have been traded with a fixed coupon at either 100 or 500 basis points with an upfront fee to offset the mispricing caused by the fixed coupon rate. Obviously, this change makes secondary market trading of CDS easier, because the upfront fee can freely move with market conditions and clear offsetting trades without having to pile new CDS on existing CDS. A fixed-coupon CDS with an upfront fee can be easily quoted as a CDS par spread. In this paper, we will stick to the CDS par spread in expressing the price of a CDS much like using effective yield instead of coupon rate to quote the cost/return of a bond.

When probabilities of default (PDs) exhibit a term structure behavior, CDS spreads become some complex aggregate of the PDs over the segment of the term structure defined by the tenor of CDS. For a 5-year CDS, one should note that the CDS spread may not be closely aligned with the 5-year PD (annualized) because CDS premiums are only payable up to the time of default. Since the maximum loss given default is 100% and the highest possible PD is also 100%, one would think that the CDS spread should be capped at 10,000 basis points. But Greek sovereign CDS were actually traded at a spread beyond 20,000 basis points prior to its default in the early part of 2012. This is because with Greece's imminent default, the protection buyer was only expected to pay a fraction of the premium determined by a short accrual period, but the protection seller was expected to soon incur a big loss whose amount was not tied to the accrual period. Pushing up the CDS premium beyond 20,000 basis points was to offset the likely short accrual period.

Instead of focusing on PDs over various periods extending out from the point of prediction, one can consider forward PDs (a fixed duration, say, one month, but with different forward starting times). Forward PDs work much like forward interest rates. Due to their contractual features, CDS spreads are expected to be more in line with short-term (long-term) forward PD when shorter-term forward PDs are higher (lower) than longer-term forward PDs. This is because an imminent default suggests high shorter-term forward PDs being coupled with lower longer-term forward PDs. As in the preceding discussion on the Greek default, CDS spreads will have to be high enough to reflect a shorter accrual period due to the imminent default.

The complexity of having to use the term structure of forward PDs to analyze CDS spreads highlights the need for a simpler summary measure. Indeed, that is precisely the objective of this paper. We envisage a CDS premium rate that would have been charged if market participants were risk-neutral and no money changed hands initially. In short, it is equivalent to pricing CDS purely based on their actuarial values. Such a premium rate is referred to as an actuarial par spread and can be computed with availability of the term structure of physical PDs. We show by a numerical example the mechanics of its computation and explain how it can be operationalized on a daily and live basis by leveraging the corporate default prediction system developed and maintained by the Risk Management Institute (RMI) of the National University of Singapore.

As an example to demonstrate this new measure, this paper will look at Eastman Kodak, which filed for Chapter 11 bankruptcy protection on January 19, 2012. Kodak later emerged from bankruptcy on September 3, 2013, and its stocks under a different ticker began to trade in NYSE on November 1, 2013. We use the actuarial par spread to study the CDS spreads of Kodak over the one-year period leading to the day of its bankruptcy filing. The results suggest that the log-ratio of CDS spread over its corresponding actuarial par spread is highly predictable with its lagged value, and this predictive relationship can form a good basis for empirical pricing of CDS.

I. TERM STRUCTURE OF PHYSICAL PDs AND ACTUARIAL PAR SPREADS

A CDS contract comprises the premium and protection legs. The protection buyer typically pays premiums on a quarterly basis to the seller, which are calculated based on the fixed spread until the reference entity defaults. In exchange, the protection buyer receives a contingent lump sum payment at the default time of the reference entity, and the settlement amount is by convention based on the recovery rate on the reference instrument determined at the credit event auction held specifically for the defaulted obligor within one month of default. Consider at time t a CDS contract to be terminated at time $T > t$. The premium leg comes with periodic future payments at $\{t_1, t_2, \ldots, t_k\}$ with $t_k = T$. The payment date at or immediately before t is denoted by t_0. The protection leg pays an amount set according to one minus a random recovery rate, R_τ at the random default time $\tau > t$ if default occurs before T, at which time all scheduled premium payments beyond the default time cease to apply.

CDS premiums are subject to day count conventions similar to coupon bonds. Adding to the complexity is the fact that accrual periods do not always end on payment dates. Differences are typically one day, and may be ignored for many practical purposes. For a more precise modeling of CDS, however, we introduce a set of accrual period end dates, $\{t'_1, t'_2, \ldots, t'_k\}$. Let $A(t_{i-1}, t'_i)$ stand for the length of an accrual period measured as the fraction of a year using the appropriate day count convention. For a typical CDS and if a particular quarterly accrual period from t_{i-1} to t'_i inclusive has, say, 91 calendar days, the actual/360 day count convention will give rise to $A(t_{i-1}, t'_i) = 91/360$, a factor that determines the fraction of the annualized spread applicable to this particular quarter.

Let $D_t(T - t)$ denote the appropriate money market discount factor starting from time t to some future date T. This discount factor is typically random. To deal with randomness in discount factor, default and recovery rate, we adopt the familiar derivatives pricing theory with which there exists a risk-neutral pricing measure, and derivatives can be priced by taking expectation of its contingent payment with respect to the risk-neutral pricing measure as if economic agents were not risk adverse. We denote such a risk-neutral expectation operator at time t by $E_t^Q(\cdot)$ to reflect the time-t information set.

I.1. CDS Par Spread and Actuarial Par Spread

The CDS par spread, $S_t(T - t)$, is known to satisfy the following condition, which reflects the fact that no money has changed hands initially between the protection buyer and seller.[1]

$$\begin{aligned} E_t^Q[(1 - R_\tau)D_t(\tau - t)1_{\{t<\tau\le t'_k\}}] &= S_t(T-t)\sum_{i=1}^{k}\{A(t_{i-1}\vee t, t'_i) \\ &\quad \times E_t^Q[D_t(t_i - t)1_{\{t'_i<\tau\}}] \\ &\quad + E_t^Q[A(t_{i-1}\vee t, \tau)D_t(\tau - t)1_{\{t'_{i-1}<\tau\le t'_i\}}]\}, \end{aligned} \tag{1}$$

where $t_{i-1} \vee t$ denotes the maximum of t_{i-1} and t so that the partial accrual for the first payment period, i.e., from t_0 to t, is taken out. Note that the left-hand side is the present value of the payment for the protection leg up to and including the final accrual end date, whereas the right-hand side is the present value of the payments for the premium leg with the amount determined by the CDS par spread that is known when the contract is entered. One needs to note that for all pre-scheduled payments, we have used the payment date, t_i, for discounting and the accrual end date, t'_i, for computing probability to reflect the actual default protection coverage period. Also implicit in the above equation is the assumption that at default, the payments for both premium and protection legs are made immediately. Any delay in payment can in effect be incorporated into the recovery rate.

Equation (1) can be used to state the CDS par spread as:

$$S_t(T - t) = \frac{E_t^Q\left[(1 - R_\tau)D_t(\tau - t)1_{\{t<\tau\le t'_k\}}\right]}{\begin{aligned}&\textstyle\sum_{i=1}^{k}\Big\{A(t_{i-1}\vee t, t'_i)E_t^Q\left[D_t(t_i - t)1_{\{t'_i<\tau\}}\right] \\ &\quad + E_t^Q\left[A(t_{i-1}\vee t, \tau)D_t(\tau - t)1_{\{t'_{i-1}<\tau\le t'_i\}}\right]\Big\}\end{aligned}}. \tag{2}$$

Let $r_t(s, q)$ be the time-t risk-free forward discount rate starting at time $t + s$ with a duration of $q - s$, where $q \ge s$. The standard term structure theory implies that $r_t(0, T - t) = -\frac{1}{T-t}\ln(E_t^Q[D_t(T - t)])$. If we further assume that R_τ, τ and $D_t(t_i - t)$ (for all i's) are all independent and let $\bar{R}_t = E_t^Q(R_\tau)$, then

$$S_t(T - t) = \frac{(1-\bar{R}_t)E_t^Q\left[e^{-r_t(0,\tau-t)(\tau-t)}1_{\{t<\tau\le t'_k\}}\right]}{\begin{aligned}&\textstyle\sum_{i=1}^{k}\Big\{A(t_{i-1}\vee t, t'_i)e^{-r_t(0,t_i-t)(t_i-t)}E_t^Q\left[1_{\{t'_i<\tau\}}\right] \\ &\quad + E_t^Q\left[A(t_{i-1}\vee t, \tau)e^{-r_t(0,\tau-t)(\tau-t)}1_{\{t'_{i-1}<\tau\le t'_i\}}\right]\Big\}\end{aligned}}. \tag{3}$$

Now we are in a position to define the actuarial par spread, denoted by $S_t^{(a)}(T - t)$, which is the par spread computed by replacing the risk-neutral probability measure Q with the physical probability measure P. In other words, the actuarial par spread would become the CDS par spread when economic agents were truly risk-neutral and valuation were conducted purely on an actuarial basis. That is to mean

$$
\begin{aligned}
&S_t^{(a)}(T-t) \\
&= \frac{(1-\bar{R}_t)E_t^P\left[e^{-r_t(0,\tau-t)(\tau-t)}1_{\{t<\tau\le t'_k\}}\right]}{\sum_{i=1}^k\left\{A(t_{i-1}\vee t, t'_i)e^{-r_t(0,t_i-t)(t_i-t)}E_t^P\left[1_{\{t'_i<\tau\}}\right]\right.}. \\
&\quad \left. + E_t^P\left[A(t_{i-1}\vee t, \tau)e^{-r_t(0,\tau-t)(\tau-t)}1_{\{t'_{i-1}<\tau\le t'_i\}}\right]\right\}
\end{aligned} \tag{4}
$$

I.2. Term Structure of Physical PDs

In order to compute the actuarial spread, we need a model for term structure of PDs with respect to the physical probability law that governs occurrences of default. Like interest rates, term structure of PDs can be stated in terms of spot or forward PDs. Here, we adopt the forward intensity approach of Duan *et al.* (2012) to characterize term structure of PDs. Before proceeding further, it is important to note that a corporate exit can be caused by default/bankruptcy or simply merger/aquisition. However, exits for reasons other than default/bankruptcy are in the literature typically left un-modeled except for a few papers like Duffie *et al.* (2007), Duan *et al.* (2012) and Duan and Fulop (2013). The resulting censoring bias of course depends on the occurrence rate of other exits. Based on Table 1 of Duan *et al.* (2012) which documents defaults/bankruptcies and other types of firm exit for the US exchange-listed firms over 1991 to 2011, the censoring bias is likely significant; for example in 2007, 0.5% of the firms defaulted whereas 9.34% of them exited for other reasons.

This huge gap implies that ignoring other exits in default models could grossly inflate the predicted default probability, because it is the only factor for tuning both survival and default occurrences. Suppose p is the default probability for one period and the default rate is time homogeneous. Depending on how the data sample is treated, the consequences may differ. If the firms due to other exits are left out of the sample, p will be overestimated simply because the sample shows an upward biased default rate. If those firms are kept in the sample and treated as survived ones, p will be correctly estimated. Even if p is estimated properly, there will be distorted consequences in applications; for example, the probability of a firm defaulting in two periods will be erroneously calculated as $p+(1-p)p$, but the correct PD should be lower because the right formula is $p+(1-p-q)p$ with q being the probability of other exits over one period. In the case of CDS, other exit does not mean termination because the successor entity will be assigned to replace the reference entity. Naturally, the relevant default probability must factor in the default probability of the successor; for example, qp^* should be added to $p+(1-p-q)p$ with p^* denoting the successor's default probability over the second period.

Envision a continuous-time setting where corporate obligors evolve dynamically with their individual attributes changing along with macroeconomic factors. Some obligors default, some exit for other reasons, but the rest survive. The occurrence of default and that of other exits for each obligor are governed by two Poisson processes that are independent when conditioning on their Poisson intensities. But these two intensities are correlated because they are functions of some common variables (obligor's attributes and macroeconomic factors). Across obligors, the default and other-exit processes are also independent once being conditioned on their Poisson intensities. Such processes are known as the Cox doubly stochastic processes, which serve as the modeling foundation for Duffie *et al.* (2007), Duan *et al.* (2012) and many others. The departing point for Duan *et al.* (2012) is the use of forward Poisson intensities to model the occurrence of default or other exits. Here, we simply apply the results directly and refer readers to Duan *et al.* (2012) for more technical details.

Let $f_t(s)$ and $h_t(s)$ be, respectively, the time-t forward default and other-exit intensities with the forward starting time of $t+s$. Define $\psi_t(s,q)=\frac{\int_s^q[f_t(u)+h_t(u)]du}{q-s}$ for $s\le q$, which is in a way much like the standardized time-t forward interest rate starting at time $t+s$ with a duration of $q-s$. Recall our earlier definition for forward interest rates, $r_t(s,q)$. Note that the instantaneous forward interest rate starting at time $t+s$ can be expressed as $r_t(s,s)$, and it can be related to forward rates with longer durations by $r_t(s,q)=\frac{\int_s^q r_t(u,u)du}{q-s}$. In a pure sense of corporate default, the default probability over $[t,t'_i]$ should equal $\int_0^{t_i'-t} e^{-\psi_t(0,u)u} f_t(u)du$ and the discounted default probability would be $\int_0^{t_i'-t} e^{-[r_t(0,u)+\psi_t(0,u)]u} f_t(u)du$. However, they are not the right default and discounted default probabilities for CDS, because substitution typically takes place when the reference entity is merged with or acquired by another corporate entity. In that case, the CDS protection is typically shifted to the merged or acquiring entity, and the successor entity will then face subsequent default or other exit. Therefore, one must be careful in applying a suitable treatment.

Let $P_t(s, q; r_t(0, u), s \le u \le q)$ denote the time-t discounted forward probability of the reference entity of the CDS being terminated, including successions, over the period $[t + s, t + q]$, where $0 \le s \le q$. This termination probability is meant to capture an intricate sequence of potential defaults by the original reference entity and its successors. This probability ultimately determines the likelihood of the CDS seller having to make a default payment. Similarly, $P_t^*(s, q; r_t(0, u), s \le u \le q)$ stands for the termination probability of the successor. When there is no ambiguity, we will simply express these discounted forward termination probabilities as $P_t(s, q)$ and $P_t^*(s, q)$. What we mean by discounted probability is the integration of the forward probability rate at, say, time $t + u$ (with $s \le u \le q$) being discounted by the time-t forward risk-free rate from time $t + s$ to time $t + u$. The related quantities for the successor are similarly denoted by $f_t^*(s), h_t^*(s)$ and $\psi_t^*(s, q)$. Let $1_{\{Sub\}}$ be an indicator with 1 for the CDS contract that is subject to substitution and 0 otherwise.

The succession entity of course cannot be determined beforehand. Therefore, some reasonable rules will be needed for implementation. One can, for example, assume the successor to be an entity that shares the same forward termination probability as the reference obligor, or an entity that is of median quality. In principle, succession may occur multiple times, which in turn requires us to make a further assumption on all subsequent substitutions. For analytical tractability, our maintained assumption is that the successor's forward termination probability may differ from that of the original reference entity, but all successors must be of the same type in terms of the forward termination probability. We show in Appendix A that the solution to the CDS discounted forward termination probability with or without substitution for $0 \le s \le q$ can be expressed as

$$\begin{aligned} P_t(s, q) = &\int_s^q e^{-[r_t(s,u)+\psi_t(s,u)](u-s)} f_t(u)du \\ &+ \int_s^q e^{-[r_t(s,u)+\psi_t(s,u)](u-s)} h_t(u) \\ &\times \left[1_{\{Sub\}} P_t^*(u, q) + 1 - 1_{\{Sub\}}\right] du, \end{aligned} \tag{5}$$

where

$$P_t^*(s, q) = \int_s^q e^{-\int_s^v [r_t(u,u)+f_t^*(u)]du} f_t^*(v)dv. \tag{6}$$

In general, formulas in (5) and (6) can be used repeatedly to compute the following quantity in the first term of the denominator of Eq. (4) by temporarily setting forward interest rates to zero:

$$\begin{aligned} E_t^P\left(1_{\{t_i'<\tau\}}\right) = 1 - P_t(0, t_i' - t; r_t(0, u) = 0 \\ \text{for } 0 \le u \le t_i' - t). \end{aligned} \tag{7}$$

When the substitution feature is disabled as in Case 2 of Appendix B, the above quantity naturally reduces to $\exp[-\psi_t(0, t_i' - t)(t_i' - t)]$, a standard result for the probability of surviving default and other exits over the period $[t, t_i']$.

The solutions to the two remaining terms in Eq. (4) again depend on $P_t^*(s, q)$ in Eq. (6). They can be expressed as

$$\begin{aligned} &E_t^P\left[e^{-r_t(0,\tau-t)(\tau-t)} 1_{\{t<\tau\le t_k'\}}\right] \\ &= \int_0^{t_k'-t} e^{-[r_t(0,s)+\psi_t(0,s)]s} f_t(s)ds \\ &\quad + \int_0^{t_k'-t} e^{-[r_t(0,s)+\psi_t(0,s)]s} h_t(s) 1_{\{Sub\}} \\ &\quad \times P_t^*(s, t_k' - t)ds \end{aligned} \tag{8}$$

and

$$\begin{aligned} &E_t^P\left[A(t_{i-1} \vee t, \tau) e^{-r_t(0,\tau-t)(\tau-t)} 1_{\{t_{i-1}'<\tau\le t_i'\}}\right] \\ &= \int_{t_{i-1}'\vee t}^{t_i'} A(t_{i-1} \vee t, s) e^{-[r_t(0,s-t)+\psi_t(0,s-t)](s-t)} \\ &\quad \times f_t(s - t)ds \end{aligned}$$

$$+\int_{t'_{i-1}\vee t}^{t'_i} A(t_{i-1}\vee t, s)e^{-[r_t(0,s-t)+\psi_t(0,s-t)](s-t)}$$

$$\times h_t(s-t)1_{\{Sub\}}P_t^*(s-t, t'_i-t)ds. \quad (9)$$

Note that forward interest rate, $r_t(s, u)$, used in Eqs. (5) and (6) can always be deduced from the spot interest rate curve.

In Appendix B, we provide the specific solutions for two special cases of interest. One of which (with substitution and its successors sharing the same forward intensities as the original obligor) will be used for the numerical example and empirical study later because substitution is a built-in feature of standard CDS contracts.[2]

The actuarial par spread formula can be readily computed daily by leveraging the Credit Research Initiative (CRI) infrastructure created and maintained by the Risk Management Institute (RMI) of the National University of Singapore since July 2010. The RMI-CRI system has implemented the forward intensity model of Duan *et al.* (2012). It currently makes available and allows free access by all legitimate users to daily updated PDs ranging from one month to five years for over 60,000 exchange-listed firms in 106 economies around the world. The forward intensity functions used to generate the RMI-CRI PDs are exponential linear functions of some input variables (2 macroeconomic factors and 10 firm-specific attributes) where the coefficients depend on the forward starting time, and are subject to the Nelson–Siegel type of smooth term structure restriction. Estimation of the parameters and statistical inference for the constrained system rely on the pseudo-Bayesian sequential Monte Carlo technique and self-normalized statistics devised in Duan and Fulop (2013). For details on the specific RMI-CRI implementation, please refer to RMI-CRI Technical Report (2013). The RMI-CRI model's parameters are re-calibrated monthly and the inputs to the functions are updated daily.

II. A NUMERICAL EXAMPLE

We will compute a 5-year actuarial par spread by daily discretization and the convention of quarterly payments subject to the actual/360 day count. Thus, all integrals above are just some simple sums with the term, ds, being approximated by $1/365$. $A(t_{i-1}\vee t, t'_i)$ in the formula is simply the fraction of a year defined by the actual number of days in an accrual period (a quarter or shorter) over 360, which reflects the CDS day count convention. It should be noted that for all accrual periods, $A(t_{i-1}\vee t, t'_i)$ or $A(t_{i-1}\vee t, \tau)$, should be inclusive of the start and end dates.

For the numerical example and the empirical analysis later, we assume that the successor to replace the reference entity has the same discounted forward termination probability, i.e., $P_t^*(s, T-t) = P_t(s, T-t)$ for $0 \le s \le T-t$. The relevant formulas are given in Case 1 of Appendix B. Now, we are in a position to show how to compute the actuarial par spread using the 5-year CDS referencing Eastman Kodak on November 16, 2011. Note that Eastman Kodak filed for Chapter 11 bankruptcy protection on January 19, 2012. The CDS traded at 4,009.84 basis points (bps) on November 16, 2011. Our calculation later shows that the actuarial par spread is estimated to be only 422.66 bps based on the standard recovery rate of 40%. Assuming that the term structure of PDs and the recovery assumption used in our analysis are reasonably accurate, the huge gap of 3,587.17 bps could only be attributed to a combination of very high risk aversion, very low market liquidity (extremely tight supply condition) and an overestimation by the market of the PDs. It is also possible that the huge gap is due to an underestimation of the PDs by the physical default prediction model and/or using an overstated recovery rate.

The typical assumption of a 40% recovery rate may indeed be too optimistic, leading to an understated actuarial par spread.[3] But even using the extreme case of zero recovery, the actuarial par spread would still be just around 700 bps. The point of this discussion is not about whether a particular estimate is correct or not; rather the actuarial par spread can be a useful device for decomposing the observed CDS spread so as to help us gain better understanding of the CDS market behavior.

The 5-year CDS traded on November 16, 2011 has its maturity on December 20, 2016 and potentially up to 21 quarterly premium payments on 20th of March/June/September/December if the 20th is a business day and otherwise the first business day after that 20th.[4] For the last payment date, however, the adjustment is capped at 20th plus at most two calendar days. Since December 20, 2016 is a business day, no adjustment is needed. The first premium payment date is the closest coupon payment date after the trade date plus one day, and in this case the first payment date is December 20, 2011. Reported in Table 1 are the actual payment dates (after adjusting the official payment dates) for this CDS. These dates of course determine the applicable length of time and discount rate for the discounting purpose. However, they differ from the accrual end dates by one calendar day except for the final payment date.

The accrual period for the first payment starts on September 20, 2011, which is the closest standard quarterly payment date prior to the first payment date of this 5-year CDS. Subsequent accrual periods are spaced according to the official payment dates with the accrual period ending one calendar day prior to the payment date except for the last payment period which actually ends on the official maturity date. Naturally, these accrual periods are not exactly identical in the number of calendar days, and the number of days will have to be computed according to the business day calendar. For this particular 5-year CDS, the accrual period and the number of calendar days in each period are given in Table 1. The number of days as reported in Table 1 for each period divided by 360 should be used for $A(t_{i-1} \vee t, t_i')$ in Eq. (4). For $A(t_{i-1} \vee t, \tau)$ in the same equation, it is the actual number of days elapsed (inclusive of the default day) and then divided by 360; for example, default on January 19, 2012 means an accrual period of 41 days (from December 20, 2011 to January 19, 2012 inclusive).

Table 1. The 5-year CDS payment dates, accrual periods, and number of days in each period for the trade date of November 16, 2011.

Payment #	Payment Date	Accrual Start Date (inclusive)	Accrual End Date (inclusive)	# of Days
1	20.12.2011	20.09.2011	19.12.2011	33[a]
2	20.03.2012	20.12.2011	19.03.2012	91
3	20.06.2012	20.03.2012	19.06.2012	92
4	20.09.2012	20.06.2012	19.09.2012	92
5	20.12.2012	20.09.2012	19.12.2012	91
6	20.03.2013	20.12.2012	19.03.2013	90
7	20.06.2013	20.03.2013	19.06.2013	92
8	20.09.2013	20.06.2013	19.09.2013	92
9	20.12.2013	20.09.2013	19.12.2013	91
10	20.03.2014	20.12.2013	19.03.2014	90
11	20.06.2014	20.03.2014	19.06.2014	92
12	22.09.2014	20.06.2014	21.09.2014	94
13	22.12.2014	22.09.2014	21.12.2014	91
14	20.03.2015	22.12.2014	19.03.2015	88
15	22.06.2015	20.03.2015	21.06.2015	94
16	21.09.2015	22.06.2015	20.09.2015	91
17	21.12.2015	21.09.2015	20.12.2015	91
18	21.03.2016	21.12.2015	20.03.2016	91
19	20.06.2016	21.03.2016	19.06.2016	91
20	20.09.2016	20.06.2016	19.09.2016	92
21	20.12.2016	20.09.2016	20.12.2016	92

Note: [a]This value reflects the number of days in the first accrual period that is applicable to this CDS contract, i.e., from November 17, 2011 (trade date plus one day) to December 19, 2011 inclusive.

As mentioned in the preceding section, daily updated PD term structures for nearly all exchange-listed firms around the world are currently provided by RMI. We extract Eastman Kodak's PD term structure on November 16, 2011. RMI computes all PDs using data obtained after each market close. Data preparation and computation take several hours and the PDs become publicly available on the next calendar day. For a small set of firms, however, the PDs can be computed on a real time basis with access to, say, a Bloomberg terminal. Our use of the PD information on the trade date is actually operationally feasible.

There are two sets of forward intensity functions at time t (i.e., November 16th), $f_t(s)$ for default and $h_t(s)$ for other exits where s stands for forward starting time from t. The set of prediction variables (covariates) used by RMI for both default and other exits comprises, as of the time of this writing, 12 variables (2 macro-financial and 10 firm-specific) and their values are based on the most current and publicly available information. In our case, it is at the market close of November 16, 2011. The variables and their values on November 16, 2011 for Eastman Kodak are provided in Table 2, which are based on the March 2014 calibration by RMI.

The forward intensity functions implemented by RMI-CRI are in the following form:

$$f_t(s) = \exp\{\alpha_0(s) + \alpha_1(s)x_{1,t} + \cdots + \alpha_{12}(s)x_{12,t}\}, \quad (10)$$

$$h_t(s) = \exp\{\beta_0(s) + \beta_1(s)x_{1,t} + \cdots + \beta_{12}(s)x_{12,t}\}. \quad (11)$$

The coefficients as functions of forward starting time are constrained by the Nelson–Siegel function of four or three parameters, depending on whether the covariate is stochastic or not. For the coefficients in the default intensity function, the RMI-CRI system, as of the time of this writing, imposes

$$\begin{aligned}
&\alpha_i(s; \varrho_{i,0}, \varrho_{i,1}, \varrho_{i,2}, d_i) \\
&= \varrho_{i,0} + \varrho_{i,1}\frac{1-\exp(-s/d_i)}{s/d_i} \\
&\quad + \varrho_{i,2}\left[\frac{1-\exp(-s/d_i)}{s/d_i} - \exp(-s/d_i)\right] \\
&\quad \text{for } i = 0, 1, 2, \ldots, 12 \text{ and } \varrho_{i,0} = 0 \\
&\quad \text{for } i = 1, 2, \ldots, 12.
\end{aligned} \quad (12)$$

Similar constraints are placed on the coefficients of the other-exit intensity function. The relevant parameter values needed to obtain the PDs for American firms with the trade date of November 16, 2011 are given in Table 3.[5]

Table 2. The variables (covariates) used in the forward intensity functions (default and other exits) and their values on November 16, 2011 extracted from the RMI-CRI database as of February 28, 2014, which may reflect data revisions post November 16, 2011. Trend stands for the current value minus one-year moving average. DTD is distance to default which is an estimate based on a structural credit risk model. Please refer to RMI-CRI Technical Report (2013) for details on this measurement along with other variables.

Prediction Variable	Value
S&P500 Index Return (1 year)	0.0497
3-month US Treasury Rate (demeaned)	−3.1928
DTD (Level)	−0.0288
DTD (Trend)	−0.6534
Cash/Total Assets (Level)	0.2163
Cash/Total Assets (Trend)	−0.0369
Net income/Total Assets (Level)	−0.0146
Net income/Total Assets (Trend)	0.0035
Relative Size (Level)	0.4176
Relative Size (Trend)	−0.6963
Market/Book	1.3303
Sigma	0.3236

The parameter values in Table 3 allow us to compute, for example, the probability of not defaulting before the first premium payment date of December 20, 2011. Daily discretization is employed, which means $\Delta s = 1/365$. This discretization matches well with the operational reality of counting days. The integral in Eq. (B.1) thus becomes a sum of 33 terms corresponding to 33 calendar days between November 16, 2011 and December 19, 2011. By Eq. (B.2), we have

$$\begin{aligned}
&E^P_{11/16/2011}\left(1_{\{12/19/2011<\tau\}}\right) \\
&= 1 - P_{11/16/2011}(0, 33\Delta s) \\
&= 1 - \Delta s \sum_{i=0}^{32} f_{11/16/2011}(i\Delta s) \\
&\quad \times \exp\left(-\Delta s \sum_{j=0}^{i} f_{11/16/2011}(j\Delta s)\right).
\end{aligned}$$

The values for the forward intensities in the above expression can be computed with Eqs. (10)–(12) and the values in Tables 2 and 3.

Several quantities in Eq. (4) for the actuarial par spread need an appropriate interest rate term structure. The standard practice in pricing CDS is to use the interest rate term structure extracted from a combination of LIBOR rates and Swap rates by a bootstrap technique. The missing rates are set by linearly interpolating the available interest rates (in continuously compounded form). Readers can refer to Markit (2013) for details of constructing such a term structure. Table 4 provides the LIBOR and Swap rates on November 16, 2011 that were retrieved from Bloomberg.[6] Since daily discretization is used, we have to compute the discount rates for maturities ranging from one calendar day (November 17, 2011) to 1861 calendar days (December 20, 2016) with daily increments. The one-day continuously compounded rate by applying the LIBOR day count convention turns out to be 0.1416% whereas the 1861-day continuously compounded rate is 1.3441%. With the term structure of interest rates in place, one can proceed to compute forward interest rates (different forward starting times but always with one-day duration) needed in the formulas.

Other formulas needed to compute the actuarial par spread are in Eqs. (B.3) and (B.4). With the term

Table 3. The parameter values used to determine the forward intensity functions for the listed American firms for the trade date of November 16, 2011.

Variable #	$\varrho_{i,0}$	$\varrho_{i,1}$	$\varrho_{i,2}$	d_i
Default Intensity Function				
Intercept	−4.8004	1.2312	3.8558	0.6316
S&P500 Index Return (1 year)	0	−0.0538	90.3545	88.2970
3-month US Treasury Rate (demeaned)	0	−7.5111	47.1087	0.9615
DTD (Level)	0	−1.2931	−0.0168	0.8524
DTD (Trend)	0	−1.0767	−0.0106	0.9322
Cash/Total Assets (Level)	0	−0.9887	0.9456	0.5911
Cash/Total Assets (Trend)	0	−2.1815	0.3087	2.8732
Net income/Total Assets (Level)	0	−4.2162	−10.9831	7.7829
Net income/Total Assets (Trend)	0	−1.1745	0.2412	8.1014
Relative Size (Level)	0	−0.0288	0.2506	0.5198
Relative Size (Trend)	0	−1.7689	2.5739	1.9547
Market/Book	0	−0.0424	0.0679	0.6598
Sigma	0	−0.1883	−137.2612	2570.6303
Other-Exit Intensity Function				
Intercept	−2.4898	−0.6837	0.5232	1.1805
S&P500 Index Return (1 year)	0	−0.1455	2.4191	0.8112
3-month US Treasury Rate (demeaned)	0	0.8581	5.4323	1.3832
DTD (Level)	0	0.0214	−0.2274	1.9629
DTD (Trend)	0	0.2734	−0.4832	0.3040
Cash/Total Assets (Level)	0	−0.3705	1.5446	1.4461
Cash/Total Assets (Trend)	0	−0.6143	0.9736	6.5312
Net income/Total Assets (Level)	0	−3.9779	5.3066	5.2265
Net income/Total Assets (Trend)	0	−2.3135	0.0711	0.4868
Relative Size (Level)	0	−0.1781	−0.1221	4.3556
Relative Size (Trend)	0	−0.5261	1.5800	11.5417
Market/Book	0	−0.0290	0.0722	4.5704
Sigma	0	1.9060	−1.4790	0.9276

Table 4. LIBOR and Swap rates (in %) on November 16, 2011.

LIBOR		Swap	
Tenor	Rate	Tenor	Rate
1 D	0.14167	2 Y	0.7590
1 W	0.19189	3 Y	0.8646
2 W	0.21039	4 Y	1.0697
1 M	0.25172	5 Y	1.3180
2 M	0.35706	6 Y	1.5623
3 M	0.47111		
4 M	0.54417		
5 M	0.60722		
6 M	0.67694		
7 M	0.73278		
8 M	0.78100		
9 M	0.83222		
10 M	0.88322		
11 M	0.93744		
1 Y	0.99700		

structure of interest rates and the intensity functions in place, the numerator of Eq. (4) is computed to be 0.1670 and the two terms in the denominator are 3.9204 and 0.0296, respectively. Thus, the actuarial par spread becomes 0.042266 (or 422.66 bps).

III. EMPIRICAL PRICING OF CDS VIA DECOMPOSITION

CDS spreads have been used in the literature as an instrument to understand corporate bond yields; for example, Longstaff *et al.* (2005) and Li *et al.* (2011), among others. The literature on the theoretical and empirical pricing of CDS is quite large. Our focus in this section is to provide an easy-to-implement empirical pricing tool for CDS through a decomposition with the actuarial par spread. Our approach differs substantially from, say, Ericsson *et al.* (2009) in which CDS is related to leverage, volatility and interest rate. Although these are theoretical determinants of CDS price, they are indirect and incomplete. They are indirect because although leverage and volatility do affect an obligor's default likelihood, they are not as close to it as the physical default probability. They are also incomplete because CDS price is expected to be closely tied to recovery rate and risk aversion.

We use a time series of Eastman Kodak CDS to demonstrate the idea of our empirical pricing through decomposition. A year-long time series of daily CDS spreads, obtained from Bloomberg and exhibited in Fig. 1, shows a dramatic rise of CDS premiums leading up to its Chapter 11 bankruptcy filing on January 19, 2012. Of course, this rising pattern is not surprising in light of Kodak's subsequent default. In the same figure, we plot the actuarial par spread over the same time period. Generally speaking, the two time series move in tandem although the CDS spread is much larger than the corresponding actuarial par spread.[7] This cursory evidence points to the possibility of establishing some empirical relationship between these two quantities.

In Fig. 2, we plot the log-ratio of the CDS spread over its corresponding actuarial par spread. As the figure shows, the log spread ratio hovers around its mean of 2.0867 with a standard deviation of 0.2968. Moreover, we can compute its skewness and excess kurtosis, and their values of 0.0953 and −0.2369 seem to suggest that the log spread ratio is not far from being normally distributed. A quick way of pricing CDS is to first look up its actuarial par spread and add on top an amount that reflects the mean of 2.0867 for the log spread ratio. The mean log spread ratio is likely to be firm-specific. For the CDS without a sufficiently long history, one could use a cross-sectional sample of mean log spread ratios corresponding to different obligors to come up with a suitable estimate.

The plot also suggests some degree of autocorrelation, and with autocorrelation one may actually come up with a workable prediction model for the log spread ratio. Indeed, our analysis suggests that a simple lagged regression can yield a high R^2 of 85% and give rise to the following predictive equation:

$$\ln\left(\frac{S_t}{S_t^{(a)}}\right) \approx 0.1487 + 0.9296 \times \ln\left(\frac{S_{t-1}}{S_{t-1}^{(a)}}\right). \qquad (13)$$

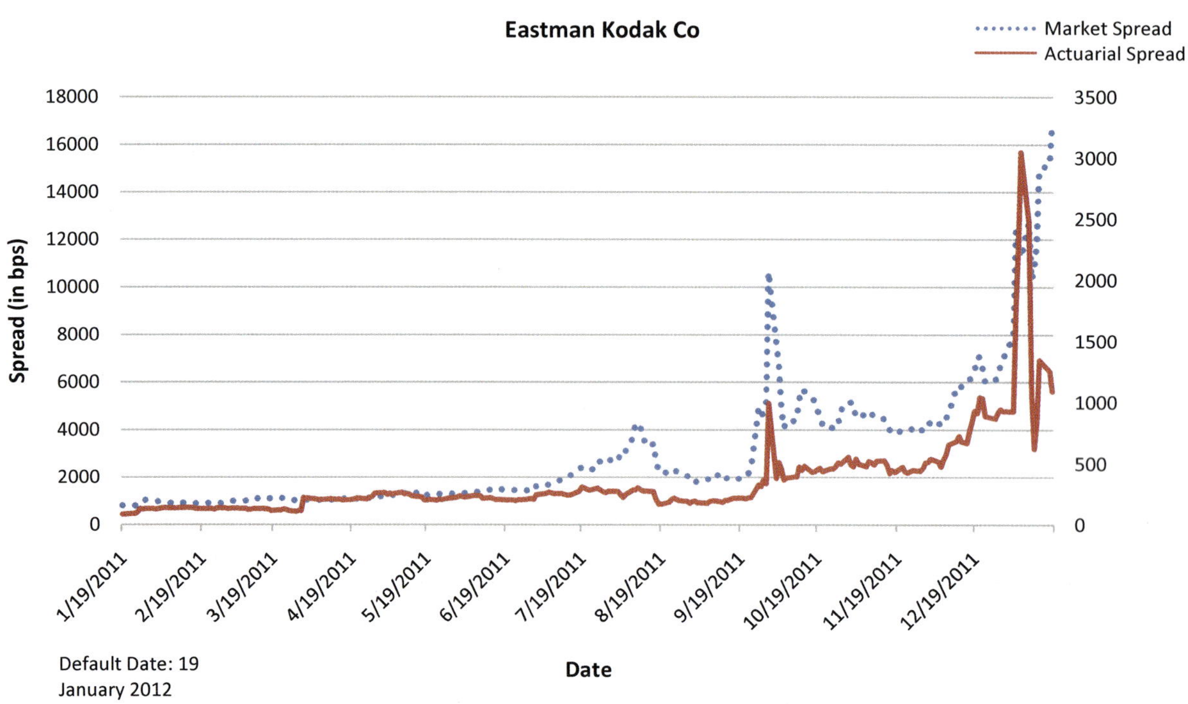

Figure 1. One-year daily time series of 5-year CDS spreads (the left axis) and actuarial par spreads (the right axis) for Eastman Kodak.

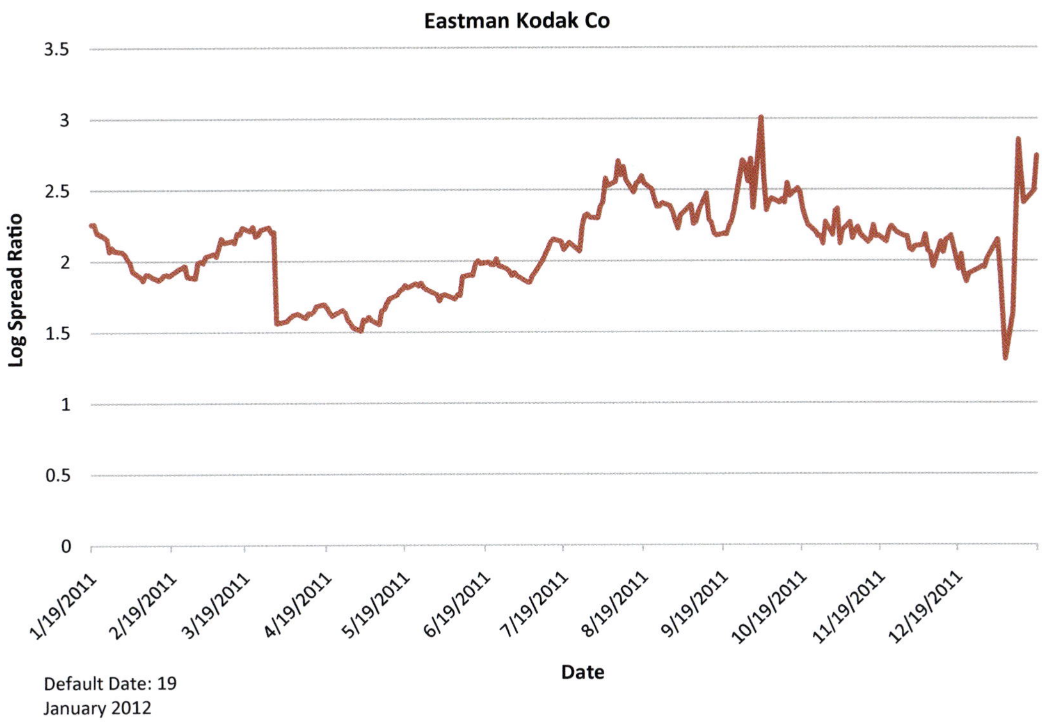

Figure 2. Time series of the log-ratio of the 5-year CDS spreads over their corresponding actuarial par spreads for Eastman Kodak.

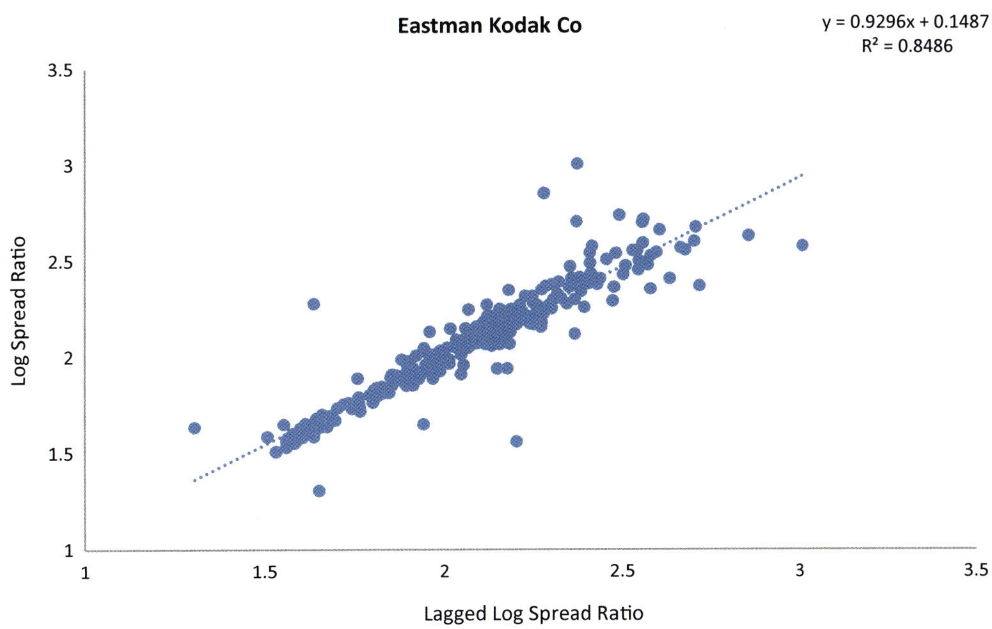

Figure 3. The log-ratio of the 5-year CDS spread over its corresponding actuarial par spread versus the log-ratio being lagged one trading day.

In Fig. 3, the visual relationship is clearly reflective of the above lagged regression. With the exception of a few scattered points, the log spread ratio seems to be tightly centered around the regression line. For pricing CDS, the predicted log spread ratio based on Eq. (13), instead of the unconditional mean of 2.0867, can be applied to produce a better estimate of CDS spread that is in principle much lower in pricing error. If we were to price the CDS on the trade date of November 16, 2011 using the actuarial par spread of 422.66 and the average log spread ratio of 2.0867, we would obtain a predicted CDS spread of 3406.03 bps (i.e., 422.66 × exp(2.0867)). Alternatively, we could price this CDS by its predicted log spread ratio of 2.1522 computed with the log spread ratio of 2.1552 on November 15, 2011 (CDS spread = 4228.85 bps and actuarial par spread = 490.01 bps). Doing so gives rise to a predicted CDS spread of 3636.56 bps (i.e., 422.66 × exp(2.1522)). As compared to 3406.03 bps, this alternative predicted spread is 230.53 bps closer to the observed CDS spread of 4009.84 bps on November 16, 2011.

In the above example, we considered the CDS pricing at the end of the trade date. Actually, empirical pricing can be performed throughout the day as the relevant information (stock price, LIBOR curve, etc.) arrives at the trading desk. While the parameter values of the PD model remains fixed, the input values to the PD model change according to the new information. The revised default and other-exit probabilities then lead to a new actuarial par spread which in turn yields a new estimate of the CDS spread through the same predicted log spread ratio.

ACKNOWLEDGMENT

Some earlier versions of this paper used the title of "CDS-equivalent physical par spread and empirical pricing of CDS by decomposition." The author would like to thank Siyuan Huang for her excellent research assistance work. This paper benefits from a discussion with Michael Gordy and the comments by the participants of the 2014 Meiji University/Kyoto University International Conference on Finance and Financial Econometrics & Engineering and the seminar at the National Taiwan University.

NOTES

1 The CDS pricing discussed here is quite standard; see for example, Hull (2012, Chapter 24). Later when we compute with survival and default probabilities, we will depart from the standard model to a more appropriate one that factors in a corporate obligor's exit due to reasons other than default (say, merger/acquistion).

2 This case essentially implies that all successors are firms of the same forward termination probability as that of the original obligor, which is a sensible assumption and simplifies the implementation task considerably. It is sensible because there is no way of predetermining which firm will end up being the successor several years before an acquisition. Having a successor with the same quality on a forward basis as the original obligor seems to be a good compromise. Operationally speaking, it is more manageable because the calculation can be completed without referencing the forward termination probability of another firm.

3 Recovery rates and PDs may also be correlated, which has been ruled out by an assumption earlier. With a suitable conditional recovery rate model, it is possible to incorporate this correlation into the actuarial par spread formula.

4 See ISDA (2012).

5 The specific parameter values in Table 3 are taken from the RMI-CRI March 2014 calibration which used its database as of February 28, 2014. Thus, the parameter values have naturally reflected some data revisions post November 16, 2011, and the model calibration has also used some data that were beyond November 16, 2011.

6 According to the ISDA standard CDS converter specification (ISDA, 2009), the interest rate curve used in the CDS discounting is locked on the trade date minus one day. Note that the ISDA specification is for the purpose of quotation conversion. Fixing the discount curve from a day earlier can avoid confusion arising from different discount curves in a trading day. Here, we choose to use the curve on the trade date instead, because it is actually operationally feasible to use updated information throughout the trade day for the purpose of CDS pricing. Typically, the interest curve does not change drastically over one day, and it will thus make no material difference for a typical day.

7 In the final month, i.e., January 2012, Kodak's actuarial par spreads have swung widely. In light of the CDS behavior over the same period, intuition leads one to question the quality of the physical PDs used to produce those actuarial par spreads. One possible reason is our use of extrapolation to produce default and other-exit probabilities for periods shorter than one month. Since the RMI-CRI PD model is calibrated to data by predictions ranging from 1 to 60 months, any prediction for a horizon less than one month must use the extrapolated parameter values obtained via the functional restriction in Eq. (12). When an obligor approaches default, shorter-term PDs naturally play a more prominent role in determining actuarial par spreads. Small random changes to the input data (such as DTD, size, etc.) over Kodak's waning days get magnified through extrapolated model parameters. A potential fix is to run calibration by incorporting shorter-period predictions to avoid using extrapolation.

APPENDIX

Appendix A

The discounted forward termination probability for a CDS reference entity can be written as

$$P_t(s,q) = \int_s^q e^{-[r_t(s,u)+\psi_t(s,u)](u-s)} f_t(u)du + \int_s^q e^{-[r_t(s,u)+\psi_t(s,u)](u-s)} h_t(u) \times \left[1_{\{Sub\}} P_t^*(u,q) + 1 - 1_{\{Sub\}}\right] du.$$

The first term on the right-hand side is the typical time-t cumulative discounted forward probability of termination due to default from time $t+s$ to $t+q$, whereas the second term is the one for other-exits over the same period but modified by the discounted forward termination probability of the successor entity, if substitution is in force. This modification reflects default by the successor after it replaces the reference entity.

To obtain a solution to the forward termination probability of the successor, we assume that substitution is in force. In addition, the successor and all its subsequent successors are required to share the same forward termination probability, but this forward termination probability can differ from that of the original reference entity. Under these assumptions, we have

$$P_t^*(s,q) = \int_s^q e^{-[r_t(s,u)+\psi_t^*(s,u)](u-s)} f_t^*(u)du + \int_s^q e^{-[r_t(s,u)+\psi_t^*(s,u)](u-s)} h_t^*(u) P_t^*(u,q)du.$$

Taking a partial derivative with respect to s gives rise to the following linear first-order differential equation:

$$\begin{aligned}\frac{\partial P_t^*(s,q)}{\partial s} &= -f_t^*(s) + [r_t(s,s) + f_t^*(s) + h_t^*(s)] \times \int_s^q e^{-[r_t(s,u)+\psi_t^*(s,u)](u-s)} f_t^*(u)du \\ &\quad - h_t^*(s)P_t^*(s,q) + [r_t(s,s) + f_t^*(s) + h_t^*(s)] \times \int_s^q e^{-[r_t(s,u)+\psi_t^*(s,u)](u-s)} h_t^*(u)P_t^*(u,q)du \\ &= -f_t^*(s) + [r_t(s,s) + f_t^*(s)]P_t^*(s,q).\end{aligned}$$

Recall that $r_t(s,s)$ is the time-t instantaneous forward rate for time $t+s$. Naturally, this differential equation must obey the terminal condition: $P_t^*(q,q) = 0$.

The general solution to this linear first-order differential equation is

$$P_t^*(s,q) = e^{-\int_s^q [r_t(u,u)+f_t^*(u)]du} \times \left(\int_s^q e^{\int_v^q [r_t(u,u)+f_t^*(u)]du} f_t^*(v)dv + C\right).$$

By the terminal condition, we have $C = 0$. Thus,

$$\begin{aligned}P_t^*(s,q) &= e^{-\int_s^q [r_t(u,u)+f_t^*(u)]du} \times \int_s^q e^{\int_v^q [r_t(u,u)+f_t^*(u)]du} f_t^*(v)dv \\ &= \int_s^q e^{-\int_s^v [r_t(u,u)+f_t^*(u)]du} f_t^*(v)dv.\end{aligned}$$

Appendix B

Case 1. Substitution is in force, i.e., $1_{\{Sub\}} = 1$, and the successor entity is assumed to always share the same default and other-exits intensities of the reference entity, i.e., $P_t^*(s,q) = P_t(s,q)$.

Under the conditions and applying the result in Appendix A, we obtain

$$P_t(s, q) = \int_s^q e^{-\int_s^v [r_t(u,u)+f_t(u)]du} f_t(v)dv. \quad \text{(B.1)}$$

The relevant formulas for the actuarial par spread are

$$E_t^P\left(1_{\{t_i' < \tau\}}\right) = 1 - P_t(0, t_i' - t; r_t(0, u) = 0 \quad \text{for } 0 \leq u \leq t_i' - t) \quad \text{(B.2)}$$

and

$$E_t^P\left[e^{-r_t(0,\tau-t)(\tau-t)} 1_{\{t<\tau\leq t_k'\}}\right] = \int_0^{t_k'-t} e^{-[r_t(0,s)+\psi_t(0,s)]s} f_t(s)ds + \int_0^{t_k'-t} e^{-[r_t(0,s)+\psi_t(0,s)]s} h_t(s) P_t(s, t_k' - t)ds = P_t(0, t_k' - t). \quad \text{(B.3)}$$

The last equality in the above is due to the result in Appendix A. In numerical evaluations of this paper, we actually use the first equality so as to be consistent with the expression below. Daily discretization used in the numerical evaluation can cause a minor difference between the first equality and the final expression.

The final quantity of interest is

$$E_t^P\left[A(t_{i-1} \vee t, \tau)e^{-r_t(0,\tau-t)(\tau-t)} 1_{\{t_{i-1}' < \tau \leq t_i'\}}\right] = \int_{t_{i-1}' \vee t}^{t_i'} A(t_{i-1} \vee t, s)e^{-[r_t(0,s-t)+\psi_t(0,s-t)](s-t)} \times f_t(s-t)ds + \int_{t_{i-1}' \vee t}^{t_i'} A(t_{i-1} \vee t, s)e^{-[r_t(0,s-t)+\psi_t(0,s-t)](s-t)} \times h_t(s-t) P_t(s-t, t_i' - t)ds. \quad \text{(B.4)}$$

Note that we cannot remove $h_t(s)$, the forward intensity for other exits, from the system in the way like for the other expression. This is simply due to the presence of $A(t_{i-1} \vee t, s)$, the day-count factor.

Case 2. No substitution takes place, i.e., $1_{\{Sub\}} = 0$, and the CDS contract terminates when exit for reasons other than default occurs. In this case, $P_t^*(s, q)$ becomes irrelevant.

Under the conditions, we obtain

$$P_t(s, q) = 1 - e^{-[r_t(s,q)+\psi_t(s,q)](q-s)}. \quad \text{(B.5)}$$

The relevant formulas for the actuarial par spread are

$$E_t^P\left(1_{\{t_i' < \tau\}}\right) = 1 - P_t(0, t_i' - t; r_t(0, u) = 0 \quad \text{for } 0 \leq u \leq t_i' - t), \quad \text{(B.6)}$$

$$E_t^P\left[e^{-r_t(0,\tau-t)(\tau-t)} 1_{\{t<\tau\leq t_k'\}}\right] = \int_0^{t_k'-t} e^{-[r_t(0,s)+\psi_t(0,s)]s} f_t(s)ds \quad \text{(B.7)}$$

and

$$E_t^P\left[A(t_{i-1} \vee t, \tau)e^{-r_t(0,\tau-t)(\tau-t)} 1_{\{t_{i-1}' < \tau \leq t_i'\}}\right] = \int_{t_{i-1}' \vee t}^{t_i'} A(t_{i-1} \vee t, s)e^{-[r_t(0,s-t)+\psi_t(0,s-t)](s-t)} \times f_t(s-t)ds. \quad \text{(B.8)}$$

REFERENCES

Duan, J. C. and A. Fulop (2013), Multiperiod Corporate Default Prediction with Partially-Conditioned Forward Intensity. National University of Singapore Working Paper.

Duan, J. C., J. Sun and T. Wang (2012), Multiperiod Corporate Default Prediction — A Forward Intensity Approach. *Journal of Econometrics*, 170, pp. 191–209.

Duffie, D., L. Saita and K. Wang (2007), Multi-Period Corporate Default Prediction with Stochastic Covariates. *Journal of Financial Economics*, 83, pp. 635–665.

Ericsson, J., K. Jacobs and R. Oviedo (2009), The Determinants of Credit Default Swap Premia. *Journal of Financial and Quantitative Analysis*, 44, pp. 109–132.

Hull, J. (2012), Options, *Futures and Other Derivatives*, 8th edition, Prentice Hall.

ISDA (2009), ISDA Standard CDS Converter Specification. Version: May 5, 2009.

ISDA (2012), Standard CDS Examples — Supporting Document for the Implementation of the ISDA CDS Standard Model. Version: October 26, 2012.

Li, H., W. Zhang and G. H. Kim (2011), The CDS-Bond Basis Arbitrage and the Cross Section of Corporate Bond Returns. University of Michigan Working Paper.

Longstaff, F., S. Mithal and E. Neis (2005), Corporate Yield Spreads: Default Risk or Liquidity? New Evidence from the Credit Default Swap Market. *Journal of Finance*, 60, pp. 2213–2253.

Markit (2013), Markit Interest Rate Curve — XML Specifications. Version 1.16, October 15.

RMI-CRI Technical Report (2013), Version 2013 Update 2b. National University of Singapore Risk Management Institute. http://d.rmicri.org/static/pdf/2013update2.pdf. 03/06/2014.

Fast Approximation of Loan Portfolio Loss

Jenny Bai*
Risk Management Institute (RMI)
National University of Singapore
rmibh@nus.edu.sg

Heikki Seppälä
Department of Mathematics and Statistics
University of Jyväskylä, Finland
heikki.i.seppala@jyu.fi

Ser-Huang Poon†,‡
Manchester Business School
University of Manchester, UK
ser-huang.poon@mbs.ac.uk

INTRODUCTION

The challenge in modeling loan portfolio loss is the multiple dependencies between obligors and on external factors. In the case when loss is classified by default instead of marked to market losses, the dependencies are non-linear and are much harder to estimate and model. To this end, the Merton structural model is popular as risky debt is valued as a short put and will be exercised when the firm value drops below a threshold. Vasicek (1991), in his seminal paper, extends the analytical result to loan portfolio loss in the limiting case when the portfolio is homogeneous and the number of loans tends to infinity.[1] Indeed the Vasicek (1991) solution has such a high impact that it became the basis of Basel II capital requirement for credit exposure. This result is generalized to non-homogeneous portfolios by Vasicek (2002) and Gordy (2003) and to small portfolio using *granularity (or concentration) adjustment* by Wilde (2001) and Martin and Wilde (2002). However, all these extensions are based on the assumption that a single factor drives all the asset returns. In practice, asset returns and default probabilities are driven by many factors. The most commonly used factors are country factors, industry factors and rating class factors. Pykhtin (2004) shows how the one factor model solution can be extended to incorporate multiple factors in addition to the granularity adjustment. The advantage of the Pykhtin's approach is that it is relatively easy to set up and it can, in certain cases, be much faster than brute force simulation.

In practice, many vendors' software allow the lender to select risk factors from a list of observed index returns. Value at Risk[2] (VaR) and Expected Shortfall[3] (ES), defined as:

$$\mathrm{VaR}_q(L) = \inf\{l \in \mathbb{R} : \mathbb{P}(L > l) \le 1 - q\}$$

Keywords: Risk factor extraction, economic capital, value at risk, expected shortfall, multi-factor adjustment.

*Marie Curie fellows funded by the European Community's Seventh Framework Programme FP7-PEOPLE-ITN-2008 under grant agreement number PITN-GA- 2009-237984 (project name: RISK). The funding is gratefully acknowledged.
†Corresponding author.
‡We are very grateful to Thomas Ribarits and Axel Clement at the European Investment Bank for many helpful comments and suggestions, Reza Abdolreza Nazemi and Lin Juan at the RMI for help in data collection, and Elisabeth Van Laere, Oliver Chen (the deputy editors of Global Credit Review), Jin Chuan Duan (the editor of Global Credit Review) and an anonymous referee for detailed reading and constructive editorial advice.

$$\mathrm{ES}_q(L) = \frac{1}{1-q}\int_q^1 \mathrm{VaR}_\gamma(L)d\gamma,$$

are calculated based on large scale simulations and some assumed values of correlation. In this paper, we provide a practical guide on how Pykhtin (2004) might be implemented in practice to provide quick ballpark figures for qth quantile portfolio loss. We assume the users have access to factors returns, historical default probabilities and their future forecasts. We first demonstrate how risk factors can be extracted from obligors' time series of default probability estimates. These risk factors are then used in the derivation of correlations needed in VaR and ES calculation. Our fast approximation should be very useful for small establishments that are not well supported by quantitative analysts and research data, or credit officers who temporarily have no access to these facilities, e.g., when screening the loan requests while on the road. At the very least, our approximation can be used as a sanity check against VaR and ES estimates produced from brute force simulations.

The remainder of this paper is organized as follows. Section I introduces the model framework and the closed form methodology of Pykhtin (2004) for calculating portfolio VaR and ES. Section II explains how risk factor time series can be estimated from observed default probabilities using a two-step iterative regression, and compares the results with proxy factors based on observed index returns. Section III demonstrates how portfolio VaR and ES can be calculated using the closed form formula and risk factors from Sec. II. Finally, we summarise and conclude in Sec. IV.

I. CLOSED FORM METHODOLOGY FOR ECONOMIC CAPITAL CALCULATION

Suppose the portfolio consists of M obligors, where obligor i, $i \in \{1, \ldots, M\}$, has a loan of w_i dollars (or percents of the portfolio size) and suppose that we have specified the default probabilities p_i of all obligors in the portfolio. Under the Merton-type (Merton, 1974) default-mode multi-factor model, the log asset returns of obligor i are given by

$$X_i = r_i Y_i + \sqrt{1 - r_i^2}\xi_i, \tag{1}$$

where $\xi_i \sim N(0, 1)$ (standard normal) is the idiosyncratic shock, r_i is obligor i's sensitivity to the obligor specific systematic risk $Y_i \sim N(0, 1)$. Risk factors Y_i are inter-correlated for the different i and the correlation structure is described by writing Y_i as a weighted sum of n independent standard normally distributed factors Z_k, $k = 1, \ldots, n$, so that

$$Y_i = \sum_{k=1}^{n} \alpha_{ik} Z_k, \quad \sum_{k=1}^{n} \alpha_{ik}^2 = 1, \tag{2}$$

α_{ik}'s are coefficients such that $\sum_{k=1}^{n} \alpha_{ik}^2 = 1$.

Borrower i defaults if its asset returns X_i drop below a threshold d_i, that is, default probability p_i and the threshold d_i are related via equation

$$p_i = \mathbb{P}(X_i \leq d_i). \tag{3}$$

Hence, the (unknown) portfolio loss can be written as

$$L = \sum_{i=1}^{M} w_i L_i = \sum_{i=1}^{M} w_i \mathbb{1}_{\{X_i \leq d_i\}} \mathrm{LGD}_i,$$

where $\mathbb{1}_{\{X_i \leq d_i\}}$ is the default indicator and $\mathrm{LGD}_i \in [0, 1]$ is the loss given default of firm i with mean μ_i and standard deviation σ_i. In order to calculate VaR or ES of the portfolio, the expected value and the variance of the LGD need to be specified, but the shape of its distribution does not enter into the calculations if the closed form approximation is used. If the variance of the LGD is set to zero, then the loss distribution is not continuous and the closed form approximation of VaR can be inaccurate, especially if the portfolio is small. This is due to the fact that the derivation of the closed form approximation assumes the continuity of the loss distribution. For ES the error is much smaller, because it considers the entire tail of the loss distribution and not just one quantile, as in the case of VaR.

The closed form formula for calculating portfolio VaR and ES given in Pykhtin (2004) is based on the second order Taylor approximation of the q-quantile of the distribution of the portfolio loss L around a random variable $\bar{L}$, for which the q-quantile can be calculated in closed form. It is known from Vasiceck (1991) and

Gordy (2003) that the q-quantile of the loss distribution of the infinitely large portfolio has a closed form solution under the one factor model. Hence, a natural choice for $\bar{L}$ is the limiting loss of the portfolio under single risk factor, where the (stochastic) benchmark risk factor $\bar{Y}$ is a linear combination of the same factors Z_k, $k = 1, \ldots, n$ that constitute the original risk factors Y_i, $i = 1, \ldots, M$. The choice of $\bar{Y}$ (or the multipliers b_k such that $\bar{Y} = \sum_{k=1}^{n} b_k Z_k$, $\sum_{k=1}^{n} b_k^2 = 1$) is not obvious and a natural choice, that appears to work well, is to maximize the sum of weighted correlations between $\bar{Y}$ and Y_i's, where the weights are chosen such that riskier obligors have larger weights. (See Eq. (A.6) in Appendix A for further details.)

The formula for calculating VaR on confidence level q is given by

$$t_q(L) = t_q(\bar{L}) + \Delta t_q^{\infty}(L) + \Delta t_q^{GA}(L),$$

where $t_q(\bar{L})$ is the q-quantile of one factor approximation, $\Delta t_q^{\infty}(L)$ is the multi-factor adjustment and $\Delta t_q^{GA}(L)$ is the granularity adjustment.

The portfolio ES is calculated as

$$\mathrm{ES}_q = \mathrm{ES}_q(\bar{L}) + \Delta \mathrm{ES}_q^{\infty}(L) + \Delta \mathrm{ES}_q^{GA}(L),$$

where $\mathrm{ES}_q(\bar{L})$ is the ES under one factor, $\Delta \mathrm{ES}_q^{\infty}(L)$ is the multi-factor adjustment and $\Delta \mathrm{ES}_q^{GA}(L)$ is the granularity adjustment. See Appendix A for technical details.

Required inputs for VaR and ES calculations are default probabilities p_i, loan amounts w_i, expectations μ_i and variances σ_i of LGDs, factor loadings $(r_i)_{i=1}^{M}$ and coefficients $(\alpha_{i,k})_{(i,k)=(1,1)}^{(M,N)}$. Indeed, the risk factors are not needed as an input for the formula, but factor loadings $(r_i)_{i=1}^{M}$ and coefficients $(\alpha_{i,k})_{(i,k)=(1,1)}^{(M,N)}$ must be estimated. In following sections, we show how factor loadings and alpha-coefficients can be estimated by first extracting the relevant risk factors from relevant time series.

Notice that if correlations between risk factors Y_i are small, then the roles of multi-factor adjustments $\Delta t_q^{\infty}(L)$ and $\Delta \mathrm{ES}_q^{\infty}(L)$ are bigger and the approximation error can get larger. On the other hand, granularity adjustments $\Delta t_q^{GA}(L)$ and $\Delta \mathrm{ES}_q^{GA}(L)$ vanish with the rate $\frac{1}{M}$ as the number of loans M grows. Closed form approximations lead to accurate results in most cases, even when the portfolio is relatively small. On the other hand, the formula is practically exact if there is only one factor and the size of the portfolio is very large. Furthermore, the computation speed can be significantly reduced if there are identical loans in the portfolio, that is, there are many loans with identical sizes, default probabilities, factor loadings and systematic risk factors. See Pykhtin (2004) and Hibbeln (2010) for further analysis about the performance of the closed form approximation.

II. RISK FACTORS EXTRACTION

In this section, we explain how risk factors, or latent factors for defaults, can be extracted from the time series of default probability estimates. In theory, most models for defaults start with asset return correlation and risk factor returns distribution. But since asset returns and factors are not observable, we use log changes in default probability estimates instead. Note that these default probabilities do not have to be the same as those used for VaR calculations, because the purpose here is just to estimate the behavior of obligors' asset returns. Moreover, the default probabilities used in the factor extraction may be physical or risk neutral so long as the two sets of probabilities are strongly correlated and are driven by the same factors. If the two sets of probabilities are not strongly correlated, then the decision has to be based on the purpose of the VaR calculation. Any physical default probability that is modeled using historical data will suffer from back-mirror driving problem and lacks forecasting power.[4] The Credit Default Swap (CDS) implied risk neutral default probabilities will be more sensitive to market condition and sentiment. But it is affected by investors' risk aversion in addition to the firm's default probabilities. We will address this issue further in the empirical analyses in Sec. II.2.

II.1. Two-Step Regressions

To extract the risk factors, we first write

$$\Delta p_{it} = \gamma_i + \beta_{i0} G_t + \beta_{j(i)} I_{j(i)t} + \beta_{k(i)} C_{k(i)t} + \epsilon_{it}, \quad t = 1, \ldots, T, \tag{4}$$

where Δp_{it}'s are the log changes of obligor i's default probability[5] with $i = 1, \ldots, M$; G is the global factor, $I_{j(i)}$ and $C_{k(i)}$ are, respectively, the industry j and the country k that obligor i belongs to with $j = 1, \ldots, J$ and $k = 1, \ldots, K$; $\gamma_i, \beta_{i0}, \beta_{j(i)}, \beta_{k(i)}$ and ϵ_{it} are constant term, factor loadings and the idiosyncratic risk factor associated with obligor i.

Since all the factors in (4) are latent variables, to extract their values, a random coefficient approach is used together with a two-step estimation procedure following Heston and Rouwenhorst (1994) and Marsh and Pfleiderer (1997). The two-step estimation involves a cross-sectional regression in the first step as follows[6]:

$$\begin{bmatrix} \Delta p_{11} & \Delta p_{12} & \cdots & \Delta p_{1T} \\ \Delta p_{21} & \Delta p_{22} & \cdots & \Delta p_{2T} \\ \vdots & \vdots & \ddots & \vdots \\ \Delta p_{M1} & \Delta p_{M2} & \cdots & \Delta p_{MT} \end{bmatrix} = \begin{bmatrix} B_{10} & B_{11} & B_{12} & \cdots & B_{1n} \\ B_{20} & B_{21} & B_{22} & \cdots & B_{2n} \\ \vdots & \vdots & \vdots & \ddots & \vdots \\ B_{M0} & B_{M1} & B_{M2} & \cdots & B_{Mn} \end{bmatrix} \times \begin{bmatrix} Z_{01} & Z_{02} & \cdots & Z_{0T} \\ Z_{11} & Z_{12} & \cdots & Z_{1T} \\ \vdots & \vdots & \ddots & \vdots \\ Z_{n1} & Z_{n2} & \cdots & Z_{nT} \end{bmatrix},$$

where $\Delta\mathbf{p}$ is the $M \times T$ matrix of exogenous default probabilities, $\mathbf{B}$ is the $M \times (n+1)$ matrix of factor loadings and $n = J + K$ is the number of industry and country factors, $\mathbf{Z}$ is the $(n+1) \times T$ matrix of factor time series, i.e., $\mathbf{Z_0}$. is the global factor, $\mathbf{Z}_\iota$. with $\iota = 2, \ldots, J+1$ are industry factors and $\mathbf{Z}_\iota$. with $\iota = J+2, \ldots, n+1$ are country factors.

The purpose of this first step is to extract values of factor $\mathbf{Z}$ from $\Delta\mathbf{p}$ given some starting values of $\mathbf{B}$, i.e., $\mathbf{Z} = \mathbf{B}^{-1} \times \Delta\mathbf{p}$. The starting values of $\mathbf{B}$ are set such that the element $B_{i\iota}$ is 1 for industry (or country) that obligor i belongs to, and zero otherwise. For the first column, B_{i0} equal to 1 for all i as $\mathbf{B}_{\cdot 0}$ is the factor loading for the global factor.

In the second step, $\mathbf{B}$ is revised based on the factors returns $\mathbf{Z}$ estimated in the first step according to the time series regression for obligor i below:

$$\begin{bmatrix} \Delta p_{i1} \\ \Delta p_{i2} \\ \vdots \\ \Delta p_{iT} \end{bmatrix} = \begin{bmatrix} \gamma_i & \beta_{i0} & \beta_{j(i)} & \beta_{k(i)} \end{bmatrix} \times \begin{bmatrix} 1 & 1 & \cdots & 1 \\ Z_{01} & Z_{02} & \cdots & Z_{0T} \\ Z_{j(i)1} & Z_{j(i)2} & \cdots & Z_{j(i)T} \\ Z_{k(i)1} & Z_{k(i)2} & \cdots & Z_{k(i)T} \end{bmatrix}, \tag{5}$$

with $B_{i0} = \beta_{i0}$, $B_{ij} = \beta_{j(i)}$ and $B_{ik} = \beta_{k(i)}$ and $B_{i\iota} = 0$ for all other values of ι. The regression described by Eq. (5) is repeated for $i = 1, \ldots, M$. The factor loadings for country and industry that obligor i does not belong to are all set equal to zero.

Most of the random coefficient models assume that the factor loadings of common factors are scaled to unity, which is too restrictive according to Marsh and Pfleiderer (1997), who suggest the scaling of the systematic factors to unit variance instead. The two-step regressions above, i.e., Eq. (5) and $\mathbf{Z} = \mathbf{B}^{-1} \times \Delta\mathbf{p}$, are repeated until the following variance ratios converged:

$$\frac{\mathrm{var}(\Delta p_{it} \mid G_t)}{\mathrm{var}(\Delta p_{it} \mid G_t, I_{j(i)t}, C_{k(i)t})} = \frac{\beta_{i0}^2}{\beta_{i0}^2 + \beta_{j(i)}^2 + \beta_{k(i)}^2},$$

$$\frac{\mathrm{var}(\Delta p_{it} \mid C_{k(i)t})}{\mathrm{var}(\Delta p_{it} \mid G_t, I_{j(i)t}, C_{k(i)t})} = \frac{\beta_{k(i)}^2}{\beta_{i0}^2 + \beta_{j(i)}^2 + \beta_{k(i)}^2},$$

$$\frac{\mathrm{var}(\Delta p_{it} \mid I_{j(i)t})}{\mathrm{var}(\Delta p_{it} \mid G_t, I_{j(i)t}, C_{k(i)t})} = \frac{\beta_{j(i)}^2}{\beta_{i0}^2 + \beta_{j(i)}^2 + \beta_{k(i)}^2}.$$

II.2. Empirical Analyses

In this section, we estimate and study the factor structures for large and small portfolios; both consist of European obligors. For the large portfolio example, we use the daily 1-year CDS spread for all European obligors contained in the Markit database for the periods from January 1, 2008 to June 30, 2010 and from July 1, 2010 to May 29, 2012.[7] The number

Table 1. CDS tickers included in sample portfolios.

	Sovereign	Financial	Industrial	Total	# Countries	# Industries
Large portfolio (daily)						
1 Jan 2008 to 30 Jun 2010	51	175	332	558	35	11
1 Jul 2010 to 29 May 2012	55	196	373	624	36	11
Whole period	49	153	307	509	35	11
Small portfolio (weekly and monthly)						
7 Jan 2009 to 2 Jan 2013	7	9	10	26	10	6

of CDS tickers included in each sub-period and the whole period is presented in Table 1. The large portfolio sample covers 11 industries spread over 36 countries. About 60% of the sample consists of corporate CDS, 30% is financial CDS and the remaining 10% is sovereign CDS.

In practice, not all loan portfolios are large. Here, we illustrate the issues one faces when the portfolio consists of a small number of loans. Obviously, if the number of loans becomes too small, then the portfolio approach based on asymptotic theory may no longer be appropriate. As shown in Table 1, the small portfolio consists of 26 obligors, with 7 sovereigns, 9 banks and 10 corporates spreading over 10 countries and 6 sectors.[8]

To investigate the sensitivity of the factor extraction results with respect to risk neutral versus physical default probabilities, for the portfolio of 26 obligors, we obtain the physical default probability estimates provided by the Risk Management Institute (RMI) at the National University of Singapore.[9] We manually match the company's name of the CDS tickers with RMI's company names database.[10] We were able to match 17 out of 26 tickers, except 7 sovereigns and 2 non-sovereigns. Since RMI's database does not cover sovereign entities, we use the RMI aggregate default probability by economy to proxy for the sovereign's default probability. Further, as country aggregates for Poland and Hungary were not available when the data was first retrieved, we use the CDS spread changes correlation to find a proxy country. As a result Poland is proxied by Germany. The default probability estimate for Poland is then set equal to Germany economy wide default probability estimate multiplied by the CDS implied default probability ratio of Poland to Germany. Here, we assume that the correlation between the two risk neutral estimates will be the same as that between the two physical estimates. We use the same procedure to identify proxy default probability estimates for the two non-sovereigns.

II.2.1. *Large portfolio*

Table 2, panel (a) shows the global, country and industry effect in the portfolio of 509 European obligors. To conserve space, we report the variance ratios by type of factors instead of reporting the regression coefficients for all 17 factors, viz. 1 global, 10 country and 6 industry factors. The results of the variance decomposition indicates that the global factor dominates in the full period as well as in the sub-sample periods, and that the country factors are marginally stronger than the industry factors. The explanatory power as measured by $R^2 \simeq 20\%$ is relatively stable across sectors and over the two sub-periods. Our findings here correspond to the findings in Aretz and Pope (2011) who find that the global economic crisis strongly affects corporate bankruptcy rates especially in the recession states. Earlier studies such as Heston and Rouwenhorst (1994) and Griffin and Karolyi (1998) find country factor dominates and explains most of the variations in default probabilities in their sample period. Whether the country factor or the global factor dominates, this is bad news for lenders as it means reduction in portfolio diversification and a higher chance for a greater loss.

We also test a simpler model containing only three factors, viz. global, financial and industrial factors, in which sovereign obligors are exposed to global factor only, financial firms are exposed to both global and financial factors, and corporates are exposed to global and industrial factors. The results of the random coefficient model estimation are shown in panel (b)

Table 2. Large portfolio — variance decomposition and factor analyses.

	Whole Period				Period 1	Period 2
	Sovereign	Financial	Industrial	All	All	All
(a) 17-factor (latent)						
Global factor variance	0.917	0.598	0.833	0.739	0.747	0.686
Country factor variance	0.004	0.259	0.085	0.156	0.146	0.159
Industry factor variance	0.079	0.143	0.082	0.105	0.107	0.154
R^2	0.207	0.143	0.190	0.177	0.211	0.195
AIC				2.919	2.982	3.030
BIC				3.380	3.763	4.056
(b) 3-factor (latent)						
Global	1.000	0.878	0.946	0.931	0.900	0.862
Financial		0.122		0.122	0.139	0.211
Industrial			0.054	0.054	0.095	0.120
R^2	0.094	0.039	0.123	0.097	0.110	0.093
AIC				2.844	2.850	2.853
BIC				2.844	2.916	2.939
(c) MSCI factor R^2	0.090	0.019	0.045	0.042	0.041	0.042

of Table 2. Compared with the result in panel (a), the simple model has a much lower R^2 and bigger Akaike Information Criterian (AIC) and Bayesian Information Criterion (BIC) which means that the simple model is less accurate. Table 3(a) shows that the correlations among the three factors are low and sometimes slightly negative. Although the model structures are different between the comprehensive 17-factor model in (a) and the simplified 3-factor model in (b), both sets of results show clearly the dominance of the global factor, especially in the first sub-period during the financial crisis.[11]

Since the factors are latent and extracted from CDS implied default probabilities, we perform further analysis by relating the factors to a large sample of MSCI Euro and World indices. It is a common practice in the industry to use observable index returns as default risk factors. Table 3(b) reports the average correlation between the global factor from the 17-factor model and a range of MSCI Euro's and World's sector and region index returns. The correlations are all negative and range between −0.350 to −0.564; slightly stronger for Euro index returns with MSIEEUE (Europe Investable Market Euro) producing the highest correlation (−0.5895) with the global factor. This result is reasonable since our large portfolio consists of hundreds of European obligors, the negative correlation

Table 3. Large portfolio — factor correlation.

	Whole Periods		Period 1		Period 2	
	Financial	Industrial	Financial	Industrial	Financial	Industrial
(a) 3-factor latent						
Global	−0.050	−0.019	0.125	0.040	0.076	−0.062
Financial		−0.056		0.064		0.094
			Euro Sector	Euro Region	World Sector	World Region
(b) MSCI indices						
Global factor (average correlation)			−0.473	−0.564	−0.350	−0.417

Note: The names of the MSCI indices are listed in the note to Table 5.

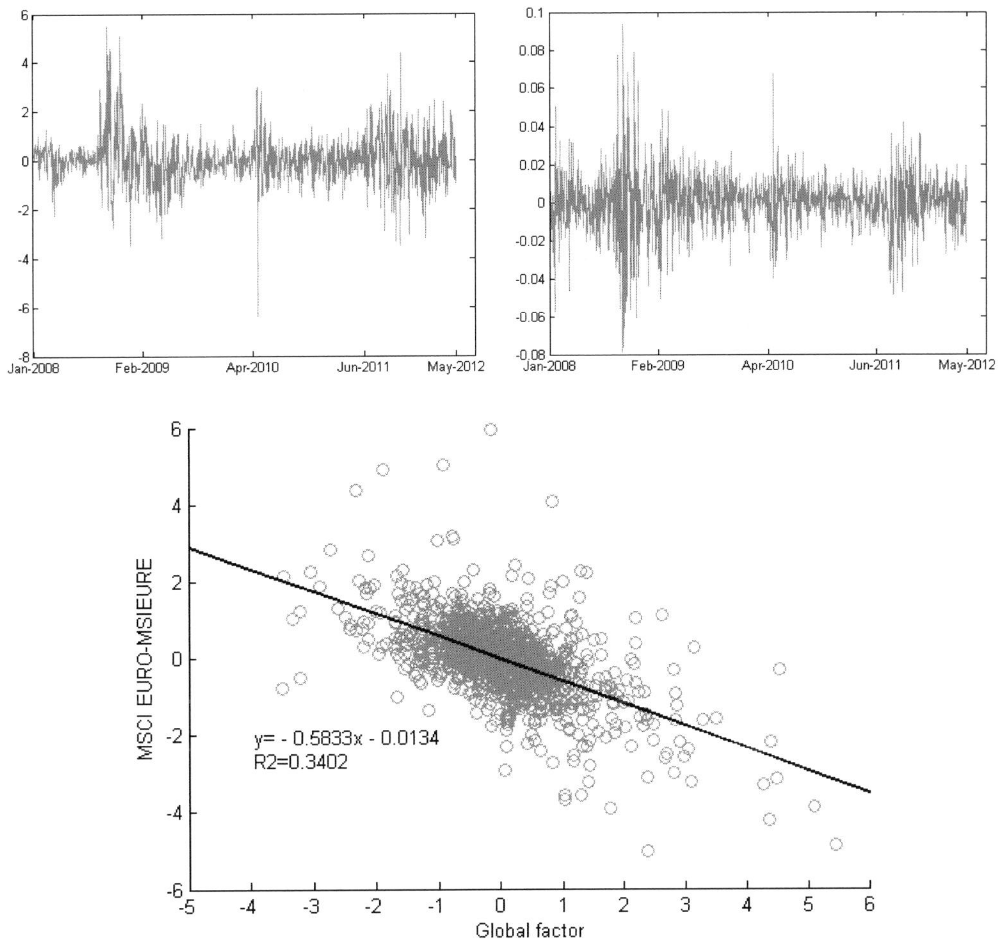

Figure 1. Large portfolio — global risk factor and log return of MSCI Europe investable market (MSIEURE).

means that the lower the MSCI market index returns, the higher the value of the global factor and the higher the individual firms' default probabilities.[12]

Figure 1 plots the time series of global factor returns and the MSCI MSIEEUE index returns showing that they share the same volatile periods in late 2008, in April 2010 and in late 2011. Figure 1 presents the scatter plot of the two series, which clearly show they are negatively correlated. While the MSCI Europe Investable Market index returns is highly correlated with the global factor, its explanatory power is not as strong as the latent factors extracted from CDS implied default probability as shown in Table 2, panel (c).

Unlike the global factor, the country factors extracted from CDS implied default probabilities are not so related to MSCI index returns. The average correlation between country factors and the MSCI index returns is -0.016. However, we noticed that country factors are more highly correlated in clusters. Table 4 puts countries into groups according to the intergroup correlations. We identify four country groups in Europe (Groups A to D); Czech Republic, Luxembourg, Greece, Hungary and Sweden do not belong to any country group. Some of the groupings are as expected; Group B, for example, consists of 15 Eastern European countries.

With the new country group information above, we reduced the country factors from 35 to 9. Then we repeat the two-step regressions described previously and extract new country factors. The correlation of these nine countries factors and the MSCI index returns are reported in Table 5. The correlation in the top panel of Table 5 are very low, which indicates that it is not possible to reduce the number of country factors

Table 4. Large portfolio country groups.

Group A		Group C	Group E
Finland		Germany	Czech Republic
Norway		Italy	
Switzerland		Netherlands	Group F
Ave Corr 0.286		*Ave Corr 0.321*	Luxembourg
Group B		Group D	Group G
Bulgaria	Poland	Austria	Greece
Croatia	Romania	Belgium	
Cyprus	Serbia	Denmark	Group H
Estonia	Slovakia	France	Hungary
Iceland	Slovenia	Ireland	
Latvia	Ukraine	Kazakhstan	
Lithuania	Malta	Portugal	Group I
Russian Federation		Spain	Sweden
		United kingdom	
Ave Corr 0.502		*Ave Corr 0.251*	

further. The bottom panel of Table 5 shows a strong pattern between country groups and the MSCI index returns. Group A, consisting of mostly Nordic countries, and Group B, consisting of mainly Eastern European countries, are strongly and negatively correlated with MSCI Euro index returns. In contrast, Czech Republic produced a strong positive correlation with all MSCI index returns.

II.2.2. *Small portfolio*

With the monthly RMI and CDS default probability estimates of the 26 obligors, we estimate the random coefficient model using a 17-factor structure and a 3-factor structure as before and the results are reported in Table 6. Unlike Table 2 which is based entirely on CDS default probability estimates, Table 6 also reports results based on RMI physical default probability estimates. Indeed, Table 6 reveals that the strong dominance of the global factor could be a feature associated more strongly with the risk neutral measures of default probability extracted from CDS (see endnote 11). While there is a strong global factor at work driving the CDS default probabilities, the results based on RMI default probabilities show that the sovereign (proxy by the respective

Table 5. Large portfolio — factor correlations between country groups and MSCI euro indices.

Country Groups		**B**	**C**	**D**	**E**	**F**	**G**	**H**	**I**
A (Nordic)		0.022	0.104	0.008	−0.076	−0.016	0.032	−0.017	−0.027
B (Eastern)			−0.044	0.050	0.028	0.064	−0.007	0.031	0.024
C (Germanic)				0.011	−0.010	−0.024	0.016	0.016	0.015
D (UK etc)					−0.057	0.229	0.143	0.089	0.032
E (Czech)						0.015	−0.069	0.170	0.080
F (Lux)							0.084	0.035	0.007
G (Greece)								0.036	0.030
H (Hungary)									0.006
I (Sweden)									1.000
	A	B	C	D	E	F	G	H	I
MSEURIL	−0.137	−0.136	−0.020	−0.013	0.161	−0.011	−0.013	0.036	0.066
MSPEURE	−0.121	−0.141	−0.025	−0.014	0.156	−0.007	−0.011	0.037	0.059
MSEROPE	−0.120	−0.144	−0.022	−0.015	0.158	−0.013	−0.011	0.038	0.060
MSIEURE	−0.121	−0.146	−0.021	−0.017	0.159	−0.016	−0.011	0.038	0.060
MSEURIE	−0.137	−0.136	−0.020	−0.013	0.161	−0.011	−0.013	0.036	0.066
MSECOME	−0.119	−0.145	−0.016	−0.017	0.158	−0.014	−0.008	0.039	0.063
MSEURZE	−0.116	−0.131	−0.045	−0.015	0.150	−0.011	−0.005	0.042	0.055
MSEEUZE	−0.114	−0.135	−0.038	−0.018	0.149	−0.007	−0.001	0.046	0.056
MSIEEUE	−0.119	−0.146	−0.015	−0.018	0.160	−0.017	−0.009	0.040	0.063
MSEFCCE	−0.137	−0.177	−0.097	−0.022	0.118	−0.034	−0.013	0.032	0.054

Note: MSEURIL is MSCI Europe, MSPEURE is MSCI Pan-Europe Euro, MSEROPE is MSCI Europe Market Euro, MSIEURE is MSCI Europe Investable Market Euro, MSEURIE is MSCI Europe Large Cap Euro, MSECOME is MSCI European Union Euro, MSEURZE is MSCI EFM Europe + CIS (Euro + C) Investable Market Euro, MSEEUZE is MSCI EFM Control and East Europe + CIS: Stock Exchange, MSIEEUE is MSCI Europe Investable Market Euro, MSEFCCE is MSCI EFM Central and Eastern Europe + CIS Euro.

Table 6. Small portfolio variance decomposition and factor analyses.

	CDS Implied Default Probability				RMI Default Probability Estimates			
	Sovereign	**Financial**	**Industrial**	**All**	**Sovereign**	**Financial**	**Industrial**	**All**
(*a*) *17-factor* (*latent*)								
Global factor variance	0.560	0.711	0.413	0.556	0.433	0.256	0.293	0.318
Country factor variance	0.210	0.226	0.257	0.233	0.284	0.425	0.162	0.286
Industry factor variance	0.230	0.063	0.331	0.211	0.283	0.319	0.545	0.396
R^2	0.962	0.950	0.961	0.958	0.873	0.870	0.909	0.886
AIC				3.637				4.629
BIC				4.306				5.298
(*b*) *3-factor* (*latent*)								
Sovereign	0.838			—	0.737			—
Financial		0.857		—		0.609		—
Industrial			0.795	—			0.611	—
R^2	0.705	0.741	0.638	0.691	0.549	0.400	0.385	0.435
AIC				1.643				2.284
BIC				1.722				2.363
(*c*) *iTraxx factors* R^2	0.385	0.637	0.568	0.543	0.106	0.184	0.127	0.141
(*d*) *Factor correlation*	iTraxx Sov	iTraxx Fin	iTraxx Ind	CDS Sov	CDS Fin	CDS Ind	RMI Sov	RMI Fin
iTraxx Financial	0.828							
iTraxx Industrial	0.927	0.789						
CDS Sovereign	−0.749	−0.665	−0.732					
CDS Financial	−0.927	−0.761	−0.895	0.797				
CDS Industrial	−0.781	−0.943	−0.752	0.633	0.716			
RMI Sovereign	−0.328	−0.414	−0.387	0.258	0.289	0.446		
RMI Financial	−0.641	−0.674	−0.718	0.665	0.642	0.648	0.622	
RMI Industrial	−0.428	−0.516	−0.451	0.376	0.379	0.528	0.555	0.535

aggregate economy) default probability is driven by the global factor, but the financial firms defaults are driven by the country factor, and the defaults of industrial firms are driven by industry sectors. The more unusual result for the small portfolio reported in Table 6 is the extremely high R^2 which is approximately 96% for the CDS default probabilities and 89% for the RMI default probabilities. A closer examination of the detailed results indicate that this is clearly due to over fitting, as some of the country factor and industry factor has a dummy variable associated with only one obligor. That is, some factors are single obligor factors, or idiosyncratic risks in another words. Next, in panel (b), we report the simplified 3-factor model where there are only three industry factors; sovereign, financial and industrial. The R^2 now drops to 69% for the CDS sample and to 44% for the RMI sample.

Again, to understand the nature of the latent factors extracted from Table 6, panel (b), we correlate these latent factors with three iTraxx sector returns, matching these three sector factors, and repeat the regressions using these iTraxx returns.[13] Table 6, panel (c) shows that the R^2 derived from the regression of log-changes of default probability on the iTraxx returns are lower, averaging 54% for the CDS sample and 14% for the RMI sample. That is, with the much lower explanatory power, the observed index returns are not a good proxy for the latent risk factors. Finally, Table 6, panel (d) reports the correlation between the latent factors returns and the three iTraxx sector returns. As before the latent factors are negatively correlated with iTraxx sector returns. The iTraxx returns are much strongly correlated with each other than with the latent factors; the same is true, to a lesser extent, for the other two sets of latent factors. Moreover, the iTraxx returns are more correlated with the CDS factors than with the RMI factors. Indeed, there are a lot of multi-way correlation and sometimes, a sovereign factor could be most highly correlated with the financial sector of another set and vice versa. The analyses here indicate that as the number of loans in a portfolio reduces, it is harder to identify a unique factor structure. Nevertheless, we will show later that this does not severely hamper the portfolio VaR and ES calculation. The interdependencies of the factors will be orthogonalized when estimating the portfolio VaR and ES.

III. EXAMPLE: LOAN PORTFOLIO VaR

As an illustration, we continue with the portfolio of 26 European obligors and calculate the portfolio VaR and ES in two different ways. In the first approach we assume that there are three (correlated) systematic risk factors proxied by iTraxx sector returns, while in the second approach we assume that there are three (correlated) latent risk factors, viz. global, country and industry factors extracted from CDS default probabilities or RMI default probabilities. Please refer to Sec. I, Eq. (1) for asset returns and Eq. (2) for the risk factor structure. Assuming that we know exposures (or loan amounts), default probabilities and expectations and variances of LGD's, we only need to estimate factor loadings r_i, $i = 1, \ldots, M$ in (1) and coefficients $(\alpha_{i,k})_{(i,k)=(1,1)}^{(M,N)}$ in (2) to be able to calculate portfolio VaR and ES. In theory, this is achieved by regressing asset return time series, x_{it}, against time series of factors, y_{it},

$$x_{it} = \gamma_i + \hat{b}_i y_{it} + e_{it}, \tag{6}$$

where γ_i is the intercept and e_{it} is the error term. Then $r_i = \text{sign}(\hat{\beta}_i)\sqrt{R_i^2}$, where R_i^2 is the regression R-square of (6). Estimation of $(\alpha_{i,k})_{(i,k)=(1,1)}^{(M,N)}$ is described in the following subsections.

Unfortunately, asset returns X_i are not directly observable, which forces us to approximate their behavior with some suitable proxy. A potential candidate is the default probability returns, since asset returns and default probability returns ought to be strongly (negatively) correlated. Based on this reasoning and the fact that all factors and coefficients will be normalized, we replace x_{it} in Eq. (6) by default probability log-returns, and y_{it} by log-returns of risk factors extracted in Sec. II or some observed index returns.

III.1. Fixed Factor Approach

Here, we assume that there are three systematic risk factors proxied by iTraxx sector returns (see endnote 13). Then the time series of the obligor-specific systematic risk factors are given by

$$y_{it} = \begin{cases} \hat{z}_{1t} & \text{for } i = 1, \ldots, 7 \text{ (Sovereign entities)} \\ \hat{z}_{2t} & \text{for } i = 8, \ldots, 16 \text{ (Financial firms)} \\ \hat{z}_{3t} & \text{for } i = 17, \ldots, 26 \text{ (Industrial firms),} \end{cases} \tag{7}$$

where $\hat{z}_{kt}$'s, for $k = 1, 2, 3$, are the normalized log-returns of the observed iTraxx sector returns.

As mentioned above, since we are not able to observe asset returns, we assume that the relationship between asset returns and systematic factors in (1) can be approximated by regressing the log-changes of default probabilities (from CDS or RMI) against the y_{it} in (7) as follows:

$$\Delta p_{it} = \log\left(\frac{p_{it}}{p_{i(t-1)}}\right) = \gamma_i + \hat{\beta}_i y_{it} + e_{it}. \tag{8}$$

The factor loading r_i in (1) can then be proxied by $r_i = \text{sign}(\hat{\beta}_i)\sqrt{R_i^2}$, where R_i^2 is the regression R-square of (8).

The next step is to find the time series of **independent** systematic risk factors z_k, for $k = 1, 2, 3$, and we do this by orthonormalizing $\hat{z}_1$, $\hat{z}_2$ and $\hat{z}_3$ with Gram-Schmidt orthogonalisation method.[14] The transformation matrix $\mathbf{V}$ from $\mathbf{z} = (z_1, z_2, z_3)$ to $\hat{\mathbf{z}} = (\hat{z}_1, \hat{z}_2, \hat{z}_3)$, which we need for finding α_{ik}-coefficients of Eq. (2), is given by $\mathbf{V} = \mathbf{z}^T\hat{\mathbf{z}}$, or $\hat{\mathbf{z}} = \mathbf{z}\mathbf{V}$. Since $\hat{\beta}$ is the coefficient of $\hat{\mathbf{z}}$, the transformation must also be applied to $\hat{\beta}$ to produce $\beta = \frac{1}{\sqrt{T-1}}\hat{\beta}\mathbf{V}^T$, where $\hat{\beta}$ is a 26×3 matrix with ith row vector as

$$\hat{\beta}_{i\cdot} = \begin{cases} (\hat{\beta}_i \quad 0 \quad 0) & \text{for } i = 1, \ldots, 7, \\ (0 \quad \hat{\beta}_i \quad 0) & \text{for } i = 8, \ldots, 16, \\ (0 \quad 0 \quad \hat{\beta}_i) & \text{for } i = 17, \ldots, 26. \end{cases}$$

From (1) and (2), $r_i\alpha_{ik} = \hat{\beta}_{ik}$. Hence, the α-coefficients are given by

$$\alpha_{ik} = \frac{\hat{\beta}_{ik}}{r_i},$$

for $i = 1, \ldots, 26$, $k = 1, 2, 3$.

III.2. Latent Factor Approach

Here, we assume that each loan is exposed to the global factor, one country factor and one industry factor. In total, there are $N = 17$ risk factors; one global, 10 country and 6 industry factors (we have also tested two cases of $N = 3$). Description on how these risk factors are estimated is given in Sec. II and from now on we assume that we already have the time series of normalized risk factors Z_k.

Given the orthogonalized risk factors, we do the regression equivalent to (8), which can be written as

$$\Delta p_{it} = \gamma_i + \sum_{k=1}^{17} \hat{\beta}_{ik} z_{kt} + e_{it},$$

where $\beta_{ik} = 0$ if the risk factor k is not related to obligor i. We take the R^2 values from the regression and set $r_i = \sqrt{R^2}$. Moreover, α_{ik} in Eq. (2) can be calculated as

$$\alpha_{ik} = \frac{\beta_{ik}}{\sqrt{\sum_{k=1}^{17} \beta_{ik}^2}}.$$

III.3. Numerical Results

The test portfolio of 26 obligors is heterogeneous and highly granular with default probabilities varying from 0.2% to over 10%, LGD's are between 0.05–0.5 and largest obligor has an exposure of over 20% of the total exposure. VaR and ES figures are calculated using formulas given in Appendix A. To calculate portfolio VaR and ES, the physical measure of default probabilities p_i, weights w_i of individual loans in the portfolio, and the expected value μ_i and volatility σ_i^2 of LGD are input values; $\bar{Y}$ is specified by (A.5) and ρ_i is specified by (A.6) and (A.7). In the examples below p_i's are estimated default probabilities, that are considerably lower than CDS-implied default probabilities p used for regression. The physical measures of default probabilities could be from Moody's Analytics or S&P Capital IQ. The default probabilities from traditional credit rating agencies, such as Moody's, S&P or Fitch, are less appropriate as these PDs are not point-in-time estimates and are not updated often enough. The RMI at the National University of Singapore (http://rmicri.org/home/) provides historical default probabilities estimates and forecasts for default in 1 to 24 months (see also Duan and Van Laere (2012); note that at the time of writing RMI forecast horison has been extended to 60 months).

Table 7. Economic capital and Expected Shortfall for small portfolio.

	99.9%				99.99%			
VaR	**ECap$_{99.9\%}$**	**VaR_{single}**	**VaR$_\infty$**	**VaR$_{GA}$**	**ECap$_{99.99\%}$**	**VaR_{single}**	**VaR$_\infty$**	**VaR$_{GA}$**
3-factor (CDS_iTraxx)	2.757	1.946	0.041	0.769	6.179	5.143	0.040	0.996
3-factor (CDS)	3.276	2.433	0.179	0.665	7.545	6.586	0.166	0.792
17-factor (CDS)	3.497	2.594	0.631	0.272	7.629	6.864	0.450	0.315
3-factor (RMI_iTraxx)	1.945	0.370	0.002	1.574	2.637	0.697	0.003	1.937
3-factor (RMI)	2.246	1.188	0.104	0.953	3.933	2.561	0.124	1.249
17-factor (RMI)	2.551	1.453	0.403	0.695	4.651	3.197	0.599	0.855
Expected Shortfall	**ES$_{99.9\%}$**	**ES$_{single}$**	**ES$_\infty$**	**ES$_{GA}$**	**ES$_{99.99\%}$**	**ES$_{single}$**	**ES$_\infty$**	**ES$_{GA}$**
3-factor (CDS_iTraxx)	4.172	3.258	0.046	0.868	7.954	6.842	0.025	1.087
3-factor (CDS)	5.034	4.100	0.206	0.727	9.568	8.613	0.106	0.849
17-factor (CDS)	5.205	4.297	0.611	0.298	9.604	8.926	0.345	0.333
3-factor (RMI_iTraxx)	2.245	0.508	0.003	1.734	2.996	0.890	0.004	2.103
3-factor (RMI)	2.968	1.768	0.113	1.086	4.766	3.309	0.107	1.350
17-factor (RMI)	3.460	2.231	0.453	0.776	5.657	4.146	0.607	0.904

Table 7 reports the economic capital (ECap), VaR and ES calculated for the portfolio of 26 obligors at $q =$ 99.9% and 99.99%. Both measures are broken down into the *single factor approximation*, the *adjustment for limiting multi-factor distribution* and the *adjustment for granularity*. We compare the estimates using regression inputs of five different specifications, which include different choices of factors (index returns or latent factors), two types of default probability estimates (risk neutral from CDS and physical measures from RMI) and two types of factor structures (3 sectors versus 17 global-country-sector factors). Apart from the regression coefficients and the correlation of the factors, which are different for the five cases, the same set of next period default probability forecasts for the 26 obligors is used in all five cases. This is done so that we can narrow the comparison to only the model choice.

The results in Table 7 reveal several important observations. (i) VaR and ES figures are smaller when observed index returns from iTraxx are used as risk factors. The industry practice as implemented in many vendors' software is to allow the lender to choose from a list of observed market indices as factor returns. Our findings here show clearly that index returns often do not fully explain obligors' asset returns variations (proxied by changes in obligors' default probabilities) and this will lead to an underestimation of tail risk. This underestimation problem is more severe for the lower explanatory power of index returns (as in the case for RMI-PD regression) and for the more extreme percentile (99.99% versus of 99.9%). The amount of VaR and ES underestimation can be close to 40%. Hence, we strongly recommend the use of risk factors extracted from changes in log difference of PD, asset returns or equity returns. At least, one should use results produced from extracted risk factors as a sanity check. (ii) For the latent factor models, the VaR and ES estimates produced from CDS-PD regressions are not sensitive to the number of factors. The 3-factor and 17-factor models produced almost identical VaR and ES values at both 99.9 and 99.99 percentiles. The larger number of factors leads to a slightly higher single factor approximation and a higher multi-factor correction, but a much smaller granularity adjustment. This is due to the fact that much of the idiosyncratic risks have already been captured as 1-obligor systematic risk factor. The same pattern can be observed from the RMI-PD factor results. But unlike the CDS-PD, the RMI-PD factors involve a much higher granularity adjustment. The RMI-PD also has a greater underestimation from the 3-factor model compared to the 17-factor model. The likely explanation is that the RMI-PD has a greater undiversifiable idiosyncratic component which is better captured by a model with a larger number of factors. The CDS-PD are more market driven and a 3-factor structure is sufficient in capturing the CDS-PD changes for all obligors. (iii) In all cases, the single factor approximation did a fairly good job. The approximation is better at 99.99 percentile (versus 99.9%) for ES (versus VaR), and for defaults or asset returns that have less undiversifiable idiosyncratic risks as in CDS-PD (versus RMI-PD). For the 99.99% VaR and ES, the single factor approximation from CDS-PD is about 90% of the full value. In the worst case scenario, for the RMI-PD, the single factor approximation captured only 52% of the 99.9% VaR.

The other salient feature in the results presented in Table 7 is that VaR and ES values are much higher when CDS-PD are used in the factors extraction instead of RMI-PD. This is to be expected. First of all, CDS-PD are risk neutral PDs which, in theory, should be higher than the RMI-PD under the physical measure and are estimated using historical time series data.[15] The variations of CDS-PD will be greater and more volatile. Moreover, given that CDS-PD are under the pricing measure, its changes can also be driven by risk aversion which is likely to be acute during the crisis period. We used these two sets of PDs to proxy for firm asset returns physical correlation and distributions. It is reasonable to expect that the true value is between the two estimates produced, respectively, from CDS-PD factors and from RMI-PD factors.

IV. CONCLUSION

In this paper, we provide a step-by-step guide on how portfolio loss and economic capital may be calculated using a simple analytical approximation, factor estimation and without simulations. We illustrate all the calculations using a small portfolio of 26 obligors. Our findings indicate that observed index returns may not explain default variations well and could lead to an underestimation of risk. Risk neutral default probability captures market conditions and changes in market sentiment well, but could lead to over estimation of risk due to the embedded risk premium that is driven by investors' risk aversion. Another argument for using RMI probabilities is practical: RMI provides default probability estimates for over 60,000 entities around the world, whereas CDSs are actively traded for only about 2,000 names. Finally, we show that even though a 17-factor model may, at times, produce similar risk measures as those from a 3-factor model, the large number of factors are useful in capturing non-diversifiable idiosyncratic risks. This is important for a small portfolio, and when a portfolio suffers from concentration risk and has high non-diversifiable idiosyncratic risks.

NOTES

1 Homogeneous in this context means all loans in the same portfolio have the same size, default probability and asset correlation.

2 The amount that the loss L is not exceeded on a confidence level q.

3 The average of the loss on condition that VaR is exceeded.

4 Note that the Risk Management Institute (RMI) physical PDs used here contain market data, so can also be sensitive to market conditions and sentiment.

5 Since default probabilities are bounded between 0 and 1, and are typically very small and highly autoregressive, we use log changes of default probabilities, $\log(p_t/p_{t-1})$, in the regression. The log transformation also scales the regression coefficients into a range that is easier to work with.

6 Here, we follow Heston and Rouwenhorst (1994) by merging the constant and the global factors for setting the starting value.

7 We derive the 1-year default probability from the 1-year CDS spread using the formula $[p \times LGD = (1-p) \times s$, or $PD = \frac{s}{LGD+s}$, where p is the probability of default, s is the spread for 1-year CDS, and LGD is the market estimate of LGD provided in Markit's CDS data. The choice of 1-year CDS is so that the PD derived is comparable to the 1-year PD downloaded from the RMI at the National University of Singapore.

8 The small sample is obtained from a case study made during the first two authors' industry secondment.

9 The RMI PD is based on the forward intensity model introduced by Duan *et al.* (2012) which is a reduced-form model in which the probability of default is computed as a function of different input variables (i.e., firm-specific and common variables). In the current Credit Research Initiative (CRI) implementation, PDs are forecasted for a horizon of one month up to 5 years. As of December 2013, the RMI-CRI generates daily updated PDs for around 34,000 currently active, exchange-listed firms in 106 economies in Asia-Pacific, Europe, Americas, Middle East and Africa. In addition, historical time series of PDs for the delisted firms in these economies are also available, making the total number of exchange-listed firms in excess of 60,400. For the purpose of comparison with the CDS implied PD, we use the 1-year RMI PD. The PD data was collected through http://rmicri.org [accessed on 11/12/2012].

10 Due to the laborious process in matching sample firms in the two databases, we did not implement this test on the larger European portfolio. We have done a similar analysis using a large portfolio of matched pair US entities, and reached a similar conclusion. Detailed results can be obtained on request.

11 Given that the default probabilities are all estimated from CDS spread, they are risk neutral estimates and include the risk aversion premium. It is plausible that it is the risk aversion premium, rather than the default probabilities *per se*, that is driven by the global factor.

12 Note that, here, the global factor is extracted from common movements of default probabilities. It will have a negative relationship with the stock market returns. If the global factor is constructed from obligors' asset returns, its relationship with the stock market returns will be positive, but its relationship with individual firms' defaults will then be negative.

13 The three iTraxx indices used are JITXE5FF JPM iTraxx Europe 5 year Financial Senior Funded Index (for financial firms), JITXE5NU JPM iTraxx Europe 5 year Non-Financial Unfunded Index (for industrial firms), and JITXE0BF JPM iTraxx Europe 10 year

Financial Sub Funded Index (for Sovereign). These are three observed index returns that are most highly correlated with the latent risk factors. The MSCI index returns are not used here as their correlations with the latent factors of the small portfolio are much lower. The large portfolio on the other hand is better diversified and is more correlated with the stock market index returns.

14 Other methods, such as Cholesky decomposition or singular value decomposition could be used as well as the results do not depend on the decomposition method.

15 For the 26-obligor portfolio, the CDS-PD is on average, across time and across firms, 8 times larger than the RMI-PD. For each obligor, the 1–99% range of the CDS-PD can be up to 38 times wider than RMI-PD.

APPENDIX A. PYKHTIN'S CLOSED FORM FORMULA

Under the setting described in Sec. I, the approximate formula for calculating VaR on confidence level q is given by

$$t_q(L) = t_q(\bar{L}) + \Delta t_q^{\infty}(L) + \Delta t_q^{GA}(L),$$

where $t_q(\bar{L})$ is the q-quantile of one factor approximation. The multi-factor adjustment $\Delta t_q^{\infty}(L)$ and the granularity adjustment $\Delta t_q^{GA}(L)$ are given by

$$t_q(\bar{L}) = \ell(y) := \sum_{i=1}^{M} w_i \mu_i \bar{p}_i(y),$$

$$\Delta t_q^{\infty}(L) := -\frac{1}{2\ell'(y)}\left[\nu'_{\infty}(y) - \nu_{\infty}(y)\left(\frac{\ell''(y)}{\ell'(y)} + y\right)\right]\Bigg|_{y=\Phi^{-1}(1-q)},$$

$$\Delta t_q^{GA}(L) := -\frac{1}{2\ell'(y)}\left[\nu'_{GA}(y) - \nu_{GA}(y)\left(\frac{\ell''(y)}{\ell'(y)} + y\right)\right]\Bigg|_{y=\Phi^{-1}(1-q)},$$

where Φ is the cumulative distribution function (cdf) of the standard normal distribution,

$$y = \Phi^{-1}(1-q), \quad \ell'(y) = \sum_{i=1}^{M} w_i \mu_i \bar{p}'_i(y), \quad a_i := r_i \rho_i, \quad \rho_i := \mathrm{cor}(Y_i, \bar{Y}) = \sum_{k=1}^{N} \alpha_{ik} b_k,$$

$$b_k := \sum_{i=1}^{M} (c_i/\lambda)\alpha_{ik}, \quad \lambda := \sqrt{\sum_{k=1}^{N}\left(\sum_{i=1}^{M} c_i \alpha_{ik}\right)^2}, \quad c_i := w_i \mu_i N\left[\frac{\Phi^{-1}(p_i) + r_i \Phi^{-1}(q)}{\sqrt{1-r_i^2}}\right],$$

$$\ell''(y) = \sum_{i=1}^{M} w_i \mu_i \bar{p}''_i(y), \quad \bar{p}_i(y) := \Phi\left(\frac{\Phi^{-1}(p_i) - a_i y}{\sqrt{1-a_i^2}}\right) \quad \text{(conditional PD on condition } \bar{Y} = y\text{)},$$

$$\bar{p}'_i(y) = -\frac{a_i}{\sqrt{1-a_i^2}}\Phi'\left(\frac{\Phi^{-1}(p_i) - a_i y}{\sqrt{1-a_i^2}}\right), \quad \bar{p}''_i(y) = \frac{a_i^2}{1-a_i^2}\frac{\Phi^{-1}(p_i) - a_i y}{\sqrt{1-a_i^2}}\Phi'\left(\frac{\Phi^{-1}(p_i) - a_i y}{\sqrt{1-a_i^2}}\right),$$

$$\nu_{\infty}(y) := \sum_{i=1}^{M}\sum_{j=1}^{M} w_i w_j \mu_i \mu_j \left[\Phi_2\left(\Phi^{-1}(\bar{p}_i(y)), \Phi^{-1}(\bar{p}_j(y), \rho_{ij}^{Y}\right) - \bar{p}_i(y)\bar{p}_j(y)\right],$$

$$\nu_{GA}(y) := \sum_{i=1}^{M} w_i^2\left(\mu_i^2\left[\bar{p}_i(y) - \Phi_2\left(\Phi^{-1}(\bar{p}_i(y)), \Phi^{-1}(\bar{p}_i(y)), \rho_{ii}^{Y}\right)\right] + \sigma_i^2 \bar{p}_i(y)\right),$$

$$\nu'_\infty(y) = 2\sum_{i=1}^{M}\sum_{j=1}^{M} w_i w_j \mu_i \mu_j \bar{p}_i(y)\left[\Phi\left(\frac{\Phi^{-1}(\bar{p}_j(y)) - \rho^Y_{ij}\Phi^{-1}(\bar{p}_i(y))}{\sqrt{1-(\rho^Y_{ij})^2}}\right) - \bar{p}_j(y)\right],$$

$$\nu'_{GA}(y) = \sum_{i=1}^{M} w_i^2 \bar{p}_i(y)\left(\mu_i^2\left[1-\Phi\left(\frac{\Phi^{-1}(\bar{p}_i(y)) - \rho^Y_{ii}\Phi^{-1}(\bar{p}_i(y))}{\sqrt{1-(\rho^Y_{ii})^2}}\right)\right] + \sigma_i^2\right),$$

$$\rho^Y_{ij} := \frac{r_i r_j \sum_{k=1}^{N}\alpha_{ik}\alpha_{jk} - a_i a_j}{\sqrt{\left(1-a_i^2\right)\left(1-a_j^2\right)}} \quad \text{(conditional asset correlation).}$$

The portfolio expected shortfall is calculated as

$$\mathrm{ES}_q = \mathrm{ES}_q(\bar{L}) + \Delta\mathrm{ES}_q^\infty(L) + \Delta\mathrm{ES}_q^{GA}(L),$$

where

$$\mathrm{ES}_q(\bar{L}) = \frac{1}{1-q}\sum_{i=1}^{M} w_i \mu_i \Phi_2(\Phi^{-1}(p_i), \Phi^{-1}(1-q), a_i),$$

$$\Delta\mathrm{ES}_q^\infty(L) := -\frac{1}{2(1-q)}\Phi'(\Phi^{-1}(1-q))\frac{\nu_\infty(\Phi^{-1}(1-q))}{\ell'(\Phi^{-1}(1-q))},$$

$$\Delta\mathrm{ES}_q^{GA}(L) := -\frac{1}{2(1-q)}\Phi'(\Phi^{-1}(1-q))\frac{\nu_{GA}(\Phi^{-1}(1-q))}{\ell'(\Phi^{-1}(1-q))},$$

and Φ_2 is the cumulative distribution of the bivariate standard normal distribution. Required inputs are default probabilities p_i, loan amounts w_i, expectations μ_i and variances σ_i of LGDs, factor loadings $(r_i)_{i=1}^M$ and coefficients $(\alpha_{i,k})_{(i,k)=(1,1)}^{(M,N)}$.

A.1. Ideas Behind the Formula

Vasicek (1991) derived a closed form expression for the loss L under the one-factor model (i.e., $N = 1$ in (1) or Y_i is the same for all i) when the portfolio is homogeneous and the number of loan tends to infinity. To retain the analytical result in the multi-factor setting, we first approximate the true L by $\bar{L}$, the loss under single factor $\bar{Y}$ such that

$$\bar{L} = \mathbb{E}[L \mid \bar{Y}].$$

Note that the quantile of $\bar{L}$ has a closed form solution, because it is formally equivalent to the one factor model in Vasicek (1991; 2002) and Gordy (2003). As shown in the next subsection, the factor $\bar{Y}$ is constructed from Y_i such that L is explained as much as possible by $\bar{Y}$.

Given $\bar{Y}$, Eq. (1) can be re-written as

$$X_i = a_i\bar{Y} + \sqrt{1-a_i^2}\zeta_i, \tag{A.1}$$

$$a_i = r_i\rho_i. \tag{A.2}$$

where ρ_i is the correlation between Y_i and $\bar{Y}$ and ζ_i's are correlated standard normally distributed random variables. From this expression, the conditional default probability of obligor i condition on $\bar{Y} = y$ is given by

$$\begin{aligned}\bar{p}_i(y) &= \mathbb{P}(X_i \le \Phi^{-1}(p_i) \mid \bar{Y} = y)\\ &= \mathbb{P}\left(\zeta_i \le \frac{\Phi^{-1}(p_i) - a_i\bar{Y}}{\sqrt{1-a_i^2}} \,\middle|\, \bar{Y} = y\right)\\ &= \Phi\left(\frac{\Phi^{-1}(p_i) - a_i y}{\sqrt{1-a_i^2}}\right),\end{aligned} \tag{A.3}$$

where Φ is the cumulative distribution function of the standard normal distribution and p_i is the default probability from (3). The quantile $t_q(\bar{L})$ is close to the quantile $t_q(L)$ if the bench mark factor $\bar{Y}$ is chosen such that the tail behavior of $\bar{L}$ closely resembles the tail of L around the qth quantile. The approximation is poorer if the portfolio is not very large and there are multiple risk factors. To get better approximation, L is formulated as $\bar{L}$ plus the perturbation term, $U = L - \bar{L}$. Defining $L_\epsilon = \bar{L} + \epsilon U$ and following Martin and Wilde (2002), $t_q(L)$ can be approximated by second order Taylor polynomial of $t_q(L_\epsilon)$ with respect to ϵ around $\epsilon = 0$: indeed, $\bar{L} = L_{\epsilon=0}$ and $L = L_{\epsilon=1}$ so that

$$t_q(L) = t_q(L_\epsilon) + \frac{dt_q(L_\epsilon)}{d\epsilon}(1 - \epsilon U)\bigg|_{\epsilon=0} + \frac{1}{2}\frac{d^2 t_q(L_\epsilon)}{d\epsilon^2}(1 - \epsilon U)^2\bigg|_{\epsilon=0}$$

$$= t_q(\bar{L}) + \frac{dt_q(L_\epsilon)}{d\epsilon}\bigg|_{\epsilon=0} + \frac{1}{2}\frac{d^2 t_q(L_\epsilon)}{d\epsilon^2}\bigg|_{\epsilon=0}.$$

According to Lemmas 1 and 3 of Gouriéroux *et al.* (2000):

$$\frac{dt_q(L_\epsilon)}{d\epsilon}\bigg|_{\epsilon=0} = \mathbb{E}[U|\bar{L} = t_q(\bar{L})],$$

$$\frac{d^2 t_q(L_\epsilon)}{d\epsilon^2}\bigg|_{\epsilon=0} = -\frac{1}{f_{\bar{L}}(l)}\frac{d}{dl}\left(f_{\bar{L}}(l)\,\mathrm{var}[U|\bar{L} = l]\right)\bigg|_{l=t_q(\bar{L})}, \tag{A.4}$$

where $f_{\bar{L}}$ is the probability density function of $\bar{L}$ and $\mathrm{var}[U|\bar{L} = l]$ is the variance of U conditional on $\bar{L} = l$.

Since $t_q(\bar{L}) = \{\ell(y) : \mathbb{P}(\bar{L} \leq \ell(y)) = q\}$, it implies that $t_q(\bar{L}) = \{\ell(y) : \mathbb{P}(\bar{Y} \leq y) = 1 - q\}$ given that $\bar{L}$ is a monotonically decreasing function of $\bar{Y}$. Moreover, since $\bar{Y}$ is normally distributed, we have

$$t_q(\bar{L}) = \ell(\Phi^{-1}(1 - q))$$

and we can rewrite the set of Eqs. (A.4) as:

$$\frac{dt_q(L_\epsilon)}{d\epsilon}\bigg|_{\epsilon=0} = \mathbb{E}[U|\bar{Y} = \Phi^{-1}(1 - q)],$$

$$\frac{d^2 t_q(L_\epsilon)}{d\epsilon^2}\bigg|_{\epsilon=0} = -\frac{1}{N'(y)}\frac{d}{dl}\left(N'(y)\frac{\nu(y)}{\ell'(y)}\right)\bigg|_{y=\Phi^{-1}(1-q)},$$

where $\nu(y) = \mathrm{var}[U \mid \bar{L} = l]$ is the conditional variance of U.

A.2. Constructing $\bar{Y}$

We can relate $\bar{Y}$ to Y_i through the set of systematic factors:

$$\bar{Y} = \sum_{k=1}^{N} b_k Z_k, \tag{A.5}$$

where $\sum_{k=1}^{N} b_k^2 = 1$ to make sure that $\bar{Y}$ has unit variance.

Given that Z_k are independent factors and all have unit variance, ρ_i, the correlation between Y_i and $\bar{Y}$, can be written as

$$\rho_i = \sum_{k=1}^{N} \alpha_{ik} b_k. \tag{A.6}$$

Now the task is to find factor loadings b_k, $k = 1, \ldots, N$ that will maximize a weighted sum of ρ_i's, that is, solve

$$\max_{(b_k)_{k=1}^N} \sum_{i=1}^{M} c_i \sum_{k=1}^{N} \alpha_{ik} b_k = \max_{(b_k)_{k=1}^N} \sum_{k=1}^{N} b_k \sum_{i=1}^{M} c_i \alpha_{ik}.$$

The positions of c_i and b_k are swapped because $c_i\alpha_{ik}$ are fixed constants. Next, optimizing with Lagrange multipliers yields

$$b_k = \sum_{i=1}^{M} (c_i/\lambda)\alpha_{ik}, \tag{A.7}$$

where the Lagrange multiplier

$$\lambda = \sqrt{\sum_{k=1}^{N}\left(\sum_{i=1}^{M} c_i \alpha_{ik}\right)^2}$$

to ensure that $\sum_{k=1}^{N} b_k^2 = 1$. Note that there is no unique solution for b_k, which means that there is no unique set of ρ_i. The choice of coefficients c_i is not obvious, but one option is to use the following coefficients as suggested by Pykhtin

$$c_i = w_i \mu_i \Phi\left(\frac{\Phi^{-1}(p_i) + r_i \Phi^{-1}(q)}{\sqrt{1 - r_i^2}}\right). \tag{A.8}$$

The rationale behind this choice is to give larger weights for those obligors who have highest individual VaR's.

A.3. Portfolio VaR

According to Pykhtin (2004), the portfolio VaR at the confidence level q can be calculated as

$$t_q(L) = t_q(\bar{L}) - \frac{1}{2\ell'(y)}\left[\nu'(y) - \nu(y)\left(\frac{\ell''(y)}{\ell'(y)} + y\right)\right],$$

where

$$\ell'(y) = \sum_{i=1}^{M} w_i \mu_i \bar{p}_i'(y),$$

$$\ell''(y) = \sum_{i=1}^{M} w_i \mu_i \bar{p}_i''(y),$$

$$\bar{p}_i'(y) = -\frac{a_i}{\sqrt{1-a_i^2}}\Phi'\left(\frac{\Phi^{-1}(p_i) - a_i y}{\sqrt{1-a_i^2}}\right),$$

$$\bar{p}_i''(y) = \frac{a_i^2}{1-a_i^2}\frac{\Phi^{-1}(p_i) - a_i y}{\sqrt{1-a_i^2}}\Phi'\left(\frac{\Phi^{-1}(p_i) - a_i y}{\sqrt{1-a_i^2}}\right),$$

μ_i is the expectation of stochastic LGD and a_i is the factor loading of the constructed factor in (A.1), $\bar{p}_i$ is given in (A.2) and (A.3) is defined through (A.6), (A.7) and (A.8). The conditional variance of portfolio loss condition on $\bar{Y} = y$ can be decomposed into

$$\nu(y) = \nu_\infty(y) + \nu_{GA}(y),$$

where $\nu_\infty(y)$ represents the conditional variance of limiting portfolio loss condition on $\bar{Y} = y$ as the number of loans tends to infinity and $\nu_{GA}(y)$ is the conditional variance of idiosyncratic part of the portfolio loss (see Chapter 5 of Hibbeln (2010) for details). These are used to quantify the limiting multi-factor adjustment and the granularity adjustment and are given as follows:

$$\nu_\infty(y) = \sum_{i=1}^{M}\sum_{j=1}^{M} w_i w_j \mu_i \mu_j \left[\Phi_2(\Phi^{-1}[\bar{p}_i(y)], \Phi^{-1}[\bar{p}_j(y)], \rho_{ij}^Y]\right],$$

$$\nu_{GA}(y) = \sum_{i=1}^{M} w_i^2 \left(\mu_i^2\left[\bar{p}_i(y) - \Phi_2(\Phi^{-1}[\bar{p}_i(y)], \Phi^{-1}[\bar{p}_i(y)], \rho_{ii}^Y)\right] + \sigma_i^2 \bar{p}_i(y)\right),$$

$$\nu_\infty'(y) = 2\sum_{i=1}^{M}\sum_{j=1}^{M} w_i w_j \mu_i \mu_j \bar{p}_i(y)\left[\Phi\left(\frac{\Phi^{-1}[\bar{p}_j(y)] - \rho_{ij}^Y \Phi^{-1}[\bar{p}_i(y)]}{\sqrt{1-(\rho_{ij}^Y)^2}}\right) - \bar{p}_j(y)\right],$$

$$\nu_{GA}'(y) = \sum_{i=1}^{M} w_i^2 \bar{p}_i(y)\left(\mu_i^2\left[1 - \Phi\left(\frac{\Phi^{-1}[\bar{p}_i(y)] - \rho_{ii}^Y \Phi^{-1}[\bar{p}_i(y)]}{\sqrt{1-(\rho_{ii}^Y)^2}}\right)\right] + \sigma_i^2\right),$$

where

$$\rho_{ij}^Y = \frac{r_i r_j \sum_{k=1}^{N} \alpha_{ik}\alpha_{jk} - a_i a_j}{\sqrt{(1-a_i^2)(1-a_j^2)}}$$

is the conditional asset correlation, Φ_2 is the cumulative distribution function of two-dimensional standard normal distribution and σ_i^2 is the volatility of LGD.

The formula for VaR follows from this and the formula for ES is obtained by

$$\mathrm{ES}_q(L) = \frac{1}{1-q}\int_q^1 \mathrm{VaR}_\gamma(L)d\gamma,$$

see Sec. 5.2 of Hibbeln (2010) for details.

REFERENCES

Aretz, K. and Pope, P. F. (2011), Common Factors in Default Risk Across Countries and Industries. *Journal of European Financial Management*. doi: 10.1111/j.1468-036X.2010.00571.x.

Duan, J. C., Sun, J. and Wang, T. (2012), Multiperiod Corporate Default Prediction — A Forward Intensity Approach. *Journal of Econometrics*, 170, pp. 191–209.

Duan J. and Van Laere, E. (2012), A Public Good Approach to Credit Ratings — From Concept to Reality. *Journal of Banking and Finance*, 36, pp. 3239–3247.

Gordy, M. (2003), A Risk-Factor Model Foundation for Ratings-Based Bank Capital Rules. *Journal of Financial Intermediation*, 12(3), pp. 199–232.

Gouriéroux, C., Laurent, J.-P. and Scaillet, O. (2000), Sensitivity Analysis of Values at Risk. *Journal of Empirical Finance*, 7, pp. 225–245.

Griffin, J. M. and Karolyi, G. A. (1998), Another Look at the Role of Industrial Structure of Markets for International Diversification Strategies. *Journal of Financial Economics*, 50, pp. 351–373.

Heston, S. L. and Rouwenhorst, K. G. (1994), Does Industrial Structure Explain the Benefits of International Diversification? *Journal of Financial Economics*, 36, pp. 3–27.

Hibbeln, M. (2010), *Risk Management in Credit Portfolios Concentration Risk and Basel II*, Springer.

Marsh, T. and Pfleiderer, P. (1997), The Role of Country and Industry Effects in Explaining Global Stock Returns. Working Paper (Stanford University).

Martin, R. and Wilde, T. (2002), Unsystematic Credit Risk. *Risk*, November, pp. 123–128.

Merton, R. C. (1974), On the Pricing of Corporate Debt: The Risk Structure of Interest Rates. *Journal of Finance*, 7, pp. 141–183.

Pykhtin, M. (2004), Multi-Factor Adjustment. *Risk*, March, pp. 17–31.

Vasicek, O. (1991), Limiting Loan Loss Probability Distribution. Working Paper, KMV Corporation.

Vasicek, O. (2002), Loan Portfolio Value. *Risk*, December pp. 160–162.

Wilde, T. (2001), Probing Granularity. *Risk*, August, pp. 103–106.

Rejection and Partial Rejection of Consumer Credit Applications

Steven E. Plaut
Graduate School of Management
University of Haifa
Haifa 31905, Israel
splaut@econ.haifa.ac.il

Keywords: Credit rejection, bank lending, loan application, credit rationing.

INTRODUCTION

Credit rationing in the real-world practice of banks is part and parcel of risk control and management. It plays an integral role in asset management. While charging higher risk premiums is one way to control for risk, banks also routinely design their internal capital allocation mechanisms to discourage its units from taking up unsuitably high credit risk exposure, even when borrowers are willing to pay higher interest rates. When banks have the ability to identify risky borrowers, they may choose to turn down applications altogether, as opposed to charging them higher interest rates.

Banks are one, but not the only, type of institution commonly using both pricing and rationing methods to control risks. Insurance companies also commonly deny coverage for life insurance and some other forms of insurance when risks are deemed too high.[1]

The bulk of the literature on consumer bank lending (and other forms of bank lending as well) focuses on bank management of customer risk by means of pricing the risk. Yet it is well known that banks also commonly control for risk by denying loan applications altogether. There are theoretical questions about why this is done. Credit rejection in full or in part may reflect market imperfections in which banks are unable to adjust pricing with sufficient flexibility (for example, according to Greer (1974), when usury laws are in effect). At the same time there is a literature that posits that credit rejection is likely to take place for some applicants in unregulated markets due to adverse selection. This is the position of much of the research on credit rationing, beginning with Stiglitz and Weiss (1981).

Credit rationing, whose literature is reviewed by Allen (1987), may be a plausible explanation for some forms of *partial* credit rejection, in which a loan applicant is rationed, but is not as persuasive an explanation for cases where credit is refused altogether. De Meza and Webb (1987; 2000; 2006), De Meza (1992) and others have described how banks ration credit quantitatively in order to control for problems associated with adverse selection and asymmetric information. Recent empirical papers on rationing include Drakos and Giannakopoulos (2011), Jappelli (1990), Munnell *et al.* (1996). In this paper, survey data of US households who have been rejected or partially rejected for credit are used to identify factors that appear to have influenced the rejection decisions.

Numerous issues in credit markets can manifest themselves in either pricing or rejection rates or both. For example, if discrimination against a group exists, it is possible that it manifests itself in either pricing or in approval rates, or both. This is essentially the position of Brent *et al.* (1995), Munnell *et al.* (1996) and Tootell (1993) for mortgage market discrimination. Much of the literature on credit rejection has been driven by concern with discrimination in mortgage markets, and particularly "redlining".[2] Pricing of credit for the discriminated group and the residual population could be similar while approval rates are different, or vice versa. There has long been interest in the existence and extent of racial/ethnic discrimination in credit markets. In mortgage markets, discrimination in loan approval is often dubbed "redlining". Duca and Rosenthal (1993) and Ladd (1998) review this literature. These approval rate disparities are the focus here.

This paper analyzes consumer credit rejection empirically using the 2010 data from the American Survey of Consumer Finances (SCF). 2010 of course was a year in the middle of the recent recession. Credit rejection rates and bank concerns over default may have been unusually acute that year. We will return to this point in the conclusions. The Survey includes information on loan applications by households, approval and rejection, and also on "partial rejections". The latter is where a loan is approved for less than the full amount for which the household applied. Little is known from earlier empirical research about such partial rejections, and these cases may be more difficult to explain theoretically, aside from the credit rationing explanation.

Factors that explain total or partial credit rejection could operate in complex ways. They may trigger credit rejection, but may also cause lower rates of application for bank credit in the first place on the part of those who anticipate rejection, such as those analyzed by Kon and Storey (2003). An issue that has not been explored extensively in empirical research is how anticipation of being rejected affects application rates for credit. This will be addressed empirically below, with some unexpected results.

In the next section, summary statistics are presented for groups of loan applicants, showing those who were approved, partially approved, rejected altogether, and who never applied. The latter are in fact a heterogeneous group of people who may not need credit at all, mixed in with those who do not apply for fear of being turned down. This heterogeneity may explain some of the signs of coefficients in the empirical section. Following this, the factors that explain loan rejection and loan application are explored empirically, using logistic regression analysis of the American SCF data.

I. SUMMARY STATISTICS FOR CREDIT APPLICANT REJECTIONS AND APPROVALS

Table 1 shows the summary statistics for four categories of credit applicants, using the 2010 SCF data. The credit for which applicants are applying includes loans and credit facilities such as lines of credit. The total sample size is 32,410 households, and is designed to represent the general American population. Of these, approximately 62% had responded that they have applied for bank credit in one form or another. Of those who applied, just over two thirds were approved for the full amount they requested. The remainder however either were turned down completely for credit or were approved for a reduced amount of credit, less than the amount they had requested. The data on "partial rejections" do not provide information on what proportion was approved.

There is clearly an element of self-selection in the credit application process. Those who never applied at all have lower total incomes and lower total salary incomes on average than any of the other groups. This suggests that these are predominantly *not* people who do not need credit at all. They differ from applicants in other ways as well. They are less likely to be married or have a male head of household, compared with all the other groups.[3] They are older than the others on average and considerably more likely to be receiving social security income. They are also more likely to be

Table 1. Summary statistics of the four subsamples.

	Application for Credit Rejected	Partial Rejection (Approval of Less Credit than Requested)	Full Approval of Application for Credit	Did not Apply at All for Credit
N	5,356	1,132	13,740	12,182
Mean (SD) Total Total Household Income	56,028 (113,584)	80,464 (311,528)	103,759 (315,620)	55,309 (243,704)
Mean (SD) Salary Income received by Household	41,542 (51,575)	61,877 (81,589)	75,321 (183,195)	30,561 (97,462)
Mean (SD) Number of Persons in Household	2.94 (1.65)	2.94 (1.80)	2.70 (1.38)	2.28 (1.41)
Mean (SD) Age of Head of Household	43.4 (14.5)	41.9 (12.4)	48.9 (15.2)	56.3 (18.5)
Percent of Column who are Male	73.2%	75.1%	79.6%	65.5%
Percent Married	46.5%	49.6%	61.4%	40.3%
Percent who are White	65.4	65.9	79.3	64.7
Percent who are Hispanic	16.4	17.3	9.2	15.3
Percent who are Black	18.4	16.2	8.2	17.5
Percent who Own their Own Home	51.0	60.7	74.7	52.6
Of non-owners, percent who once owned	14.7	14.5	9.7	13.4
Percent who Receive some Dividend Income	4.0	10.1	17.3	11.0
Percent who have some Line of Credit	11.4	16.6	20.6	7.36
Percent who Receive some Taxable Interest	8.6	14.3	26.8	18.3
Percent who receive Foodstamps	14.5	6.2	4.5	17.4
Percent Receiving Social Security Stipend	14.0	10.0	20.8	42.4
Percent who have Ever Been Declared Bankrupt	24.4	17.0	10.2	10.5
Percent who have ever been Late on Debt Payments	19.2	15.8	4.4	6.4
Percent who have completed High School	88.8	92.8	91.9	79.6
Percent who have a BA Degree	16.8	24.8	25.5	13.5
Percent who Completed Post-graduate Degree	7.9	12.6	17.6	9.7
Percent who Served in the Military	8.9	12.3	18.9	20.9
Percent who have been turned down for Credit Before	34.5	27.0	0	0
Percent who had Not Applied for Credit at some point for Fear of being Turned Down	43.59	34.4	7.8	16.9
Mean (SD) Charges last month to Credit Card with Largest Balance	371 (1,722)	695 (2,411)	1,199 (4,912)	478 (1,907)
Mean (SD) Charges last month to Credit Card with second Largest Balance	74.5 (632)	84.0 (338)	116 (501)	55.7 (452)
Mean (SD) Outstanding Balance Largest Credit Card Debt	3,529 (9,806)	5,478 (11,677)	2,990 (7,990)	917 (4,730)
Mean (SD) Sum of Credit Ceilings on All Credit Cards	9,210 (19,859)	17,381 (30,611)	24,689 (39,312)	12,204 (44,082)

Source: SCF (2010). "Head of Household" refers to member of household with highest income.

receiving foodstamps. They tend to be less educated than people in the other groups, and more likely to be military veterans.

While whites are represented in greater numbers among those fully approved, the other categories (those who never apply or who are rejected in whole or in part for credit) are fairly similar to one another in terms of racial/ethnic composition. Those receiving full approval have higher incomes and salaries than the other groups. They also are more likely to be receiving dividend income or taxable interest or to have a line of credit.

The decision to turn people down for credit appears to be generally consistent with other indicators of default risk. Households who never applied or who were completely turned down for credit were the least likely to be home-owners. These households were not simply charged higher risk premiums in interest rates but appear to anticipate being denied credit altogether should they apply. These same households are more likely to report that at some point they had opted not to apply at all for fear of being turned down. Households completely or partly turned down for credit were more likely to have been declared bankrupt in the past than members of the other groups and to have been late in making payments on debt. Those rejected for credit report having been turned down in previous applications much more often than members of the other groups.

On the other hand, in some cases having other debts appears to be associated with higher chances for approval of the loan application. Those approved report having larger outstanding credit card debt balances than do households in other groups, larger amounts of charges to their credit card in the past month, as well as a larger sum of all credit card debt ceilings. As noted, these households also tend to have higher incomes.

II. FACTORS AFFECTING THE LIKELIHOOD OF CREDIT REJECTION

The various factors that are associated with credit rejection are explored in Tables 2–5. Variables include demographic, ethnic, and financial factors.[4] Credit rejection is first analyzed for all households who applied for credit, where all possible outcomes are considered: full approval, full rejection, and partial approval.

In Table 2, logistic regression analysis is shown for the subsample of households who had applied for credit. The regression analyzes the factors that affect the allocation of households among three categories: those fully approved for credit, those fully rejected, and those partially rejected (who were approved for less than the amount of credit that they requested). The two intersect terms refer to the full and partial rejection decisions, respectively. For the other variables, a positive (negative) coefficient for an explanatory variable indicates that it contributes to an increase (decrease) in the logit of the likelihood of one of these two forms of rejection relative to the likelihood of full approval.

As can be seen, a number of economic and demographic variables appear to be playing a significant role. A higher level of salary is associated with lower likelihood of some form of credit rejection, as is home ownership. Likelihood of rejection drops with age and with being married, while it rises with household size and with being black or Hispanic. Somewhat strangely, the educational level of the head of the household is not a significant explanatory factor, perhaps because its effect is captured by the income term, but the education level of the spouse does seem to be significant. Rejection drops when the spouse has a college degree.

In the same table, mortgage debt is associated with a higher likelihood of some form of credit rejection. So is non-mortgage debt and the total number of debts outstanding. Having any dividend income is associated with lower likelihood of rejection. Being on food-stamps, ever having filed for bankruptcy, or ever having been late in payments on debt are all associated with higher likelihood of rejection.

The two different forms of credit rejection, that is, full rejection versus partial rejection, are explored in separate logit regressions in Tables 3 and 4. In Table 3, for full rejection, it is seen that greater household income or salary income is associated with a lower likelihood of being rejected, as would be expected. For homeowners, a higher value of their home is associated with a lower likelihood of rejection, as is having any mortgage outstanding. The size of the mortgage balance outstanding, however, is positively associated with the likelihood of being rejected. So are the size of non-mortgage debts outstanding and credit card balances outstanding. Having dividend income or taxable interest income is associated with a lower likelihood of rejection. Having a larger sum of ceilings on credit cards is associated with a lower likelihood of rejection. But the total number of outstanding debts (separated from the debt amounts or balances in question) is associated with a higher likelihood of rejection. Having ever been late in payments on debt or having ever been declared bankrupt is unsurprisingly

Table 2. Logistic regression of rejection or partial rejection of the application for credit, for those who applied for credit.

	I **All Applicants**	II **Current Home Owners Only**
Intercept for Full Rejection	0.142	0.152
	(0.448)	(0.566)
Intercept for Partial Rejection	0.468*	0.479*
	(5.336)	(5.594)
Log of Salaries Received by Household Members	−0.018	−0.018
	(2.517)	(2.511)
Dummy if Own Home	−0.172	—
	(1.055)	
Dummy if Has any Mortgage Debt	0.302**	0.276*
	(5.454)	(4.766)
Log of Real Estate Taxes Paid	—	−0.099**
		(23.97)
Age	−0.013**	−0.013**
	(17.13)	(17.32)
Dummy for Married	−0.376**	−0.379**
	(10.25)	(10.39)
Number of Persons in Household	0.063*	0.065*
	(4.668)	(4.946)
Dummy if Has a Spouse with High School Diploma	0.314**	0.313**
	(7.211)	(7.170)
Dummy if Has Spouse with BA	−0.433**	−0.432**
	(12.85)	(12.75)
Dummy if Hispanic	0.357**	0.355**
	(10.44)	(10.37)
Dummy if Black	0.441**	0.432**
	(16.40)	(15.86)
Dummy if Served in the Military	0.213*	0.210*
	(4.316)	(4.218)
Log of Size of Non-mortgage Debts	0.133**	0.133**
	(108,5)	(109.1)
Dummy if have Dividend Income	−0.259*	−0.251*
	(2.951)	(2.793)
Total Number of Outstanding Debts	0.161**	0.162**
	(9.248)	(9.167)
Log of Credit Ceiling for Largest Credit Cards	−0.145**	−0.146**
	(121.2)	(122.0)
Dummy if Receives Foodstamps	0.236*	0.239*
	(3.004)	(3.064)
Dummy if Ever Declared Bankrupt	0.619**	0.617**
	(39.52)	(39.30)
Dummy if Ever Made Late Payment on Debt	0.865**	0.866**
	(53.36)	(53.33)
Somers' D	0.532	0.530
Percent Concordant	76.5	76.2
AIC (Intercept and Covariates)	5,496	3,409
N	20,228	13,545

Note: (Numbers in Parentheses are Wald Chi-Squares).
*Significant at 10%.
**Significant at 1%.

Table 3. Logit regression of full rejection of the application for credit, for those who applied for credit.

	I All Applicants	II All Applicants	III Current Home Owners Only
Intercept	0.028 (0.017)	0.417 (0.650)	0.877 (0.507)
Age	−0.007* (3.81)	−0.006* (2.78)	—
Dummy for Married	−0.383** (9.47)	−0.383** (9.49)	−0.754** (18.7)
Number of Persons in Household	0.491* (2.36)	0.049* (2.34)	0.070* (2.53)
Dummy if has a Spouse with High School Diploma	0.406** (10.54)	0.404** (10.34)	0.615** (11.1)
Dummy if Has Spouse with BA	−0.452** (11.38)	−0.444** (10.96)	−0.534** (10.7)
Dummy if Hispanic	0.320** (7.52)	0.230** (6.60)	0.398** (6.12)
Dummy if Black	0.390** (11.68)	0.377** (10.98)	0.402** (6.02)
Dummy if Served in the Military	0.242* (4.87)	0.243* (4.91)	—
Log of Total Household Income	—	−0.059 (1.35)	−0.103 (2.04)
Log of Salaries Received by Household Members	−0.020* (2.39)	—	—
Log of Value of Home	—	—	−0.106 (1.09)
Dummy if has any Mortgage Debt	0.290 (2.19)	0.297* (2.30)	−1.161 (1.56)
Log of Current Outstanding Mortgage Balance	—	—	0.143* (2.70)
Log of Size of Non-mortgage Debts	0.032* (2.89)	0.031* (2.72)	0.058* (5.03)
Log of Real Estate Taxes Paid	−0.067** (22.5)	−0.065** (20.8)	—
Dummy if have Dividend Income	−0.370* (4.15)	−0.348* (3.67)	−0.265 (1.70)
Total Number of Outstanding Debts	0.135** (5.92)	0.137** (6.08)	0.143* (4.99)
Log of Credit Card Debt Balance	0.118** (66.5)	0.118** (66.0)	0.123** (50.0)
Log of Sum of Credit Ceilings for All Credit Cards	−0.131** (59.9)	−0.131** (59.0)	−0.118** (28.3)
Dummy if have Taxable Interest Income	−0.222* (2.75)	−0.216* (2.59)	—
Dummy if Receives Foodstamps	0.322* (5.15)	0.332** (5.51)	0.934** (12.2)
Dummy if Receives Social Security	−0.161 (1.14)	—	—
Dummy if Ever Declared Bankrupt	0.601** (33.9)	0.596** (33.3)	0.735** (30.5)
Dummy if Ever Made Late Payment on Debt	0.759** (38.6)	0.754** (37.9)	0.596** (12.6)
Log of Charges Last Month to main Credit Card	−0.038* (4.44)	−0.037* (4.18)	−0.060** (7.32)
Somers' D	0.562	0.563	0.533

(*Continued*)

Table 3. *(Continued)*

	I All Applicants	II All Applicants	III Current Home Owners Only
Percent Concordant	78.0	78.0	76.4
AIC (Intercept and Covariates)	4,022	4,018	2,372
N	20,134	20,134	13,545

Note: (Numbers in Parentheses are Wald Chi-Squares).
Partial rejections excluded from analysis.
*Significant at 10%.
**Significant at 1%.

Table 4. Logit regression of approval of credit but for LESS than amount of loan requested, for those who applied for credit and were at least partly approved (default possibility here is full approval).

	I All Applicants	II Current Home Owners Only
Intercept	−2.314**	−3.22**
	(62.2)	(11.04)
Age	−0.023**	−0.022**
	(16.26)	(15.2)
Number of Persons in Household	0.084*	0.085*
	(2.62)	(2.70)
Dummy if has Spouse with High School Diploma	−0.447**	−0.491**
	(6.77)	(7.65)
Dummy if Wife has Postgraduate Degree	0.383*	0.344
	(2.47)	(1.93)
Dummy if Hispanic	0.335*	0.313*
	(2.89)	(2.52)
Dummy if Black	0.360*	0.352*
	(3.28)	(3.17)
Log of Total Household Income	—	0.094
		(1.02)
Log of Size of All Debts	0.095**	0.094**
	(27.4)	(28.8)
Total Number of Outstanding Debts	0.128*	0.126*
	(2.61)	(2.53)
Dummy if Receives Foodstamps	−0.522*	−0.492*
	(2.97)	(2.56)
Dummy if Ever Declared Bankrupt	0.187	—
	(0.94)	
Dummy if Ever Made Late Payment on Debt	0.533**	0.569**
	(7.15)	(8.25)
Dummy if Own Home	−0.412*	—
	(2.72)	
Dummy if have a Mortgage	—	0.444*
		(2.81)
Log of Price Paid for Home	—	−0.053*
		(4.38)
Somers' D	0.303	0.305
Percent Concordant	64.3	64.4
AIC (Intercept and Covariates)	1673.7	1671.8
N	20,228	20,134

Note: (Numbers in Parentheses are Wald Chi-Squares).
Complete rejections excluded from analysis.
*Significant at 10%.
**Significant at 1%.

Table 5. Logit regression of decision to apply for credit.

	I Whole Sample	II Whole Sample	III Current Home Owners Only	IV Current Home Renters Only
Intercept	0.752**	0.739**	−0.128	−2.172**
	(14.92)	(20.4)	(0.222)	(12.92)
Age	−0.039**	−0.037**	−0.032**	−0.037**
	(284.8)	(188.3)	(89.8)	(141.4)
Dummy for Male	−0.185*	−0.192*	−0.320**	−0.303**
	(5.02)	(5.48)	(7.50)	(7.07)
Number of Persons in Household	0.057*	0.065**	0.084*	0.078*
	(5.02)	(6.68)	(5.12)	(4.40)
Dummy if has a High School Diploma	0.116	—	0.382**	0.375**
	(1.58)		(8.81)	(8.52)
Dummy if has BA	0.198**	0.290**	0.222*	0.192
	(5.92)	(12.14)	(2.41)	(1.78)
Dummy if has Postgraduate Degree	—	0.255**	—	—
		(6.74)		
Dummy if Spouse has a High School Diploma	0.367**	0.243**	0.397**	0.337**
	(19.04)	(11.86)	(10.21)	(7.16)
Likelihood of Loan Application being Rejected	—	0.189	—	—
		(1.65)		
Dummy if Hispanic	−0.437**	−0.539**	−0.515**	−0.485**
	(22.5)	(29.1)	(15.8)	(14.2)
Dummy if Black	−0.327**	−0.425**	−0.338**	−0.328**
	(14.02)	(17.2)	(7.87)	(7.418)
Dummy if Served in the Military	—	—	0.175	—
			(1.43)	
Log of Total Household Income	—	—	—	0.272**
				(20.9)
Log of Salaries Received by Household Members	0.040**	0.043**	0.053**	—
	(26.6)	(27.7)	(17.2)	
Dummy if Own Home	0.386**	0.441**	—	—
	(28.75)	(37.7)		
Log of Balance of Total Household Debts	0.092**	0.072**	0.098**	0.106**
	(84.4)	(11.1)	(23.0)	(26.2)
Dummy if have a Line of Credit	0.620**	0.611**	0.893**	0.875**
	(40.53)	(39.2)	(13.6)	(12.9)
Total Number of Outstanding Debts	0.338**	0.321**	0.511**	0.487**
	(17.9)	(15.5)	(15.6)	(14.0)
Log of Credit Limit for Credit Card with Largest Balance	0.062**	0.113**	0.080**	0.069**
	(77.6)	(20.2)	(24.2)	(17.1)
Dummy if Receives Foodstamps	−0.432**	−0.498**	−0.284*	−0.318**
	(18.0)	(20.3)	(5.09)	(8.70)
Log of Real Estate Taxes Paid	—	—	0.122**	—
			(19.69)	
Dummy if Ever Declared Bankrupt	0.600**	0.468**	0.508**	—
	(41.5)	(12.6)	(14.0)	
Dummy if Ever Made Late Payment on Debt	0.429**	0.300*	0.497**	0.515**
	(14.4)	(3.36)	(10.5)	(11.3)
Somers' D	0.543	0.522	0.545	0.547
Percent Concordant	77.0	76.0	77.2	77.3
AIC (Intercept and Covariates)	6977.8	7028.4	2849.2	2835.5
N	32,410	32,410	12,270	12,250

Note: (Numbers in Parentheses are Wald Chi-Squares).
*Significant at 10%.
**Significant at 1%.

associated with a considerably greater likelihood of being rejected.

A number of demographic factors also appear to be important. In Table 3, age is associated with a lower likelihood of full rejection, other things equal, as is being married. Household size, which includes children, is associated with greater likelihood of rejection.[5] This does not appear to be discrimination, but simply a reflection of the fact that larger households have higher expenses (controlling for income) and presumably save less. A spouse having a high school degree alone is associated with a higher likelihood of rejection (compared with those having less schooling than that), but having a BA is associated with a lower likelihood.[6] The two coefficients are of similar size, but opposite sign. Black and Hispanic households are more likely to be rejected, other things equal. Military veterans are *more* likely to be rejected than non-veterans, other things equal.

Table 4 is similar to Table 3 but shows logistic regressions for partial credit rejection. (The specific proportion approved is not reported in the data set.) The default outcome is full approval. The likelihood of partial rejection rises with age. It falls with household size. Once again, the educational level of the head of the household does not appear to be statistically significant, while the spouse's educational level is. Home owners are considerably less likely to be partially rejected. Households with spouses having a high school diploma are less likely to be partially rejected than households with no spouse or with spouse not having such a degree; where the spouse has an advanced degree, rejection becomes more likely than for those where the spouse has a high school degree. The signs are different from those in Table 3. As in Table 3, blacks and Hispanics are more likely to be rejected, other things equal. Curiously, household income is not a statistically significant explanatory factor, unlike Table 3.

Having other debts and a larger size of those debts are both positively correlated with partial credit rejection. Strangely, households on foodstamps are *less* likely to be partially rejected, perhaps because they are more likely to select themselves out by not applying for credit in the first place. For home owners, having a mortgage raises the likelihood of partial rejection, while the value of the home itself lowers it. Previous bankruptcy or delinquent payments on previous debt increase the likelihood of partial rejection.

Finally, in Table 5, the decision to apply for bank credit is analyzed using logistic regression. Separate estimates are shown for home owners, home renters, and the two combined. As noted, the credit application decision may reflect in part self-selection, as those who expect to be turned down are less likely to apply in the first place. In regression II, this possibility is explored empirically; the likelihood of being rejected (estimated for the subsample of those who apply for credit) is included as an explanatory variable for the decision to apply for credit in the first place. This allows differentiation between those who do not apply because they anticipate being turned down and those who simply are not in "need" of credit. The impact of various explanatory factors could affect likelihood of loan application in different ways for each of these two subsets of households.

As is seen in Table 5, loan application likelihood tends to drop with age, other things equal. Households whose heads are male are significantly less likely to apply than others, even controlling for salary income, probably because they have more (non-salary) resources of their own without credit. Application is more likely when household size increases, probably reflecting increased demand for and reliance upon credit. Education is positively associated with likelihood to apply. Households whose heads have a high school diploma or a BA or where the spouse has a BA apply more often.[7]

The inclusion of the likelihood of being turned down for credit in Equation II of Table 5 produces some interesting results. The coefficient is not statistically significant, with an "alpha" of only 20%. However the sign of the coefficient is positive. This means that among those who face a higher (lower) likelihood of being turned down for credit if they apply for it, the inclination to apply for credit anyway is higher (lower), other things equal. In essence, applicants of "poorer quality" who are in greater danger of being rejected are also people with a greater demand for credit, other things equal. This raises thought associations with the old folk adage that holds that banks lend to people who do not "need" credit but tend to reject those who do "need" it. People confident that they will *not* be turned down are those who are less likely to apply for credit in the first place.

The inclusion of the likelihood of being rejected also sheds some interesting light on the role of race in the credit application process. In Table 5, it is seen that black and Hispanic households are significantly less likely to apply for credit, other things equal, for all equations and subsamples examined. The reason for this does *not* appear to be because of anticipation of being turned down. While blacks and Hispanics are indeed more likely to be turned down for credit once they apply for it, as seen above, the inclusion of this likelihood as an explanatory variable in the estimate of application likelihood (column II) actually INCREASES the disparity between these minority groups and whites. The coefficient for the racial groups increases in absolute value when this likelihood of rejection is included as an explanatory factor. This means that after taking into account the likelihood of being rejected, minorities are even less likely (compared to whites) to apply for credit!

So why do blacks and Hispanics apply less often for credit? It does not appear to be because of fear of being rejected! This casts doubt on discrimination as the main factor explaining the disparity in credit seeking behavior. The pattern could be because of factors affecting approval likelihood that have nothing at all to do with race itself but are differentially distributed across ethnic groups, such as urban–rural residential patterns or differences in regional distribution.

Household income or salary income is positively associated with the likelihood to apply for credit. This may be because these households have a higher appetite for credit-financed consumption, or it could be because they are less apprehensive about being turned down. Similarly, homeownership increases the likelihood of applying.

It is possible that credit application for bank loans is part of a general reliance upon credit in all its forms, making bank loans and other forms of debt complements. This may explain why loan application increases in likelihood with the total balance of outstanding household debts, with having a line of credit, or with having a larger credit ceiling on credit cards. Those on foodstamps are less likely to apply, probably expecting to be turned down. Interestingly, loan application is higher for those who have been declared bankrupt in the past or who have made late payments on debt. Since we are including those who will later be turned down in this sample, perhaps we are picking up a "debt splurging" sub-population in these coefficients, those who seek credit even though they have had financial problems or rejections in the past.

Interestingly, past credit problems, like bankruptcy, appear to increase the likelihood of application for credit. Having other credit balances outstanding in various forms also seems to increase "appetite" for bank credit in the form of higher likelihood of applying for loans.

III. CONCLUSIONS

While the "jury is still out" on the theoretical explanation for why rejection of loan applications is a common means by which lending institutions deal with risk, as opposed to pricing the risk, it is useful to explore the phenomenon of credit rejection empirically. It appears to be rather complex. Using SCF data, rates of rejection and partial rejection of applications for consumer loans from banks appear to be affected by a wide set of demographic, social, and economic variables.[8]

In many cases, the factors that make rejection more likely are unsurprising. Previous bankruptcy, previous history of late payments on debt, the total number of loans outstanding, and some other indicators of riskiness are all associated with higher rejection rates. Household income is a significant factor in explaining total rejection of credit application, other things equal, but — curiously — does not seem to explain the partial rejections. Education also seems to play a bizarre role in the rejection functions. In cases where it is not a significant factor, this is probably because education is indirectly being captured in salary levels. Home ownership generally is associated with lower likelihood of rejection, while mortgage debt outstanding is associated with a higher likelihood.

The role of race is complex and intriguing. Black and Hispanic applicants are more likely to be turned down, and are also less likely to apply for credit. But the reason that they are less likely to apply does NOT seem to be because they anticipate being turned down. When this likelihood is included as an explanatory variable, the disparity between white and racial minority credit application rates increases. Moreover, the sign of the coefficient of the likelihood of rejection is a bit surprising: other things equal, those who face higher (lower) likelihood of being turned down are *more* likely (less likely) to apply for credit in the first place.

Female applicants and applicants with larger households are more likely to apply for credit, other things equal. This could reflect discrimination but could also reflect the disparate distribution of some characteristics across demographic groups not otherwise being picked up by the Survey interviews forming the data set.

There are still many questions outstanding about rejection of credit applications. To what extent is it caused by existing regulation, and what can regulatory changes do to affect it? Is it even a social problem at all? Is it a mechanism for improving efficiency of capital allocation or is it a market distortion?

Finally, the year chosen for analysis was one in the midst of the recent global turndown and recession, when default rates were relatively high. It is not clear how representative the results here would be for other years or other sets of macroeconomic conditions. Hopefully, these and other questions will be addressed in future research.

ACKNOWLEDGMENT

Author wishes to thank Uri Geberger for statistical and computer assistance and guidance.

NOTES

1 The empirical literature on insurance rejection is not much richer than that on loan rejection. A review of rejection rates is in http://www.healthpocket.com/healthcare-research/infostat/health-insurance-application- rejection- rates/#.Uo3Nj68UHQw.

2 Redlining, if it exists, is reliance upon total rejection of credit applications from people in an area or belonging to some group, not partial approval of applications and not a means of differential pricing.

3 The Survey does not explicitly identify a "head of household". Instead, some of the characteristics which refer to the "head of household" are the characteristics of the member of the household with the highest salary income, who would likely be the main applicant in a credit application.

4 Household income and household salaries are closely correlated and so are not used together in the regressions. The more significant statistically of the two is used in each case. Multicollinearity among the other variables was not a major problem.

5 Curiously, while there is a large literature on lender discrimination by ethnicity or race, to my knowledge there is no analytic literature on discrimination by household size. Clearly other factors besides discrimination could be explaining the sign of the coefficient, such as household expenditure needs. But, as in the case of ethnicity, discrimination is something that should be considered.

6 In this and subsequent tables, the education dummies measure the increment above the next lower level, or in this case having a high school diploma compared with those with less than a high school diploma. The BA dummy shows the increment over those with a high school diploma, and the postgraduate dummy shows the incremental impact beyond those with a BA.

7 Other educational dummies did not have a significant incremental impact. See previous footnote.

8 The analysis is for a single year, in the midst of the US financial recession, when rejection rates may have been unusually high. Further research on other periods would help shed light on how general the findings are.

9 Based on estimation of loan rejection likelihood from separate logit regression for those who applied for loan.

REFERENCES

Allen, L. (1987), The Credit Rationing Phenomenon: A Survey of The Literature, Salomon Brothers Center for the Study of Financial Institutions. Graduate School of Business Administration, New York University.

Brent, W. A., W. T. Hughes, Jr. and P. Simmons (1995), Policy Issues Concerning Racial and Ethnic Differences in Home Loan Rejection Rates. *Journal of Housing Research*, 6(1), pp. 115–135.

De Meza, D. (1992), Efficient Credit Rationing. *European Economic Review*, 36(6), pp. 1277–1290.

De Meza, D. and D. C. Webb (1987), Too Much Investment: A Problem of Asymmetric Information. *Quarterly Journal of Economics*, 102(2), pp. 281–292.

De Meza, D. and D. C. Webb (2000), Does Credit Rationing Imply Insufficient Lending? *Journal of Public Economics*, 78, pp. 215–234.

De Meza, D. and D. C. Webb (2006), Credit Rationing: Something's Gotta Give. *Economica*, 73(292), pp. 563–578.

Drakos, K. and N. Giannakopoulos (2011), On the Determinants of Credit Rationing: Firm-Level Evidence from Transition Countries. *Journal of International Money and Finance*, 30(6), pp. 1773–1790.

Duca, J. V. and S. S. Rosenthal (1993), Borrowing Constraints, Household Debt, and Racial Discrimination in Loan Markets. *Journal of Financial Intermediation*, 3(1), pp. 77–103.

Greer, D. F. (1974), Rate Ceilings, Market Structure, and the Supply of Finance Company Personal Loans. *Journal of Finance*, 29(5), pp. 1363–1382.

Jappelli, T. (1990), Who is Credit Constrained in the U.S. Economy? *Quarterly Journal of Economics*, 105, pp. 219–234.

Kon, Y. and D. J. Storey (2003), A Theory of Discouraged Borrowers. *Small Business Economics*, 21(1), pp. 37–49.

Ladd, H. F. (1998), Evidence on Discrimination in Mortgage Lending. *Journal of Economic Perspectives*, 12(2), pp. 41–62.

Munnell, A. H., G. M. B. Tootell, L. E. Browne and J. McEneaney (1996), Mortgage Lending in Boston: Interpreting the HMDA Data. *American Economic Review*, 86(1), pp. 25–53.

SCF (2010), The American Survey of Consumer Finances. http://www.federalreserve.gov/econresdata/scf/scfindex.htm (03/06/2014)

Stiglitz, J. E. and A. Weiss (1981), Credit Rationing in Markets with Imperfect Information. *American Economic Review*, 71(3), pp. 393–410.

Tootell, G. M. B. (1993), Defaults, Denials, and Discrimination in Mortgage Lending. *New England Economic Review*, September–October, pp. 45–51.

IACPM/Oliver Wyman Survey: Perspectives on the Evolving Role of Enterprise-Wide Stress Testing

Andy McGee
Partner, Oliver Wyman
andy.mcgee@oliverwyman.com

Ilya Khaykin
Principal, Oliver Wyman
ilya.khaykin@oliverwyman.com

Keywords: Enterprise wide stress testing, stress testing, capital adequacy, economic capital.

INTRODUCTION

Enterprise-wide stress testing, as a formal discipline for risk and capital management, was born out of the financial crisis.

Stress tests had previously been carried out for certain types of risk or for specific portfolios, but rarely for all risks faced by the entire enterprise. For example, market risk stress testing was widely adopted in the 1990s to supplement Value-at-Risk (VaR) measures, whose calculation tends to underestimate extreme losses. While these narrow stress tests were useful for managing specific risks or portfolios, they shed little light on the overall effect that a "stress event" would have on an institution.

During the 2000s, some institutions began enterprise-wide stress testing, typically estimating the losses from a single risk factor, such as an equity price crash or a housing price decline. These stress tests tended to be ad-hoc, with no systematic way of articulating the scenarios or estimating the consequent losses, and they focused more on earnings than on capital or solvency.

To assess their solvency position, or capital adequacy, banks instead relied on regulatory capital and economic

IACPM/Oliver Wyman Enterprise-Wide Stress Testing Survey

In 2013, the International Association of Credit Portfolio Managers (IACPM) and Oliver Wyman jointly conducted a survey with leading financial institutions around the world focused on the existing, and planned uses of enterprise-wide stress testing. The participants include the world's largest banks and insurance companies across North America, Europe and Asia-Pacific. Throughout this document, "surveyed institutions" and "survey respondents" refer to this survey.

Key survey facts:

- 55 survey respondents, including both banks and insurers
- 59 questions, including both multiple choice as well as free form responses
- Topics covered include: scope & process, stress testing applications, organization and governance
- Follow-up interviews were held with a small set of participants

capital. Regulatory capital has been the most important lens for capital adequacy. Provided that an institution's capital exceeded the regulatory minimum, it was taken to be adequate, even though it might be inadequate to maintain solvency during a stressed period. Economic capital was developed in the 1990s to remedy some of the known shortcomings of regulatory capital, such as failing to account for all risks and conflating materially different risks. By avoiding these issues, economic capital provided banks with a better measure of relative risk and a better foundation for making business decisions.

However, economic capital took a purely probabilistic view of capital adequacy, aiming to answer the question, "How much capital is needed to ensure the institution remains economically solvent except in a very extreme event?" This approach overlooked the underlying dynamics of bank failure — both the *causes* and the *process* of failing, where the point at which creditors' confidence is lost is more important, and usually comes sooner, than the point at which the bank can no longer pay its depositors.

During the financial crisis, many banks failed despite having capital well in excess of the regulatory minimum. The market judged banks' solvency not by their current capital, but by the capital that would remain once losses were fully recognized.

Banks realized that the salient questions were: "What will your capital levels be in a year or two if this crisis continues?"; "Will the bank still be able to operate as a going concern?"; and, "Will the bank need more capital?" Regulators also demanded answers to these questions, starting with the Supervisory Capital Assessment Program (SCAP) in 2009 in the US, and soon followed by similar exercises in other jurisdictions. Enterprise-wide stress testing in roughly the form now seen at banks was born.

Since 2009, stress testing has advanced rapidly to meet increasing regulatory demands for this new perspective on capital adequacy. Because stress testing requires a projection of losses conditional on a specific macroeconomic scenario, it has required most banks to develop new methodologies, models, and infrastructure beyond those used to calculate economic capital. This has been the main focus of risk management at financial institutions in the years since the financial crisis.

This article discusses the state of enterprise-wide stress testing five years after the start of the financial crisis, with a focus on how financial institutions are using this new capability. It begins by reporting on the current role of enterprise-wide stress testing, especially the use banks make of it and the ways they combine it with measures of economic capital. Then, banks' aspirations for the next generation of stress testing are explored. Finally, this article discusses some of the challenges banks face in taking their stress testing capabilities to the next level.

What is "Enterprise-Wide Stress Testing"?

Enterprise-wide stress testing is a process that a financial firm uses to explore the impact of economic scenarios on its financial condition over multiple periods, typically using regulatory capital metrics. The impact is estimated for all businesses and risks, using models that link financial performance to macroeconomic or other factors. In capital adequacy assessment, the "test" is typically whether the institution retains sufficient capital to remain a going concern at the worst point of the forecasted period.

I. WHAT IS THE CURRENT ROLE OF ENTERPRISE-WIDE STRESS TESTING?

The impetus for setting up enterprise-wide stress testing in most jurisdictions was a regulatory requirement around capital adequacy assessment. As a result, the early use of enterprise-wide stress testing was narrow, focusing on whether there was sufficient capital to survive a stress event and which capital actions, such as making dividend payments, were possible. However, financial institutions have since built up their stress testing capabilities and have been exploring ways of using these to meet broader risk management and business objectives, such as: "For which applications or decisions will stress testing be a key input or driver?";

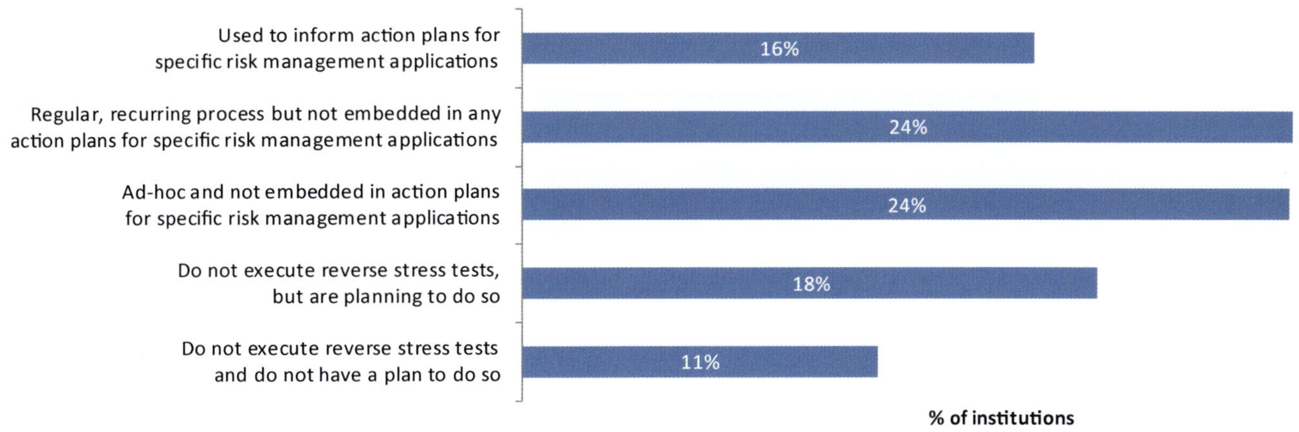

Figure 1. Use of reverse stress testing.

**Note*: That figures do not add to 100% due to assorted other responses.
Source: IACPM/Oliver Wyman Enterprise-Wide Stress Testing Survey.

"Should risk appetite be articulated based upon tolerances in a stress environment?"; and, "Should capital requirements from stress testing be used for performance management or loan pricing?"

Banks have cited a number of reasons for incorporating enterprise-wide stress testing results into a broader set of such risk and business applications:

- Binding constraint: Enterprise-wide stress testing results have now become the binding constraint for evaluating capital adequacy and the key driver of dividend policy for many institutions.
- Management attention: Given its linkage to dividend payments, as well as the governance requirements demanded by regulators, enterprise-wide stress testing now has the attention of senior management and the Board of Directors.
- Intuition: Many users find enterprise-wide stress test results to be more intuitive than other risk metrics because they are presented in an accounting framework, similar to other external communications regarding the institution's financial condition.
- Transparency: Because outcomes are linked to causal factors in enterprise-wide stress testing, such results are also more transparent and easier to understand than other risk metrics such as economic capital.
- Consistency: The enterprise-wide stress testing process usually "piggy-backs" on the budgeting and planning process, which gives it a degree of consistency with the inputs and approaches accepted already in a well-established process.

Enterprise-wide stress testing is widely employed in banking institutions — all surveyed institutions reported having some level of enterprise-wide stress testing. The objective of enterprise-wide stress testing is typically to understand the impact of a stress environment on the institution's capital position and performance. In addition, some institutions also reported employing reverse stress testing, which "works backward from the answer" to identify the scenario that leads to a particular adverse outcome. Reverse stress testing shares many of the features of traditional enterprise-wide stress testing, but is still evolving across the industry as a consistent feature or integral component of stress testing (see Fig. 1).

I.1. Current Applications of Enterprise-Wide Stress Testing

As seen in Fig. 2, almost all surveyed institutions use enterprise-wide stress testing to measure capital adequacy. Typically, this is done by assessing the impact of a stress scenario on the organization's capital base to evaluate whether post-stress, a minimum amount of capital remains to ensure the viability of the organization. Two key elements of this framework are the specification of the stress scenario and the requirements placed on post-stress capital.

In the CCAR[1] process in the US, regulators have defined requirements on both of these elements. Each year, regulators release the parameters of the Severely Adverse Scenario that institutions must apply in their capital forecasts. In addition, institutions also define scenarios tailored to their organization ("BHC scenarios"). In practice, these scenarios are typically at least as severe as the regulator-defined Severely Adverse Scenario. Regulators in the US also define the acceptable capital ratio level after incorporating the impact of the stress scenario. This minimum post-stress requirement is defined in terms of regulatory capital ratios. Likewise, European regulators have also defined these two core elements in industry stress tests, including the CEBS[2]/EBA[3] run stress tests in 2009, 2010, and 2011, as well as during the stress test in Spain in 2012, and during the Prudential Capital Assessment and Review (PCAR) in Ireland in 2011. In Asia, the Monetary Authority of Singapore approaches its annual industry-wide stress testing program similarly, specifying parameters for an adverse scenario and assessing capital adequacy of financial institutions to withstand the stress. Other Asian regulators are beginning to embrace similar approaches.

The specification of the minimum post-stress requirement may differ across institutions. For example, some insurers use minimum local capital requirements for each of their legal entities for their post-stress minimum requirement, with such requirements differing by insurer type (e.g., life versus property and casualty insurance) and jurisdiction of the legal entity. In other cases, institutions use an economic capital metric to define the minimum post-stress requirement. Multiple specifications may also be used: One institution surveyed indicated use of statutory capital requirements, economic capital, and capital required by rating agencies to define acceptable post-stress capital levels. The institution considers its risk appetite with respect to these various measures. For example, the rating agency capital stress evaluates the ability to maintain a certain range of ratings after a stress scenario.

A large share of surveyed institutions also use enterprise-wide stress testing for risk reporting, risk appetite, limit setting and management, and various planning exercises (e.g., financial, strategic, contingency).

Examples of such extended uses of enterprise-wide stress testing results include:

- *Risk reporting*: Enterprise-wide stress testing results are often used to report levels of risk in business activities, for example, by reporting the credit losses by portfolio in various stress scenarios would cause in specific portfolios, or by showing a business unit's contribution to the P&L in a stress scenario.
- *Strategic planning*: Enterprise-wide stress testing results are increasingly integrated into business planning as institutions look to understand the impact of stress scenarios on alternative strategies, and especially on the ability to pay dividends. For some institutions, the use of stress testing in strategic planning is formally required by policy, with approval of the strategy taking into account the stress results. Often, however, the linkage to strategic planning is less formal. For example, one institution described an informal process where the strategy team requests ad-hoc analysis of strategic alternatives. Creating this linkage to strategic planning can lead to a cycle of positive reinforcement of stress testing, where use in strategic decision-making highlights the value of stress testing to the most senior managers in the institution. At the same time, this level of scrutiny also drives enhancements to the approaches and results, potentially leading to further integration into decision-making.
- *Risk appetite*: Stress testing is increasingly being integrated into risk appetite, using tolerance for outcomes in a stress test to set risk appetite and cascade it down to risk tolerances for individual products/businesses. Some institutions directly tie risk appetite statements to stress results by including statements expressing a maximum loss or minimum income in a stress scenario. The stress testing process also motivates institutions to re-specify their risk appetite on an ongoing basis in a tangible manner. The range of stress scenarios that is used to test the institution's capital adequacy is itself an expression

Figure 2. Current role of stress testing by business application.

Source: IACPM/Oliver Wyman Enterprise-Wide Stress Testing Survey.

of the institution's risk appetite, with the view that scenarios outside of this range may lead to insufficient capitalization.

- *Limits*: An institution's use of stress testing in risk appetite is sometimes cascaded into limits at the enterprise level, such as limits placed on enterprise-wide credit losses. Enterprise-wide stress testing is also used to inform the magnitude of more traditional exposure-based limits. For example, one institution interviewed tests alternative limit levels by evaluating the impact of the limits on forecast losses in stress scenarios.

To a lesser extent, banks are also using enterprise-wide stress testing to inform capital allocation, credit portfolio structuring, performance measurement and management, pricing, and origination strategy. Given theoretical and practical challenges of using stress testing for these applications (further discussed in Sec. I.2), institutions tend to use stress test results informally to inform decision-making for these applications, rather than in a formalized framework. As an example, one institution noted that stress test results help inform decisions regarding credit portfolio structuring by highlighting concentrations in the portfolio that are likely to react similarly in a stress scenario.

I.2. Balancing Enterprise-Wide Stress Testing and Economic Capital

Enterprise-Wide Stress Testing

- Accounting-based
- Considers the entire P&L including revenues, losses, expenses, etc.
- Short- to medium-term forecast (e.g., typically 9 quarters in the US)
- Reveals mechanics of how potential risks arise
- Loss level defined by a specific macroeconomic scenario, loosely linked to a probability (e.g., "adverse")
- Adverse loss typically not an insolvency event

Economic Capital

- Value-based
- One-year forecast (but often embeds changes in long-term value)
- Loss level defined at a specific confidence level (i.e., probabilistic), typically not linked to a specific macroeconomic scenario
- Adverse loss typically an insolvency event

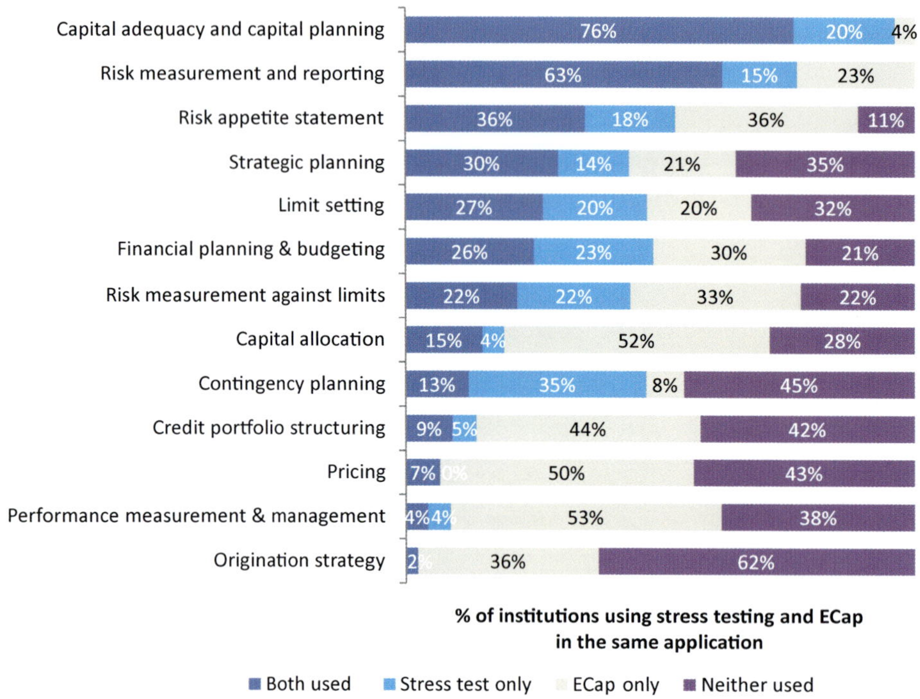

Figure 3. Use of stress testing and economic capital.

**Note*: That figures do not add to 100% for all applications due to rounding.
Source: IACPM/Oliver Wyman Enterprise-Wide Stress Testing Survey.

Banks have traditionally used economic capital metrics for many core risk management applications. Stress testing is now competing with economic capital for influence across these applications. The outcome is currently mixed, as shown in Fig. 3, with enterprise-wide stress testing being used alongside economic capital in a subset of largely top-of-the-house applications, while economic capital remains the dominant risk metric in other applications, such as performance measurement and risk-based pricing that require greater granularity and consistency in the risk metric applied across the portfolio.

Applications where economic capital and enterprise-wide stress testing are both used include risk reporting, risk appetite, limit setting and management, and strategic and financial planning. Over half of the surveyed institutions that reported using enterprise-wide stress testing in these applications also report use of economic capital as a complementary measure. Having two perspectives on potential losses or capital consumption is useful, and also can help to identify the modeling limitations of either approach. Stress test results, for example, are often considered more intuitive and actionable because they are typically less severe and more plausible than events leading to an economic capital-sized loss. A number of institutions surveyed indicated that they are more likely to make hedging decisions, portfolio composition decisions and business strategy decisions based on these more plausible outcomes. However, when enterprise-wide stress testing results and economic capital suggest different courses of action, banks must either reconcile the two perspectives to produce consistent answers or have a process for deciding which metric should guide decision-making.

For other applications, such as capital allocation, credit portfolio structuring, pricing, performance management, and origination strategy, economic capital is still the dominant risk metric. The use of stress testing in these areas faces theoretical and practical limitations (see Fig. 4 for a description of key challenges by application).

APPLICATION	DESCRIPTION	KEY CHALLENGES FOR USE OF ENTERPRISE-WIDE STRESS TESTING
Capital adequacy	Ensuring institution maintains sufficient capital in line with risk appetite	• Managing across regulatory, stress testing-based and economic capital views of required capital and risk
Risk measurement & reporting	Communicating risk exposure across the organization	
Risk appetite statement	Definition of the institution's high-level risk-related objectives and constraints	
Contingency planning	Definition of contingency measures such as capital raising and B/S reduction	• N.A.
Strategic planning	Medium-term planning of strategy and targets around business units, geographies and products	• Cultural shift in some cases to incorporate stress scenarios as a planning scenario • Some stress scenarios may be perceived as too unlikely to occur for use in planning • Organizational challenge to achieve Finance buy-in on risk metrics
Financial planning & budgeting	Annual exercise to forecast revenues, expenses and allocate budget across businesses	
Limit setting	Setting risk limits at business, product, portfolio and single-name level	• Scenario severity used for establishing limits and measuring risk against limits is difficult to define objectively
Risk measurement against limits	Measuring and monitoring usage of risk limits	
Capital allocation	Allocation of economic and regulatory capital at granular portfolio and business line level	• Stress testing produces a narrow, scenario-conditional view of risk that may not be well-suited to allocation and achieving consistency across exposures • Stress results are less accurate at granular levels at which capital allocation is needed for performance measurement and pricing purposes
Performance measurement & management	Measurement of risk-return of portfolios and business lines	
Pricing	Transaction-level pricing and decision support	
Credit portfolio structuring	Reshaping of credit portfolio based on risk metrics	• Stress results are less accurate at granular levels needed for transaction and portfolio-level decision-making
Origination strategy	Transaction level decision-making on loan origination	

Figure 4. Applications of stress testing and their challenges.

The theoretical limitations arise from the fact that stress testing looks at the short-term accounting losses caused by stress scenarios and therefore fails to consistently capture risks that materialize over a longer horizon (such as ALM risks). This is inappropriate for applications that concern long-term value creation. Economic capital captures risks that may not materialize in financial statements over the short-time horizon of a stress test, but which are required to understand the long-term value of a business or activity. Economic capital also facilitates comparisons across products and geographies because, given its calibration to a consistent confidence interval, each dollar of economic capital represents the same quantum of risk. By contrast, enterprise-wide stress testing results are conditional on specific macroeconomic scenarios; different stress scenarios of equal probability could produce different losses across products/ geographies.

And, in practice, using stress tests for purposes that require comparisons between products, regions or customer segments is limited by the fact that stress testing often does not specify losses at this level of granularity. Many uses of risk metrics require even position-level specificity and an ability to capture position-level drivers of risk. Economic

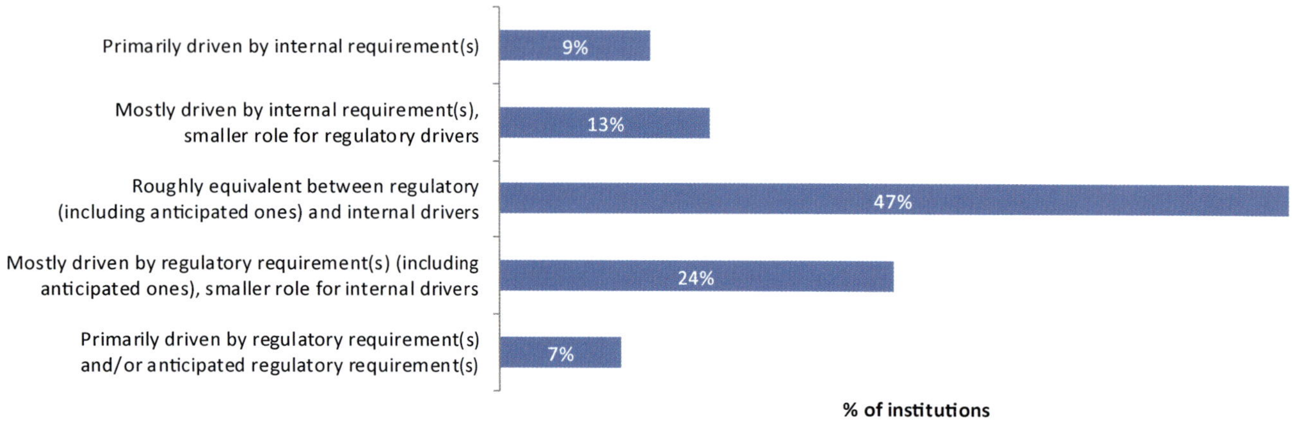

Figure 5. Motivation for enterprise-wide stress testing.

Source: IACPM/Oliver Wyman Enterprise-Wide Stress Testing Survey.

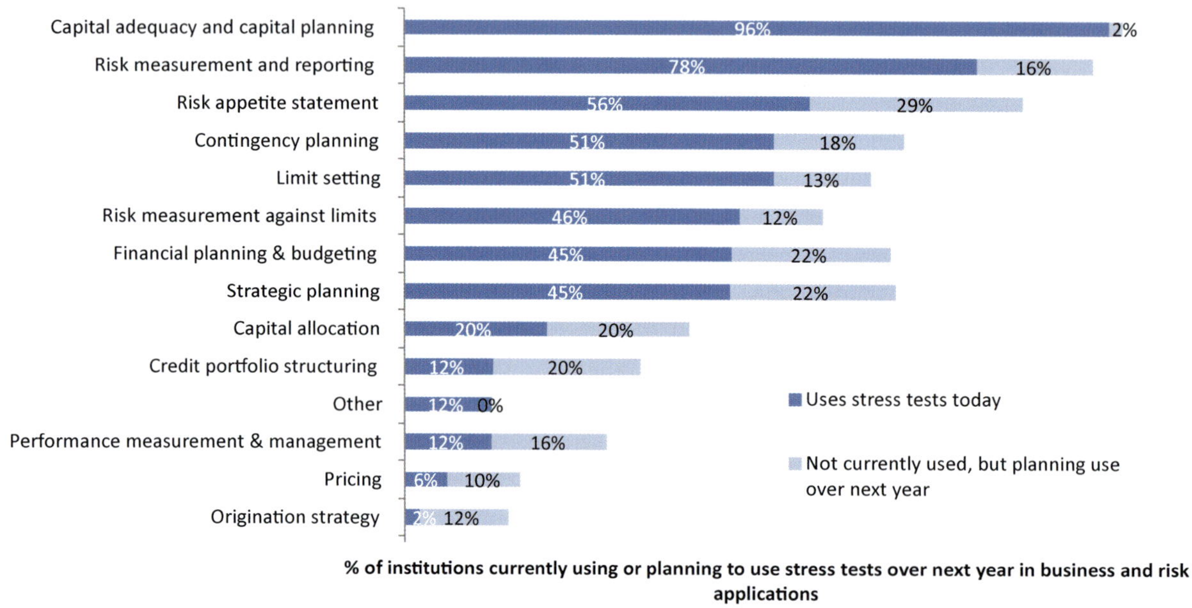

Figure 6. Current and planned use of stress testing by business application.

Source: IACPM/Oliver Wyman Enterprise-Wide Stress Testing Survey.

capital can deliver this level of granularity but so far, enterprise-wide stress testing cannot.

II. WHAT WILL BE THE FUTURE ROLE OF ENTERPRISE-WIDE STRESS TESTING?

The expectations for enterprise-wide stress testing have increased across the globe. At large US banks, the requirements and expectations have increased each year in the CCAR and CapPR[4] processes. And the Dodd-Frank Act Stress Test (DFAST) rules now require smaller banks to conduct enterprise-wide stress tests, too. Most of them will need to make rapid progress from their currently rudimentary stress testing capabilities. European regulators are also demanding the increased use of stress tests, and Asian regulators are beginning to take the same position.

Beyond regulatory pressure, financial institutions consider enterprise-wide stress testing as a valuable

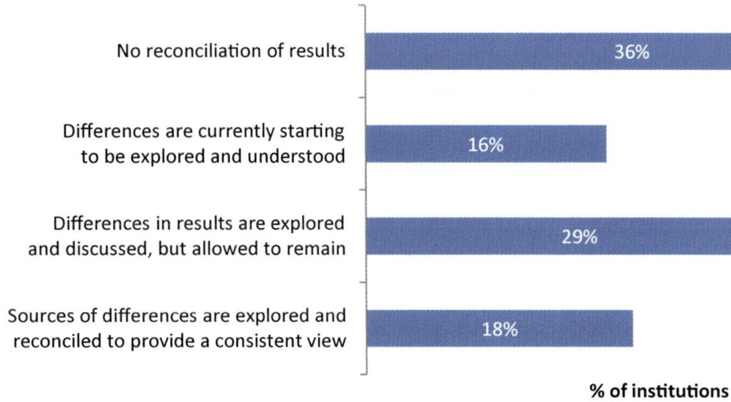

Figure 7. Reconciliation between stress testing and economic capital.

Source: IACPM/Oliver Wyman Enterprise-Wide Stress Testing Survey.

management tool in its own right. About half of the surveyed institutions characterized their current enterprise-wide stress testing as being driven equally by regulatory requirements and internal mandate. Senior managers believe that the benefits of stress testing go beyond regulatory compliance.

Finally, financial institutions now have another set of metrics (in addition to economic capital and regulatory capital) being produced, and have often made significant investment in the stress testing tools. Institutions recognize the need to have a coherent approach and framework for managing across these metrics to ensure clarity within their organizations and in decision-making processes. It should be clear within an organization how the different tools are applied to each decision, and how the answers provided should be used. In a world of multiple measures, this clarity is critical to efficiently and effectively make decisions.

II.1. For Which Applications is Enterprise-Wide Stress Testing Being Planned?

Most financial institutions plan to extend their use of enterprise-wide stress testing across the range of core risk management applications. Nearly all surveyed institutions have aspirations to incorporate enterprise-wide stress testing into capital adequacy and capital planning (if not doing so already) and into risk reporting and risk appetite statements. Approximately two-thirds either already or plan to link enterprise-wide stress testing to their planning processes and to their limit setting and management.

However, many institutions remain focused on improving the underlying approach to enterprise-wide stress testing and the infrastructure that supports it. With continued methodological improvements, and growing experience, we expect stress testing results to be further integrated into business applications. One of the institutions interviewed described recent success in achieving higher levels of business and senior management buy-in, a critical precursor to greater integration of stress testing in business applications. As methodologies are further refined, and as results can be better supported at granular levels, this institution hopes to use stress test results much more broadly for applications such as capital allocation and pricing.

II.2. Alternative Future Paths for Enterprise-Wide Stress Testing and Economic Capital

Surveyed institutions overwhelmingly expect to maintain both economic capital and enterprise-wide stress testing as risk management tools. However, maintaining multiple frameworks could lead to challenges in decision-making as they may appear to generate conflicting results. For example, approximately three-quarters of surveyed institutions intend to continue to develop and maintain both metrics, but only about a fifth report currently reconciling differences

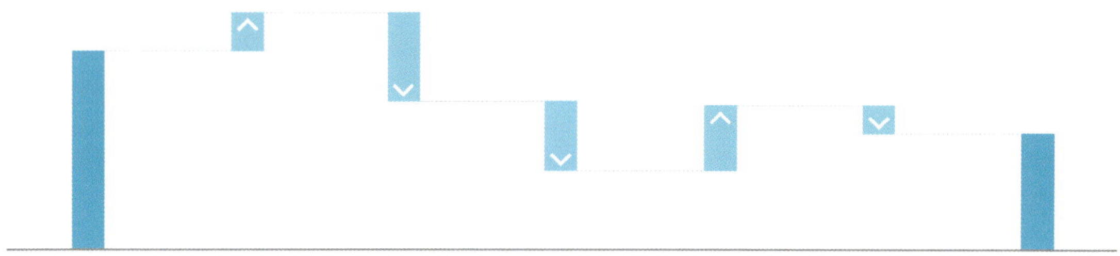

ECap (with migration)	Expected Loss	Migration Risk	Confidence Level	Time Horizon	Unexplained	Stress Test - based tail loss
Calculated using Basel II IRB formula	EL is added back to ECap for comparability	Removal of losses due to non-default economic losses ; removal of Basel maturity adjustment	Adjustment to approximate confidence level of stress scenario	Adjusted to cover a 9 quarter period	Unexplained residual factors and variables Unexplained variance can be large in many cases	Calculated using stressed rating migrations and default rates from stress scenario

Figure 8. Example reconciliation of economic capital and stress test results.

Source: Oliver Wyman analysis.

between the two approaches to provide a consistent view of risk (Fig. 7).

Moreover, economic capital and stress testing results are often challenging to reconcile. This is, in part, due to theoretical differences between the metrics, such as conditionality on specific macroeconomic scenarios, differences in time horizon, and accounting versus economic views of risk. However, even after accounting for these theoretical differences, fundamentally different methodologies and inputs can further complicate reconciliation, as Fig. 8 illustrates.

The industry has not settled on an answer to the question of how to balance stress testing and economic capital. Will the two be applied in largely separate domains, with minimal correspondence or overlap? Or will they be used as complementary metrics for the same risks and business purposes? Or will banks try to unify their underlying frameworks to the extent possible? Each of these approaches is discussed below.

ALTERNATIVE 1: Economic capital and enterprise-wide stress testing are used in separate areas.

In this approach, enterprise-wide stress testing becomes a critical tool for capital adequacy, capital management contingency planning, and strategic and financial planning. Economic capital continues to be the primary risk metric for capital allocation, performance measurement and pricing. For other applications, such as limit setting and risk reporting, institutions may make different decisions about whether enterprise-wide stress testing, economic capital or both should be used. In short, this alternative achieves a balance between enterprise-wide stress testing and economic capital by generally avoiding situations where these metrics give different answers to the same question and, hence, recommend different courses of action. However, this can obscure inconsistencies that, if seen, would prompt risk analysts to a more thorough examination of data or assumptions and a deeper understanding of the real risk situation.

ALTERNATIVE 2: Economic capital and enterprise-wide stress testing co-exist as competing measures of risk, with both informing similar applications.

In this alternative, both economic capital and enterprise-wide stress testing are used across many of the core risk management applications. Institutions would accept the various benefits and shortcomings of each metric. For cases where the two metrics suggest different courses of action, institutions would apply a framework to decide which metric should be given priority for the matter at hand. Such a framework could allow some use of management judgment. However, a well-defined process is needed to avoid bias in selecting the metric to be used.

ALTERNATIVE 3: Economic capital and enterprise-wide stress testing are integrated into a common framework.

In this alternative, institutions find ways of producing enterprise-wide stress test results and economic capital results using common underlying data, approaches and assumptions. For example, as described by McGee and Cope (2012), consistent joint approaches for credit risk could involve the combination of a stress testing platform for evaluating conditional credit losses with an economic scenario simulation generator. This alternative requires significant advancements in modeling capabilities and enterprise-wide stress testing processes (compared to where the industry is today) in order to measure economic capital.

Economic capital numbers would now be more intuitive, because they are grounded in clearly defined, causal scenarios. Differences in results can then be attributed to accounting-based versus value-based considerations and to differences in the severity of the stress scenario and the economic capital scenario.

This approach allows banks to use multiple risk metrics for risk management applications while minimizing their potential inconsistencies. Banks would still need to decide when to use which measure of risk, but such decisions could be based on fundamental differences in the metrics and then formalized in policy rather than being evaluated case-by-case.

Point of View

While we view each of these as plausible long-term alternatives, we believe that most institutions will likely end up in Alternative 2. In a post-crisis world, there are a larger number of objectives and constraints to manage, and making some decisions based on a single metric may lead to suboptimal decisions. For example, while today's binding constraint may be capital under a regulatory stress test, an institution would not want to make decisions that look favorable under this measure but less favorable on an economic basis.

Effectively managing in a world of multiple constraints and multiple measures is much more challenging than choosing a single measure — not only in terms of the measures themselves, but also in communicating to stakeholders and decision-makers across an institution. To do this effectively, each institution should develop a comprehensive metric framework that clearly articulates:

- What are the measures that are used across the institution? What are the advantages and limitations of each?
- What measures will we use for each application? Where multiple measures are used, how do we use them jointly? Is one measure primary/secondary?
- What do we do when the measures disagree? What does it mean?

III. ONGOING CHALLENGES IN STRESS TESTING?

Despite much progress in enterprise-wide stress testing across the industry, there remain challenges to greater usage in business decision-making. There are methodological and technical challenges to meeting users' demands for increasingly granular, accurate and timely information.

And there are broader process and organizational challenges that currently limit the use of enterprise-wide stress testing results within the institution.

III.1. Methodological and Technical Challenges

CHALLENGE: Increased granularity is needed for tailored use of enterprise-wide stress testing results.

Enterprise-wide stress testing results must be accurate at the portfolio or sub-portfolio levels to be effective in business applications such as capital allocation, pricing, and performance measurement. So far, however, enterprise-wide stress testing has focused mostly on capital adequacy, which requires accurate results at only the enterprise level.[5] In many institutions, enterprise-wide stress test results

	METHODOLOGY AND TECHNICAL	PROCESS AND ORGANIZATIONAL
Frequently cited	• Data limitations prevent granular customization • Poor, ad-hoc infrastructure	• Difficult to coordinate across groups • Excessive manual interventions
Occasionally cited	• Methodologies are not appropriate • Challenges with attributing stress test results to the necessary level of granularity	• Individual elements of process are too slow • Excessive review periods

Figure 9. Common stress testing challenges and "pain points".

are still relatively crude at position-level or even portfolio-level. Currently, approximately half of the institutions surveyed produce enterprise-wide stress testing results at the business unit level, and even fewer institutions produce them at the portfolio level. Several institutions interviewed indicated that the lack of accurate results at more granular levels limits the amount of buy-in achieved, which in turn limits the use of stress testing in the organization.

Getting more granular enterprise-wide stress test output requires advances in three areas:

- *Data*: Institutions identified data limitations as the top impediment to greater use of enterprise-wide stress testing. Over half the surveyed institutions report that data limitations prevent modeling and customization at a sufficiently granular level. For example, obtaining good historical data to support loss given default (LGD) modeling is well-known to be a challenge for many institutions.
- *Methodology*: In some institutions, enterprise-wide stress testing is still predominantly top-down, relying, for example, on high-level loss regressions. Such top-down approaches may be accurate for the enterprise as a whole but not at more granular portfolio levels, especially when portfolio composition has changed over time. Many of the simplest top-down approaches have now been replaced by more granular models. But even some of these granular approaches do not fully account for the characteristics of specific portfolios and changes in their quality over time. For example, commercial loan losses are often forecasted using a a credit quality migration matrix. However, many institutions have not modeled the relationship of migration and default to macroeconomic variables based on factors such as industry, or company size. To do so, models can either incorporate more loan-level characteristics into the forecast directly (that is, as independent variables in the model) or segment the macroeconomic relationships using these characteristics.
- *Segmentation*: Segmentation is a common way of tailoring models to specific portfolio segments. The segmentation process is often driven by the readily available data or business definitions of segments. Ideally, however, segmentation would explicitly consider the trade-offs between homogeneity of exposures within a segment, data availability at the granular segment level, and materiality of the exposures. In cases where homogeneity and materiality indicate the need for a distinct modeling segment, but data is not readily available, further avenues such as external data or alternative sources for internal data should be explored.

Although modeling granularity will be an ongoing challenge, we expect significant advances in this area for many institutions. In the US, regulators are pushing institutions to improve the accuracy and timeliness of granular data. They require quarterly submission of loan-level data as well as Pre-Provision Net Revenue (PPNR)-related data. Institutions continue to develop data capture mechanisms to support these demands and will benefit from the improved modeling this data allows. Recent regulatory guidance (see Federal

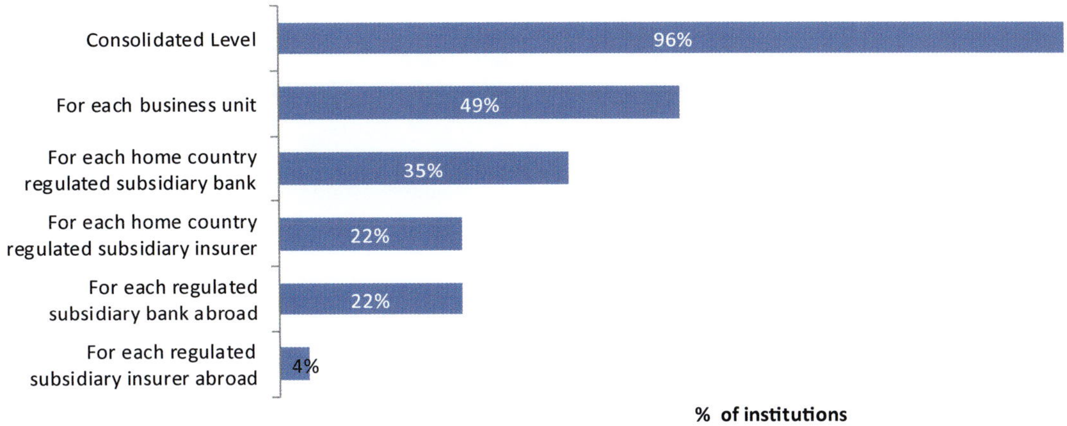

Figure 10. Granularity of enterprise-wide stress test results and reporting.
Source: IACPM/Oliver Wyman Enterprise-Wide Stress Testing Survey.

Reserve (2013)) has also emphasized the importance of appropriate and systematic segmentation. Demands for greater customization of model parameters and approaches are also likely to come from business line staff, as enterprise-wide stress testing results are used in more business applications.

CHALLENGE: Improved data and modeling infrastructure is needed to support enterprise-wide stress testing.

Institutions often cite data and modeling infrastructure as a limitation on current stress testing approaches. This infrastructure impacts both the range of approaches available to institutions and process efficiency in executing the enterprise-wide stress tests. Difficulties arise because the infrastructure used for stress testing has largely been a collage of tools developed for other processes at financial institutions, such as planning, asset liability management and ad-hoc risk modeling. Similarly, the existing data infrastructure has proven insufficient for the needs of enterprise-wide stress testing. The data is often spread across the organization and is typically unavailable in centralized systems. As a result, institutions often rely on a patchwork of systems, ad-hoc tools and manual processes to execute enterprise-wide stress tests. Many of the tools and systems used were not designed to interface with one another, and end-to-end automation that ensures the traceability of inputs through a reliable, consistent platform is not yet available.

These infrastructural weaknesses have impacted both methodologies and processes. Methodologies are stymied by the unavailability of the data needed to execute more customized and sophisticated modeling, especially in the timeframe required of stress testing. For example, while front-office systems may have the most granular position-level data, this may not be readily available to the areas executing the enterprise-wide stress testing process. Processes are also hindered by the many different tools and hand-offs required by the lack of appropriate infrastructure.

Institutions that most successfully manage the challenges of stress testing do two things:

- *Invest in integrated modeling tools*: The breadth of enterprise-wide stress testing means that institutions often employ many platforms in the process. Individual risk models, such as those that estimate credit losses, may be combined with financial forecasting platforms. Integrating these various tools greatly increases the efficiency of the process, requiring less effort to complete stress tests within the short timeframes demanded. For example, some asset-liability management (ALM) tools can also be used to house financial statement data, portfolio data, and forecasting models. With the core models embedded in a central tool, those conducting the stress tests can use their time on ensuring the models receive the right inputs rather than on running many models across the organization and then aggregating the results. This requires significant upfront investment to set up, but such platforms can reduce the cycle time from weeks to days.

- *Focus on consistent data processes*: Some institutions have designed data infrastructure and processes for enterprise-wide stress testing that are consistent with existing regulatory reporting. They rely on shared data infrastructure and thereby reduce the challenges of reconciling the various data used in enterprise-wide stress testing. Alternatively, those that rely on more ad-hoc portfolio or other data often face process inefficiencies because reconciling to reported balance sheet data can be difficult.

CHALLENGE: Modeling profitability dynamics is at a relatively early stage of sophistication for many institutions.

Forecasting profitability (i.e., PPNR in the US) under stress scenarios requires modeling net interest income, non-interest income and operating expenses. Historically, for banking institutions, PPNR forecasting has resided within financial planning functions rather than with risk management, the latter of which has typically focused on modeling credit and market risks rather than the drivers of PPNR. However, with multi-period enterprise-wide stress testing, PPNR is a major driver of the capital position of the institution in the stress scenario, and modeling PPNR increasingly needs to satisfy the requirements of rigorous, sound modeling approaches.

PPNR is driven by external market factors as well as an institution's own business plan and expected behavior, all of which can drive volume and, to a lesser extent, pricing decisions across products and markets. Forecasting of PPNR in annual planning processes also often includes a strong element of goal setting for the institution's businesses. For these reasons, PPNR forecasting for the purposes of planning and budgeting has often been heavily based on business judgment rather than empirically grounded modeling.

Over the past couple of years, institutions have focused on developing and enhancing PPNR modeling for use in enterprise-wide stress testing, but discussions with survey participants have highlighted that there is still significant work to be done in this area. The key challenge is to convert traditional PPNR forecasting into an empirically-based, analytically rigorous modeling process that satisfies the expectations of risk management functions while remaining intuitive and realistic from the perspectives of the Finance and Business teams.

Key factors to success include:

- *Linkage to the budgeting and forecasting process*: Conceptually, there should be no difference between budgeting and stress testing PPNR projections — the budget should be a PPNR scenario with different macroeconomic inputs. While conceptually simple, in practice this requires a shift towards driver-based budgeting, where a budget projection for a line item is a function of a macroeconomically-driven industry growth rate, and an institutional "share" overlay taking into account specific strategies and tactics that are planned. In a stress test, the institutions would run the models to generate a stress input for the industry growth, resulting in its stress output. Moving to this type of driver-based process is critical to ensuring ongoing alignment.
- *Rigorous model development process*: PPNR forecasts must be linked to macroeconomic variables to effectively capture the impact of the stress scenario. Development of these macroeconomic relationships should follow a rigorous approach in order to provide an accurate forecast in the stress scenario and to justify the appropriateness of the final model to regulators as well as internal constituents. Macroeconomic relationships that are developed judgmentally may not use the optimal macroeconomic variables, are more likely to be inaccurate in their forecast results, and typically fail to pass muster with regulators. A rigorous development process also leaves room to incorporate business expert judgment in the final form of the macroeconomic relationship; Fig. 11 illustrates such a development approach.
- *Appropriately granular approaches*[6]: Successfully modeling profitability requires tailored, institution-specific approaches that segment the components of the P&L across products and business activities. Insufficient granularity can obscure different sensitivities to macroeconomic factors and reduce the accuracy of stress forecasts. Segmentation should consider the components of PPNR such

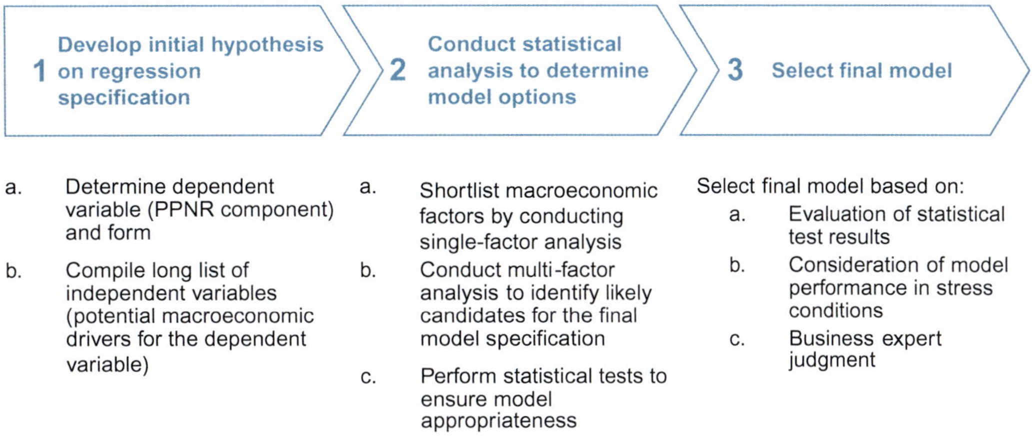

Figure 11. Example PPNR macroeconomic linkage development approach.

as business volumes, pricing and fee categories. Segmentation should also aim to distinguish drivers of PPNR that are contractual from those that are macroeconomically-driven or behavioral. For example, volume modeling should focus on new business volumes and non-contractual prepayment rather than on the modeling of aggregate balances that include contractually defined repayments. Segmentation may also consider differences in geography, business lines, products and industry sectors. P&L across these segments may be impacted differently depending on the stress scenario and may warrant separate macroeconomic relationships.

- Attention to data: A key challenge is the availability of data at a level needed to develop empirically based macroeconomic relationships. While more aggregate P&L data is commonly available from finance systems, data that splits PPNR into components such as new business volumes and pricing is often more difficult to obtain at a granular segment level. In some cases, this information is available somewhere in the institution, or suitable external proxies are available, but would require material effort to locate and adapt to the task. Institutions sometimes hesitate to make this investment in obtaining the data — to the detriment of the ultimate quality of the modeling.
- Participation in the development effort: Modeling PPNR should incorporate expertise from Risk, Finance and Business teams. Modeling efforts, without sufficient input from those with an understanding of key business drivers, may result in spurious macroeconomic relationships that may not be intuitive and ultimately have poor results and buy-in from the organization. Implementing a process for model development that explicitly incorporates all relevant parties can help mitigate these issues.

III.2. Process and Organizational Challenges

CHALLENGE: Clear ownership and governance is critical to an efficient process and to organizational buy-in.

Many institutions have struggled to define and agree on an efficient organizational and governance model for enterprise-wide stress testing. About three-quarters of surveyed institutions cite coordination among groups as the biggest "pain point" in the overall enterprise-wide stress testing process. For example, enterprise-wide stress testing requires the forecasting of new business volumes under a stress scenario. Under the baseline scenario in the budgeting processes, business units and financial planning teams often specify their anticipated volumes given market considerations, internal strategy, and some constraints, such as the limits defined by Risk. To forecast stress scenarios, however, greater involvement is needed from Risk as the forecast can have a large impact on anticipated capital ratios. An overly ambitious forecast of volume reductions can distort the view of capital adequacy.

Governance is further complicated by the fact that the key participants — Finance, Risk and the Business Units — often approach enterprise-wide stress testing with different perspectives and objectives:

- Business units may have the deepest understanding of likely behavior of the business and the market under stress, and they often have the best understanding of the underlying data needed to develop the appropriate models. On the other hand, business units may be reluctant to admit the size of losses they would incur in the stress scenario and thus might be inclined to understate risk.
- Finance generally owns the planning process that often forms the backbone of enterprise-wide stress testing and often also owns the capital management process that is a key consumer of enterprise-wide stress testing results. Given the responsibility for capital management, Finance has a tendency to focus on achieving appropriate capital returns for shareholders.
- Risk is responsible for measuring and managing the risk profile of the institution. However, it often does not house all the capabilities needed to execute the full enterprise-wide stress testing process. It needs to coordinate with Finance and the Business units; and therein can lie disagreements about the control and ownership of key parameters and processes.

The governance challenge varies significantly across institutions surveyed. Much of the success observed to date can be attributable to regulatory pressure and resulting senior management attention. The threat of a withheld dividend can be a significant motivator for overcoming organizational and governance challenges. In the US, where the regulatory focus on enterprise-wide stress testing has been very high, institutions were more than twice as likely as non-US institutions to report that they are highly satisfied with their current organizational model.

This challenge cannot be easily remedied by simply moving accountability or responsibility — the nature of the process is that it inherently cuts across functions. Firms where the organizational and governance model works best tend to have clearly defined accountabilities for each of the major stakeholders, and effective coordination processes for managing the inevitable issues as they arise.

CHALLENGE: Process integration and appropriate resourcing are needed to achieve the level of responsiveness demanded by business applications and key stakeholders.

The end-to-end stress testing process often takes significant time due to the number of participants, range of required models, and lack of turn-key solutions. However, regulators have placed increasing demands on institutions to produce results quickly. For example, CCAR institutions in the US typically have 7 to 8 weeks between the issuance of a scenario and finalization of capital plans for submission to the regulators. This allows for only a few weeks of stress testing, due to significant review and discussion needed in the capital management process.

As enterprise-wide stress testing plays an increasing role in business applications, the demand for quick execution will also increase. For example, senior management may request ad-hoc analyses to evaluate the potential impact of a business acquisition. To be a useful input into such decision-making, enterprise-wide stress testing analyses would need to be available quickly and reflect current conditions. Processes that are cumbersome and primarily anchored to annual business planning or regulatory reporting calendars will be of limited value for business applications.

Agile stress testing requires the kind of infrastructure development and governance discussed above. It also requires a process that takes account of when data becomes available, when end results are needed, and how long the Board of Directors and senior management need to review them. Institutions must design the process by "working backward" from these constraints. There is little room in the process for failed hand-offs, so the content and format required for each link in the process must be clearly specified.

Appropriate resourcing is also critical for effective and timely execution of enterprise-wide stress testing. Institutions report that having sufficient dedicated resources, as well as external advice and perspectives,

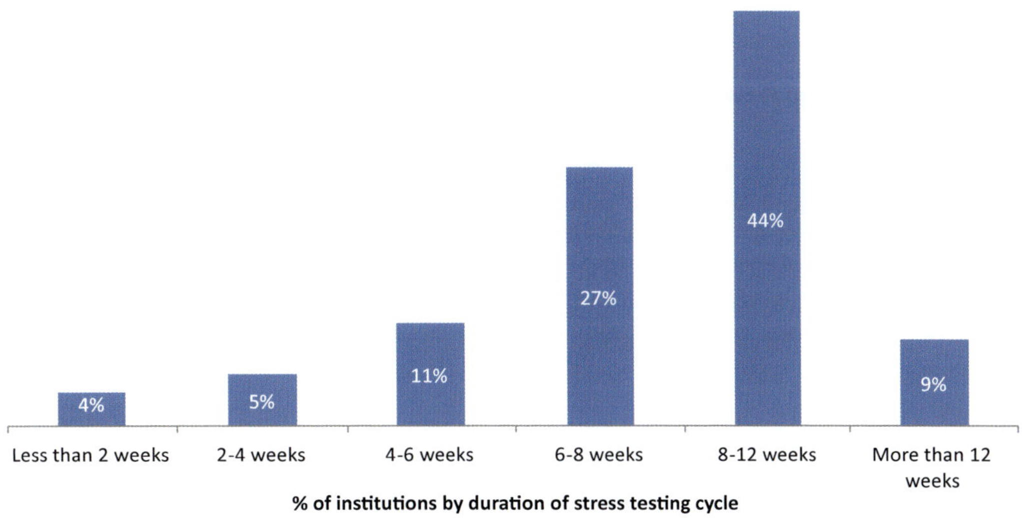

Figure 12. Enterprise-wide stress testing cycle times.*

**Note*: Cycle time here is defined as the time between scenario definition and presentation of final results.

Source: IACPM/Oliver Wyman Enterprise-Wide Stress Testing Survey.

are key lessons learned in the recent past. In general, budgets and resource allocations for stress testing have been increasing. Much of the challenge, however, remains in finding individuals with the appropriate background and skill sets.

IV. CONCLUSIONS

Enterprise-wide stress testing has been rapidly evolving and gaining prominence as an important management tool. It is now widely used as a critical tool for evaluating capital adequacy. Institutions have also begun linking enterprise-wide stress testing results to risk reporting, planning, limit setting and limit management.

As stress testing exits its infancy and becomes a "business as usual" process, institutions face the challenge of how to integrate stress testing into broader risk and capital management applications such as performance measurement, capital allocation and pricing, as well as to define the relative role for stress testing, economic capital, and (pre-stress) regulatory capital measures. Institutions need to think carefully about the strengths and limitations of each measure, and how they will utilize them together. We believe that the industry will move towards managing across multiple, co-existing measures of risk, which presents challenges not only in terms of developing and maintaining the various measures themselves, but also in communicating effectively and clearly to stakeholders and decision-makers.

More broadly, in order to continue the trajectory of increasingly using enterprise-wide stress testing in decision-making, the industry will need to tackle a number of key challenges:

- *Granularity*: Increased data and modeling granularity is needed for tailored use of enterprise-wide stress testing results.
- *Infrastructure*: Improved data and modeling infrastructure is needed to support enterprise-wide stress testing.
- *Profitability modeling*: Modeling profitability dynamics is at a relatively early stage of sophistication for many institutions.
- *Governance*: Clear governance is critical to an efficient process and to organizational buy-in.
- *Process*: Process integration and appropriate resourcing are needed to achieve the level of responsiveness demanded by business applications and key stakeholders.

Given the current and anticipated attention given to enterprise-wide stress testing, we expect to see significant developments in the coming years.

NOTES

[1] Comprehensive Capital Analysis and Review.

[2] Committee of European Banking Supervisors.

[3] European Banking Authority.

[4] Capital Plan Review.

[5] However, in many cases approaches that are developed to achieve accuracy at enterprise level may fail to achieve this if they are insufficiently granular. See Duane *et al.* (2014).

[6] For more on this topic see Duane *et al.* (2014).

REFERENCES

Cope, D. and A. McGee (2012), Improving the Measurement of Capital Adequacy — The Future of Economic Capital and Stress Testing. Oliver Wyman Point of View.

Duane, M., T. Schuermann and P. Reynolds (2014), Stress Testing Bank Profitability. *Journal of Risk Management in Financial Institutions*, 7 (2013/2014), pp. 72–84.

Federal Reserve (2013), Capital Planning at Large Bank Holding Companies: Supervisory Expectations and Range of Current Practice, August.

Contributors:
Melinda Sulewski
Partner, Oliver Wyman
melinda.sulewski@oliverwyman.com

Terry Tse
Principal, Oliver Wyman
terry.tse@oliverwyman.com

IACPM contacts:
Som-lok Leung
Executive Director, IACPM
somlok@iacpm.org

Marcia Banks
Associate Director, IACPM
marcia@iacpm.org

NUS-RMI Credit Research Initiative Technical Report

Version: 2014 Update 1

RMI staff article

For any questions or comments on this article, please contact the CRI-team at rmicri@nus.edu.sg

Keywords: Non-profit credit research initiative, credit risk, probability of default, forward intensity.

This document describes the implementation of the system which the Credit Research Initiative (CRI) at the Risk Management Institute (RMI) of the National University of Singapore (NUS) uses to produce probabilities of default (PDs). As of this version of the Technical Report, RMI covers around 60,400 listed firms (including delisted ones) in 106 economies around the world (see Table A.1). Of the around 40,000 active firms under the CRI coverage, around 34,000 firms have sufficient data to release daily updated PDs. The PD for all firms is freely available to users who can provide evidence of their professional qualifications to ensure that they will not misuse the data. General users who do not request global access are restricted to a list of 3,000 firms. The individual company PD data, along with aggregate PDs at the economy and sector level, can be accessed at http://rmicri.org.

The primary goal of this initiative is to drive research and development in the critical area of credit rating systems. As such, a transparent methodology is essential to this initiative. Having the details of the methodology available to everybody means that there is a base from which suggestions and improvements can be made. The objective of this Technical Report is to provide a full exposition of the CRI system. Readers of this document who have access to the necessary data and who have a sufficient level of technical expertise will be able to implement a similar system on their own. For a full exposition of the conceptual framework of the CRI, see Duan and Van Laere (2012).

The system used by the CRI will evolve as new innovations and enhancements are applied. The changes to the 2013 technical report and operational implementation of our model are: (1) the changes in financial statement (FS) priority rules for Australia, South-Korea and Taiwan; (2) the changes to the winsorization for market-to-book ratio; (3) some changes to the monthly calibration for the Emerging Markets Group;

(4) a reclassification of default events in Thailand; (5) a replacement for the stock index in Jordan; (6) replacements for the 3-month interest rates in Russia and Singapore; (7) a replacement for the risk-free rate in Sweden; and (8) revision to balance sheet items used in distance-to-default (DTD). This version of the technical report provides an update on the operational implementation of the CRI and includes all changes to the system that had been implemented by March 2014. More specifically, in addition to Technical Report version: 2013 update 2, the current version of the technical report specifies some revisions to the monthly parameter updates that went into effect as of the April 2014 calibration. The latest version of the Technical Report and addenda to the latest version are available via the web portal and will include any changes to the system that have been implemented since the publication of this version.

The remainder of this Technical Report is organized as follows. The next section describes the quantitative model that is currently used to compute PDs from the CRI. The model was first described in Duan *et al.* (2012). The description includes calibration procedures, which are performed on a monthly basis, and individual firm PD computations, which are performed on a daily basis.

Section II describes the input variables of the model as well as the data used to produce the variables for input into the model. This model uses both input variables that are common to all firms in an economy and input variables that are firm-specific. Another critical component when calibrating a probability of default estimation system is the default data, and this is also described in this section.

While Section I provides a broader description of the model, Section III describes the implementation details that are necessary for application, given real world issues of, for example, bad or missing data. The specific technical details needed to develop an operational system are also given, including details on the monthly calibration, daily computation of individual firm PDs and aggregation of the individual firm PDs. DTD in a Merton-type model is one of the firm-specific variables. The calculation for DTD is not the standard one, and has been modified to allow a meaningful computation of the DTD for financial firms. While most academic studies on default prediction exclude financial firms from consideration, it is important to include them given that the financial sector is a critical component in every economy. The calculation for DTD is detailed in this section.

Section IV shows an empirical analysis for those economies that are currently covered. While the analysis shows excellent results in several economies, there is room for improvement in a few others. This is because, at the CRI's current stage of development, the economies all use the variables used in the academic study of US firms in Duan *et al.* (2012). Future development within the CRI will deal with variable selection specific to different economies, and the performance is then expected to improve. Other planned developments are discussed in Sec. V.

I. MODEL DESCRIPTION

The quantitative model that is currently being used by the CRI is a forward intensity model that was introduced in Duan *et al.* (2012). Certain aspects of the model are taken from Duan and Fulop (2013). This model allows PD forecasts to be made at a range of horizons. In the current CRI implementation of this model, PDs are forecasted from a horizon of one month up to a horizon of five years. At the RMI CRI website, for every firm, the probability of that firm defaulting within one month, three months, six months, one year, two years, three years and five years is given. The ability to assess credit quality for different horizons is a useful tool for risk management, credit portfolio management, policy setting and regulatory purposes, since short- and long-term credit risk profiles can differ greatly depending on a firm's liquidity, debt structures and other factors.

The forward intensity model is a reduced form model in which the PD is computed as a function of different input variables. These can be firm-specific or common to all firms within an economy. The other category of the default prediction model is the structural model, whereby the corporate structure of a firm is modeled in order to assess the firm's PD.

A similar reduced form model by Duffie *et al.* (2007) relies on modeling the time series dynamics of the input variables in order to make PD forecasts for different horizons. However, there is little consensus on assumptions for the dynamics of variables such as accounting ratios, and the model output will be highly dependent on these assumptions. In addition, the time series dynamics will be of very high dimension. For example, with the two common variables and two firm-specific variables that Duffie *et al.* (2007) use, a sample of 10,000 firms gives a dimension of the state variables of 20,002.

Given the complexity in modeling the dynamics of variables such as accounting ratios, this model will be difficult to implement if different forecast horizons are required. The key innovation of the forward intensity model is that PD for different horizons can be consistently and efficiently computed based only on the value of the input variables at the time the prediction is made. Thus, the model specification becomes far more tractable.

Fully specifying a reduced form model includes the specification of the function that computes a PD from the input variables. This function is parameterized, and finding appropriate parameter values is called calibrating the model. The forward intensity model can be calibrated by maximizing a pseudo-likelihood function. The calibration is carried out by groups of economies and all firms within a group of economies will use the same parameter values along with each firm's variables in order to compute the firm's PD.

Subsection I.1 will describe the modeling framework, including the way PDs are computed based on a set of parameter values for the economy and a set of input variables for a firm. Subsection I.2 explains how the model can be calibrated. Subsection I.3 details the way parameters are estimated based on the SMC technique.

I.1. Modeling Framework

While the model can be formulated in a continuous time framework, as done in Duan *et al.* (2012), an operational implementation requires discretization in time. Since the model is more easily understood in discrete time, the following exposition of the model will begin in a discrete time framework.

Variables for default prediction can have vastly different update frequencies. Financial statement data is updated only once a quarter or even once a year, while market data like stock prices are available at frequencies of seconds. A way of compromising between these two extremes is to have a fundamental time period Δt of one month in the modeling framework. As will be seen later, this does not preclude updating the PD forecasts on a daily basis. This is important since, for example, large daily changes in a firm's stock price can signal changes in credit quality even when there is no change in FS data.

Thus, for the purposes of calibration and subsequently for computing time series of PD, the input variables at the end of each month will be kept for each firm. The input variables associated with the ith firm at the end of the nth month (at time $t = n\Delta t$) is denoted by $X_i(n)$. This is a vector consisting of two parts: $X_i(n) = (W(n), U_i(n))$. Here, $W(n)$ is a vector of variables at the end of month n that is common to all firms in the economy and $U_i(n)$ is a vector of variables specific to firm i.

In the forward intensity model, a firm's default is signaled by a jump in a Poisson process. The probability of a jump in the Poisson process is determined by the intensity of the Poisson process. The forward intensity model draws an explicit dependence of intensities at time periods in the future (that is, forward intensities) to the values of input variables at the time of prediction. With forward intensities, PDs for any forecast horizon can be computed knowing only the values of the input variables at the time of prediction, without needing to simulate future values of the input variables.

There is a direct analogy in interest rate modeling. In spot rate models where dynamics on a short-term spot rate are specified, bond pricing requires expectations on realizations of the short rate. Alternatively, bond prices can be computed directly if the forward rate curve is known.

One issue in default prediction is that firms can exit public exchanges for reasons other than default. For example, in mergers and acquisitions involving two public companies, there will be one company that delists from its stock exchange. This is important in predicting defaults because a default cannot happen if a firm has been previously delisted. An exception is if the exit is a distressed exit and is followed soon after by a credit event. See Subsec. II.4 for details on how this case is handled in the CRI system.

In order to take these other exits into account, defaults and other exits are modeled as two independent Poisson processes, each with their own intensity. While defaults and exits classified as non-defaults are mutually exclusive by definition, the assumption of independent Poisson processes does not pose a problem since the probability of a simultaneous jump in the two Poisson processes is negligible. In the discrete time framework, the probability of simultaneous jumps in the same time interval is non-zero. As a modeling assumption, a simultaneous jump in the same time interval by both the default Poisson process and the non-default type exit Poisson process is considered as a default. In this way, there are three mutually exclusive possibilities during each time interval: survival, default and non-default exit. As with defaults, the forward intensity of the Poisson process for other exits is a function of the input variables. The parameters of this function can also be calibrated.

To further illustrate the discrete framework, the three possibilities for a firm at each time point are diagrammed. Either the firm survives for the next time period Δt, or it defaults within Δt, or it has a non-default exit within Δt. This setup is pictured in Fig. 1. Information about firm i is known up until time $t = m\Delta t$ and the figure illustrates possibilities in the future between $t = (n-1)\Delta t$ and $(n+1)\Delta t$. Here, m and n are integers with $m < n$.

The probabilities of each branch are, for example: $p_i(m,n)$ the conditional probability viewed from $t = m\Delta t$ that firm i will default before $(n+1)\Delta t$, conditioned on firm i surviving up until $n\Delta t$. Likewise, $\bar{p}_i(m,n)$ is the conditional probability viewed from $t = m\Delta t$ that firm i will have a non-default exit before $(n+1)\Delta t$, conditioned on firm i surviving up until $n\Delta t$. It is the modeler's objective to determine $p_i(m,n)$ and $\bar{p}_i(m,n)$, but for now it is assumed that these quantities are known. With the conditional default and other exit probabilities known, the corresponding conditional survival probability of firm i is $1 - p_i(m,n) - \bar{p}_i(m,n)$.

With this diagram in mind, the probability that a particular path will be followed is the product of the conditional probabilities along the path. For example, the probability at time $t = m\Delta t$ of firm i surviving until $(n-1)\Delta t$ and then defaulting between $(n-1)\Delta t$ and $n\Delta t$ is:

$$\begin{aligned}\text{Prob}_{t=m\Delta t}[\tau_i = n, \tau_i < \bar{\tau}_i] \\ = p_i(m,n-1)\prod_{j=m}^{n-2}[1 - p_i(m,j) - \bar{p}_i(m,j)].\end{aligned} \tag{1}$$

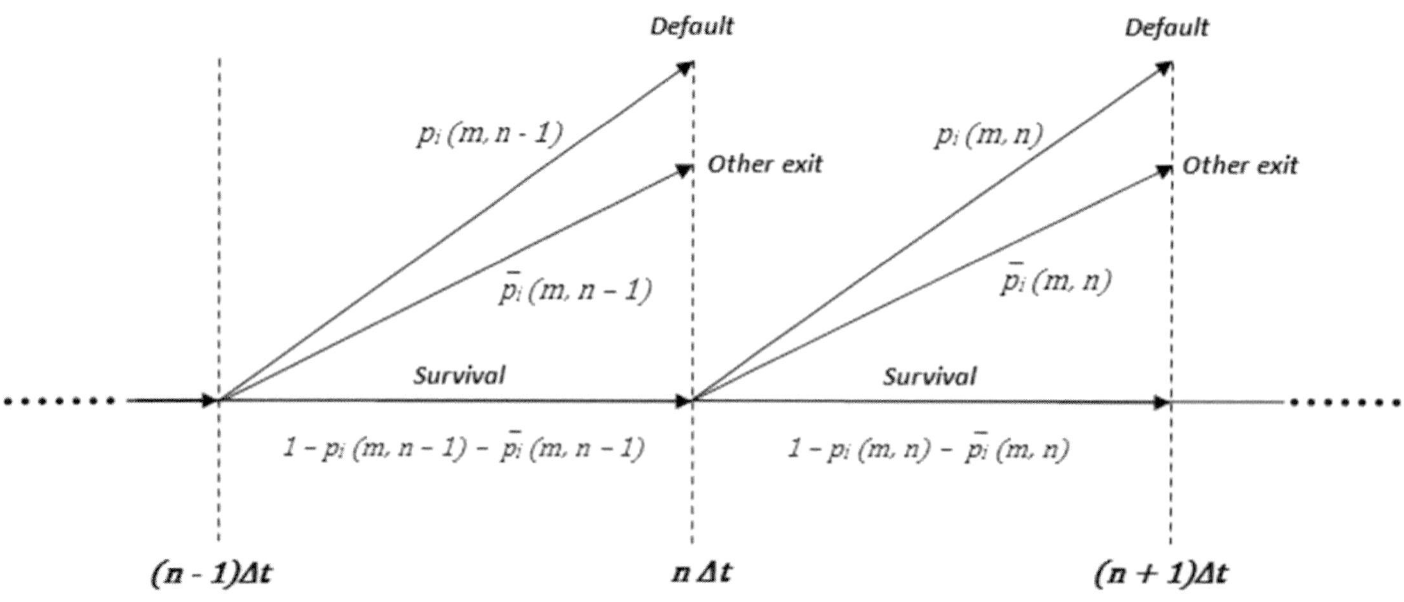

Figure 1. Default-other exit-survival tree for firm i, viewed from time $t = m\Delta t$.

Here, τ_i is the default time for firm i measured in units of months, $\bar{\tau}_i$ is the other exit time measured in units of months, and the product is equal to 1 if there is no term in the product. The condition $\tau_i < \bar{\tau}_i$ is the requirement that the firm defaults before it has a non-default type of exit. Note that by measuring exits in units of months, if, for example, a default occurs at any time in the interval $[(n-1)\Delta t, n\Delta t]$, then $\tau_i = n$.

Using Eq. (1), cumulative default probabilities can be computed. At $m\Delta t$ the probability of firm i defaulting at or before $n\Delta t$ and not having an other exit before $t = n\Delta t$ is obtained by taking the sum of all of the paths that lead to default at or before $n\Delta t$:

$$\begin{aligned}&\text{Prob}_{t=m\Delta t}[m < \tau_i \leq n, \tau_i < \bar{\tau}_i] \\ &= \sum_{k=m}^{n-1} \left\{ p_i(m,k) \prod_{j=m}^{k-1} [1 - p_i(m,j) - \bar{p}_i(m,j)] \right\}.\end{aligned} \tag{2}$$

While it is convenient to derive the probabilities given in Eqs. (1) and (2) in terms of the conditional probabilities, expressions for these in terms of the forward intensities need to be found, since the forward intensities will be functions of the input variable $X_i(m)$. The forward intensity for the default of firm i that is observed at time $t = m\Delta t$ for the forward time interval from $t = n\Delta t$ to $(n+1)\Delta t$, is denoted by $h_i(m,n)$, where $m \leq n$. The corresponding forward intensity for a non-default exit is denoted by $\bar{h}_i(m,n)$. Because default is signaled by a jump in a Poisson process, its conditional probability is a simple function of its forward intensity:

$$p_i(m,n) = 1 - \exp[-\Delta t\, h_i(m,n)]. \tag{3}$$

Since joint jumps in the same time interval are assigned as defaults, the conditional other exit probability needs to take this into account:

$$\begin{aligned}\bar{p}_i(m,n) &= \exp[-\Delta t\, h_i(m,n)] \\ &\quad \times \{1 - \exp[-\Delta t\, \bar{h}_i(m,n)]\}.\end{aligned} \tag{4}$$

The conditional survival probabilities in Eqs. (1) and (2) are computed as the conditional probability that the firm does not default in the period and the firm does not have a non-default exit either:

$$\begin{aligned}&\text{Prob}_{t=m\Delta t}[\tau_i, \bar{\tau}_i > n+1 \mid \tau_i, \bar{\tau}_i > n] \\ &\quad = \exp\{-\Delta t[h_i(m,n) + \bar{h}_i(m,n)]\}.\end{aligned} \tag{5}$$

It remains to be specified the dependence of the forward intensities on the input variable $X_i(m)$. The forward intensities need to be positive so that the conditional probabilities are non-negative. A standard way to impose this constraint is to specify the forward intensities as exponentials of a linear combination of the input variables:

$$\begin{aligned}h_i(m,n) &= \exp[\beta(n-m)\cdot Y_i(m)], \\ \bar{h}_i(m,n) &= \exp[\bar{\beta}(n-m)\cdot Y_i(m)].\end{aligned} \tag{6}$$

Here, β and $\bar{\beta}$ are coefficient vectors that are functions of the number of months between the observation date and the beginning of the forward period $(n-m)$, and $Y_i(m)$ is simply the vector $X_i(m)$ augmented by a preceding unit element: $Y_i(m) = (1, X_i(m))$. The unit element allows the linear combination in the argument of the exponentials in Eq. (6) to have a non-zero intercept.

In the current implementation of the forward intensity model in the CRI, the maximum forecast horizon is 60 months (5 years) and there are 12 input variables plus the intercept, so there are 60 sets of β and $\bar{\beta}$. While this is a large set of parameters, as will be seen in Subsecs. I.2 and I.3, the calibration is tractable because the default parameters can be calibrated separately from the other exit parameters, and the total number of parameters are greatly reduced after constraining the term-structure of the parameter estimates to be Nelson–Siegel functions.

Before expressing the probabilities in Eqs. (1) and (2) in terms of the forward intensities, a notation H is introduced for the forward intensities so that it becomes clear which parameters the forward intensity depends on:

$$H(\beta(n-m), X_i(m)) = \exp[\beta(n-m)\cdot Y_i(m)]. \tag{7}$$

This is the forward default intensity. The corresponding notation for other exit forward intensities is then just $H(\bar{\beta}(n-m), X_i(m))$. So, the probability in Eq. (1) is expressed in terms of the forward intensities, using Eq. (3) as the conditional default probability and

Eq. (5) as the conditional survival probability:

$$
\begin{aligned}
&\text{Prob}_{t=m\Delta t}[\tau_i = n, \tau_i < \bar{\tau}_i] \\
&\quad = \{1 - \exp[-\Delta t\, H(\beta(n-1-m), X_i(m))]\} \\
&\qquad \times \prod_{j=m}^{n-2} \exp\{-\Delta t[H(\beta(j-m), X_i(m)) \\
&\qquad + H(\bar{\beta}(j-m), X_i(m))]\} \\
&\quad = \{1 - \exp[-\Delta t\, H(\beta(n-m-1), X_i(m))]\} \\
&\qquad \times \exp\left\{ -\Delta t \sum_{j=m}^{n-2} [H(\beta(j-m), X_i(m)) \right. \\
&\qquad \left. + H(\bar{\beta}(j-m), X_i(m))] \right\}.
\end{aligned} \tag{8}
$$

This probability will be relevant in the next part during the calibration. The cumulative default probability given in Eq. (2) in terms of the forward intensities is then:

$$
\begin{aligned}
&\text{Prob}_{t=m\Delta t}[m < \tau_i \le n, \tau_i < \bar{\tau}_i] \\
&\quad = \sum_{k=m}^{n-1} \left\{ \{1 - \exp[-\Delta t\, H(\beta(k-m), X_i(m))]\} \right. \\
&\qquad \times \exp\left\{ -\Delta t \sum_{j=m}^{k-1} [H(\beta(j-m), X_i(m)) \right. \\
&\qquad \left.\left. + H(\bar{\beta}(j-m), X_i(m))] \right\} \right\}.
\end{aligned} \tag{9}
$$

This formula is used to compute the main output of the CRI: an individual firm's PD within various time horizons. The β and $\bar{\beta}$ parameters are obtained when the firm's economy is calibrated, and using those together with the firm's input variables yields the firm's PD.

I.2. Pseudo-Likelihood Function

The empirical data set used for calibration can be described as follows. For the economy as a whole, there are N end of month observations, indexed as $n = 1, \ldots, N$. Of course, not all firms will have observations for each of the N months as they may start later than the start of the economy's data set or they may exit before the end of the economy's data set. There are a total of I firms in the economy, and they are indexed as $i = 1, \ldots, I$. As before, the input variables for the ith firm in the nth month is $X_i(n)$. The set of all observations for all firms is denoted by X.

In addition, the default times τ_i and non-default exit times $\bar{\tau}_i$ for the ith firm are known if the default or other exit occurs after time $t = \Delta t$ and at or before $t = N\Delta t$. The possible values for τ_i and $\bar{\tau}_i$ are integers between 2 and N, inclusive. If a firm exits before the month end, then the exit time is recorded as the first month end after the exit. If the firm does not exit before $t = N\Delta t$, then the convention can be used that both of these values are infinite. If the firm has a default type of exit within the data set, then $\bar{\tau}_i$ can be considered as infinite. If instead the firm has a non-default type of exit within the data set, then τ_i can be considered as infinite. The set of all default times and non-default exit times for all firms is denoted by τ and $\bar{\tau}$, respectively. The first month in which firm i has an observation is denoted by t_{0i}. Except for cases of missing data, these observations continue until the end of the data set if the firm never exits. If the firm does exit, the last needed input variable $X_i(n)$ is for $n = \min(\tau_i, \bar{\tau}_i) - 1$.

The calibration of the β and $\bar{\beta}$ parameters is done by maximizing a pseudo-likelihood function. The function to be maximized violates the standard assumptions of likelihood functions, but Appendix A in Duan *et al.* (2012) derives the large sample properties of the pseudo-likelihood function.

In formulating the pseudo-likelihood function, the assumption is made that the firms are conditionally independent from each other. In other words, correlations arise naturally from shared common factors $W(n)$ and any correlations between different firms' firm-specific variables. With this assumption, the pseudo-likelihood function for the horizon of ℓ months, a set of parameters β and $\bar{\beta}$ and the data set $(\tau, \bar{\tau}, X)$ is:

$$
\begin{aligned}
&\mathcal{L}_\ell(\beta, \bar{\beta}; \tau, \bar{\tau}, X) \\
&\quad = \prod_{m=1}^{N-1} \prod_{i=1}^{I} P_{\min(N-m,\ell)}(\beta, \bar{\beta}; \tau_i, \bar{\tau}_i, X_i(m)).
\end{aligned} \tag{10}
$$

Here, $P_{\min(N-m,\ell)}(\beta, \bar{\beta}; \tau_i, \bar{\tau}_i, X_i(m))$ is a probability for the ith firm, with the nature of the probability depending on what happens to the firm during the period from month m to month $m + \min(N - m, \ell)$. This is defined as:

$$
\begin{aligned}
&P_\ell(\beta, \bar{\beta}; \tau_i, \bar{\tau}_i, X_i(m)) \\
&\quad = 1_{\{t_{0i} \le m, \min(\tau_i, \bar{\tau}_i) > m+\ell\}} \\
&\qquad \times \exp\left\{ -\Delta t \sum_{j=0}^{\ell-1} [H(\beta(j), X_i(m)) + H(\bar{\beta}(j), X_i(m))] \right\} \\
&\quad + 1_{\{t_{0i} \le m, \tau_i \le \bar{\tau}_i, \tau_i \le m+\ell\}} \\
&\qquad \times \{1 - \exp[-\Delta t\, H(\beta(\tau_i - m - 1), X_i(m))]\} \\
&\qquad \times \exp\left\{ -\Delta t \sum_{j=0}^{\tau_i - m - 2} [H(\beta(j), X_i(m)) + H(\bar{\beta}(j), X_i(m))] \right\} \\
&\quad + 1_{\{t_{0i} \le m, \bar{\tau}_i \le \tau_i, \bar{\tau}_i \le m+\ell\}} \\
&\qquad \times \{1 - \exp[-\Delta t\, H(\bar{\beta}(\bar{\tau}_i - m - 1), X_i(m))]\} \\
&\qquad \times \exp[-\Delta t\, H(\beta(\tau_i - m - 1), X_i(m))] \\
&\qquad \times \exp\left\{ -\Delta t \sum_{j=0}^{\bar{\tau}_i - m - 2} [H(\beta(j), X_i(m)) + H(\bar{\beta}(j), X_i(m))] \right\} \\
&\quad + 1_{\{t_{0i} > m\}} + 1_{\{\min(\tau_i, \bar{\tau}_i) \le m\}}.
\end{aligned} \tag{11}
$$

In words, if the ith firm survives from the observation time at month m for the full horizon ℓ until at least $m + \ell$, then the probability is the model-based survival probability for this period. This is the first term in Eq. (11). The second term handles the cases where the firm has a default within the horizon, in which case the probability is the model-based probability of the firm defaulting at the month that it ends up defaulting, as given in Eq. (8). The third term handles the cases where the firm has a non-default exit within the horizon, in which case the probability is the model-based probability of the firm having a non-default type exit at the month that the exit actually does occur. The expression for this probability uses the conditional non-default type exit probability given in Eq. (4). The final two terms handle the cases where the firm is not in the data set at month m — either the first observation for the firm is after m or the firm has already exited. A constant value is assigned in this case so that this firm will not affect the maximization at this time point.

The pseudo-likelihood function given in Eq. (10) can be numerically maximized to give estimates for the coefficients β and $\bar{\beta}$. Notice though that the sample observations for the pseudo-likelihood function are overlapping if the horizon is longer than one month. For example, when $\ell = 2$, default over the next two periods from month m is correlated to default over the next two periods from month $m + 1$ due to the common month in the two sample observations. However, in Appendix A of Duan *et al.* (2012), the maximum pseudo-likelihood estimator is shown to be consistent, in the sense that the estimators converge to the "true" parameter value in the large sample limit.

Notice though that each of the terms in Eq. (11) can be written as a product of terms containing only β and terms containing only $\bar{\beta}$. This will allow separate maximizations with respect to β and with respect to $\bar{\beta}$, that is, the defaults and other exits.

The β and $\bar{\beta}$ specific versions of Eq. (11) are:

$$
\begin{aligned}
&P_\ell^{\beta}(\beta; \tau_i, \bar{\tau}_i, X_i(m)) \\
&\quad = 1_{\{t_{0i} \le m, \min(\tau_i, \bar{\tau}_i) > m+\ell\}} \exp\left\{ -\Delta t \sum_{j=0}^{\ell-1} H(\beta(j), X_i(m)) \right\} \\
&\quad + 1_{\{t_{0i} \le m, \tau_i \le \bar{\tau}_i, \tau_i \le m+\ell\}} \exp\left\{ -\Delta t \sum_{j=0}^{\tau_i - m - 2} H(\beta(j), X_i(m)) \right\} \\
&\qquad \times \{1 - \exp[-\Delta t\, H(\beta(\tau_i - m - 1), X_i(m))]\} \\
&\quad + 1_{\{t_{0i} \le m, \bar{\tau}_i \le \tau_i, \bar{\tau}_i \le m+\ell\}} \exp\left\{ -\Delta t \sum_{j=0}^{\bar{\tau}_i - m - 2} H(\beta(j), X_i(m)) \right\} \\
&\qquad \times \exp[-\Delta t\, H(\beta(\tau_i - m - 1), X_i(m))] \\
&\quad + 1_{\{t_{0i} > m\}} + 1_{\{\min(\tau_i, \bar{\tau}_i) \le m\}}, \\
&P_\ell^{\bar{\beta}}(\bar{\beta}; \tau_i, \bar{\tau}_i, X_i(m)) \\
&\quad = 1_{\{t_{0i} \le m, \min(\tau_i, \bar{\tau}_i) > m+\ell\}} \exp\left\{ -\Delta t \sum_{j=0}^{\ell-1} H(\bar{\beta}(j), X_i(m)) \right\} \\
&\quad + 1_{\{t_{0i} \le m, \tau_i \le \bar{\tau}_i, \tau_i \le m+\ell\}} \exp\left\{ -\Delta t \sum_{j=0}^{\tau_i - m - 2} H(\bar{\beta}(j), X_i(m)) \right\} \\
&\quad + 1_{\{t_{0i} \le m, \bar{\tau}_i \le \tau_i, \bar{\tau}_i \le m+\ell\}} \exp\left\{ -\Delta t \sum_{j=0}^{\bar{\tau}_i - m - 2} H(\bar{\beta}(j), X_i(m)) \right\} \\
&\qquad \times \{1 - \exp[-\Delta t\, H(\bar{\beta}(\bar{\tau}_i - m - 1), X_i(m))]\} \\
&\quad + 1_{\{t_{0i} > m\}} + 1_{\{\min(\tau_i, \bar{\tau}_i) \le m\}}.
\end{aligned} \tag{12}
$$

Then, the β and $\bar{\beta}$ specific versions of the pseudo-likelihood function are given by:

$$
\begin{aligned}
\mathcal{L}_\ell^{\beta}(\beta; \tau, \bar{\tau}, X) &= \prod_{m=1}^{N-\ell} \prod_{i=1}^{I} P_\ell^{\beta}(\beta; \tau_i, \bar{\tau}_i, X_i(m)), \\
\mathcal{L}_\ell^{\bar{\beta}}(\bar{\beta}; \tau, \bar{\tau}, X) &= \prod_{m=1}^{N-\ell} \prod_{i=1}^{I} P_\ell^{\bar{\beta}}(\bar{\beta}; \tau_i, \bar{\tau}_i, X_i(m)).
\end{aligned} \tag{13}
$$

With the definitions given in Eqs. (12) and (13), it can be seen that:

$$\mathcal{L}_\ell(\beta, \bar{\beta}; \tau, \bar{\tau}, X) = \mathcal{L}_\ell^{\beta}(\beta; \tau, \bar{\tau}, X)\mathcal{L}_\ell^{\bar{\beta}}(\bar{\beta}; \tau, \bar{\tau}, X). \tag{14}$$

Thus, $\mathcal{L}_\ell^{\beta}$ and $\mathcal{L}_\ell^{\bar{\beta}}$ can be separately maximized to find their respective parameters. Subsection I.3 will further explain how the optimum parameters can be estimated.

I.3. Parameter Estimation

Previously, the CRI system produced default predictions to a horizon of two years (RMI, 2012). An extension of the forecast horizon has been implemented as of the PD released on April 1, 2013. With this update, horizons of up to five years are now being computed. Technically speaking, horizons of arbitrary length can be calculated.

This extension to a five-year horizon is done by constraining the term-structure of the parameter estimates to be Nelson–Siegel (Nelson and Siegel (1987); hereafter NS) functions of the forward-starting time. Horizon-specific parameters $\beta, \bar{\beta}$ can be obtained from the continuous NS function by using the forward prediction horizon as an input. The term-structures are further constrained so that the effect of risk factors on the forward intensity goes to zero as the horizon increases. This allows tractable and parsimonious extrapolations for horizons beyond five years.

The parameter estimation for the NS functions is based on a new numerical method (a pseudo-Bayesian SMC technique) developed in a working paper by Duan and Fulop (2013). The remainder of this section details the new parameter estimation. Subsection I.3.1 describes the parameterization of the parameters by NS functions, Subsec. I.3.2 gives an overview of the SMC method that is used to estimate the NS functions, Subsec. I.3.3 details the calculation of the confidence intervals for the parameter estimation, and Subsec. I.3.4 describes how the parameters can be re-estimated given new data or updates of old data.

I.3.1. *Smoothed parameters*

Duan *et al.* (2012) formulate the forward intensity model in which the forward default intensity for a firm is a function of a number of covariates. The forward default intensities for different forward starting periods are computed using different sets of parameters.

In Duan *et al.* (2012), the sets of parameters are estimated separately for each forward starting time. Parameters at different forward starting times that are associated with each covariate can be approximated by a function of the forward starting time using NS type term structure functions. Duan *et al.* (2012) show that this approximation by NS functions does not negatively affect prediction performance. The RMI implementation follows Duan and Fulop (2013) to impose the functional restriction during the estimation as opposed to the method used in Duan *et al.* (2012) of fitting the curve after parameter estimates have been obtained. This is done for two reasons.

First, it will significantly reduce the number of parameters. For example, using 12 covariates for forward default intensities up to 60 months would require a joint estimation of $13 \times 60 = 780$ parameters. Here, 13 comes from adding an intercept to the intensity function with 12 covariates. If the coefficients corresponding to each covariate are represented by the NS function of 4 parameters, there will be at most $13 \times 4 = 52$ parameters. In fact, there will be fewer parameters as some of the NS parameters will be constrained to zero.

Second, the NS function will allow extrapolation. For example, the 13 NS functions estimated with predictions up to 60 months can be used for prediction, say, over 72 months.

The NS function with four free parameters is:

$$\begin{aligned} r(t; \varrho_0, \varrho_1, \varrho_2, d) &= \varrho_0 + \varrho_1 \frac{1 - \exp(-t/d)}{t/d} \\ &\quad + \varrho_2 \left[\frac{1 - \exp(-t/d)}{t/d} - \exp(-t/d) \right], \end{aligned} \tag{15}$$

where t is the forecast horizon (measured in years). In the RMI implementation, the horizon is 60 months (5 years) so that t ranges from 0 to $59/12$. Once the four NS parameters are estimated, individual horizon-specific parameters β, $\bar{\beta}$ are obtained from the NS function r using the forecast horizon as input to the NS function. In our current implementation with forecast horizons extending to 60 months (5 years), 120 sets of month specific β and $\bar{\beta}$ are obtained. For all covariates, the restriction $d > 0$ is imposed so that the functions converge to a value for large t. This formulation will be used for forward intensities for both defaults and other types of exit.

For the coefficients of all stochastic covariates, the long-run level ϱ_0 is restricted to zero, because the current value of a stochastic covariate should be uninformative of default or other exits when the forward starting time goes to infinity. In other words, the coefficient of such a stochastic covariate should approach zero when t goes to infinity.

The intercept of the forward intensity function is of course non-stochastic. Thus, ϱ_0 can have non-zero values for the intercept. With these restrictions on the NS parameters, take the example of 12 covariates, there will be a total of $12 \times 3 + 1 \times 4 = 40$ parameters.

In the RMI implementation, the NS function is further constrained to be non-positive for certain covariates: DTD level and trend, liquidity level and trend, and profitability level and trend. Refer to Sec. II for descriptions of these covariates.

I.3.2. *Parameter estimation by SMC*

Reliably estimating a system involving 40 parameters presents a numerical challenge. Moreover, the number of parameters can be greater than 40 if there are more than 12 covariates. The RMI implementation follows Duan and Fulop (2013) who use the SMC pseudo-Bayesian method for estimation and self-normalized statistics for inference.

Due to decomposability, the analysis can be performed separately on the forward default and other exit intensities. The data in the RMI implementation are refreshed with monthly frequency, and the sample likelihood used in estimation relies on default predictions running from 1 month to 60 months with a one-month increment. Naturally, default prediction is subject to data availability. Towards the end of the period with available data, the prediction horizon naturally decreases and stops at one-month predictions.

The following exposition closely follows the Appendix in Duan and Fulop (2013). It is important to note that the RMI implementation uses the model described in Duan and Fulop (2013), which does not contain any latent frailty or partial conditioning variable, and hence is technically much simpler in parameter estimation. For example, there is no nonlinear filtering problem.

According to the current modeling framework, where for a particular economy there are N end of the month observations, the input variables of the ith firm in the mth month is given by $X_i(m)$. Let θ denote a set of NS parameters and ℓ denote the forecast horizon ($\ell = 60$). Then the pseudo-likelihood function at step m, denoted by $\mathcal{L}_{m,\min(N-m,\ell)}(\theta)$, takes the form:

$$\mathcal{L}_{m,\min(N-m,\ell)}(\theta) = \prod_{i=1}^{I} P_{\min(N-m,\ell)}(\beta(\theta), \bar{\beta}(\theta); \tau_i, \bar{\tau}_i, X_i(m)), \quad (16)$$

where I is the number of firms, $\beta(\theta)$ and $\bar{\beta}(\theta)$ are the coefficient vectors from Eq. (6) generated from the NS functions with parameter θ. One may notice that $\mathcal{L}_{m,\min(N-m,\ell)}(\theta)$ is one of the terms in the outer-most product in Eq. (10).

Let $\pi(\theta)$ denote the prior. Following the notation from Sec. I.1, consider the following pseudo-posterior distribution at time n after one makes the ℓ-period prediction:

$$\gamma_n(\theta) \propto \prod_{m=1}^{n-1} \mathcal{L}_{m,\min(N-m,\ell)}(\theta)\pi(\theta), \quad \text{for } n = 2, \ldots, N. \quad (17)$$

One can apply the sequential batch-resampling routine of Chopin (2012) together with tempering steps as in Del Moral *et al.* (2006) to advance the system. For each n, this procedure yields a weighted sample of K particles, $(\theta^{(k,n)}, w^{(k,n)})$ for $k = 1, \ldots, K$, whose empirical distribution function will converge to $\gamma_n(\theta)$ as K increases. In the following paragraphs, the superscript k

denotes the particle index. Note that in the RMI implementation, $K = 1{,}000$.

Initialization: Draw an initial random sample from the prior: $(\theta^{(k,0)} \sim \pi(\theta), w^{(k,0)} = 1/K)$. Here, the only role of the prior $\pi(\theta)$, is to provide the initial particle cloud from which the algorithm can start. Of course, the support of $\pi(\theta)$ must contain the true parameter value θ_0. In the RMI implementation, normal/truncated normal priors are used. Truncation applies in order to impose the restriction $d > 0$. To obtain the means of the priors for the SMC method, a least square fit of the MLE parameter estimates to the NS function is conducted. The standard deviations of the priors are set to 5.

Recursions and defining the tempering sequence: Assume there is a particle cloud $\left(\theta^{(k,n)}, w^{(k,n)}\right)$ whose empirical distribution represents $\gamma_n(\theta)$. Then, a cloud representing $\gamma_{n+1}(\theta)$ will be reached by combining importance sampling and the Markov Chain Monte Carlo (MCMC) steps. Sometimes moving directly from $\gamma_n(\theta)$ to $\gamma_{n+1}(\theta)$ is too ambitious as the two distributions are too far from each other. This will be reflected in highly variable importance weights if one resorts to direct importance sampling. Hence, following Duan and Fulop (2013) which in turn followed Del Moral *et al.* (2006), a tempered bridge is built between the two densities and the particles are evolved through the resulting sequence of densities. In particular, assume that at time $n+1$, there are P_{n+1} intermediate densities:

$$\overline{\gamma}_{n+1,p}(\theta) \propto \gamma_n(\theta)\mathcal{L}^{\xi_p}_{n,\min(N-n,\ell)}(\theta), \quad \text{for } p = 1, \ldots, P_{n+1}. \tag{18}$$

This construction defines an appropriate bridge: $\xi_0 = 0$ so that $\overline{\gamma}_{n+1,0}(\theta) = \gamma_n(\theta)$, and $\xi_{P_{n+1}} = 1$ so that $\overline{\gamma}_{n+1,P_{n+1}}(\theta) = \gamma_{n+1}(\theta)$. For p between 0 and P_{n+1}, ξ_p is chosen from a grid of points to evenly distribute the weights, as decribed below. A particle cloud representing $\overline{\gamma}_{n+1,0}(\theta)$ can be initialized as $(\overline{\theta}^{(k,n+1,0)}, \overline{w}^{(k,n+1,0)}) = (\theta^{(k,n)}, w^{(k,n)})$. Then, for $p = 1, \ldots, P_{n+1}$ the sequence proceeds as follows:

- *Reweighting Step*: In order to arrive at a representation of $\overline{\gamma}_{n+1,p}(\theta)$, the particles representing $\overline{\gamma}_{n+1,p-1}(\theta)$ and the importance sampling principle can be used. This leads to:

$$\overline{\theta}^{(k,n+1,p)} = \overline{\theta}^{(k,n+1,p-1)}, \tag{19}$$

$$\begin{aligned}\overline{w}^{(k,n+1,p)} &= \overline{w}^{(k,n+1,p-1)} \times \frac{\overline{\gamma}_{n+1,p}(\overline{\theta}^{(k,n+1,p)})}{\overline{\gamma}_{n+1,p-1}(\overline{\theta}^{(k,n+1,p)})} \\ &= \overline{w}^{(k,n+1,p-1)} \times \mathcal{L}^{\xi_p-\xi_{p-1}}_{n+1,\min(N\Delta t-(n+1)\Delta t,\ell)}(\overline{\theta}^{(k,n+1,p)}).\end{aligned} \tag{20}$$

To avoid particle impoverishment in sequential importance sampling where most of the weight is concentrated in a small number of particles, a resample-move step is run, which is triggered whenever a measure of particle diversity — the efficient sample size (ESS) defined as

$$\text{ESS} = \frac{\left(\sum_{k=1}^{N} \overline{w}^{(k,n+1,p)}\right)^2}{\sum_{k=1}^{N} (\overline{w}^{(k,n+1,p)})^2}, \tag{21}$$

falls below some preset value B. Here, resampling directs the particle cloud towards more likely areas of the sampling space, while the move step enriches particle diversity.

In the RMI implementation, B is set to 50%. Thus, if ESS $< 50\%$, the following resampling and move steps are performed.

- *Resampling Step*: The particles are resampled proportional to their weights. If $I^{(k,n+1,p)} \in (1, \ldots, K)$ are particle indices sampled proportional to $\overline{w}^{(k,n+1,p)}$, the equally weighted particles are obtained as

$$\overline{\theta}^{(k,n+1,p)} = \overline{\theta}^{(I^{(k,n+1,p)},n+1,p)}, \tag{22}$$

$$\overline{w}^{(k,n+1,p)} = \frac{1}{K}. \tag{23}$$

- *Move Step*: Each particle is passed through a Markov kernel $\mathcal{K}_{n+1,p}(\overline{\theta}^{(k,n+1,p)}, \cdot)$ that leaves $\overline{\gamma}_{n+1,p}(\theta)$ invariant, typically a Metropolis–Hastings kernel:

(1) Propose $\theta^{*(k)} \sim \mathcal{Q}_{n+1,p}\left(\cdot \mid \overline{\theta}^{(k,n+1,p)}\right)$.

(2) Compute the acceptance weight α, where:

$$\alpha = \min\left(1, \frac{\overline{\gamma}_{n+1,p}\left(\theta^{*(k)}\right) Q_{n+1,p}\left(\overline{\theta}^{(k,n+1,p)} \,\middle|\, \theta^{*(k)}\right)}{\overline{\gamma}_{n+1,p}\left(\overline{\theta}^{(k,n+1,p)}\right) Q_{n+1,p}\left(\theta^{*(k)} \,\middle|\, \overline{\theta}^{(k,n+1,p)}\right)}\right). \tag{24}$$

(3) With probability α, set $\overline{\theta}^{(k,n+1,p)} = \theta^{*(k)}$, otherwise keep the old particle.

This step will enrich the support of the particle cloud while conserving its distribution. If the particle set is a poor representation of the target distribution, the move step can also help adjust the location of the support. Crucially, given the importance of the sampling setup, the proposal distribution $Q_{n+1,p}(\cdot \mid \overline{\theta}^{(k,n+1,p)})$ can be adapted using the existing particle cloud.

In the RMI implementation, block independent normal distribution proposals using the means and the standard deviations implied by the particle set are fitted to the particle cloud before the move. Three (or four) NS parameters corresponding to each covariate form one block. To ensure that the NS parameter d remains positive, any block with a non-positive value for d is discarded. To ensure the smoothness of the term structure of the forward intensity parameters, any block that does not produce an increasing or decreasing structure of the NS function for the first five months is also discarded. Once some block is discarded, the particle is regenerated until it meets the requirements. Note that the likelihood ratio in the Metropolis–Hastings algorithm is not affected by this because the truncated normal creates a common adjustment term in both numerator and denominator.

As mentioned previously, the coefficients for some covariates are also required to be non-positive over all forward starting times. This is achieved by checking whether the NS curve at a particular set of three (or four) parameters meets the condition. If not, the parameter set will be discarded.

To improve the support of the particle cloud, one can execute multiple such Metropolis–Hastings steps each time. In the RMI implementation, such Metropolis–Hastings steps are consecutively performed in each resampling-move step until the number of unique particles exceeds $K/2$.

When $p = P_{n+1}$ is reached, a representation of $\gamma_{n+1}(\theta)$ is:

$$(\theta^{(k,n+1)}, w^{(k,n+1)}) = (\overline{\theta}^{(k,n+1,P_{n+1})}, \overline{w}^{(k,n+1,P_{n+1})}). \tag{25}$$

Following Duan and Fulop (2013), the tempering sequence ξ_p is automatically set to ensure that the ESS stays close to 50%. This is done by a grid search, where the ESS is evaluated at a grid of candidate ξ_p and the one that produces the closest ESS to 50% is chosen.

After the recursion procedure (i.e., ξ_p reaches 1), additional moves using the means implied by the particle set but all standard deviations increased by a factor of 30% are further performed to enrich the support and adjust the location of the particle set. The number of such moves is set to 20 for the first time point and exponentially declines to 3 mid-way to the sample period and stays at 3 for the remainder. After that, if the number of unique particles is still below $K/2$, more moves using the means and the standard deviations implied by the particle set (without expansions) are consecutively performed until the particle set meets the requirement. (This case could only happen when ESS $\geq B$ for $\xi_p = 1$.)

I.3.3. *Statistical inference*

The full sample size has N time series data points but one can only make default prediction at $N - 1$ time points; for example, at time point 2, the data is only available for making one-period default prediction at time point 1. Denote the pseudo-posterior mean of the parameter of the whole sample by $\hat{\theta}_N$ and for $n = 2, \ldots, N$,

$$\hat{\theta}_n = \frac{1}{\sum_{k=1}^{K} w^{(k,n)}} \sum_{k=1}^{K} w^{(k,n)} \theta^{(k,n)}. \tag{26}$$

Note that $(\overline{\theta}^{(k,n+1,0)}, \overline{\omega}^{(k,n+1,0)}) = (\theta^{(k,n)}, \omega^{(k,n)})$ is not a true posterior because the likelihood function in Eq. (17) is not a true likelihood function. Thus, it cannot directly provide valid Bayesian inference. But following Duan and Fulop (2013) — which is in turn based on Shao's self-normalized statistic (Shao, 2010) — inference can be performed using the t-like statistic. To test, for example, the hypothesis of the kth element of $\overline{\theta}^{(k,n+1,p)} = \overline{\theta}^{(I^{(k,n+1,p)},n+1,p)}$, denoted by $\overline{\omega}^{(k,n+1,p)} = \frac{1}{K}$, equal to a, one has:

$$t^* = \frac{\sqrt{N-1}\left(\hat{\theta}_N^{(k)} - a\right)}{\sqrt{\hat{\delta}_{k,N}}} \xrightarrow{d} \frac{W(1)}{[\int_0^1 (W(r) - rW(1))^2 dr]^{1/2}}, \tag{27}$$

where $W(r)$ is a Wiener process, $\hat{\delta}_{k,N}$ is the kth diagonal element of $\hat{C}_N$, and

$$\hat{C}_N = \frac{1}{(N-1)^2} \sum_{n=2}^{N} n^2 (\hat{\theta}_n - \hat{\theta}_N)(\hat{\theta}_n - \hat{\theta}_N)'. \tag{28}$$

The right-hand-side random variable for t^* does not have a known distribution, but can be easily simulated. Kiefer *et al.* (2000) reported that the 95% quantile is 5.374 and the 97.5% quantile is 6.811. These values can also be used to set up confidence intervals.

I.3.4. *Periodic updating*

In reality, portfolio credit risk models need to be updated periodically as new data arrive and/or old data are revised. With one new month of data, this means that the final date index N is increased to $N + 1$. A particular strength of Duan and Fulop (2013)'s methodology is that the estimation routine does not need to be re-initialized from the prior as the pseudo-posterior using data up to $N\Delta t$ will provide a much better proposal distribution.

Let the pseudo-posterior at time N (based on the old data set available at time N) be denoted by

$$\gamma_N^{(N)}(\theta) \propto \prod_{m=1}^{N-1} \mathcal{L}_{m,\min(N-m,\ell)}^{(N)}(\theta)\pi(\theta), \tag{29}$$

and the pseudo-posterior at time $N + 1$ (based on the new data set available at time $N + 1$) by

$$\gamma_{N+1}^{(N+1)}(\theta) \propto \prod_{m=1}^{N} \mathcal{L}_{m,\min((N+1)-m,\ell)}^{(N+1)}(\theta)\pi(\theta). \tag{30}$$

The superscript is introduced to differentiate the data set available at time N and $N + 1$, respectively. It is important to note that $\mathcal{L}_{m,k}^{(N+1)}(\theta) \neq \mathcal{L}_{m,k}^{(N)}(\theta)$ can be caused by revisions to the old data set. More importantly, there is a generic difference between the pseudo-posterior distribution up to time N under the new data set and the corresponding quantity under the old data set specifically due to multiperiod prediction; that is, $\gamma_{N+1}^{(N)}(\theta) \neq \gamma_N^{(N)}(\theta)$ even without any data revisions to the period covered by the old data set. To put it concretely, using the new data set and at, say, one period before the last (i.e., time $N - 1$), one can make default predictions up to two periods, whereas at the same time point, it was only possible to make one-period predictions under the old data set because there were no data beyond time N. Adjustments to the weights are thus necessary to reflect the change in data set before making any sequential updates.

There are several possible ways of advancing the system. The RMI implementation decomposes the move into two steps. First, we take care of data revision up to time N and then act as if we were making predictions with data only up to time N. Doing it this way is meant to maintain the same default prediction setting; that is, for example, only makes one-period default prediction at time $N - 1$ even though the new data set permits predictions up to two periods. Thus, we introduce

$$\gamma_N^{(N+1,N)}(\theta) \propto \prod_{m=1}^{N-1} \mathcal{L}_{m,\min(N-m,\ell)}^{(N+1)}(\theta)\pi(\theta) \tag{31}$$

to denote this pseudo-posterior when the superscript $(N + 1, N)$ stands for the updated data set available at time $N+1$ but making default predictions as if the data were only available up to time N.

From the previous run up to time N, one already has a weighted set of particles $(\theta^{(k,N)}, w^{(k,N)})$ representing the pseudo-posterior distribution $\gamma_N^{(N)}(\theta)$. Next, preform a reweighting by

$$\theta^{*(k,N)} = \theta^{(k,N)}, \tag{32}$$

$$w^{*(k,N)} = w^{(k,N)} \times \frac{\gamma_N^{(N+1,N)}\left(\theta^{(k,N)}\right)}{\gamma_N^{(N)}\left(\theta^{(k,N)}\right)}. \tag{33}$$

Since the denominator is available from the previous run, one only needs to compute the numerator using the new data set up to time N. Then, the weighted set $(\theta^{*(k,N)}, w^{*(k,N)})$ represents the revised pseudo-posterior distribution at time N, i.e., $\gamma_N^{(N+1,N)}(\theta)$, specifically to account for data revisions. From this point onward, one can apply the same recursive procedure described in Subsec. I.3.2, starting from Eq. (18), to complete the updating task.

Reweighting may substantially alter the ESS of the particle set due to a large volume of data changes. If the reweighting leads to a satisfactory ESS, i.e., ESS $\geq B$, advancing to $N+1$ continues as usual. Otherwise, the weighted sample will be discarded to prevent the support from degeneration. One can return to the particle set before reweighting and perform resampling to create an equally-weighted particle set. Then, make the Metropolis–Hastings moves by targeting $\gamma_N^{(N+1,N)}(\theta)$ using the Gaussian-type sampler described earlier and starting with the mean and variance implied by the resampled particle set. One should make these Metropolis–Hastings moves until the particle set reaches a desirable level of distinctiveness, and perhaps with a preset minimum number of moves to ensure that the resulting particle set is close enough to the target distribution. In the RMI implementation, the number of moves is set to be 20.

Furthermore, one can update all self-normalized statistics in the way as described earlier to reflect the additional one more pseudo-posterior means to the sequence.

The initial parameter estimation is carried out for all calibration groups using the data up to the end of January 2013. Relevant quantities (parameter estimates, the 1,000 parameter particles and corresponding weights and sample likelihoods) are saved for periodic updating for all future months. Additional implementation details on the calibration are given in Sec. III.

II. INPUT VARIABLES AND DATA

Subsection II.1 describes the input variables used in the quantitative model. Currently, the same set of input variables is common to all of the economies under the CRI's coverage. Future enhancements to the CRI system will allow different input variables for different economies. The effect of each of the variables on the PD output will be discussed in the empirical analysis of Sec. IV.

Subsection II.2 gives the data sources and relevant details of the data sources. There are two categories of data sources: current and historical. Data sources used for current data need to be updated in a timely manner so that daily updates of PD forecasts are meaningful. They also need to be comprehensive in their current coverage of firms. Data sources that are comprehensive for current data may not necessarily have comprehensive historical coverage for different economies. Thus, other data sources are merged in order to obtain comprehensive coverage of historical and current data.

Subsection II.3 indicates the fields from the data sources that are used to construct the input variables. For some of the fields, proxies need to be used for a firm if the preferred field is not available for that firm.

Subsection II.4 discusses the definition and sources of defaults and of other exits used in the CRI.

II.1. Input Variables

Following the notation that was introduced in Sec. I, firm i's input variables at time $t = n\Delta t$ are represented by the vector $X_i(n) = (W(n), U_i(n))$ consisting of a vector $W(n)$ that is common to all firms in the same economy, and a firm-specific vector $U_i(n)$ which is observable from the date the firm's first FS is released, until the month end before the month in which the firm exits, if it does exit.

In Duan *et al.* (2012), different variables that are commonly used in the literature were tested as candidates for the elements of $W(n)$ and $U_i(n)$. The 2 common variables and 10 firm-specific variables, as described below, were selected as having the greatest predictive power for corporate defaults in the United States. In the current stage of development, this same set of 12 input variables is used for all economies. Future development will include variable selection for firms in different economies.

- Common variables

  The vector $W(n)$ contains two elements, which are:

  (1) Stock index return: the trailing one-year simple return on a major stock index of the economy;

(2) Interest rate: a representative 3-month short term interest rate.

- Firm-specific variables

The 10 firm-specific input variables are transformations of measures of 6 different firm characteristics. The six firm characteristics are:

(1) volatility-adjusted leverage;
(2) liquidity;
(3) profitability;
(4) relative size;
(5) market misvaluation/future growth opportunities; and
(6) idiosyncratic volatility.

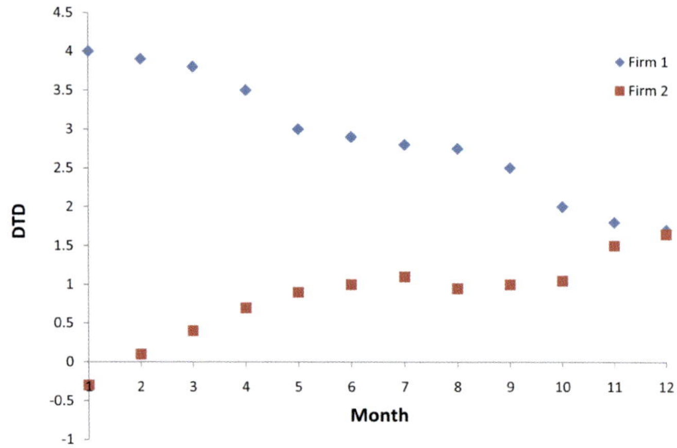

Figure 2. Two firms with all current values equal to each other, but DTD trending in the opposite direction.

Volatility-adjusted leverage is measured as the DTD in a Merton-type model. The calculation of DTD used by the CRI allows a meaningful DTD for financial firms, a critical sector that must be excluded from most DTD computations. This calculation is detailed in Sec. III.

Liquidity is measured as a ratio of cash and short-term investments to total assets. Profitability is measured as a ratio of net income to total assets. Relative size is measured as the logarithm of the ratio of market capitalization to the economy's median market capitalization.

Duan *et al.* (2012) transformed these first four characteristics into level and trend versions of the measures. For each of these characteristics, the level is computed as the one-year average of the measure, and the trend is computed as the current value of the measure minus the one-year average of the measure. The level and trend of a measure has seldom been used in the academic or industry literature for default prediction, and Duan *et al.* (2012) found that using the level and trend significantly improves the predictive power of the model for short-term horizons.

To understand the intuition behind using level and trend of a measure as opposed to using just the current value, consider the case of two firms with the same current value for all measures. If the level and trend transformations were not performed, only the current values would be used and the two firms would have identical PD. Suppose that for the first firm the DTD had reached its current level from a high level, and for the second firm the DTD had reached its current level from a lower level (see Fig. 2). The first firm's leverage is increasing (worsening) and the second firm's leverage is decreasing (improving). If there is a momentum effect in DTD, then firm 1 should have a higher PD than firm 2.

Duan *et al.* (2012) found evidence of the momentum effect in DTD, liquidity, profitability and size. For the other two firm characteristics, applying the level and trend transformation did not improve the predictive power of the model.

One of the remaining two firm characteristics is the market mis-valuation/future growth opportunities characteristic, which is taken as the market-to-book asset ratio and measured as a ratio of market capitalization and total liabilities to total assets. One can see whether the market mis-valuation effect or the future growth opportunities effect dominates this measure by looking at whether the parameter for this variable is positive or negative. This will be further discussed in the empirical analysis of Sec. IV.

The last firm characteristic is the idiosyncratic volatility which is taken as SIGMA, following Shumway (2001). SIGMA is computed by regressing the daily returns of the firm's market capitalization against the daily returns of the economy's stock index, for the previous 250 days. SIGMA is defined to be the standard deviation of the residuals of this regression. Using daily returns is to ensure that SIGMA provides an accurate and timely measure of idiosyncratic risk of individual companies. Shumway (2001) reasons that SIGMA should be logically related to bankruptcy since firms with more variable cash flows and therefore more variable stock returns relative to a market index are likely to have a higher probability of bankruptcy.

Finally, the vector $U_i(n)$ contains 10 elements, consisting of:

(1) Level of DTD.
(2) Trend of DTD.
(3) Level of (Cash + Short term investments)/Total assets, abbreviated as CASH/TA.
(4) Trend of CASH/TA.
(5) Level of Net income/Total assets, abbreviated as NI/TA.
(6) Trend of NI/TA.
(7) Level of log (Firm market capitalization/Economy's median market capitalization), abbreviated as SIZE.
(8) Trend of SIZE.
(9) Current value of (Market capitalization + Total liabilities)/Total asset, abbreviated as M/B.
(10) Current value of SIGMA.

The data fields that are needed to compute DTD and short-term investments are described in Subsec. II.3. The remaining data fields required are straightforward and standard. The computation for DTD is explained in Sec. III.

II.2. Data Sources

There are two data sources that are used for the daily PD forecast updates: Thomson Reuters Datastream and the Bloomberg Data License Back Office Product. Many of the common factors such as short-term interest rates and macroeconomic data are retrieved from Datastream.

Firm-specific data comes from Bloomberg's Back Office Product which delivers daily update files by region via FTP after respective market closes. All relevant data is extracted from the FTP files and uploaded into the CRI database for storage. From this, the necessary fields are extracted and joined with previous months of data.

The Back Office Product includes daily market capitalization data based on closing share prices and also includes new FSs as companies release them. Firms will often have multiple versions of FSs within the same period, with different accounting standards, filing statuses (most recent, preliminary, original, reclassified or restated), currencies or consolidated/unconsolidated indicators. A major challenge lies in prioritizing these FSs to decide which data should be used. The priority rules are described in Sec. III.

The firm coverage of the Back Office Product is of sufficient quality that nearly 34,000 firms can be updated on a daily basis in the 106 economies under the CRI's coverage. While the current coverage is quite comprehensive, historical data from the Back Office Product can be sparse for certain economies. For this reason, various other databases are merged in order to fill out the historical data. The other databases used for historical data are: a database from the Taiwan Economics Journal (TEJ) for Taiwanese firms; a database provided by Korea University for South Korean firms; and data from Prowess for Indian firms.

With all of the databases merged together and for the 106 economies under CRI's coverage, over 60,000 exchange listed firms are in the CRI database. This includes over 30,000 firms that have been delisted at some point in time. The historical coverage of the firm data goes back to the early 1990s. In order to be included in our coverage, a company needs to have common equity traded on a stock exchange. Of these 106 economies, 71 economies have their own stock exchange (see Table A.2). For the other 35 economies under the RMI coverage, we cover companies domiciled in the economy that are quoted on a foreign exchange, either because those economies do not have a stock exchange or because data issues are preventing us from including the companies listed on the local exchange.

II.3. Constructing Input Variables

The chosen stock indices and short-term interest rates for the 71 economies with their own stock exchange under the CRI's current coverage are listed in Tables A.5 and A.6, respectively. All economies are listed by their three letter ISO code given in Table A.4.

Most of the firm-specific variables can be readily constructed from standard fields from firms' FSs in addition to daily market capitalization values. The only two exceptions are the DTD and the liquidity measure.

The calculation for DTD is explained in Sec. III. In the calculation, several variables are required. One variable is a proxy for a one-year risk-free interest rate, and the choices for each of the 71 economies are listed in Table A.7. Total assets, long-term borrowing and total liabilities are also required, but can be obtained from standard FS fields easily.

Total current liabilities are also required, and due to the relatively large numbers of firms that are missing this value, proxies have to be found. The preferred Bloomberg field for this is BS_CUR_LIAB. If this is missing, then the sum of BS_ST_BORROW, BS_OTHER_ST_LIAB, BS_CUST_ACCPT_LIAB_CUSTDY_SEC (customers' acceptance and liabilities/custody securities) and BS_SEC_SOLD_REPO_AGRMNT is used. If one, two or three of these are missing, zero is inserted for those fields, but at least one of the four fields is required.

The liquidity measure requires different fields for financial and non-financial firms. For non-financial firms, the numerator of the ratio (Cash + Short-term investments) is taken as the sum of BS_CASH_NEAR_CASH_ITEM and BS_MKT_SEC_OTHER_ST_INVEST (marketable securities and other short-term investments). If BS_MKT_SEC_OTHER_ST_INVEST is missing, substitute zero (but BS_CASH_NEAR_CASH_ITEM is required).

It was found that this sum frequently overstated the liquidity for financial firms. In place of BS_MKT_SEC_OTHER_ST_INVEST, financial firms use the sum of ARD_SEC_PURC_UNDER_AGR_TO_RESELL (securities purchased under agreement to re-sell), ARD_ST_INVEST and BS_INTERBANK_ASSET. If one or two of these are missing, zero is inserted for those fields, but at least one field is required. The "ARD" prefix indicates that these are "as reported" numbers directly from the FSs. As such, for some firms these fields may need to be adjusted to the same units before adding them to other fields.

To summarize, the firm-specific variables include: DTD, Cash/TA, NI/TA, SIZE, M/B, and SIGMA, and the statistics grouped by economy are listed in Table A.8.

II.4. Data for Defaults

The CRI database contains credit events of over 4,000 firms from 1990 to the present. The default events come from numerous sources, including Bloomberg, Compustat, CRSP, Moodys reports, TEJ, exchange websites and news sources.

The default events that are recognized by the CRI can be classified under one of the following events:

(1) Bankruptcy filing, receivership, administration, liquidation or any other legal impasse to the timely settlement of interest and/or principal payments;
(2) A missed or delayed payment of interest and/or principal, excluding delayed payments made within a grace period;
(3) Debt restructuring/distressed exchange, in which debt holders are offered a new security or package of securities that result in a diminished financial obligation (e.g., a conversion of debt to equity, debt with lower coupon or par amount, debt with lower seniority, debt with longer maturity).

The more precise sub-categories of default corporate actions are listed in Table A.9.

Delisting due to other reasons such as failure to meet listing requirements, inactive stock prices or M&A are counted as "other exits" and are not considered as default. However, firms that are delisted from an exchange and then experience a default event within 365 calendar days of the delisting will have an exit event reclassified as credit default. Technical defaults such as covenant violations are not included in our definition of default. The exit events that are not considered as defaults in the CRI system are listed in Table A.10.

In addition to the aforementioned events, there are still cases that require special attention and will be assessed on a case-by-case basis, e.g., subsidiary default. As a general rule, the CRI does not consider related party-default (e.g., subsidiary bankruptcy) as a default event. However, when a non-operating holding parent company relies heavily on its subsidiary, bankruptcy by the subsidiary will cause a considerable economic impact on the parent company. Such cases will be reviewed and final classifications made.

Complete statistics of the total number of firms, number of defaults and number of other exits in each of the 71 economies from 1992 to 2012 are listed in Table A.11.

III. IMPLEMENTATION DETAILS

Section I described the modeling framework underlying the current implementation of the CRI system. It focused on theory rather than the details encountered in an operational implementation. The present section describes how the CRI system handles more specific issues.

Subsection III.1 describes implementation details related to data, mainly dealing with data cleaning and missing data. Subsection III.2 describes the specific computation of DTD used by the CRI system that leads to meaningful DTD for financial firms. Subsection III.3 explains how the calibration previously described in Subsec. I.2 can be implemented. Subsection III.4 gives the implementation details relevant to the daily output. This includes an explanation of the various modifications needed to compute daily PD so that the daily PD is consistent with the usual month end PD, and a description of the computation of the aggregate PDs provided by the CRI.

III.1. Data Treatment

Fitting data to monthly frequency: Historical end of month data for every firm in an economy is required to calibrate the model. For daily data such as market capitalization, interest rates and stock index values, the last day of the month for which there is valid data is used.

Up to the October 2012 calibration, FS variables data were used, starting from the period end of the statement lagged by 3 months. This is to ensure that predictions are made based on information that was available at the time the prediction was made. However, this treatment can be over-conservative, and many companies actually release their FSs quicker than 3 months. Therefore, we implement a new logic and we start using the values in an FS as soon as its latest revision was put into the RMI database, unless the FS' release was delayed for more than 3 months. If there was no revision to an FS, the originally released FS is used. Whenever the latest revision is available more than 3 months after the period end, we revert to the previous logic. We start including the FS before the latest revision is actually available as a compromise, to avoid situations like later minor revisions of the FS holding back more up-to-date information. It should be noted that the new approach was only applied for FS input into the RMI database after February 2011, as the revision dates were not accurately recorded before this date. The CRI considers FS variables to be valid for one year without restriction, after they were first used.

Priority of FSs: As described in Subsec. II.2, data provided in Bloomberg's Back Office Product can include numerous versions of FSs within the same period. If there are multiple FSs with the same period end, priority rules must be followed in order to determine which to use. The formulation and implementation of these rules are major challenges and areas of continuing development.

The first rule is to prioritize by consolidated/unconsolidated status. This status is relevant only to firms in India, Japan, South Korea and Taiwan, so this rule is only relevant in those economies. Most firms in these economies issue unconsolidated FSs more frequently than consolidated ones, so these are given higher priority. This simple prioritization can, however, lead to cases where the FSs used switch from consolidated statements to unconsolidated statements and back again. More specifically, in South Korea and Taiwan, where corporate structures are biased toward large holding companies, the effect of this switching means that the DTD calculation is not meaningful for these holding companies. Therefore, as of October 2013 calibration, in the case of South Korea, and November 2013 calibration, in the case of Taiwan, if a company has released at least one consolidated FS over the last 12 months, all unconsolidated FS will be ignored.

If, after the first prioritization rule has been applied, there are still multiple FSs, the second rule is applied. This is prioritization by fiscal period. In most economies, annual statements are required to be audited, whereas other fiscal periods are not necessarily audited. The order of priority from highest to lowest is, therefore: annual, semi-annual, quarterly, cumulative, and finally other fiscal periods. We have observed that the capital structure breakdown reported by Australian domiciled-banks differs between annual and semi-annual reports, leading to DTD calculations that are not meaningful. Because of this, as of October 2013 calibration, we only use data from annual FSs for Australian banks.

The third prioritization rule is based on filing status. The "Most Recent" statement is used before the "Original" statement, which is used before the "Preliminary" statement.

The final prioritization rule is based on the accounting standard. Here, FSs that are reported using Generally Accepted Accounting Principles (GAAP) are given higher priority than FSs that are reported using International Financial Reporting Standards (IFRS). If an accounting standard is not indicated at all, the FS is not used.

Financial statement entries with all other descriptors the same but with different filing statuses will be grouped together. For each variable separately, the variable value is taken from the highest priority FS within the group where the value is non-null.

For example, we may consider two FS entries having the same period end, and they both are from annual, consolidated statements, and both use the same accounting standard, but the first entry is classified as the "Most Recent" entry and the second is "Original" entry. Suppose the total assets and total liabilities are reported in the "Original" entry, and in the "Most Recent" entry only the total liabilities have been updated but the total assets have been replaced with a null value, then the total liabilities will be taken from the "Most Recent" entry while the total assets will be taken from the "Original" entry.

The rule mentioned above allows us to group the "Most Recent" and the "Original" entries together, as Bloomberg occasionally only updates values that change without updating other values. If the entries are not grouped, most of the variables would have null values.

One variable that requires special attention is the net income. Net income is a flow variable and needs to be adjusted based on the period of the FS. More specifically, we transform the net income into a monthly net income by dividing the net income by the number of months that the FS covers. Due to the different coverage periods, several types of net income can still be used. For example, the monthly net income can be computed from the annual net income divided by 12, the semi-annual net income divided by 6 and the quarterly net income divided by 3. When the monthly net income can be obtained from different sources simultaneously, the quarterly net income will have higher priority than any others because it covers a more recent period of time.

Treatment of stale market capitalization prices: The market capitalization of a firm is required in a few input variables: DTD, SIZE, M/B and SIGMA. For most firms, the market capitalization is available from Bloomberg on a daily basis.

A check on the trading volume of shares is used to remove stale prices. Specifically, if there are more than two consecutive days of identical market capitalization prices, subsequent identical prices are removed only if the trading volume is equal to zero. This is to avoid, for example, cases where the shares of a company are under a trading suspension but the market capitalization data is incorrectly carried forward.

An exception is for Indian companies, where it is common for some companies to have market capitalizations reported only once a month with several consecutive months having identical prices and positive trading volume. These prices are very likely not to be accurate reflections of the firms' value. So, the trading volume is not checked for Indian firms and market capitalizations are excluded after more than two repeated prices.

For some firms, there are gaps in the market capitalization data provided by Bloomberg. Previously, the first recourse was to use the share price multiplied by the shares outstanding listed in the balance sheet and multiplied by an adjustment factor that Bloomberg provides to account for splits, dividends, etc. However, this data is frequently in error and using the shares outstanding as the previous available market capitalization divided by the price on that day was found to be more reliable.

If the gap in market capitalization data is more than a year, then the previous computation using the shares outstanding from the balance sheet is again used. If there are still remaining gaps in the data, then shares outstanding from Compustat data is used.

Currency conversion: Currency conversions are required if the market capitalization or any of the FS variables are reported in a currency different than the currency of the economy. If a currency conversion is required, the foreign exchange rate used is that reported at the relevant market close. For firms traded in Asia and Asia-Pacific, the Tokyo closing rate is used; for firms traded in Western Europe, the London closing rate is used; and for firms traded in North America, the New York closing rate is used. For market capitalizations, the FX rate used is for the date that the market capitalization is reported. For FS variables, the FX rate used is for the date of the period end of the statement.

Provisions for missing values and outliers: Missing values and outliers are dealt with by a three-step procedure. In the first step, the 10 firm-specific input variables are computed for all firms and all months. In the second step, outliers are eliminated by winsorization. In the final step, missing values are replaced under certain conditions.

The first step is to compute the input variables and to determine which are missing. As mentioned previously, FS variables are carried forward for one year after the date that they are first used. This is generally three months after the period end of the statement. If no FS is available for the company within this year, then the FS variable will be missing. For market capitalization, if there is no valid market capitalization value within the calendar month, then the value is set to missing.

For illiquid stocks, if there has been no valid market capitalization value for a firm within the last 90 calendar days, then the market capitalization is deemed to not properly reflect the value of the firm. The firm is considered to have exited with a non-default event. Once the firm starts trading again and a new FS is released, the firm can enter back into the calibration. With regard to historical PD, the PD can be reported again once there are enough valid variables.

With regard to the level variables, the current month and the last 11 months are averaged to compute the level. A minimum of six observations are required to calculate the level variables. However, this condition is not enforced during the first six months of a firm. In the absence of six valid observations after the initial six months of a company, the level variable will be considered as missing.

To compute the trend variables, the level is subtracted from the current month value. If the current month value is missing, the trend variable is set to be the last valid value during the previous one year.

The value of M/B is set to be missing if any of the following values are missing: market capitalization, total liabilities or total assets of the firm. For the computation of SIGMA, at least 50 valid returns over the last 250 days of possible returns are required for the regression. If there are less than 50 valid returns, SIGMA is set to be missing.

In this way, the eight trend and level variables as well as M/B and SIGMA are computed and identified as missing or present. Winsorization can then be performed as a second step to eliminate outliers. The volume of outliers is too large to be able to determine whether each one is valid or not, so winsorization applies a floor and a cap on each of the variables. The historical 0.1 percentile and 99.9 percentile for all firms in the economy are recorded for each of the 10 variables. Any values that exceed these levels are set to equal these boundary values.

With a winsorization level and 0.1 percentile and 99.9 percentile, the boundary values still may not be reasonable. For example, NI/TA levels of nearly −25, meaning an annual net income −25 times larger than the total assets of a firm, has been observed at this stage. In these cases, a more aggressive winsorization level is applied, until the boundary values are reasonable. Thus, the winsorization level is economy — and variable-specific, and will depend on the data quality for that economy and variable. Winsorization levels different from the default of 0.1 percentile and 99.9 percentile are indicated in Table A.8. In addition to the special winsorization levels indicated in this table, as of October 2013 calibration; we also apply a winsorization of 0.1 and 99.5 percentile for market-to-book ratio in the Emerging Markets and Europe calibration group.

A third and final step can be taken to deal with missing values. If during a particular month, no variable is missing for a particular firm, the PD can then be computed. If six or more of these 10 variables are missing, there is deemed to be too many missing observations and no replacement shall be made.

If between 1 and 5 variables are missing out of the 10, the first step is to trace back for at most 12 months to use previous values of these variables instead. If this does not succeed in replacing all of the variables, a replacement by sector medians is done. The median is for the financial or non-financial firms (as indicated by their Bloomberg industry sector code) within the economy during that month. Replacement by the sector median should have a neutral effect on the PD of the firm; the firm is assessed by the other variables that it does have values for. This sector median is always performed in calibration. However, when reporting historical PD, the sector replacement is not done if it results in a relative change in PD of 10% or more where the initial PD was at or above 100 bps, or an absolute change in PD of 10 bps or more where the initial PD was below 100 bps.

However, this treatment of missing values is not always meaningful and occasionally results in counter intuitive patterns in a company's historical PD. Accordingly, the RMI CRI team is reconsidering the treatment of missing values in two stages of development, with the first stage focusing on the replacement of missing values in the initial phase of a company, and the second stage of development focusing on later periods in the company's time series. The first stage has been implemented and is explained below.

In the initial phase of a company — up until 6 months after IPO — it can be expected that the company's data availability and quality is relatively low due to, for example, a delay in the issuance of FSs or illiquid trading. So, many companies require missing value replacements during that period. However, as observed in our data, replacing the missing values during these first six months with a sector median affects a company's PD in an unmeaningful way, sometimes resulting in extreme spikes and falls in the company's PD. Since this occurs at the beginning of a company's history, there are no previous PD values to compare to as can be done at later periods in a company's history.

Hence, in order to avoid this, as of the 2013 February calibration, we set a criterion to start the missing value treatment only six months after the beginning of a company's data. Doing so ensures that PDs in the beginning of a company's history are more reflective of the true creditworthiness of that individual company.

The RMI CRI team is currently developing a method to deal with missing values later in the history of a company in a more meaningful way. This second stage of development for treating missing values will be completed in the coming months.

Inclusion/exclusion of companies for calibration: Firms are included within an economy for calibration when the primary listing of the firm is on an exchange in the economy. This ensures that all firms within the economy are subject to the same disclosure and accounting rules.

There are a relatively small number of firms that are dually listed, in which two corporations listed in different exchanges operate as a single entity but retain separate legal status. In the CRI system, a combined company will be assigned to the single economy it is most associated with. An example is the Rio Tinto Group. This consists of Rio Tinto plc, listed in the UK; and Rio Tinto Limited, listed in Australia. Most of Rio Tinto's operations are in Australia rather than the UK, so Rio Tinto is assigned to Australia.

In the US, firms traded on the OTC markets or the Pink Sheets are not considered as exchange listed so are not included in calibration or in the reporting of PD forecasts. Many of these firms are small or start-up firms. Including this large group of companies would skew the calibration and the aggregate results. The TSX Venture Exchange in Canada also contains only small and start-up firms, so firms listed here are also excluded.

Other examples include Taiwan's GreTai Securities Market and Singapore's Catalist. The challenge for markets outside of the US or Canada is that the data on whether firms are listed on the smaller markets rather than the main board is difficult to obtain. For all economies besides the US and Canada, there is continuing work being done in the CRI system to exclude firms that are not listed on major exchanges within a country.

Firms that record an exit (other than due to no trading for 90 calendar days) will not enter back into the calibration even if the firm continues to trade and issues FSs, as that can happen after the firms declare bankruptcy. There are two exceptions to this exclusion. The first, determined on a case by case basis, is if the firm should be deemed to have re-emerged from bankruptcy. The second exception is for all firms in China, where two situations are prevalent. The first situation is that the firm experiences few repercussions from the default and continues operating normally. The other situation is for one firm to take over a defaulted firm's listing. This happens due to the limited supply of exchange listings. Both of these situations can be considered as emerging from default, so the CRI system enters all of these companies back into the calibration as new companies.

III.2. DTD Computation

The DTD computation used in the CRI system is not a standard one. Standard computations exclude financial firms, which is of course a critical part of any economy. Thus, the standard DTD computation must be extended to give meaningful estimates for financial firms as well. Duan and Wang (2012) have provided a review of different DTD calculations with several examples for financial and non-financial firms.

The description of the specialized DTD computation starts with a brief description of the Merton (1974) model. Merton's model makes the simplifying assumption that firms are financed by equity and a single zero-coupon bond with maturity date T and principal L. The asset value of the firm V_t follows a geometric Brownian motion:

$$dV_t = \mu V_t dt + \sigma V_t dB_t. \tag{34}$$

Here, B_t is the standard Brownian motion, μ is the drift of the asset value in the physical measure, and σ is the volatility of the asset value. Equity holders receive the excess value of the firm above the principal of the zero-coupon bond and have limited liability, so the equity value at maturity is: $E_t = \max(V_t - L, 0)$. This is just a call option payoff on the asset value with a strike value of L. Thus, the Black–Scholes option pricing formula can be used to calculate the equity value at times t before T,

$$E_t = V_t N(d_+) - e^{-r(T-t)} L N(d_-), \tag{35}$$

where r is the risk-free rate, $N(\cdot)$ is the standard normal cumulative distribution function, and

$$d_\pm = \frac{\log\left(\frac{V_t}{L}\right) + \left(r \pm \frac{\sigma^2}{2}\right)(T-t)}{\sigma\sqrt{T-t}}. \tag{36}$$

Following the Merton (1974) model, the probability of the company's default at time T evaluated at time t is $N(-\text{DTD}_t)$, where DTD at time t is defined as:

$$\text{DTD}_t = \frac{\log\left(\frac{V_t}{L}\right) + \left(\mu - \frac{\sigma^2}{2}\right)(T-t)}{\sigma\sqrt{T-t}}. \tag{37}$$

The standard KMV assumptions given in Crosbie and Bohn (2003) are to set the time to maturity $T-t$ at a value of one year, and the principal of the zero-coupon bond L to a value equal to the firms current liabilities plus one half of its long-term debt. Here, the current liabilities and long-term debt are taken from the firm's FSs. If the firm is missing the current liabilities field, then various substitutes for this field can be used, as described in Subsec. II.3.

This is a poor assumption of the debt level for financial firms, since they typically have large liabilities, such as deposit accounts, that are neither classified as current liabilities nor long-term debt. Thus, using these standard assumptions means ignoring a large part of the debt of financial firms.

To properly account for the debt of financial firms, Duan (2010) included a fraction δ of a firm's other liabilities. The other liabilities are defined as the firm's total liabilities minus both the short and long-term debt. The debt level L then becomes the current liabilities plus half of the long-term debt plus the fraction δ multiplied by the other liabilities, so that the debt level is a function of δ. The standard KMV assumptions are then a special case where $\delta = 0$.

The fraction δ can be optimized along with μ and σ in the maximum likelihood estimation method developed in Duan (1994; 2000) Following Duan *et al.* (2012), the firm's market value of assets is standardized by its book value A_t, so that the scaling effect from a major investment or financing by the firm will not distort the time series from which the parameter values are estimated. Thus, the log-likelihood function is:

$$\mathcal{L}(\mu, \sigma, \delta) = -\frac{n-1}{2}\log(2\pi) - \frac{1}{2}\sum_{t=2}^{n}\log(\sigma^2 h_t) - \sum_{t=2}^{n}\log\left(\frac{\hat{V}_t(\sigma,\delta)}{A_t}\right) - \sum_{t=2}^{n}\log[N(\hat{d}_+(\hat{V}_t(\sigma,\delta),\sigma,\delta))] - \frac{1}{2\sigma^2}\sum_{t=2}^{n}\frac{1}{h_t}\left[\log\left(\frac{\hat{V}_t(\sigma,\delta)}{A_t} \times \frac{A_{t-1}}{\hat{V}_{t-1}(\sigma,\delta)}\right) - \left(\mu - \frac{\sigma^2}{2}\right)h_t\right]^2, \tag{38}$$

where n is the number of days with observations of the equity value in the sample, $\hat{V}_t$ is the implied asset value found by solving Eq. (35), $\hat{d}_+$ is computed with Eq. (36) using the implied asset value, and h_t is the number of trading days as a fraction of the year between observations $t-1$ and t. Notice that the implied asset value and $\hat{d}_+$ are dependent on δ by virtue of the dependence of L on δ.

Implementation of DTD computation: The DTD at the end of each month is needed for every firm in order to calibrate the forward intensity model. A moving window, consisting of the last one year of data before each month end is used to compute the month end DTD. Daily market capitalization data based on closing prices is used for the equity value in the implied asset value computation of Eq. (35). If there are fewer than 50 days of valid observations for the market capitalization, then the DTD value is set to missing. An observation is valid if there is positive trading volume that day. If the trading volume is not available, the observation is assumed to be valid if the value for the market capitalization changes often enough. The precise criterion is as follows: if the market capitalization does not change for three days or more in a row, the first day is taken as a valid observation and the remaining days with the same value are set to missing.

A straightforward idea for the DTD computation is to first estimate the three variables μ, σ and δ via maximizing the log-likelihood function (38) over $\sigma \geq 0$ and $0 \leq \delta \leq 1$, and then to calculate the DTD from Eq. (37). Let $(\hat{\mu}, \hat{\sigma}, \hat{\delta})$ be an optimal solution to the maximization problem. By direct calculation, it is not hard to see that

$$\hat{\mu} = \frac{\hat{\sigma}^2}{2} + \frac{1}{\sum_{t=2}^{n} h_t}\log\left(\frac{\hat{V}_n(\hat{\sigma},\hat{\delta})}{A_n} \times \frac{A_1}{\hat{V}_1(\hat{\sigma},\hat{\delta})}\right). \tag{39}$$

In view of this, maximizing the three-dimensional function $\mathcal{L}(\mu, \sigma, \delta)$ can be equivalently reduced to maximizing the two-dimensional function $\tilde{\mathcal{L}}(\sigma, \delta)$ taking the form

$$\tilde{\mathcal{L}}(\sigma, \delta) = -\frac{n-1}{2}\log(2\pi) - \frac{1}{2}\sum_{t=2}^{n}\log(\sigma^2 h_t) - \sum_{t=2}^{n}\log\left(\frac{\hat{V}_t(\sigma,\delta)}{A_t}\right) - \frac{1}{2\sigma^2}\left\{\sum_{t=2}^{n}\frac{1}{h_t} \times \left[\log\left(\frac{\hat{V}_t(\sigma,\delta)}{A_t} \times \frac{A_{t-1}}{\hat{V}_{t-1}(\sigma,\delta)}\right)\right]^2 - \frac{1}{\sum_{t=2}^{n} h_t} \times \left[\log\left(\frac{\hat{V}_n(\hat{\sigma},\hat{\delta})}{A_n} \times \frac{A_1}{\hat{V}_1(\hat{\sigma},\hat{\delta})}\right)\right]^2\right\}. \tag{40}$$

However, with quarterly FSs there will never be more than three changes in the corporate structure (defined in this model by L and A_t) throughout the year, leading to possibly unstable estimates of δ. This problem is mitigated by performing a two-stage optimization for σ and δ.

In the first stage, the maximization of $\tilde{\mathcal{L}}(\sigma, \delta)$ for each firm is performed over both σ and δ. For each firm, at the first month in which DTD can be computed, the maximization is constrained in $\sigma \geq 0$ and $0 \leq \delta \leq 1$. Thereafter, at month n, the maximization is still constrained in $\sigma \geq 0$ while δ is constrained in the interval $[\max(0, \hat{\delta}_{n-1} - 0.05), \min(1, \hat{\delta}_{n-1} + 0.05)]$, where $\hat{\delta}_{n-1}$ is the estimate of δ made in the previous month. In other words, a 10% band around the previous estimate of δ (where that band is floored with 0 and capped with 1) is applied so that the estimates do not fluctuate too much from month to month.

However, for many firms, the estimate of δ would frequently lie on the boundary of the constraining interval, meaning that the estimates of δ were not stable. Therefore, a second stage is implemented to impose greater stability. All financial sector firms in the same economy are assumed to share the same estimate of δ, chosen to be the average of all its individual estimates. The same is done for non-financial firms. Accordingly, with δ being fixed to be the sector average, the original maximization of $\tilde{\mathcal{L}}(\sigma, \delta)$ is reduced to a one-dimensional maximization in σ. Thus, this maximization is used to perform the estimates of σ for each firm.

Since the first stage is done to obtain a stable sector-average estimate of δ, the criteria used to include a firm-month is more strict. In the first stage, a two-year window is used instead of one year, and a minimum of 250 days of valid observations of the market capitalization are required instead of 50. If a firm has less than 250 days of valid observations within the last two years of a particular month end, δ will not be estimated for that firm and that month end.

It was found that after applying the two-stage procedure described above, the estimate of μ was frequently unstable and could lower the explanatory power of DTD. For example, suppose a firm has a large drop in its implied asset value in January 2011, so that the estimated μ is negative for the DTD calculation at the end of December 2011. If there is little change in the company in January 2012, then the drop in implied asset value in January 2011 is no longer within the observation window for the DTD calculation at the end of January 2012. There will be a large increase in the estimated μ, resulting in a substantial improvement of the DTD just because of the moving observation window. To avoid this problem, we now set μ to be equal to $\sigma^2/2$. So in calculating DTD, the second term in the numerator of Eq. (37) is eliminated.

In summary, the DTD for each firm is computed using the economy and sector (financial or non-financial) average for δ in that month, and the estimate of σ based on the last year of data for the firm.

Carrying out this two-stage procedure would take about 70 hours of computation time on a single PC, given the millions of firm months that are required. However, each of the stages is parallelizable. In the first stage the DTD can be computed independently between firms. In the second stage, once the sector averages of the δ have been computed for each month, the DTD can again be computed independently between firms. In the current CRI system, by using a computational grid administered by the NUS Computer Center, the DTD computational time for all firms over the full history of twenty years takes only about 3.5 hours.

III.3. Calibration

Implementation: As shown in Sec. I, the calibration of the forward intensity model involves multiple maximum pseudo-likelihood estimations, where the pseudo-likelihood functions are given in Eq. (13). The maximizations are on the logarithm of these expressions, and the default parameters' maximization is performed independently from the non-default exit parameters. Parameter estimates for the entire horizon up to five years for the default and non-default exits can be obtained directly from the NS function.

A few input variables have an unambiguous effect on a firm's probability of default. Increments of both the level and trend of DTD, CASH/TA, and NI/TA should indicate that a firm is becoming more creditworthy and should lead to a decreasing PD. For large and relatively clean data sets such as the US, an unconstrained optimization leads to parameter values which mostly have the expected sign. For each of the DTD level and trend, CASH/TA level and trend, and NI/TA level, the default parameters at all horizons are negative. A negative default parameter at a horizon means that if the variable increases, the forward intensity will decrease (based on Eq. (6)), so that the conditional default probability at that horizon will decrease.

Grouping for economies: There are not enough defaults in some small economies and calibrations of these individual economies are not statistically meaningful. In order to ensure that there are enough defaults for calibration, the 71 economies are categorized into groups according to similarities in their stage of development and their geographic locations. Within these groups, the economies are combined and calibrated together.

Starting from the August 2012 calibration, Canada and the US remain in the same calibration group, and the developed economies of Asia-Pacific (Australia, Hong Kong, Japan, Singapore, South Korea, Taiwan and New Zealand) form another calibration group. China and India, the two major emerging economies of Asia Pacific are each calibrated as individual groups. All the European countries covered by the CRI are in a single calibration group, which now includes Israel, Russia and Turkey. The other emerging economies of Asia Pacific (Kazakhastan, Indonesia, Malaysia, Pakistan, Philippines, Sri Lanka, Thailand and Vietnam) are grouped together with the Latin American economies (Argentina, Brazil, Colombia, Chile, Mexico, Peru, and Venezuela), Middle-East economies (Bahrain, Jordan, Kuwait, Saudi Arabia and United Arab Emirates) and African economies (Egypt, Morocco, Nigeria and South Africa), to form the "emerging markets" calibration group.

All economies in these new calibration groups share the same coefficients for all variables except for the benchmark risk-free interest rate variable. The benchmark interest rates coefficient will be allowed to vary, because different economies based in different currencies naturally have different dependencies on their interest rates and the interest rate levels can differ significantly across economies. After adopting the euro, all eurozone countries use Germany's three-month Bubill rate as this is more reflective of monetary rather than sovereign credit conditions in each economy, which is the intent of this variable. For the period before joining the eurozone, their own interest rates are used.

In addition, the benchmark interest rate is entered as the current value minus the historical month-end mean. This allows the variable to reflect its value relative to the historical average. When an economy does not have enough default events to identify a separate interest rate coefficient, the interest rate variable will be disabled for that economy by inputting a zero value for the whole time series. In fact, that is also why we de-mean all interest rate series so that setting the interest rate series of a particular economy to zero, when necessary, does not induce a bias by the base economy in the same group.

Since all eurozone countries except Germany do not have enough default events prior to joining the eurozone, their benchmark interest rate is entered as zero for that period. Among the non-eurozone members of the European group, Denmark, Norway, Sweden and the UK each have separate coefficients for the benchmark interest rate. Switzerland and Iceland do not use this variable for their whole history.

In the Developed Asia-Pacific group, all economies have their own coefficient for the benchmark interest rate, except for Japan and New Zealand who share the same coefficient. For the North American group, both Canada and the US have their own coefficient for the benchmark interest rate.

In the Emerging Markets group, there are insufficient defaults in the Latin American economies to calibrate individual economy benchmark interest rate coefficients in a statistically significant way, so all Latin American economies share the same benchmark interest rate coefficient. Among the Asian economies in the Emerging Markets group, Indonesia, Malaysia, and the Philippines have their own coefficient for the benchmark interest rate, while Vietnam does not use this variable. All the other economies in the Emerging Markets group share the same benchmark interest rate coefficient. Indonesia also has its own intercept and uses its own coefficients for the stock index return, CASH/TA level and Relative Size level. These coefficients are required because these characteristics for defaulting firms in Indonesia are substantially different than in other economies. Separate coefficients are required to improve the accuracy of the PD forecasts. In October 2013, an additional 50 default events were collected for Indonesia. With these additional events, a re-assessment of the special treatment of Indonesia was called for. Based on our analysis, as of now Indonesia only uses its own coefficients for interest rate and relative size, indicating that the two variables are still significantly different compared to other economies in the Emerging Markets group. The common Emerging Markets coefficient for the CASH/TA level is now used for Indonesian companies.

Relative size: For the calibration data set, the median market cap of firms in an economy for each month end includes the market cap from the last trading day of each firm in the month. If a firm does not trade in a particular month, the firm's market cap is not included in the median. For certain economies, many firms are illiquid and the median market cap experiences large variations due to the change in composition of firms rather than the market value of the firms. Another problem is data quality at the beginning of the historical sample: if a data provider starts including the market cap for a large number of firms in one month compared to the previous, there can be a large jump in the median market cap.

To avoid this problem, we use a combination of the economy's stock index and the economy's median market cap as the divisor in the Relative Size variable:

(1) We choose a recent month where there is a more complete set of firms in the economy that have trading activity, and calculate the ratio of the economy's median market cap to stock index value at the end of the month.
(2) For each month, the divisor for the Relative Size variable of firms in the economy is taken as the month end stock index multiplied by that ratio.

III.4. Daily Output

Individual firms' PD: In computing the pseudo-log-likelihood functions in Eq. (13), only the end of month data is needed. The data needs to be extended to daily values in order to produce daily PDs.

For the level variables, the last 12 end-of-month observations (before averaging) are combined with the current value. The current value is scaled by a fraction equal to the current day of the month divided by the number of calendar days in the month. The earliest monthly value is scaled by one minus this fraction. The sum is then divided by the number of valid monthly observations, with the current value and the earliest monthly value jointly having the weight of one observation if either or both are not missing. Not performing this scaling can lead to an artificial jump in PD at the beginning of the month. When performing the scaling, the change in level is more gradual throughout the month.

SIGMA is computed by regressing the daily returns of the firm's market capitalization against the daily returns of the economy's stock index for the previous 250 days.

Exclusion rule for Mergers & Acquisitions: Mergers & Acquisitions (M&A) events are common occurrences. When an important M&A deal is closed, the Market Capitalization (MC) of the acquirer changes immediately as the MC of the acquirer will now reflect the joint value of the acquirer and the target. However, the FS will not immediately reflect the new situation. In this case, the DTD and market-to-book ratio, which are important inputs for the PD computation, will be distorted due to a mismatch in the MC and the FS variables. In order to ensure the accuracy and reliability of our PD estimates, we apply a rule to disable PD calculations for companies that are involved in important M&A deals.

An important M&A deal is defined as an M&A event on which all the following three criteria apply:

(1) Upon the deal's completion, the acquiring company owns 20% or more of the target company.
(2) The size of the deal is material to the acquirer. This is measured in terms of total assets. If α is the percentage of the target that is being acquired, the size is considered material if the product of α and the total assets of the target is greater than or equal to 20% of the total assets of the acquirer.
(3) The change in MC is material, with the largest absolute daily MC return, within 20 days of the M&A completion day, larger than or equal to 5%.

In the event of an important M&A, the PDs of the acquirer will be not be computed until we are able to include FS variables reflecting the new situation (typically between 3 and 6 months after deal completion). The RMI CRI team is currently developing a method to deal with M&A cases more systematically, and will avoid having to disable PDs for companies involved in an important M&A deal.

Aggregating PD: The CRI provides term structures of the probability distributions for the number of defaults as well as the expected number of defaults for different groups of firms. The companies are grouped by economy (using each firm's country of domicile), by sector (using the firm's Bloomberg industrial sector code) and sectors within economies. With the individual firms' PD, the expected number of defaults is trivial to compute. The algorithm used to compute the probability distribution of the number of defaults was originally reported in Anderson *et al.* (2003). It assumes conditional independence and uses a fast recursive scheme to compute the necessary probability distribution.

Note that while this algorithm is currently used to produce the probability distribution of the number of defaults within an economy or sector, it can easily be generalized to compute loss distributions for a portfolio manager, in which case the portfolio's exposure to each firm should be aggregated.

Inclusion of firms in aggregation: As explained in Subsec. III.1, firms are included in an economy for calibration if the firms' primary listing is on an exchange in that economy. This is to ensure that all firms in an economy are subject to the same disclosure and accounting requirements. In contrast, a firm is included in an economy's aggregate results if the firm is domiciled in that economy. This is because users typically associate firms with their economy of domicile rather than the economy where their primary listing is, if they are different. For example, the Bank of China has its primary listing in Hong Kong, but its economy of domicile is China so the Bank of China is included in the aggregation forecasts for China, and is included under China when searching for the individual PDs.

Treatment of companies after a default event: When a company experiences a default event, the CRI system discontinues the PD calculation for that company. However, if the company resumes operations after some time, it will be treated as a new company, and we continue to generate PD. The new company's PDs are not affected by the FS or market cap data prior to the event. So, the PDs calculated are independent of the PDs that were generated before the default event. On our website, the PDs are however displayed on a single graph for the convenience of our users.

In order to implement the treatment, default events are classified into hard defaults and soft defaults (see Table 1).

Hard defaults are default events that are typically permanent. In other words, companies typically cannot emerge from hard defaults. An example of a hard default is a forced liquidation of a company. PDs will not be computed after the default event unless there is an exceptional circumstance that warrants a manual intervention. General Motors (GM) is an example of such an event. Although GM filed for Chapter 11 reorganization in June 2009, the company resumed operations in March 2011. As of March 2011, after the company resumed operations, we decided to treat GM as a new company.

Table 1. Classification of default events.

Default-Action Type	Subcategory
Hard Defaults (Default events that are typically permanent)	Administration, Arrangement, Canadian CCAA, Chapter 7, Chapter 11, Chapter 15, Conservatorship, Insolvency, Japanese CRL, Judicial Management, Liquidation, Pre-Negotiated Chapter 11, Protection, Receivership, Rehabilitation, Reorganization, Restructuring, Section 304, Supreme court declaration, Winding Up, Work Out, Other, Unknown.
Soft Defaults (Default events that companies can emerge from)	Coupon & Principal Payment, Coupon Payment Only, Debt Restructuring, Interest Payment, Loan Payment, Principal Payment, ADR (Japan only), Declared Sick (India only), Rehabilitation (Thailand 1997), Unknown.

Soft defaults are default events that companies can typically emerge from. An example of a soft default is a debt restructuring. More specifically, after a soft default, if there is sufficient data for the company, then the company is assumed to have been able to continue its operations and PDs are computed. The PDs are generated once sufficient history of both the market capitalization data and the new FS data (released after the event) becomes available. Take the Australian company Marion Energy Ltd as an example, which had a debt restructuring in April 2010. We stopped calculating PD after 31 March 2010. As debt restructuring is considered as a soft default, we started calculating PD again from 30 September 2010 onwards, when data requirements were met.

This treatment does not apply to Chinese companies, based on two reasons: (1) a firm typically experiences few repercussions from the default and continues operating normally; and (2) it is common for another firm to take over a defaulted firm's listing, due to the limited supply of exchange listings. Both of these situations can be considered as emerging from default, so the CRI system enters all of these companies back into the calibration as new companies.

IV. EMPIRICAL ANALYSIS

This section presents an empirical analysis of the CRI outputs for the 71 economies with their own exchange that are currently being covered. In Subsec. IV.1, an overview is given of the default parameter estimates. Subsection IV.2 explains and provides the accuracy ratios for the different countries under the CRI coverage.

IV.1. Parameter Estimates

With 60 months of forecast horizons, 13 variables and 6 different groups of economies, tables of the parameter estimates occupy over 20 pages and are not included in this Technical Report. In Figs. B.1 and B.2, the parameter estimates are from calibrations performed in April 2014 using data up until the end of March 2014. As an example, plots of the default parameters for the US are given in figures included in Figs. B.1 and B.2 in Appendix B. In this part, a brief overview is given of the general traits and patterns seen in the default parameter estimations of the economies covered by the CRI.

Recall that if a default parameter for a variable at a particular horizon is estimated to be positive (negative) from the maximum pseudo-likelihood estimate, then an increasing value in the associated variable will lead to an increasing (decreasing) value of the forward intensity at that horizon, which in turn means an increasing (decreasing) value for the conditional default probability at that horizon.

For the stock index one-year trailing return variable, most groups have default parameters that are slightly negative in the shorter horizons and then become positive in the longer horizons. When the equity market performs well, this is only a short-term positive for firms and in the longer term, firms are actually more likely to default. This seemingly counterintuitive result could be due to correlation between the market index and other firm-specific variables. For example, Duffie *et al.* (2009) suggested that a firm's DTD can overstate its creditworthiness after a strong bull market. If this is the case, then the stock index return serves as a correction to the DTD levels at these points in time.

As expected we observe a different relationship between the short-term interest rate and default across economies. This observation possibly indicates different lead-lag relationships between credit conditions and the raising and cutting of short-term interest rates.

DTD is a measure of the volatility-adjusted leverage of a firm. Low or negative DTD indicates high leverage and high DTD indicates low leverage. Therefore, PD would be expected to increase with decreasing DTD. Indeed, almost all of the calibrations for the different groups lead to negative default parameters for the DTD level.

The ratio of the sum of cash and short-term investments to total assets (CASH/TA) measures liquidity of a firm. This indicates the availability of a firm's funds and its ability to make interest and principal payments. As expected, for almost all economies (Indonesia being the only exception) the default parameters for CASH/TA level in shorter horizons are significantly negative. The magnitude of the default parameters typically decreases for longer horizons, indicating that CASH/TA level is a better indicator of a firm's ability to make payments in the short term than the long term.

The ratio of net income to total assets (NI/TA) measures profitability of a firm. The relationship between PD and NI/TA is as expected: the default parameters for NI/TA level is negative for most economies and most horizons.

The logarithm of the market capitalization of a firm over the median market capitalization of firms within the economy (SIZE) does not have a consistent effect on PD across different economies. For example, in the US the default parameters for SIZE level are positive for all horizons, suggesting that the complexity of larger firms outweighs the potential benefits, such as diversified business lines and funding sources, are a benefit in the shorter term but not in the longer term. On the other hand, in Japan the default parameters for SIZE level are negative across all horizons. These differences may reflect differences in the business environments in the respective economies.

The default parameters associated with DTD Trend, CASH/TA Trend, SIZE Trend and NI/TA Trend are negative across almost all economies and horizons. The trend variables reflect momentum. The momentum effect is a short-term effect, and evidence of this is seen in the lower magnitude of the default parameters at longer horizons than at shorter horizons. The exception is the NI/TA Trend, which for some calibration groups has a higher magnitude at longer horizons.

The ratio of the sum of market capitalization and total liabilities to total assets (M/B) can either indicate the market mis-valuation effect or the future growth effect. This default parameter is negative in most economies, indicating that higher M/B implies lower PD, and the future growth effect dominates. On the other hand, in China and in the Developed Asia-Pacific calibration group, the default parameter for M/B is positive, indicating that for these economies, the market misvaluation effect dominates.

Shumway (2001) argued that a high level of the idiosyncratic volatility (SIGMA) indicates highly variable stock returns relative to the market index, which is equivalent to highly variable cash flows. Currently, for the different economies, this variable is no longer significant.

IV.2. Prediction Accuracy

In-sample testing: Various tests are carried out to test the prediction accuracy of the RMI PD forecasts. These tests are conducted in-sample.

A single calibration is conducted for the in-sample tests, using data to the end of the data sample. As an example, one-year PD forecasts are made for December 31, 2000 by using the data at or before December 31, 2000 and the parameters from the calibration. These PD forecasts can be compared to actual defaults that occurred at any time in 2001.

Accuracy ratio: The accuracy ratio (AR) is one of the most popular and meaningful tests of the discriminatory power of a rating system (BCBS, 2005). The AR and the equivalent Area Under the Receiver Operating Characteristic (AUROC) are described in Duan and Shrestha (2011). In short, if defaulting firms had been assigned among the highest PD of all firms before they defaulted, then the model has discriminated well between safe and distressed firms. This leads to higher values of AR and AUROC. The range of possible AR values is in [0, 1], where 0 is a completely random rating system and 1 is a perfect rating system. The range of possible AUROC values is in [0.5, 1]. AUROC and AR values are related by: $\text{AR} = 2 \times \text{AUROC} - 1$.

The AR and AUROC values for different horizons are available in Table B.1 of this technical report. Only economies with more than 20 defaults entering into the AR and AUROC computation are listed. The PD are taken to be non-overlapping. For example, the one-year AR is based on PDs computed on 31/12/2000, 31/12/2001, . . . , 31/12/2009 and firms defaulting within one year of those dates, while the two-year AR is based on PDs computed on 31/12/2000, 31/12/2002, . . . , 31/12/2008 and firms defaulting within two years of those dates.

The AUROC values have been provided only for the purpose of comparison, if other rating systems report their results in terms of AUROC. The discussion will focus only on AR. The model is able to achieve strong

AR results mostly greater than 0.80 at the one and six-month horizons for developed economies. There is a drop in AR at one and two-year horizons, but the AR are still mostly acceptable. Australia, the UK and Singapore have sharp drops in AR at the two-year horizon. Hong Kong has comparatively worse AR over all horizons as compared to other developed economies.

The AR in emerging market economies such as Brazil, China, India, Indonesia, Malaysia, Philippines, Russia, and Vietnam are noticeably weaker than the results in the developed economies. This can be due to a number of issues. The quality of data is worse in emerging markets, in terms of availability and data errors. This may be due to lower reporting and auditing standards. Also, variable selection is likely to play a more important role in emerging markets. The variables were selected based on the predictive power in a developed economy, the US. Performing variable selections specific to the calibration group are expected to improve predictive accuracy, especially in emerging market economies. Finally, there could be structural differences in how defaults and bankruptcies occur in emerging market economies. If the judicial system is weak and there are no repercussions for default, firms may be less reluctant to default.

Aggregate defaults: The time series of aggregate predicted number of defaults and actual number of defaults in each calibration group are also available in Fig. B.3 to B.8. For China and India in particular, these figures show that there is room for improvement in the predictive power of the model.

V. ONGOING DEVELOPMENTS

The CRI can be developed along a number of directions. We now comment on obvious ones that in our view are likely to bring meaningful and measurable benefits. Besides modifications to the current modeling framework of the forward intensity, a change in modeling platform will be undertaken if another model proves more promising in terms of accuracy and robustness of results. For this type of development we also rely on the collective efforts by the worldwide credit research community to challenge and improve the existing modeling platform.

As an example, the CRI will soon start a parallel implementation using the partially-conditioned forward intensity approach proposed in Duan and Fulop (2013) to study its practicality and performance. In fact, the parameter constraints on the forward-intensity function essential to the implementation of that approach has already been incorporated into the current CRI system in making longer-term default predictions.

Within the current modeling framework, future developments involve, for example, variable selection where more experiments are needed to identify common risk factors and company-specific attributes that are more indicative of defaults in emerging markets.

Finally, a series of new applications and tools using the RMI PD as an input are currently being developed. More specifically, RMI is actively working with users and exploring different possibilities of taking advantage of the world class research infrastructure at the institute to propagate real world applications in credit rating and testing. Some interesting areas include research in counterparty risk management and stress testing of financial systems by policy makers. RMI also remains committed to making its vast resources available for academic research.

ACKNOWLEDGMENT

The RMI CRI is premised on the concept of credit ratings as a "public good". Being a non-profit undertaking allows a high level of transparency and collaboration that other commercial credit rating systems cannot replicate. The research and support infrastructure is in place and researchers from around the world are invited to contribute to this initiative. Any methodological improvements that researchers develop will be incorporated into the CRI system. In essence, the initiative operates as a "selective wikipedia" where many can contribute but implementation control is retained.

If you have feedback on this technical report or wish to work with us in this endeavor, please contact us at rmicri@globalcreditreview.com.

APPENDIX A: DATA

Table A.1. All countries under the RMI coverage.

Region	Economy
Asia-Pacific (21)	Australia, China, Hong Kong, Indonesia, India, Japan, Kazakhstan, Malaysia, Pakistan, Philippines, Singapore, South Korea, Sri Lanka, Taiwan, Thailand, Vietnam, New Zealand, Cambodia, Macau, Mongolia and Papua New Guinea.
North America (2)	Canada, the United States.
Europe (43)	Austria, Belgium, Bermuda, Bulgaria, Croatia, Cyprus, Czech Republic, Denmark, Estonia, Finland, France, Germany, Greece, Hungary, Iceland, Ireland, Italy, Latvia, Lithuania, Luxembourg, Macedonia, Malta, Netherlands, Norway, Poland, Portugal, Romania, Russian Federation, Slovakia, Slovenia, Spain, Sweden, Switzerland, Turkey, the United Kingdom, Ukraine, Faeroe Island, Gibraltar, Guernsey, Isle Of Man, Jersey, Liechtenstein and Monaco.
Latin America (17)	Argentina, Brazil, Columbia, Chile, Mexico, Peru, Venezuela, Bahamas, Belize, Cayman Islands, Curacao, Dominican Republic, Falkland Islands, Panama, Puerto Rico, Virgin Islands and Virgin Islands, British.
Middle-East (10)	Bahrain, Israel, Jordan, Kuwait, Saudi Arabia, United Arab Emirates, Azerbaijan, Iraq, Qatar and Sudan.
Africa (13)	Angola, Egypt, Morocco, Nigeria, South Africa, Gabon, Mauritius, Mozambique, Namibia, Sierra Leone, Tanzania, United Republic of, Togo and Zambia.

Table A.2. The 71 countries under the RMI coverage for which we cover companies listed on the exchange.

Region	Economy
Asia-Pacific (17)	Australia, China, Hong Kong, Indonesia, India, Japan, Kazakhstan, Malaysia, Pakistan, Philippines, Singapore, South Korea, Sri Lanka, Taiwan, Thailand, Vietnam and New Zealand.
North America (2)	Canada and the United States.
Europe (35)	Austria, Belgium, Bermuda, Bulgaria, Croatia, Cyprus, Czech Republic, Denmark, Estonia, Finland, France, Germany, Greece, Hungary, Iceland, Ireland, Italy, Latvia, Lithuania, Luxembourg, Macedonia, Malta, Netherlands, Norway, Poland, Portugal, Romania, Russian Federation, Slovakia, Slovenia, Spain, Sweden, Switzerland, Turkey and the United Kingdom, Ukraine.
Latin America (7)	Argentina, Brazil, Columbia, Chile, Mexico, Peru and Venezuela.
Middle-East (6)	Bahrain, Israel, Jordan, Kuwait, Saudi Arabia and United Arab Emirates.
Africa (4)	Egypt, Morocco, Nigeria and South Africa.

Table A.3. The 35 countries under the RMI coverage for which we cover companies domiciled in the economy but listed on a foreign exchange included in Table A.2. The gray boxes indicate that these economies also have their own local stock exchange.

Angola	Gibraltar	Panama
Azerbaijan	Guernsey	Papua New Guinea
Bahamas	Iraq	Puerto Rico
Belize	Isle Of Man	Qatar
Bermuda	Jersey	Sierra Leone
Cambodia	Liechtenstein	Sudan
Cayman Islands	Macau	Tanzania, United Republic of
Curacao	Mauritius	Togo
Dominican Republic	Monaco	Virgin Islands
Faeroe Island	Mongolia	Virgin Islands, British
Falkland Islands	Mozambique	Zambia
Gabon	Namibia	

Table A.4. ISO codes for economies currently covered by the CRI and the group that each economy is calibrated in.

ISO Code	Economy	Calibration Group
ARE	United Arab Emirates	Emerging
ARG	Argentina	Emerging
AUS	Australia	Developed Asia-Pacific
AUT	Austria	Europe
BEL	Belgium	Europe
BGR	Bulgaria	Europe
BHR	Bahrain	Emerging
BRA	Brazil	Emerging
CAN	Canada	North America
CHE	Switzerland	Europe
CHL	Chile	Emerging
CHN	China	China
COL	Colombia	Emerging
CYP	Cyprus	Europe
CZE	Czech Republic	Europe
DEU	Germany	Europe
DNK	Denmark	Europe
EGY	Egypt	Emerging
ESP	Spain	Europe
EST	Estonia	Europe
FIN	Finland	Europe
FRA	France	Europe
GBR	United Kingdom	Europe
GRC	Greece	Europe
HKG	Hong Kong	Developed Asia-Pacific
HRV	Croatia	Europe

(Continued)

Table A.4. (*Continued*)

ISO Code	Economy	Calibration Group
HUN	Hungary	Europe
IDN	Indonesia	Emerging
IND	India	India
IRL	Ireland	Europe
ISL	Iceland	Europe
ISR	Israel	Europe
ITA	Italy	Europe
JOR	Jordan	Emerging
JPN	Japan	Developed Asia-Pacific
KAZ	Kazakhstan	Emerging
KOR	South Korea	Developed Asia-Pacific
KWT	Kuwait	Emerging
LKA	Sri Lanka	Emerging
LTU	Lithuania	Europe
LUX	Luxembourg	Europe
LVA	Latvia	Europe
MAR	Morocco	Emerging
MEX	Mexico	Emerging
MKD	Macedonia	Europe
MLT	Malta	Europe
MYS	Malaysia	Emerging
NGA	Nigeria	Emerging
NLD	Netherlands	Europe
NOR	Norway	Europe
NZL	New Zealand	Developed Asia-pacific
PAK	Pakistan	Emerging
PER	Peru	Emerging
PHL	Philippines	Emerging
POL	Poland	Europe
PRT	Portugal	Europe
ROM	Romania	Europe
RUS	Russian Federation	Europe
SAU	Saudi Arabia	Emerging
SGP	Singapore	Developed Asia-Pacific
SVK	Slovakia	Europe
SVN	Slovenia	Europe
SWE	Sweden	Europe
THA	Thailand	Emerging
TUR	Turkey	Europe
TWN	Taiwan	Developed Asia-Pacific
UKR	Ukraine	Emerging
USA	United States	North America
VEN	Venezuela	Emerging
VNM	Vietnam	Emerging
ZAF	South Africa	Emerging

Table A.5. The stock indices used for each economy in computing the first common variable.

Country	Stock Exchange	Period Used*
ARE	FTSE NASDAQ DUB UAE 20	6/28/2006–Present
ARG	Buenos Aires Stock Exchange Merval Index	
AUS	All Ordinaries Index	
AUT	Austrian Traded ATX Index	
BEL	Belgian All Shares Return Index	
BGR	Bulgaria Stock Exchange Sofix Index	10/24/2000–Present
BHR	Bahrain Bourse All Share Index	7/8/2004–Present
BRA	Brazil Bovespa Stock Index	
CAN	S&P/TSX Composite Index	
CHE	SPI Swiss Performance Index	
CHL	Santiago Stock Exchange IPSA Index	
CHN	Shanghai Stock Exchange Composite Index	
COL	FTSE All World Series Colombia Local	
CYP	Cyprus Stock Exchange General Index	9/3/2004–Present
	Cyprus Stock Exchange General	4/2/1996–9/2/2004
CZE	Prague Stock Exch Index	4/5/1994–Present
DEU	CDAX Performance Index	
DNK	OMX Copenhagen 20 Index	
EGY	EGX 100 Index	5/1/2006–Present
ESP	IBEX 35 Index	
EST	OMX Tallinn OMXT	
FIN	OMX Helsinki Index	
FRA	CAC 40 Index	
GBR	FTSE 100 Index	
GRC	Athex Composite Share Price Index	
HKG	Hang Seng Index	
HRV	Croatia Zagreb CROBEX	6/14/2002–Present
HUN	Budapest Stock Exch Index	1/2/1991–Present
IDN	Jakarta Composite Index	
IND	BSE Sensex 30 Index	
IRL	Irish Overall Index	
ISL	OMX Iceland All-Share Price Index	
ISR	Tel Aviv 100 Index	12/31/1991–Present
ITA	Italy Stock Market BCI Comit Global	
JOR	MSCI Jordan	3/7/2011–Present
JPN	Nikkei 500	
KAZ	Kazakhstan Stock Exchange Index KASE	7/12/2000–Present
KOR	KOSPI Index	
KWT	Kuwait SE Weighted Index	1/2/2012–Present
	Kuwait Global General Index	1/2/1984–1/2/2012
LKA	Sri Lanka Colombo All-Share Index	1/2/1985–Present
LTU	OMX Vilnius OMXV	1/4/2000–Present
LUX	Luxembourg Stock Exchange LuxX Index	1/4/1999–Present
	Luxembourg Stock Exchange 13 'Dead'	1/2/1998–1/3/1999
LVA	OMX GIRA OMXR	1/2/2000–Present
MAR	CFG 25	12/31/1993–Present
MEX	Mexico Bolsa Index	
MKD	Macedonian Stock Exchange MBI 10	12/30/2004–Present
MLT	Malta Stock Exchange	
MYS	FTSE Bursa Malaysia KLCI	
NGA	NIGERIA STCK EXC ALL SHR	1/30/1998–Present
NLD	AEX Index	
NOR	OBX Price Index	

(*Continued*)

Table A.5. (*Continued*)

Country	Stock Exchange	Period Used*
NZL	NZX All Index	3/30/1992–Present
PAK	Karachi All Share Index	3/11/1998–Present
PER	Bolsa de Valores de Lima General Sector Index	
PHL	PSEI-Philippine Stock Exchange Index	
POL	WSE WIG Index	4/16/1991–Present
PRT	PSI General Index	
ROM	BSE COMPOSITE INDEX	4/17/1998–Present
RUS	MICEX INDEX	9/22/1997–Present
SAU	TADAWUL ALL SHARE INDEX	1/31/1994–Present
SGP	Straits Times Index	1/10/2008–Present
	Straits Times Old Index	8/31/1999–1/9/2008
SVK	Slovak Share Index	
SVN	HSBC Slovenia Dollar	
SWE	OMX Stockholm All-Share Index	
THA	Stock Exchange of Thailand Index	
TUR	Istanbul Stock Exchange National 100 Index	1/4/1988–Present
TWN	Taiwan Taiex Index	
UKR	Ukraine PFTS Index	1/12/1998–Present
USA	S&P 500 Index	
VEN	Caracas Stock Exchange Stock Market Index	
VNM	Ho Chi Minh Stock Index	7/28/2000–Present
ZAF	MSCI South Africa Index	12/31/1992–Present

*A blank Period Used column indicates that there is only a single interest rate that is used throughout the whole period.

Table A.6. The interest rates used for each economy as the second common variable.

Country	Short Term Interest Rate	Period Used
ARE	UAE Ibor 3 Months	5/15/2000–Present
ARG	Argentina Deposit 90 Days	
AUS	Australia Dealer Bill 90 Days	
AUT	Germany 3 Month Bubill	1/1/1999–Present
	—	–12/31/1998
BEL	Germany 3 Month Bubill	1/1/1999–Present
	—	–12/31/1998
BGR	Bulgaria Interbank 3 Months	2/17/2003–Present
BHR	Bahrain Ibor 3 Months	12/14/2006
BRA	Andima Brazil Govt Bond Fixed Rate 3 Months	4/3/2000–Present
	Brazil CDB (up to 30 Days)	10/10/1994–3/31/2000
CAN	Canada Treasury Bill 3 Months	
CHE	—	
CHL	Chile TAB UF Interbank Rate 90 Days	
CHN	China Time Deposit Rate 3 Months	
COL	Colombia CD Rate 90-Day	
CYP	Germany 3 Month Bubill	1/1/2008–Present
	—	–12/31/2007
CZE	Czech Republic Interbank 3 MTH	4/22/1992–Present
DEU	Germany 3 Month Bubill	5/25/1993–Present
	Germany Interbank 3 Months	1/2/1986–5/24/1993
DNK	Denmark Interbank 3 Months	
EGY	Egypt 91 Days T-Bill	7/6/2004–Present

(*Continued*)

Table A.6. *(Continued)*

Country	Short Term Interest Rate	Period Used
ESP	Germany 3 Month Bubill	1/1/1999–Present
	—	–12/31/1998
EST	Germany 3 Month Bubill	1/1/2011–Present
	—	–12/31/2010
FIN	Germany 3 Month Bubill	1/1/1999–Present
	—	–12/31/1998
FRA	Germany 3 Month Bubill	1/1/1999–Present
	—	–12/31/1998
GBR	UK Treasury Bill Tender 3 Months	
GRC	Germany 3 Month Bubill	1/1/2001–Present
	—	–12/31/2000
HKG	Hong Kong Exchange Fund Bill 3 Months	
HRV	Croatia Zibor Rate 3 Months	6/2/1997–Present
HUN	Hungary Interbank 3 Months	9/7/1995–Present
IDN	Indonesia SBI 90 Days	7/10/2003–Present
	Indonesia SBI/DISC 90 Days	1/1/1985–7/9/2003
IND	India T-Bill Secondary 91 Days	
IRL	Germany 3 Month Bubill	1/1/1999–Present
	—	–12/31/1998
ISL	—	
ISR	Israel T-Bill Secondary 3 Months	5/30/1995–Present
ITA	Germany 3 Month Bubill	1/1/1999–Present
	—	–12/31/1998
JOR	Amman Interbank 3 Months	3/9/2001–Present
JPN	Japan Treasury Discount Bills 3 Months	7/10/1992–Present
	Japanese Government Bond Interest Rate — 1 Year Maturity	9/24/1974–7/9/1992
KAZ	Kazakhstan KIBOR/KIBID 90 Days Interbank	9/29/2001–Present
KOR	Korea Commercial Paper 91 Days	
KWT	Kuwait Interbank 3 Months	8/17/1983–Present
LKA	Sri Lanka Treasury Bill 3 Months	1/6/1989–Present
LTU	VILNIUS Interbank Three Months	1/6/1999–Present
LUX	Germany 3 Month Bubill	1/1/1999–Present
	—	–12/31/1998
LVA	Treasury Bill Rate 3 Months	5/11/1994–Present
MAR	Morocco Deposit Rate 3 Months	6/6/2003–Present
MEX	Mexico Cetes 2ND MKT. 90 Days	6/26/1996–Present
	Mexico Cetes 91 Dat AVG.RET.AT AUC.	3/9/1989–6/25/1996
MKD	Macedonia Skibor 3 Months	7/2/2007–Present
MLT	Germany 3 Month Bubill	1/1/2008–Present
	—	–12/31/2007
MYS	Malaysia Deposit 3 Months	
NGA	Nigeria Interbank Offered Rate 3 Months	1/30/2004–Present
NLD	Germany 3 Month Bubill	1/1/1999–Present
	—	–12/31/1998
NOR	Norway Govt Treasury Bills 3 Months	6/27/1995–Present
	Norway Interbank 3 Months (effective)	1/2/1986–6/26/1995
NZL	New Zealand Dollar Deposit 3 Months	9/27/1988–Present
PAK	PKR 3 Months Repo	10/29/1999–Present
PER	Peru Savings Rate	
PHL	Philippine Treasury Bill 91 Days	
POL	Poland Interbank 3 Months (EOD)	6/4/1993–Present
PRT	Germany 3 Month Bubill	1/1/1999–Present
	—	–12/31/1998

(Continued)

Table A.6. (*Continued*)

Country	Short Term Interest Rate	Period Used
ROM	Romanian Interbank 3 Months	8/1/1995–Present
RUS	MosPime 3 Months Rate	4/18/2005–Present
	Russia Moscow Interbank Non Co	8/14/2000-4/17/2005
	Russian Federation Interbank 31–90 Days	9/1/1994-8/13/2000
SAU	Saudi Interbank 3 Months	1/1/1987–Present
SGP	Monetary Authority of Singapore Benchmark Govt Bill Yield 3 Months	9/20/2013–Present
	Singapore T-Bill 3 Months	1/8/1988–9/19/2013
SVK	Germany 3 Month Bubill	1/1/2009–Present
	—	–12/31/2008
SVN	Germany 3 Month Bubill	1/1/2007–Present
	—	–12/31/2006
SWE	Sweden T-Bill 3 Months	5/25/1993–Present
	Sweden Treasury Bill 90 Days	4/25/1989–5/24/1993
THA	Thailand Repo 3 Months (BOT)	
TUR	Turkish Interbank 3 Months	8/1/2002–Present
TWN	Taiwan Money Market 90 Days	
UKR	Ukraine Interbank 3 Months	3/1/2001–Present
USA	US Generic Govt 3-Month Yield	
VEN	Venezuela Overnight	
VNM	Vietnam Interbank 3 Months	12/11/1998–Present
ZAF	South Africa T-Bill 91 Days (Tender Rates)	12/31/1980–Present

*A blank Period Used column indicates that there is only a single interest rate that is used throughout the whole period.

Table A.7. The interest rates used for each economy in the DTD calculation.

Country	Interest Rate Name	Period Used*
ARE	UAE Ibor 1 Year	5/15/2000–Present
ARG	Aregentina Deposit 90 Days (PA.)	
AUS	Australia Govt. Bonds Generic Mid Yield 1 Year	
AUT	German Government Bonds 1 Year BKO	1/1/1999–Present
	Austria VIBOR 12 Months	6/10/1991–12/31/1998
BEL	German Government Bonds 1 Year BKO	1/1/1999–Present
	Belgium Treasury Bill 1 Year	4/2/1991–12/31/1998
BGR	Bulgaria Interbank 3 Months	2/17/2003–Present
BHR	Bahrain Ibor 1 Year	12/14/2006
BRA	Andima Brazil Govt Bond Fixed Rate 1 Year	4/3/2000–Present
	BRAZIL CDB (UP TO 30 DAYS)	10/10/1994–3/31/2000
CAN	Canada Treasury Bill 1 Year	
CHE	Swiss Interbank 1 Year (ZRC:SNB)	
CHL	Chile TAB UF Interbank Rates 360 Days	8/1/1996–Present
	Chile TAB UF Interbank Rate 90 Days	11/2/1992–7/30/1996
CHN	China Household Savings Deposits 1 Year Rate	
COL	Colombia Government Generic Bond 1 Year Yield	3/1/2001–Present
	Colombia CD Rate 360-Dat	7/12/1993–2/8/2001
CYP	Cyprus Treasury Bill Rate — 13 Weeks	
CZE	Czech Republic Interbank 3 MTH	4/22/1992–Present
DEU	German Government Bonds 1 Year BKO	1/10/1995–Present
	Germany Interbank 12 Months	11/2/1990–1/9/1995
DNK	Denmark Government Bonds 1 Year Note Generic Bid Yield	6/1/2008–Present
	Denmark Euro-Krone 1 Year (FT/ICAP/TR)	6/14/1985–5/31/2008

(*Continued*)

Table A.7. *(Continued)*

Country	Interest Rate Name	Period Used*
EGY	Egypt 364 Days T-Bill	7/6/2004–Present
ESP	German Government Bonds 1 Year BKO	1/1/1999–Present
	Spain 12 Months Treasury Bill Yield	11/30/1992–12/31/1998
	Spain Interbank 12 Months	12/19/1991–11/29/1992
EST	Estonia, Interest Rates, Prices, Production, & Labor, Interest Rates, Deposit Rate	
FIN	German Government Bonds 1 Year BKO	1/1/1999–Present
	Finland Interbank Close 12 Months	4/2/1992–12/31/1998
FRA	German Government Bonds 1 Year BKO	1/1/1999–Present
	France Treasury Bill 12 Months	1/3/1989–12/31/1998
GBR	UK Govt. Bonds 1 Year Note Generic	9/12/2001–Present
	UK Govt. Liability Nominal Spot Curve 12 Months	12/13/1985–9/11/2001
GRC	German Government Bonds 1 Year BKO	1/1/2001–Present
	Greece Treasury Bill 1 Year	1/2/1990–12/31/2000
HKG	HKMA Hong Kong Exchange Fund Bill 12 Months	
HRV	Croatia Zibor Rate 3 Months	6/2/1997–Present
HUN	Hungary Interbank 3 Months	9/7/1995–Present
IDN	Indonesia SBI 90 Days	7/10/2003–Present
	Indonesia SBI/DISC 90 Days	1/1/1985–7/9/2003
IND	India T-Bill Secondary 1 Year	
IRL	UK Govt. Liability Nominal Spot Curve 12 Months	
ISL	Iceland Interbank 12 Months	2/1/2000–Present
	Iceland Interbank 3 Months	8/4/1998–1/31/2000
	Iceland 90-day CB Notes	5/12/1987–8/3/1998
ISR	Israel T-Bill Secondary 1 Year	11/15/1994–Present
ITA	German Government Bonds 1 Year BKO	1/1/1999–Present
	Italy Bots Treasury Bill 12 Months Gross Yields	9/5/1994–12/31/1998
	Italy T-Bill Auction Gross 12 Months	3/31/1987–9/4/1994
JOR	Amman Interbank 1 Year	3/9/2001–Present
JPN	Japan Treasury Bills 12 Months	12/14/1999–Present
	Japanese Government Bond Interest Rate — 1 Year Maturity	9/24/1979–12/13/1999
KAZ	Kazakhstan KIBOR/KIBID 90 Days Interbank	9/29/2001–Present
KOR	Korea Monetary Stabilization Bonds 1 Year	
KWT	Kuwait Interbank 1 Year	8/17/1983–Present
LKA	Sri Lanka Fixed Deposit 1 Year	3/31/1988–Present
LTU	Vilnius Interbank 12 Months	3/29/2000–Present
LUX	Long Term Government Bond Yields — Maastricht Definition (Avg.)	
LVA	Treasury Bill Rate 1 Year	4/3/1998–Present
MAR	Morocco Deposit Rate 1 Year	6/6/2003–Present
MKD	Macedonia Skibor 3 Months	7/2/2007–Present
MEX	Mexico Cetes 2ND MKT. 360 Days	6/26/1996–Present
	Mexico Cete 91 DAY AVG.RET.AT AUC	3/9/1989–6/25/1996
MLT	Long Term Government Bond Yields — Maastricht Definition (Avg.)	
MYS	Bank Negara Malaysia 1 Year Govt. Securities Indicative YTM	6/21/2005–Present
	Malaysia Deposit 1 Year	1/1/1985–6/20/2005
NGA	Nigeria Interbank Offered Rate 3 Months	1/30/2004–Present
NLD	German Government Bonds 1 Year BKO	1/1/1999–Present
	Netherland Interbank 1 Year	1/2/1987–12/31/1998
NOR	Norway Govt Treasury Bills 12 Months	7/1/1997–Present
	Norway Interbank 1 Year	1/2/1986–6/30/1997
NZL	New Zealand Dollar Deposit 1 Year	9/27/1988–Present
PAK	PKR 12 Months Repo	10/29/2004–Present
PER	Peru Savings Rate	
PHL	Philippine Treasury Bill 364 Days	

(Continued)

Table A.7. *(Continued)*

Country	Interest Rate Name	Period Used*
POL	Poland Interbank 1 Year (EOD)	10/11/1995–Present
PRT	German Government Bonds 1 Year BKO	1/1/1999–Present
	Portugal 1-Year-LISBOR-Act/365 Days convention	8/16/1993–12/31/1998
ROM	Romanian Interbank 12 Months	8/1/1995–Present
RUS	MosPime 3 Months Rate	4/18/2005–Present
	Russia Moscow Interbank Non Co	8/14/2000–4/17/2005
	Russian Federation Interbank 31–90 Days	9/1/1994–8/13/2000
SAU	Saudi Interbank 1 Year	1/1/1987–Present
SGP	Monetary Authority of Singapore Benchmark Govt Bill Yield 3 Months	9/20/2013–Present
	Singapore T-Bill 3 Months	1/8/1988–9/19/2013
SVK	Slovak Rep.Interbank 1 Year	
SVN	Slovenia Treasury Bill 3 Months 'Dead'	
SWE	Sweden T Bill 3 Months	5/25/1993–Present
	Sweden Treasury Bill 90 Days	4/25/1989–5/24/1993
THA	Thailand Govt. Bond 1 Year Note	8/7/2000–Present
	Thailand Deposit 12 Months (KT)	1/2/1991–8/6/2000
TUR	Turkish Interbank 12 Months	8/1/2002–Present
TWN	Taiwan Deposit 12 Months	
UKR	UAE Ibor 1 Year	5/15/2000–Present
USA	US Treasury Constant Maturities 1 Year	
VEN	Venezuela Overnight	
VNM	Vietnam Interbank 3 Months	12/11/1998–Present
ZAF	South Africa T-Bill 91 Days (Tender Rates)	12/31/1980–Present

*A blank Period Used column indicates that there is only a single interest rate that is used throughout the whole period.

Table A.8. Summary statistics of input variables (based on data from January 1991 to March 2014).

	Min	25%	Median	75%	Max	Mean	StdDev	# Observations
				DTD Level				
ARE	−0.80	1.85	2.82	3.86	13.33	3.12	1.90	5,591
ARG	−1.75	1.37	2.67	3.84	19.82	2.88	2.24	12,873
AUS	−1.40	1.85	2.97	4.20	18.66	3.29	2.19	289,095
AUT	−2.67	1.89	3.09	4.96	24.48	3.92	3.78	20,436
BEL	−2.67	2.55	4.41	6.75	24.48	5.06	3.76	29,567
BGR	−1.78	1.08	2.02	3.22	24.48	2.46	2.30	10,386
BHR	−0.27	1.73	2.43	4.56	18.23	3.53	2.92	1,460
BRA	−1.84	0.72	1.84	3.42	24.08	2.43	2.70	51,037
CAN	−1.13	1.91	3.27	4.96	24.84	3.71	2.61	218,173
CHE	−2.67	2.68	4.11	5.98	24.48	4.58	2.91	51,381
CHL	−1.84	3.58	5.24	6.79	25.62	5.63	3.45	28,944
CHN	0.04	3.11	4.21	5.77	16.57	4.68	2.29	277,785
COL	−1.35	2.33	3.94	5.78	20.21	4.38	3.09	5,836
CYP	−1.19	0.88	1.53	2.46	23.81	2.06	2.26	16,185
CZE	−2.67	1.30	2.42	3.73	20.20	2.73	2.22	5,985
DEU	−2.67	1.61	2.90	4.42	24.48	3.32	2.68	179,036
DNK	−1.92	1.88	3.18	4.71	24.48	3.66	2.95	42,075
EGY	−1.84	1.81	2.85	4.14	25.62	3.18	2.13	14,725
ESP	−2.67	2.00	3.43	4.96	24.48	3.82	3.03	35,143
EST	−0.30	1.99	3.50	5.94	13.59	3.97	2.70	769

(Continued)

Table A.8. (*Continued*)

	Min	25%	Median	75%	Max	Mean	StdDev	# Observations
				DTD Level				
FIN	−2.67	2.26	3.44	4.97	18.16	3.79	2.40	28,399
FRA	−2.67	1.84	3.03	4.62	24.48	3.51	2.72	160,812
GBR	−2.67	2.23	3.60	5.32	24.48	4.05	2.73	382,413
GRC	−2.67	1.34	2.36	3.69	23.59	2.68	2.14	55,630
HKG	−1.40	1.54	2.57	4.01	18.66	3.07	2.31	213,945
HRV	−2.67	1.16	2.32	3.66	20.81	2.68	2.24	10,768
HUN	−0.73	1.64	2.72	4.29	24.48	3.11	2.27	7100
IDN	−1.84	0.70	1.72	2.88	25.55	2.05	2.10	60,191
IND	−1.79	0.82	1.70	2.86	19.49	2.12	2.16	463,078
IRL	−1.73	1.95	3.27	4.77	14.51	3.49	2.26	9,918
ISL	−1.48	1.76	3.01	4.34	20.01	3.35	2.37	4,368
ISR	−2.30	1.26	2.37	3.66	24.48	2.75	2.40	74,789
ITA	−2.67	1.55	2.81	4.37	24.48	3.19	2.52	59,551
JOR	−1.84	2.44	3.52	5.17	23.79	4.07	2.49	22,026
JPN	−1.40	2.09	3.16	4.52	18.66	3.56	2.21	816,444
KAZ	−1.60	0.54	1.30	3.15	25.62	2.60	4.23	850
KOR	−1.40	1.26	2.20	3.39	18.66	2.56	2.13	290,591
KWT	−0.44	2.30	3.26	4.49	25.62	3.72	2.28	22,256
LKA	−1.84	1.60	2.42	3.75	16.12	2.82	1.97	18,026
LTU	−1.30	1.45	3.17	5.36	20.95	3.74	3.27	4,361
LUX	−0.56	3.08	4.74	7.40	24.48	6.02	4.47	2,876
LVA	−1.45	1.31	2.31	3.84	24.48	2.88	2.48	3,090
MAR	−0.69	2.61	3.84	5.29	21.53	4.15	2.42	7,459
MEX	−1.84	2.05	3.70	5.61	25.62	4.17	3.12	18,962
MKD	−1.09	1.35	1.98	2.84	16.51	2.67	2.70	2,019
MLT	−0.65	2.33	3.57	5.14	14.99	4.14	2.95	951
MYS	−1.84	1.58	2.85	4.62	25.62	3.52	2.94	189,706
NGA	−1.78	1.17	2.28	3.23	25.62	2.83	3.54	14,292
NLD	−2.67	2.44	3.97	5.80	24.48	4.39	2.96	35,914
NOR	−2.63	1.24	2.37	3.81	20.49	2.66	2.06	43,504
NZL	−1.21	2.88	4.91	6.98	18.66	5.25	3.23	17,446
PAK	−1.84	0.45	1.66	3.29	14.67	2.08	2.28	24,135
PER	−1.84	1.96	3.19	4.52	22.71	3.58	2.56	11,146
PHL	−1.84	1.16	2.30	3.75	25.62	2.73	2.36	38,597
POL	−2.67	1.37	2.33	3.49	24.48	2.64	2.06	60,259
PRT	−2.67	1.09	2.30	3.83	20.10	2.73	2.36	13,696
ROM	−2.67	0.97	1.81	2.42	24.48	1.95	1.63	15,804
RUS	−2.51	1.21	2.50	3.98	24.48	2.72	2.09	21,191
SAU	−1.52	3.71	5.43	7.78	25.62	6.25	3.75	14,993
SGP	−1.19	1.55	2.67	4.30	18.66	3.20	2.39	118,629
SVK	−0.60	1.29	2.19	3.04	24.48	3.38	5.11	989
SVN	−2.47	2.14	3.37	5.34	16.84	3.87	2.89	6,793
SWE	−2.67	1.72	3.04	4.57	24.48	3.40	2.49	80,208
THA	−1.71	1.68	2.91	4.43	25.62	3.32	2.53	97,155
TUR	−2.67	1.64	2.93	4.65	24.48	3.58	3.01	40,300
TWN	−1.40	2.66	3.77	5.16	18.66	4.12	2.28	237,398
UKR	−1.69	0.87	1.69	2.73	21.76	1.88	1.73	5,067
USA	−1.13	1.80	3.07	4.75	24.84	3.56	2.64	1,482,028
VEN	−1.84	0.40	1.39	3.13	17.01	2.27	3.09	3,417
VNM	−1.84	0.97	1.73	2.82	25.62	2.07	1.74	37,816
ZAF	−1.84	1.34	2.78	4.54	25.62	3.37	3.13	78,514

(*Continued*)

Table A.8. *(Continued)*

	Min	25%	Median	75%	Max	Mean	StdDev	# Observations
				DTD Trend				
ARE	−4.43	−0.36	0.00	0.37	6.00	−0.03	0.83	5,591
ARG	−7.70	−0.50	−0.01	0.40	7.28	−0.04	1.01	12,873
AUS	−5.75	−0.48	−0.03	0.37	5.42	−0.06	0.97	289,095
AUT	−7.97	−0.53	−0.03	0.42	7.60	−0.12	1.49	20,436
BEL	−7.97	−0.60	−0.00	0.60	7.60	−0.01	1.50	29,567
BGR	−7.97	−0.43	0.00	0.34	7.60	−0.06	1.00	10,386
BHR	−7.70	−0.27	0.01	0.30	4.36	−0.07	0.89	1,460
BRA	−7.70	−0.34	0.01	0.37	7.28	0.01	1.00	51,037
CAN	−6.39	−0.53	−0.02	0.46	5.53	−0.05	1.11	218,173
CHE	−7.97	−0.58	0.01	0.62	7.60	0.02	1.28	51,381
CHL	−7.70	−0.68	0.03	0.59	7.28	−0.03	1.49	28,944
CHN	−5.87	−0.56	−0.03	0.46	5.37	−0.07	1.02	277,785
COL	−7.70	−0.40	0.03	0.65	7.28	0.10	1.32	5,836
CYP	−7.97	−0.35	−0.07	0.17	7.60	−0.12	0.76	16,185
CZE	−7.78	−0.34	0.00	0.38	5.78	0.00	0.87	5,985
DEU	−7.97	−0.48	−0.02	0.43	7.60	−0.03	1.10	179,036
DNK	−7.97	−0.49	−0.00	0.44	7.60	−0.02	1.19	42,075
EGY	−7.70	−0.41	0.02	0.54	7.28	0.05	0.99	14,725
ESP	−7.97	−0.47	0.02	0.49	7.60	0.01	1.24	35,143
EST	−3.42	−0.07	0.19	0.73	3.80	0.35	0.83	769
FIN	−7.97	−0.44	0.04	0.55	7.60	0.04	1.05	28,399
FRA	−7.97	−0.46	0.00	0.46	7.60	−0.00	1.09	160,812
GBR	−7.97	−0.54	−0.01	0.42	7.60	−0.07	1.24	382,413
GRC	−7.97	−0.51	−0.08	0.32	7.60	−0.10	0.94	55,630
HKG	−5.75	−0.46	0.00	0.45	5.42	−0.01	0.97	213,945
HRV	−4.96	−0.53	−0.03	0.26	7.60	−0.10	0.93	10,768
HUN	−7.97	−0.41	0.00	0.41	7.60	−0.05	0.91	7,100
IDN	−7.70	−0.32	0.00	0.32	7.28	−0.02	0.77	60,191
IND	−7.02	−0.36	−0.03	0.33	5.51	−0.02	0.84	463,078
IRL	−7.97	−0.46	0.00	0.48	7.36	−0.03	1.01	9,918
ISL	−7.97	−0.68	−0.06	0.42	6.70	−0.17	1.33	4,368
ISR	−7.97	−0.42	0.00	0.42	7.60	−0.01	1.05	74,789
ITA	−7.97	−0.54	−0.01	0.49	7.60	−0.03	1.13	59,551
JOR	−7.70	−0.46	−0.02	0.38	7.28	−0.06	1.05	22,026
JPN	−5.75	−0.46	−0.02	0.42	5.42	−0.02	0.88	816,444
KAZ	−7.70	−0.50	0.00	0.41	7.28	−0.01	1.22	850
KOR	−5.75	−0.43	0.00	0.42	5.42	−0.01	0.91	290,591
KWT	−7.70	−0.43	0.00	0.40	7.28	−0.03	1.05	22,256
LKA	−7.70	−0.33	0.00	0.42	7.28	0.06	0.87	18,026
LTU	−6.23	−0.62	0.00	0.65	7.60	0.02	1.36	4,361
LUX	−7.97	−0.63	0.02	0.55	7.60	−0.09	1.38	2,876
LVA	−7.97	−0.34	0.05	0.34	7.60	−0.03	1.07	3,090
MAR	−7.70	−0.56	−0.06	0.39	7.28	−0.09	1.06	7,459
MEX	−7.70	−0.44	0.05	0.58	7.28	0.06	1.16	18,962
MKD	−6.14	−0.35	−0.04	0.32	6.55	0.04	0.87	2,019
MLT	−6.66	−0.57	−0.01	0.72	4.26	0.08	1.28	951
MYS	−7.70	−0.46	−0.00	0.42	7.28	−0.03	1.07	189,706
NGA	−7.70	−0.38	0.00	0.38	7.28	−0.00	1.43	14,292
NLD	−7.97	−0.62	−0.02	0.55	7.60	−0.05	1.21	35,914
NOR	−7.97	−0.40	0.00	0.39	7.60	−0.02	0.91	43,504

(Continued)

Table A.8. *(Continued)*

	Min	25%	Median	75%	Max	Mean	StdDev	# Observations
				DTD Trend				
NZL	−5.75	−0.58	0.01	0.60	5.42	0.00	1.42	17,446
PAK	−6.29	−0.25	0.04	0.35	6.17	0.04	0.74	24,135
PER	−7.70	−0.41	0.00	0.51	7.28	0.04	1.22	11,146
PHL	−7.70	−0.35	0.00	0.34	7.28	−0.01	0.94	38,597
POL	−7.97	−0.47	−0.02	0.38	7.60	−0.06	0.91	60,259
PRT	−7.97	−0.42	−0.01	0.35	7.60	−0.03	0.94	13,696
ROM	−7.97	−0.26	0.00	0.25	7.60	0.00	0.74	15,804
RUS	−7.97	−0.45	0.00	0.41	7.60	−0.08	1.05	21,191
SAU	−7.70	−0.72	0.16	1.04	7.28	0.12	1.82	14,993
SGP	−5.75	−0.44	−0.00	0.41	5.42	−0.03	0.97	118,629
SVK	−7.97	−0.14	0.06	0.32	7.60	0.04	1.59	989
SVN	−5.13	−0.56	−0.08	0.21	7.60	−0.15	0.98	6,793
SWE	−7.97	−0.46	−0.01	0.45	7.60	−0.00	1.04	80,208
THA	−7.70	−0.52	−0.02	0.45	7.28	−0.05	1.05	97,155
TUR	−7.97	−0.59	0.04	0.62	7.60	0.03	1.36	40,300
TWN	−5.75	−0.53	0.01	0.57	5.42	0.02	1.03	237,398
UKR	−5.71	−0.51	−0.01	0.33	6.49	−0.14	0.89	5067
USA	−6.39	−0.47	0.00	0.47	5.53	−0.01	1.00	1,482,028
VEN	−6.72	−0.30	−0.00	0.29	7.28	0.01	0.96	3,417
VNM	−7.70	−0.37	−0.02	0.28	7.28	−0.04	0.67	37,816
ZAF	−7.70	−0.45	−0.01	0.37	7.28	−0.06	1.18	78,514
				CASH/TA Level				
ARE	0.00	0.07	0.14	0.23	0.94	0.17	0.14	6,700
ARG	0.00	0.02	0.05	0.11	0.69	0.08	0.08	13,407
AUS	0.00	0.04	0.13	0.35	0.97	0.23	0.25	300,910
AUT	0.00	0.03	0.07	0.15	0.99	0.11	0.13	22,520
BEL	0.00	0.03	0.07	0.18	0.99	0.14	0.18	32,089
BGR	0.00	0.01	0.03	0.08	0.58	0.06	0.08	10,687
BHR	0.00	0.09	0.18	0.26	0.91	0.20	0.15	2,956
BRA	0.00	0.02	0.08	0.17	0.94	0.12	0.13	54,565
CAN	0.00	0.01	0.06	0.21	0.99	0.16	0.21	224,124
CHE	0.00	0.05	0.10	0.20	0.99	0.15	0.16	56,712
CHL	0.00	0.01	0.03	0.08	0.94	0.06	0.09	30,854
CHN	0.00	0.08	0.15	0.25	0.89	0.19	0.16	283,560
COL	0.00	0.03	0.06	0.09	0.76	0.07	0.07	6,358
CYP	0.00	0.01	0.05	0.15	0.93	0.10	0.14	16,765
CZE	0.00	0.02	0.05	0.11	0.99	0.09	0.12	6,720
DEU	0.00	0.03	0.08	0.19	0.99	0.14	0.18	187,269
DNK	0.00	0.03	0.08	0.18	0.99	0.14	0.17	46,304
EGY	0.00	0.04	0.12	0.22	0.94	0.15	0.14	16,211
ESP	0.00	0.02	0.05	0.11	0.82	0.09	0.10	39,354
EST	0.00	0.03	0.05	0.12	0.53	0.09	0.09	2,579
FIN	0.00	0.03	0.08	0.16	0.99	0.12	0.14	30,053
FRA	0.00	0.03	0.08	0.17	0.99	0.13	0.14	168,024
GBR	0.00	0.03	0.09	0.22	0.99	0.17	0.21	388,884
GRC	0.00	0.02	0.05	0.13	0.83	0.10	0.11	57,391
HKG	0.00	0.06	0.14	0.26	0.97	0.19	0.17	220,051
HRV	0.00	0.01	0.02	0.05	0.52	0.05	0.08	12,668
HUN	0.00	0.02	0.06	0.13	0.74	0.09	0.10	7,739

(Continued)

Table A.8. *(Continued)*

	Min	25%	Median	75%	Max	Mean	StdDev	# Observations
				CASH/TA Level				
IDN	0.00	0.03	0.08	0.17	0.90	0.12	0.12	64,011
IND	0.00	0.01	0.03	0.07	0.83	0.06	0.10	625,463
IRL	0.00	0.05	0.09	0.21	0.97	0.15	0.17	10,545
ISL	0.00	0.02	0.04	0.08	0.53	0.06	0.06	4,794
ISR	0.00	0.03	0.10	0.22	0.99	0.18	0.21	75,988
ITA	0.00	0.03	0.06	0.14	0.99	0.10	0.11	63,019
JOR	0.00	0.01	0.05	0.18	0.94	0.13	0.16	25,814
JPN	0.00	0.08	0.13	0.22	0.97	0.17	0.14	820,518
KAZ	0.00	0.07	0.13	0.17	0.36	0.13	0.08	1,035
KOR	0.00	0.04	0.09	0.18	0.97	0.13	0.13	294,250
KWT	0.00	0.03	0.07	0.20	0.94	0.15	0.18	23,325
LKA	0.00	0.02	0.05	0.10	0.94	0.09	0.13	18,344
LTU	0.00	0.01	0.03	0.07	0.51	0.06	0.09	4,528
LUX	0.00	0.05	0.11	0.18	0.97	0.14	0.14	3,267
LVA	0.00	0.01	0.04	0.12	0.44	0.08	0.09	3,325
MAR	0.00	0.01	0.05	0.12	0.78	0.09	0.11	10,983
MEX	0.00	0.03	0.06	0.11	0.77	0.08	0.08	20,690
MKD	0.00	0.02	0.05	0.17	0.59	0.11	0.13	2,517
MLT	0.00	0.03	0.08	0.20	0.50	0.14	0.14	1,418
MYS	0.00	0.02	0.07	0.16	0.94	0.12	0.13	192,519
NGA	0.00	0.03	0.07	0.20	0.73	0.13	0.15	15,623
NLD	0.00	0.02	0.05	0.12	0.99	0.10	0.13	38,264
NOR	0.00	0.04	0.09	0.19	0.99	0.15	0.18	45,681
NZL	0.00	0.01	0.03	0.10	0.97	0.10	0.17	18,399
PAK	0.00	0.01	0.05	0.14	0.90	0.10	0.12	30,696
PER	0.00	0.01	0.04	0.13	0.71	0.09	0.11	12,167
PHL	0.00	0.02	0.09	0.18	0.94	0.13	0.15	40,574
POL	0.00	0.03	0.06	0.14	0.99	0.11	0.12	61,773
PRT	0.00	0.01	0.03	0.07	0.54	0.06	0.08	14,762
ROM	0.00	0.01	0.03	0.08	0.73	0.07	0.10	16,508
RUS	0.00	0.02	0.06	0.15	0.99	0.11	0.12	23,448
SAU	0.00	0.04	0.09	0.18	0.94	0.16	0.19	15,690
SGP	0.00	0.06	0.13	0.24	0.97	0.17	0.15	120,532
SVK	0.00	0.02	0.05	0.10	0.59	0.08	0.09	1,498
SVN	0.00	0.01	0.03	0.08	0.41	0.06	0.07	7,371
SWE	0.00	0.04	0.09	0.20	0.99	0.16	0.19	83,062
THA	0.00	0.02	0.06	0.14	0.88	0.10	0.12	99,324
TUR	0.00	0.02	0.06	0.15	0.99	0.11	0.14	62,996
TWN	0.00	0.06	0.12	0.22	0.97	0.16	0.14	239,883
UKR	0.00	0.01	0.02	0.07	0.88	0.06	0.12	5,861
USA	0.00	0.03	0.07	0.24	0.99	0.18	0.22	1,536,923
VEN	0.00	0.04	0.07	0.18	0.94	0.12	0.11	3,980
VNM	0.00	0.03	0.08	0.17	0.93	0.13	0.15	39,343
ZAF	0.00	0.03	0.08	0.16	0.94	0.12	0.14	82,366

(Continued)

Table A.8. *(Continued)*

	Min	25%	Median	75%	Max	Mean	StdDev	# Observations
				CASH/TA Trend				
ARE	−0.36	−0.02	−0.00	0.01	0.40	−0.01	0.06	6,700
ARG	−0.36	−0.01	0.00	0.01	0.40	0.00	0.04	13,407
AUS	−0.42	−0.03	−0.00	0.01	0.44	−0.01	0.09	300,910
AUT	−0.46	−0.01	0.00	0.00	0.46	−0.00	0.04	22,520
BEL	−0.46	−0.01	0.00	0.00	0.46	−0.00	0.05	32,089
BGR	−0.25	−0.00	0.00	0.00	0.46	−0.00	0.03	10,687
BHR	−0.36	−0.02	0.00	0.01	0.40	−0.00	0.06	2,956
BRA	−0.36	−0.01	0.00	0.01	0.40	−0.00	0.05	54,565
CAN	−0.44	−0.02	0.00	0.01	0.42	−0.00	0.07	224,124
CHE	−0.46	−0.01	0.00	0.01	0.46	−0.00	0.04	56,712
CHL	−0.36	−0.01	−0.00	0.00	0.40	−0.00	0.04	30,854
CHN	−0.30	−0.03	−0.00	0.01	0.30	−0.01	0.05	283,560
COL	−0.36	−0.01	0.00	0.01	0.40	0.00	0.04	6,358
CYP	−0.46	−0.01	0.00	0.00	0.46	−0.00	0.04	16,765
CZE	−0.33	−0.00	0.00	0.00	0.46	0.00	0.04	6,720
DEU	−0.46	−0.01	0.00	0.00	0.46	−0.00	0.06	187,269
DNK	−0.46	−0.01	−0.00	0.01	0.46	−0.00	0.05	46,304
EGY	−0.36	−0.02	−0.00	0.01	0.40	−0.00	0.05	16,211
ESP	−0.46	−0.01	0.00	0.01	0.46	−0.00	0.04	39,354
EST	−0.25	−0.01	0.00	0.01	0.17	−0.00	0.03	2,579
FIN	−0.46	−0.01	−0.00	0.01	0.46	−0.00	0.05	30,053
FRA	−0.46	−0.01	0.00	0.01	0.46	−0.00	0.04	168,024
GBR	−0.46	−0.02	0.00	0.01	0.46	−0.01	0.07	388,884
GRC	−0.46	−0.01	−0.00	0.01	0.46	−0.00	0.04	57,391
HKG	−0.42	−0.02	0.00	0.01	0.44	−0.00	0.07	220,051
HRV	−0.18	−0.00	−0.00	0.00	0.44	0.00	0.03	12,668
HUN	−0.46	−0.01	−0.00	0.01	0.46	−0.00	0.04	7,739
IDN	−0.36	−0.01	0.00	0.01	0.40	−0.00	0.04	64,011
IND	−0.35	−0.00	0.00	0.00	0.37	−0.00	0.04	625,463
IRL	−0.46	−0.01	0.00	0.01	0.46	−0.00	0.05	10,545
ISL	−0.36	−0.01	0.00	0.00	0.40	−0.00	0.03	4,794
ISR	−0.46	−0.02	−0.00	0.01	0.46	−0.00	0.08	75,988
ITA	−0.46	−0.01	−0.00	0.01	0.46	−0.00	0.04	63,019
JOR	−0.36	−0.01	0.00	0.00	0.40	−0.00	0.05	25,814
JPN	−0.42	−0.01	0.00	0.01	0.44	−0.00	0.04	820,518
KAZ	−0.17	−0.02	0.00	0.01	0.30	−0.00	0.04	1,035
KOR	−0.42	−0.02	−0.00	0.01	0.44	−0.00	0.06	294,250
KWT	−0.36	−0.01	−0.00	0.01	0.40	−0.00	0.06	23,325
LKA	−0.36	−0.01	−0.00	0.01	0.40	−0.00	0.05	18,344
LTU	−0.20	−0.01	−0.00	0.00	0.31	−0.00	0.03	4,528
LUX	−0.39	−0.01	0.00	0.00	0.26	0.00	0.04	3,267
LVA	−0.21	−0.01	0.00	0.01	0.32	−0.00	0.04	3,325
MAR	−0.36	−0.01	0.00	0.01	0.40	−0.00	0.04	10,983
MEX	−0.30	−0.01	−0.00	0.01	0.40	−0.00	0.03	20,690
MKD	−0.18	−0.00	0.00	0.00	0.31	0.00	0.04	2,517
MLT	−0.32	−0.01	0.00	0.00	0.18	−0.00	0.03	1,418
MYS	−0.36	−0.01	0.00	0.01	0.40	−0.00	0.04	192,519
NGA	−0.36	−0.01	0.00	0.00	0.40	−0.00	0.06	15,623
NLD	−0.46	−0.01	0.00	0.00	0.46	−0.00	0.04	38,264
NOR	−0.46	−0.02	−0.00	0.01	0.46	−0.00	0.06	45,681
NZL	−0.42	−0.01	0.00	0.00	0.44	−0.00	0.06	18,399

(Continued)

Table A.8. *(Continued)*

	Min	25%	Median	75%	Max	Mean	StdDev	# Observations
				CASH/TA Trend				
PAK	−0.36	−0.01	0.00	0.00	0.40	−0.00	0.04	30,696
PER	−0.32	−0.01	0.00	0.01	0.39	0.00	0.04	12,167
PHL	−0.36	−0.01	0.00	0.01	0.40	−0.00	0.06	40,574
POL	−0.46	−0.01	0.00	0.00	0.46	−0.00	0.05	61,773
PRT	−0.40	−0.01	0.00	0.00	0.46	−0.00	0.03	14,762
ROM	−0.46	−0.00	0.00	0.00	0.46	−0.00	0.03	16,508
RUS	−0.46	−0.01	0.00	0.01	0.46	0.00	0.06	23,448
SAU	−0.36	−0.02	0.00	0.01	0.40	−0.00	0.06	15,690
SGP	−0.42	−0.02	0.00	0.01	0.44	−0.00	0.06	120,532
SVK	−0.13	−0.01	0.00	0.00	0.15	−0.00	0.02	1,498
SVN	−0.30	−0.00	0.00	0.00	0.28	−0.00	0.02	7,371
SWE	−0.46	−0.01	−0.00	0.01	0.46	−0.00	0.06	83,062
THA	−0.36	−0.01	−0.00	0.01	0.40	−0.00	0.04	99,324
TUR	−0.46	−0.01	−0.00	0.01	0.46	−0.00	0.06	62,996
TWN	−0.42	−0.02	0.00	0.02	0.44	0.00	0.05	239,883
UKR	−0.23	−0.00	0.00	0.00	0.32	0.00	0.03	5,861
USA	−0.44	−0.02	−0.00	0.01	0.42	−0.00	0.06	1,536,923
VEN	−0.18	−0.01	0.00	0.00	0.31	−0.00	0.03	3,980
VNM	−0.36	−0.02	−0.00	0.01	0.40	−0.00	0.05	39,343
ZAF	−0.36	−0.01	0.00	0.01	0.40	−0.00	0.05	82,366
				NI/TA Level				
ARE*	−0.04	0.00	0.00	0.01	0.03	0.00	0.01	6,740
ARG*	−0.04	−0.00	0.00	0.01	0.03	0.00	0.01	13,460
AUS*	−0.47	−0.02	−0.00	0.00	0.10	−0.02	0.05	301,452
AUT	−0.60	0.00	0.00	0.00	0.13	−0.00	0.02	22,647
BEL	−0.35	0.00	0.00	0.01	0.13	0.00	0.01	32,183
BGR	−0.19	−0.00	0.00	0.01	0.13	0.00	0.02	11,634
BHR*	−0.03	0.00	0.00	0.01	0.03	0.01	0.01	3,011
BRA*	−0.04	−0.00	0.00	0.01	0.03	0.00	0.01	54,622
CAN	−0.42	−0.01	0.00	0.00	0.20	−0.01	0.04	224,767
CHE	−0.60	0.00	0.00	0.00	0.13	0.00	0.02	56,930
CHL*	−0.04	0.00	0.00	0.01	0.03	0.00	0.01	30,950
CHN	−0.15	0.00	0.00	0.01	0.15	0.00	0.01	283,803
COL*	−0.04	0.00	0.00	0.01	0.03	0.00	0.01	6,403
CYP	−0.60	−0.00	0.00	0.00	0.13	−0.00	0.03	17,300
CZE	−0.29	0.00	0.00	0.00	0.04	0.00	0.01	6,778
DEU	−0.60	−0.00	0.00	0.00	0.13	−0.00	0.02	188,244
DNK	−0.60	0.00	0.00	0.00	0.13	−0.00	0.03	46,529
EGY*	−0.04	0.00	0.00	0.01	0.03	0.01	0.01	16,258
ESP	−0.60	0.00	0.00	0.00	0.13	0.00	0.03	39,413
EST	−0.09	−0.00	0.00	0.01	0.05	0.00	0.01	2,601
FIN	−0.22	0.00	0.00	0.01	0.13	0.00	0.01	30,106
FRA	−0.60	0.00	0.00	0.00	0.13	0.00	0.02	168,783
GBR*	−0.60	−0.01	0.00	0.01	0.13	−0.01	0.04	390,110
GRC	−0.60	−0.00	0.00	0.01	0.13	0.00	0.02	57,500
HKG	−0.47	−0.00	0.00	0.01	0.10	−0.00	0.03	220,088
HRV	−0.11	−0.00	0.00	0.00	0.13	0.00	0.01	12,933
HUN	−0.15	−0.00	0.00	0.01	0.03	0.00	0.01	7,763
IDN*	−0.04	0.00	0.00	0.01	0.03	0.00	0.01	64,103
IND*	−0.04	0.00	0.00	0.01	0.03	0.00	0.01	631,104

*Winsorization levels are at 1 and 99 percentiles instead of 0.1 and 99.9 percentiles.

(Continued)

Table A.8. *(Continued)*

	Min	25%	Median	75%	Max	Mean	StdDev	# Observations
				NI/TA Level				
IRL	−0.60	−0.00	0.00	0.01	0.13	0.00	0.02	10,609
ISL	−0.13	0.00	0.00	0.01	0.02	0.00	0.01	4,827
ISR	−0.60	−0.00	0.00	0.00	0.13	−0.01	0.05	76,032
ITA	−0.49	−0.00	0.00	0.00	0.13	0.00	0.01	63,074
JOR*	−0.04	−0.00	0.00	0.00	0.03	0.00	0.01	26,045
JPN	−0.47	0.00	0.00	0.00	0.10	0.00	0.01	820,562
KAZ*	−0.04	0.00	0.00	0.00	0.03	0.00	0.01	1,048
KOR	−0.47	−0.00	0.00	0.01	0.10	−0.00	0.02	297,303
KWT*	−0.04	0.00	0.00	0.01	0.03	0.00	0.01	23,403
LKA*	−0.04	0.00	0.00	0.01	0.03	0.00	0.01	18,408
LTU	−0.05	−0.00	0.00	0.01	0.05	0.00	0.01	4,537
LUX	−0.20	0.00	0.00	0.01	0.09	0.00	0.02	3,417
LVA	−0.10	−0.00	0.00	0.01	0.13	0.00	0.01	3,444
MAR*	−0.04	0.00	0.00	0.01	0.03	0.00	0.01	11,058
MEX*	−0.04	0.00	0.00	0.01	0.03	0.00	0.01	20,826
MKD	−0.50	0.00	0.00	0.00	0.03	−0.00	0.03	2,620
MLT	−0.14	0.00	0.00	0.00	0.04	0.00	0.01	1,436
MYS*	−0.04	0.00	0.00	0.01	0.03	0.00	0.01	192,568
NGA*	−0.04	0.00	0.00	0.01	0.03	0.00	0.01	15,946
NLD	−0.60	0.00	0.00	0.01	0.13	0.00	0.03	38,290
NOR	−0.60	−0.00	0.00	0.00	0.13	−0.00	0.03	45,933
NZL	−0.47	−0.00	0.00	0.01	0.10	−0.01	0.05	18,434
PAK*	−0.04	0.00	0.00	0.01	0.03	0.00	0.01	30,785
PER*	−0.04	0.00	0.00	0.01	0.03	0.01	0.01	12,247
PHL*	−0.04	−0.00	0.00	0.01	0.03	0.00	0.01	40,643
POL	−0.54	−0.00	0.00	0.01	0.11	0.00	0.02	61,982
PRT	−0.22	−0.00	0.00	0.00	0.06	0.00	0.01	14,870
ROM	−0.60	−0.00	0.00	0.01	0.13	0.00	0.02	18,411
RUS	−0.60	0.00	0.00	0.01	0.13	0.00	0.02	23,853
SAU*	−0.04	0.00	0.00	0.01	0.03	0.00	0.01	15,741
SGP	−0.47	0.00	0.00	0.01	0.10	0.00	0.02	120,617
SVK	−0.02	0.00	0.00	0.00	0.03	0.00	0.01	1,609
SVN	−0.11	−0.00	0.00	0.00	0.03	0.00	0.01	7,437
SWE	−0.60	−0.01	0.00	0.01	0.13	−0.01	0.03	83,478
THA*	−0.04	0.00	0.00	0.01	0.03	0.00	0.01	99,368
TUR	−0.60	−0.00	0.00	0.01	0.13	0.00	0.03	63,007
TWN	−0.47	0.00	0.00	0.01	0.10	0.00	0.01	239,925
UKR	−0.10	−0.00	0.00	0.01	0.06	0.00	0.01	6,012
USA	−0.42	−0.00	0.00	0.01	0.20	−0.00	0.03	1,536,308
VEN*	−0.04	0.00	0.00	0.01	0.03	0.00	0.01	4,038
VNM*	−0.04	0.00	0.00	0.01	0.03	0.01	0.01	39,594
ZAF*	−0.04	0.00	0.00	0.01	0.03	0.00	0.01	82,657

*Winsorization levels are at 1 and 99 percentiles instead of 0.1 and 99.9 percentiles.

(Continued)

Table A.8. *(Continued)*

	Min	25%	Median	75%	Max	Mean	StdDev	# Observations
				NI/TA Trend				
ARE*	−0.03	−0.00	0.00	0.00	0.03	−0.00	0.01	6,740
ARG*	−0.03	−0.00	0.00	0.00	0.03	−0.00	0.01	13,460
AUS*	−0.38	−0.00	0.00	0.00	0.29	−0.00	0.04	301,452
AUT	−0.35	−0.00	0.00	0.00	0.31	−0.00	0.01	22,647
BEL	−0.35	−0.00	0.00	0.00	0.31	−0.00	0.01	32,183
BGR	−0.35	−0.00	0.00	0.00	0.31	−0.00	0.02	11,634
BHR*	−0.03	−0.00	0.00	0.00	0.03	−0.00	0.00	3,011
BRA*	−0.03	−0.00	0.00	0.00	0.03	−0.00	0.01	54,622
CAN	−0.32	−0.00	0.00	0.00	0.25	0.00	0.03	224,767
CHE	−0.35	−0.00	0.00	0.00	0.31	−0.00	0.01	56,930
CHL*	−0.03	−0.00	0.00	0.00	0.03	−0.00	0.01	30,950
CHN	−0.18	−0.00	-0.00	0.00	0.15	−0.00	0.01	283,803
COL*	−0.03	−0.00	0.00	0.00	0.03	−0.00	0.00	6,403
CYP	−0.35	−0.00	0.00	0.00	0.31	−0.00	0.02	17,300
CZE	−0.27	−0.00	0.00	0.00	0.26	−0.00	0.01	6,778
DEU	−0.35	−0.00	0.00	0.00	0.31	−0.00	0.02	188,244
DNK	−0.35	−0.00	0.00	0.00	0.31	−0.00	0.02	46,529
EGY*	−0.03	−0.00	0.00	0.00	0.03	−0.00	0.01	16,258
ESP	−0.35	−0.00	0.00	0.00	0.31	−0.00	0.02	39,413
EST	−0.32	−0.00	0.00	0.00	0.11	−0.00	0.02	2,601
FIN	−0.20	−0.00	0.00	0.00	0.31	−0.00	0.01	30,106
FRA	−0.35	−0.00	0.00	0.00	0.31	−0.00	0.01	168,783
GBR*	−0.35	−0.00	0.00	0.00	0.31	−0.00	0.03	390,110
GRC	−0.35	−0.00	-0.00	0.00	0.31	−0.00	0.01	57,500
HKG	−0.38	−0.00	0.00	0.00	0.29	−0.00	0.03	220,088
HRV	−0.22	−0.00	0.00	0.00	0.10	−0.00	0.01	12,933
HUN	−0.10	−0.00	0.00	0.00	0.11	−0.00	0.01	7,763
IDN	−0.03	−0.00	0.00	0.00	0.03	−0.00	0.01	64,103
IND*	−0.14	−0.00	0.00	0.00	0.12	−0.00	0.01	631,104
IRL	−0.35	−0.00	0.00	0.00	0.31	−0.00	0.02	10,609
ISL	−0.12	−0.00	0.00	0.00	0.13	−0.00	0.01	4,827
ISR	−0.35	−0.00	-0.00	0.00	0.31	−0.00	0.04	76,032
ITA	−0.35	−0.00	0.00	0.00	0.31	−0.00	0.01	63,074
JOR*	−0.03	−0.00	0.00	0.00	0.03	−0.00	0.01	26,045
JPN	−0.38	−0.00	0.00	0.00	0.29	−0.00	0.01	820,562
KAZ*	−0.03	−0.00	0.00	0.00	0.03	−0.00	0.01	1,048
KOR	−0.38	−0.00	0.00	0.00	0.29	−0.00	0.03	297,303
KWT*	−0.03	−0.00	0.00	0.00	0.03	−0.00	0.01	23,403
LKA*	−0.03	−0.00	0.00	0.00	0.03	−0.00	0.01	18,408
LTU	−0.12	−0.00	0.00	0.00	0.11	0.00	0.01	4,537
LUX	−0.09	−0.00	0.00	0.00	0.15	0.00	0.01	3,417
LVA	−0.19	−0.00	0.00	0.00	0.08	−0.00	0.01	3,444
MAR*	−0.03	−0.00	0.00	0.00	0.03	−0.00	0.00	11,058
MEX*	−0.03	−0.00	0.00	0.00	0.03	0.00	0.01	20,826
MKD	−0.35	−0.00	0.00	0.00	0.31	−0.00	0.02	2,620
MLT	−0.04	−0.00	-0.00	0.00	0.03	−0.00	0.00	1,436
MYS*	−0.03	−0.00	-0.00	0.00	0.03	−0.00	0.01	192,568
NGA*	−0.03	−0.00	0.00	0.00	0.03	−0.00	0.01	15,946
NLD	−0.35	−0.00	0.00	0.00	0.31	−0.00	0.02	38,290
NOR	−0.35	−0.00	0.00	0.00	0.31	−0.00	0.02	45,933
NZL	−0.38	−0.00	0.00	0.00	0.29	−0.00	0.03	18,434

*Winsorization levels are at 1 and 99 percentiles instead of 0.1 and 99.9 percentiles.

(Continued)

Table A.8. (*Continued*)

	Min	25%	Median	75%	Max	Mean	StdDev	# Observations
				NI/TA Trend				
PAK*	−0.03	−0.00	0.00	0.00	0.03	0.00	0.01	30,785
PER*	−0.03	−0.00	0.00	0.00	0.03	−0.00	0.01	12,247
PHL*	−0.03	−0.00	0.00	0.00	0.03	−0.00	0.01	40,643
POL	−0.35	−0.00	0.00	0.00	0.31	−0.00	0.02	61,982
PRT	−0.35	−0.00	0.00	0.00	0.21	−0.00	0.01	14,870
ROM	−0.35	−0.00	0.00	0.00	0.31	−0.00	0.02	18,411
RUS	−0.35	−0.00	0.00	0.00	0.31	0.00	0.02	23,853
SAU*	−0.03	−0.00	0.00	0.00	0.03	−0.00	0.01	15,741
SGP	−0.38	−0.00	-0.00	0.00	0.29	−0.00	0.02	120,617
SVK	−0.05	−0.00	0.00	0.00	0.06	−0.00	0.01	1,609
SVN	−0.17	−0.00	0.00	0.00	0.06	−0.00	0.01	7,437
SWE	−0.35	−0.00	0.00	0.00	0.31	−0.00	0.03	83,478
THA*	−0.03	−0.00	0.00	0.00	0.03	−0.00	0.01	99,368
TUR	−0.35	−0.00	-0.00	0.00	0.31	−0.00	0.03	63,007
TWN	−0.38	−0.00	-0.00	0.00	0.29	−0.00	0.01	239,925
UKR	−0.11	−0.00	0.00	0.00	0.13	−0.00	0.01	6,012
USA	−0.32	−0.00	0.00	0.00	0.25	−0.00	0.02	1,536,308
VEN*	−0.03	−0.00	0.00	0.00	0.03	−0.00	0.00	4,038
VNM*	−0.03	−0.00	-0.00	0.00	0.03	−0.00	0.01	39,594
ZAF*	−0.03	−0.00	0.00	0.00	0.03	−0.00	0.01	82,657
				SIZE Level				
ARE	−4.80	−0.88	0.08	1.15	4.25	0.14	1.51	7,608
ARG	−6.52	−1.41	0.25	1.57	7.06	0.14	2.06	14,787
AUS	−6.46	−1.24	-0.12	1.53	6.96	0.30	2.06	322,712
AUT	−6.75	−1.39	-0.15	1.32	4.50	−0.08	2.01	23,771
BEL	−6.75	−1.40	0.10	1.54	6.91	0.11	2.26	38,826
BGR	−6.75	−1.69	-0.32	0.91	7.97	−0.36	1.84	17,793
BHR	−3.60	−1.13	-0.27	1.05	3.23	−0.09	1.49	3,646
BRA	−6.52	−1.73	-0.07	1.31	7.37	−0.14	2.56	61,159
CAN	−6.08	−1.53	-0.23	1.25	6.00	−0.10	2.10	245,557
CHE	−6.75	−1.30	-0.06	1.26	6.31	0.06	1.97	55,797
CHL	−6.52	−1.11	0.07	1.27	4.30	−0.00	1.83	33,888
CHN	−2.46	−0.73	-0.24	0.32	3.84	−0.14	0.89	305,899
COL	−5.42	−1.44	-0.09	1.10	4.43	−0.25	1.69	7,487
CYP	−4.64	−1.02	0.03	1.07	6.87	0.05	1.65	20,814
CZE	−6.75	−1.51	-0.17	0.88	5.36	−0.25	1.90	8,969
DEU	−6.75	−0.40	1.10	2.75	7.97	1.16	2.51	215,855
DNK	−6.75	−0.27	0.91	2.23	7.41	1.03	1.90	46,715
EGY	−6.52	−1.05	0.02	1.50	5.40	0.21	1.76	19,275
ESP	−6.75	−1.69	-0.29	1.15	5.31	−0.32	2.12	41,717
EST	−3.62	−0.46	0.27	1.33	5.13	0.43	1.67	2,766
FIN	−6.36	−1.77	-0.47	1.11	6.40	−0.31	1.98	30,384
FRA	−6.75	−1.33	0.11	1.86	7.66	0.35	2.32	195,181
GBR	−6.75	−1.15	0.23	1.87	7.97	0.46	2.24	422,563
GRC	−6.75	−0.46	0.49	1.58	6.55	0.65	1.61	60,289
HKG	−8.79	−1.50	-0.49	0.87	6.96	−0.20	1.85	234,889
HRV	−6.75	−0.72	0.42	1.63	6.10	0.47	1.80	16,063
HUN	−6.75	−1.16	0.56	2.14	6.23	0.53	2.28	8,581
IDN	−6.52	−1.03	0.14	1.41	6.08	0.25	1.83	71,672

*Winsorization levels are at 1 and 99 percentiles instead of 0.1 and 99.9 percentiles.

(*Continued*)

Table A.8. *(Continued)*

	Min	25%	Median	75%	Max	Mean	StdDev	# Observations
				SIZE Level				
IND	−5.27	−1.22	0.21	2.02	8.39	0.53	2.32	556,040
IRL	−6.75	−2.06	-0.84	0.65	4.79	−0.71	1.97	10,853
ISL	−6.75	−1.98	-1.05	-0.08	2.76	−1.05	1.53	5,981
ISR	−6.75	−0.77	0.29	1.59	7.97	0.50	1.85	98,621
ITA	−6.75	−0.91	0.22	1.66	6.36	0.40	1.93	63,750
JOR	−3.88	−0.88	-0.09	1.08	6.17	0.18	1.51	29,987
JPN	−9.57	−0.79	0.25	1.53	6.96	0.47	1.73	841,659
KAZ	−6.07	−2.15	-0.58	1.19	5.50	−0.52	1.92	1,548
KOR	−11.23	−0.49	0.29	1.34	6.96	0.48	1.80	345,407
KWT	−2.55	−0.33	0.58	1.41	5.14	0.65	1.34	25,848
LKA	−6.52	−0.82	0.12	1.29	5.26	0.26	1.54	20,509
LTU	−4.47	−0.89	0.19	1.16	4.08	0.15	1.55	5,876
LUX	−6.75	−2.35	-0.55	0.43	4.33	−0.84	2.07	4,590
LVA	−5.38	−1.43	-0.22	2.16	5.91	0.25	2.39	4,849
MAR	−6.52	−1.29	-0.13	1.65	4.76	0.10	1.81	11,560
MEX	−6.52	−1.19	0.17	1.53	5.16	0.10	1.97	22,526
MKD	−6.46	−1.26	0.20	1.37	5.37	0.11	1.86	4,456
MLT	−4.07	−0.98	-0.10	1.18	2.31	−0.00	1.36	2,007
MYS	−4.25	−0.21	0.68	1.78	6.47	0.84	1.58	204,304
NGA	−6.52	−1.40	-0.21	1.62	6.17	−0.00	2.15	19,030
NLD	−6.75	−1.89	-0.35	1.11	5.99	−0.26	2.18	38,602
NOR	−6.75	−0.93	0.15	1.39	6.65	0.26	1.74	48,794
NZL	−5.78	−1.54	-0.07	1.07	5.12	−0.21	1.89	20,373
PAK	−6.52	−1.12	0.77	2.77	7.37	0.78	2.53	49,297
PER	−6.52	−1.03	0.33	1.80	5.54	0.33	2.01	14,474
PHL	−6.52	−1.44	-0.32	1.07	5.31	−0.09	1.82	44,162
POL	−5.61	−1.15	0.11	1.53	7.97	0.26	2.06	73,226
PRT	−6.75	−1.95	-0.33	1.28	4.56	−0.43	2.47	16,646
ROM	−6.75	−1.00	0.26	1.58	7.97	0.26	2.11	48,073
RUS	−6.75	−1.74	-0.28	1.26	7.97	−0.19	2.23	30,678
SAU	−4.48	−0.75	0.14	1.46	5.34	0.42	1.57	17,144
SGP	−4.35	−0.63	0.35	1.59	6.96	0.58	1.71	129,749
SVK	−6.14	−0.40	1.02	3.01	7.97	1.47	2.61	4,265
SVN	−6.75	−0.52	0.82	2.34	7.97	1.12	2.44	11,200
SWE	−6.75	−0.72	0.98	2.57	7.97	1.05	2.38	88,335
THA	−5.99	−0.87	0.10	1.24	6.48	0.30	1.60	109,062
TUR	−5.21	−1.23	-0.03	1.25	6.88	0.09	1.86	67,078
TWN	−5.78	−0.72	0.24	1.27	6.90	0.36	1.51	262,305
UKR	−6.75	−0.97	0.10	1.06	7.97	−0.01	1.64	9,013
USA	−6.08	−1.99	-0.65	0.79	6.00	−0.53	2.01	1,598,295
VEN	−6.52	−1.68	-0.15	1.17	7.37	−0.42	2.60	5,450
VNM	−4.93	−1.21	-0.27	0.78	6.46	−0.11	1.63	45,171
ZAF	−6.52	−1.57	0.18	1.89	6.55	0.16	2.34	88,296

(Continued)

Table A.8. *(Continued)*

	Min	25%	Median	75%	Max	Mean	StdDev	# Observations
				SIZE Trend				
ARE	−0.83	−0.13	−0.01	0.09	1.81	−0.00	0.23	7,608
ARG	−1.81	−0.16	−0.02	0.10	2.01	−0.02	0.32	14,787
AUS	−1.58	−0.18	−0.00	0.17	1.82	0.00	0.38	322,712
AUT	−2.03	−0.12	−0.02	0.08	2.11	−0.02	0.27	23,771
BEL	−2.03	−0.11	−0.02	0.07	2.11	−0.02	0.26	38,826
BGR	−2.03	−0.15	0.00	0.15	2.11	0.01	0.36	17,793
BHR	−0.80	−0.06	0.01	0.09	2.01	0.03	0.17	3,646
BRA	−1.81	−0.15	0.00	0.14	2.01	−0.01	0.35	61,159
CAN	−1.90	−0.16	0.00	0.16	1.84	−0.00	0.37	245,557
CHE	−2.03	−0.11	−0.01	0.08	2.11	−0.02	0.24	55,797
CHL	−1.81	−0.10	−0.00	0.09	2.01	−0.00	0.22	33,888
CHN	−0.96	−0.10	−0.00	0.11	1.13	0.01	0.19	305,899
COL	−1.34	−0.09	0.00	0.10	1.85	0.01	0.21	7,487
CYP	−2.03	−0.18	−0.00	0.17	2.11	0.00	0.35	20,814
CZE	−2.03	−0.13	0.00	0.12	2.11	−0.01	0.26	8,969
DEU	−2.03	−0.17	−0.03	0.09	2.11	−0.06	0.35	215,855
DNK	−2.03	−0.14	−0.02	0.09	2.11	−0.03	0.28	46,715
EGY	−1.81	−0.13	−0.01	0.11	2.01	0.02	0.27	19,275
ESP	−2.03	−0.11	−0.00	0.10	2.11	0.01	0.26	41,717
EST	−1.99	−0.13	−0.01	0.12	2.11	−0.00	0.27	2,766
FIN	−2.03	−0.13	0.00	0.14	2.11	0.00	0.27	30,384
FRA	−2.03	−0.12	0.00	0.12	2.11	0.00	0.28	195,181
GBR	−2.03	−0.15	0.00	0.13	2.11	−0.02	0.34	422,563
GRC	−2.03	−0.19	−0.03	0.13	2.11	−0.02	0.32	60,289
HKG	−1.58	−0.17	−0.02	0.14	1.82	0.00	0.35	234,889
HRV	−2.03	−0.14	−0.01	0.08	2.11	−0.02	0.24	16,063
HUN	−1.80	−0.19	−0.05	0.09	2.11	−0.05	0.30	8,581
IDN	−1.81	−0.18	−0.03	0.13	2.01	−0.01	0.34	71,672
IND	−1.71	−0.22	−0.04	0.13	2.08	−0.03	0.36	556,040
IRL	−2.03	−0.10	0.01	0.13	2.11	0.00	0.30	10,853
ISL	−2.03	−0.11	0.00	0.12	2.11	0.02	0.30	5,981
ISR	−2.03	−0.15	−0.02	0.10	2.11	−0.03	0.31	98,621
ITA	−2.03	−0.11	−0.01	0.09	2.11	−0.00	0.23	63,750
JOR	−1.81	−0.10	0.00	0.12	2.01	0.02	0.24	29,987
JPN	−1.58	−0.12	−0.01	0.09	1.82	−0.01	0.22	841,659
KAZ	−1.81	−0.11	0.00	0.13	2.01	0.03	0.41	1,548
KOR	−1.58	−0.18	−0.03	0.13	1.82	−0.02	0.34	345,407
KWT	−1.81	−0.12	−0.01	0.09	2.01	−0.01	0.24	25,848
LKA	−1.81	−0.13	−0.02	0.09	2.01	−0.00	0.23	20,509
LTU	−2.03	−0.14	−0.01	0.12	2.11	−0.01	0.32	5,876
LUX	−2.03	−0.08	0.00	0.10	2.11	0.01	0.21	4,590
LVA	−2.03	−0.12	0.01	0.17	2.11	0.04	0.32	4,849
MAR	−1.81	−0.09	−0.00	0.08	2.01	−0.00	0.20	11,560
MEX	−1.81	−0.13	−0.01	0.09	2.01	−0.02	0.25	22,526
MKD	−1.45	−0.10	0.00	0.07	1.26	−0.01	0.19	4,456
MLT	−1.23	−0.07	0.00	0.08	1.85	0.01	0.23	2,007
MYS	−1.81	−0.14	−0.03	0.09	2.01	−0.02	0.26	204,304
NGA	−1.81	−0.16	−0.02	0.13	2.01	0.01	0.34	19,030
NLD	−2.03	−0.11	0.00	0.11	2.11	−0.01	0.26	38,602
NOR	−2.03	−0.13	−0.00	0.13	2.11	0.00	0.33	48,794
NZL	−1.58	−0.09	0.01	0.11	1.82	0.02	0.25	20,373

(Continued)

Table A.8. (*Continued*)

	Min	25%	Median	75%	Max	Mean	StdDev	# Observations
				SIZE Trend				
PAK	−1.81	−0.19	−0.04	0.10	2.01	−0.03	0.29	49,297
PER	−1.81	−0.13	0.00	0.12	2.01	0.00	0.27	14,474
PHL	−1.81	−0.15	−0.01	0.13	2.01	0.01	0.32	44,162
POL	−2.03	−0.21	−0.04	0.13	2.11	−0.04	0.36	73,226
PRT	−2.03	−0.14	−0.02	0.09	2.11	−0.02	0.25	16,646
ROM	−2.03	−0.13	0.00	0.20	2.11	0.05	0.39	48,073
RUS	−2.03	−0.14	0.00	0.11	2.11	−0.01	0.30	30,678
SAU	−1.81	−0.11	−0.01	0.10	2.01	0.01	0.22	17,144
SGP	−1.58	−0.14	−0.02	0.10	1.82	−0.01	0.26	129,749
SVK	−2.03	−0.06	0.01	0.12	2.11	0.04	0.30	4,265
SVN	−2.03	−0.16	−0.03	0.07	1.98	−0.06	0.31	11,200
SWE	−2.03	−0.15	−0.01	0.14	2.11	−0.00	0.34	88,335
THA	−1.81	−0.15	−0.02	0.12	2.01	−0.00	0.28	109,062
TUR	−2.03	−0.17	−0.03	0.12	2.11	−0.01	0.29	67,078
TWN	−1.58	−0.13	−0.02	0.11	1.82	−0.01	0.24	262,305
UKR	−2.03	−0.16	0.00	0.17	2.11	0.00	0.42	9,013
USA	−1.90	−0.15	−0.01	0.13	1.84	−0.02	0.33	1,598,295
VEN	−1.81	−0.17	−0.02	0.11	2.01	0.01	0.42	5,450
VNM	−1.81	−0.19	−0.04	0.09	2.01	−0.04	0.26	45,171
ZAF	−1.81	−0.16	−0.01	0.13	2.01	−0.03	0.36	88,296
				M/B				
ARE*	0.34	0.87	1.03	1.30	8.35	1.18	0.60	6,657
ARG*	0.18	0.83	1.01	1.27	32.77	1.54	2.90	13,152
AUS*	0.18	0.92	1.32	2.37	14.76	2.26	2.64	296,870
AUT*	0.20	0.94	1.06	1.37	19.59	1.31	1.11	21,066
BEL*	0.16	0.94	1.09	1.44	19.59	1.44	1.49	30,712
BGR*	0.16	0.66	0.92	1.28	19.59	1.21	1.39	10,689
BHR*	0.40	0.93	1.06	1.25	5.54	1.17	0.47	2,929
BRA*	0.18	0.84	1.07	1.60	32.77	2.71	6.29	53,136
CAN	0.22	0.98	1.31	2.08	64.92	2.26	4.35	220,867
CHE*	0.16	0.99	1.14	1.63	19.59	1.57	1.44	52,059
CHL*	0.18	0.86	1.14	1.68	32.77	1.63	2.82	30,256
CHN	0.67	1.46	2.07	3.11	44.08	2.69	2.49	282,397
COL*	0.23	0.79	1.03	1.28	32.77	1.21	1.10	6,218
CYP*	0.16	0.61	0.80	1.04	19.59	1.06	1.41	16,753
CZE*	0.16	0.65	0.92	1.16	9.28	1.02	0.60	6,516
DEU*	0.16	1.00	1.21	1.67	19.59	1.69	1.85	182,025
DNK*	0.16	0.96	1.06	1.42	19.59	1.53	1.72	43,387
EGY*	0.21	0.98	1.23	1.81	32.77	1.67	1.85	16,110
ESP*	0.16	0.95	1.10	1.46	19.59	1.41	1.24	37,683
EST*	0.17	0.95	1.17	1.75	19.59	1.67	1.85	2,569
FIN*	0.20	1.00	1.22	1.73	19.59	1.64	1.61	28,827
FRA*	0.16	0.94	1.13	1.56	19.59	1.55	1.66	162,873
GBR*	0.16	0.97	1.33	2.08	19.59	2.06	2.50	384,927
GRC*	0.16	0.86	1.09	1.60	19.59	1.65	1.98	56,715
HKG*	0.18	0.72	0.99	1.55	14.76	1.54	1.91	219,231
HRV*	0.16	0.71	0.93	1.18	19.59	1.09	1.07	12,551
HUN**	0.16	0.74	0.99	1.35	19.59	1.20	0.98	7,530
IDN*	0.18	0.87	1.07	1.50	32.77	1.44	1.48	63,044

*Winsorization levels are 0.1 and 99.5 percentiles instead of 0.1 and 99.9 percentiles.
**Winsorization levels are at 1 and 99 percentiles instead of 0.1 and 99.9 percentiles.

(*Continued*)

Table A.8. *(Continued)*

	Min	25%	Median	75%	Max	Mean	StdDev	# Observations
				M/B				
IND**	0.19	0.77	0.99	1.48	12.11	1.48	1.67	478,324
IRL*	0.16	0.99	1.21	1.70	19.59	1.68	1.74	10,121
ISL*	0.31	1.09	1.28	1.63	19.59	1.67	2.02	4,786
ISR*	0.16	0.91	1.04	1.37	19.59	1.57	2.17	75,612
ITA*	0.19	0.95	1.06	1.35	19.59	1.30	1.05	60,786
JOR*	0.18	0.84	1.05	1.40	32.77	1.28	1.21	25,439
JPN*	0.18	0.85	1.00	1.24	14.76	1.22	1.02	819,528
KAZ*	0.23	0.89	1.00	1.20	9.35	1.16	0.61	951
KOR*	0.18	0.80	0.99	1.32	14.76	1.32	1.35	294,834
KWT*	0.18	0.89	1.15	1.56	32.77	1.36	0.93	23,232
LKA*	0.24	0.94	1.13	1.57	32.77	1.56	1.74	18,128
LTU*	0.31	0.81	0.99	1.36	5.32	1.17	0.60	4,529
LUX*	0.33	0.74	0.97	1.19	9.28	1.09	0.66	3,166
LVA*	0.16	0.55	0.76	1.00	6.80	0.87	0.63	3,316
MAR*	0.18	1.07	1.28	1.84	15.95	1.64	0.99	10,855
MEX*	0.18	0.78	1.04	1.44	10.84	1.23	0.72	19,943
MKD*	0.16	0.67	0.92	1.17	19.59	1.53	3.23	2,510
MLT*	0.25	0.99	1.09	1.53	15.76	1.39	0.94	1,418
MYS*	0.18	0.77	0.99	1.41	32.77	1.37	1.64	192,047
NGA*	0.18	0.91	1.20	1.81	32.77	1.74	1.84	15,636
NLD*	0.16	1.00	1.21	1.67	19.59	1.64	1.63	36,682
NOR*	0.16	0.95	1.14	1.71	19.59	1.76	2.06	44,242
NZL*	0.18	0.97	1.27	1.96	14.76	1.92	2.17	18,208
PAK*	0.18	0.84	1.00	1.32	32.77	1.32	1.57	30,060
PER*	0.18	0.80	1.11	1.64	29.63	1.49	1.35	11,734
PHL*	0.18	0.77	1.06	1.71	32.77	2.31	4.96	39,566
POL*	0.16	0.86	1.11	1.65	19.59	1.61	1.89	61,443
PRT*	0.16	0.90	1.02	1.24	19.59	1.16	0.69	14,381
ROM*	0.16	0.66	0.91	1.23	19.59	1.21	1.79	16,500
RUS*	0.16	0.82	1.08	1.56	19.59	1.45	1.63	21,980
SAU*	0.19	1.19	1.73	2.86	32.77	2.46	2.28	15,677
SGP*	0.18	0.82	1.03	1.45	14.76	1.37	1.30	120,119
SVK*	0.21	0.71	0.87	1.03	3.18	0.89	0.29	1,466
SVN*	0.16	0.67	0.84	1.02	19.59	0.92	0.64	7,352
SWE*	0.16	1.03	1.38	2.17	19.59	2.11	2.36	80,849
THA*	0.18	0.86	1.06	1.46	32.77	1.32	1.00	98,910
TUR*	0.16	0.87	1.10	1.59	19.59	1.74	2.65	62,842
TWN*	0.29	0.93	1.17	1.65	14.76	1.49	1.08	239,779
UKR*	0.16	0.87	1.20	1.93	19.59	1.80	2.06	5,729
USA	0.22	1.03	1.31	2.09	64.92	2.12	3.32	1,533,990
VEN*	0.18	0.60	0.90	1.18	32.77	5.38	10.98	3,860
VNM*	0.18	0.81	0.94	1.17	18.99	1.13	0.76	39,271
ZAF*	0.18	0.89	1.19	1.84	32.77	1.84	2.93	81,822

*Winsorization levels are 0.1 and 99.5 percentiles instead of 0.1 and 99.9 percentiles.
**Winsorization levels are 1 and 99 percentiles instead of 0.1 and 99.9 percentiles.

(Continued)

Table A.8. *(Continued)*

	Min	25%	Median	75%	Max	Mean	StdDev	# Observations
				SIGMA				
ARE	0.01	0.09	0.11	0.16	0.43	0.13	0.06	6,687
ARG	0.03	0.09	0.11	0.14	0.65	0.12	0.06	13,453
AUS	0.02	0.13	0.22	0.32	0.95	0.25	0.15	305,684
AUT	0.01	0.07	0.09	0.14	1.16	0.12	0.10	21,938
BEL	0.02	0.07	0.09	0.12	1.42	0.11	0.08	34,242
BGR	0.02	0.14	0.18	0.28	1.11	0.23	0.14	11,719
BHR	0.03	0.07	0.09	0.12	0.24	0.10	0.03	2,937
BRA	0.01	0.10	0.14	0.20	1.19	0.18	0.14	54,021
CAN	0.03	0.11	0.17	0.27	1.02	0.21	0.15	233,281
CHE	0.01	0.07	0.09	0.13	1.42	0.11	0.07	52,914
CHL	0.01	0.06	0.08	0.10	0.73	0.09	0.06	30,512
CHN	0.03	0.08	0.10	0.13	0.43	0.11	0.04	298,453
COL	0.01	0.06	0.09	0.12	0.48	0.10	0.06	6,327
CYP	0.02	0.16	0.21	0.28	1.42	0.25	0.17	17,755
CZE	0.03	0.09	0.13	0.18	0.42	0.14	0.05	7,163
DEU	0.01	0.10	0.15	0.24	1.42	0.22	0.22	199,451
DNK	0.01	0.07	0.10	0.15	1.29	0.13	0.11	43,966
EGY	0.01	0.09	0.12	0.18	1.19	0.15	0.09	17,118
ESP	0.01	0.06	0.09	0.12	0.95	0.10	0.06	38,560
EST	0.01	0.08	0.13	0.20	0.66	0.15	0.10	2,625
FIN	0.01	0.08	0.11	0.16	1.42	0.13	0.09	29,360
FRA	0.01	0.08	0.11	0.16	1.42	0.13	0.09	175,793
GBR	0.01	0.08	0.12	0.18	1.31	0.15	0.10	394,731
GRC	0.01	0.10	0.14	0.19	0.90	0.16	0.08	58,457
HKG	0.02	0.11	0.16	0.24	0.95	0.19	0.11	227,865
HRV	0.01	0.11	0.14	0.18	0.78	0.16	0.08	12,824
HUN	0.02	0.09	0.13	0.18	0.67	0.16	0.09	7,863
IDN	0.01	0.12	0.17	0.26	1.19	0.21	0.13	64,782
IND	0.05	0.15	0.19	0.24	1.00	0.22	0.13	503,137
IRL	0.03	0.08	0.11	0.17	1.42	0.16	0.14	10,209
ISL	0.03	0.08	0.11	0.14	0.61	0.12	0.07	5,064
ISR	0.01	0.10	0.13	0.20	1.15	0.16	0.09	83,567
ITA	0.01	0.07	0.10	0.13	0.76	0.11	0.05	62,136
JOR	0.01	0.09	0.12	0.15	0.74	0.13	0.05	26,803
JPN	0.02	0.08	0.11	0.16	0.95	0.13	0.07	827,007
KAZ	0.01	0.11	0.14	0.23	1.03	0.19	0.12	946
KOR	0.02	0.11	0.15	0.21	0.81	0.17	0.08	336,766
KWT	0.01	0.10	0.12	0.16	0.76	0.13	0.05	23,541
LKA	0.03	0.11	0.15	0.20	1.00	0.17	0.09	19,075
LTU	0.03	0.09	0.13	0.18	1.02	0.15	0.10	5,387
LUX	0.02	0.07	0.09	0.13	0.51	0.11	0.05	3,286
LVA	0.03	0.11	0.14	0.22	0.97	0.17	0.09	3,412
MAR	0.02	0.08	0.10	0.12	0.54	0.10	0.05	10,993
MEX	0.01	0.07	0.10	0.13	1.19	0.11	0.07	20,320
MKD	0.01	0.08	0.11	0.16	0.54	0.13	0.07	2,601
MLT	0.02	0.05	0.07	0.09	0.55	0.08	0.05	1,496
MYS	0.02	0.10	0.14	0.21	1.19	0.17	0.11	199,915
NGA	0.01	0.11	0.14	0.17	0.55	0.14	0.06	16,608
NLD	0.02	0.07	0.09	0.13	1.26	0.11	0.08	37,636
NOR	0.03	0.10	0.14	0.20	1.10	0.17	0.11	45,236
NZL	0.02	0.07	0.09	0.14	0.95	0.13	0.11	18,831

(Continued)

Table A.8. *(Continued)*

	Min	25%	Median	75%	Max	Mean	StdDev	# Observations
				SIGMA				
PAK	0.03	0.11	0.15	0.24	1.19	0.22	0.19	39,752
PER	0.02	0.09	0.12	0.16	0.62	0.13	0.07	11,811
PHL	0.01	0.12	0.17	0.25	0.94	0.20	0.12	40,571
POL	0.01	0.12	0.16	0.24	1.42	0.20	0.13	69,339
PRT	0.01	0.07	0.10	0.15	1.18	0.12	0.09	14,641
ROM	0.01	0.17	0.22	0.33	1.42	0.26	0.15	21,425
RUS	0.03	0.10	0.13	0.20	1.25	0.17	0.11	22,077
SAU	0.02	0.06	0.09	0.13	0.64	0.11	0.06	16,584
SGP	0.02	0.10	0.15	0.23	0.95	0.19	0.14	125,699
SVK	0.01	0.08	0.11	0.16	0.59	0.13	0.08	1,458
SVN	0.01	0.08	0.10	0.14	1.14	0.14	0.12	8,758
SWE	0.01	0.10	0.14	0.25	1.42	0.20	0.17	84,418
THA	0.01	0.09	0.13	0.18	1.19	0.15	0.10	105,776
TUR	0.01	0.10	0.14	0.19	1.25	0.15	0.07	65,671
TWN	0.02	0.08	0.11	0.14	0.88	0.12	0.05	255,014
UKR	0.01	0.15	0.19	0.29	1.05	0.24	0.16	5,690
USA	0.03	0.09	0.15	0.23	1.02	0.18	0.12	1,559,843
VEN	0.01	0.13	0.18	0.23	0.69	0.19	0.10	4,118
VNM	0.01	0.11	0.15	0.19	0.69	0.16	0.07	41,373
ZAF	0.01	0.09	0.13	0.22	1.19	0.19	0.18	83,354

Table A.9. Exits classified as "Defaults".

Default	
Action Type	**Subcategory**
Bankruptcy filling	Administration, Arrangement, Canadian CCAA, Chapter 7, Chapter 11, Chapter 15, Conservatorship, Insolvency, Japanese CRL, Judicial Management, Liquidation, Pre-Negotiation Chapter 11, Protection, Receivership, Rehabilitation, Rehabilitation (Thailand 1997), Reorganization, Restructuring, Section 304, Supreme court declaration, Winding up, Work out, Other, Unknown.
Delisting	Bankruptcy
Default Corporate Action	Bankruptcy, Coupon & Principal Payment, Coupon Payment Only, Debt Restructuring, Interest Payment, Loan Payment, Principal Payment, ADR (Japan only), Declared Sick(India Only), Unknown.

Table A.10. Exits classified as "Other Exits".

Other Exits	
Action Type	**Subcategory**
Delisting	Unknown,Acquired/Merged, Assimilated with underlying shares,Bid price below minimum, Cancellation of listing, End of When- issued trading, Expired, Failure to meet listing requirements, Failure to pay listing fees, Inactive security, Insufficient assets, Insufficient capital and surplus, Insufficient number of market makers, Issue postponed, Lack of market maker interest, Lack of public interest, Liquidated, Matured, Not available, Not current in required filings, NP/FP finished, Privatized, Reorganization security called for redemptions, the company's request, Scheme of arrangement, Insufficient spread of holders, Selective capital reduction of the company

Table A.11. Number of defaults and other exits of 71 economies from 1992 to 2013.

Economy: ARE					
		Defaults		Others	
Year	Active	#	%	#	%
1992	0	0	NaN	0	NaN
1993	0	0	NaN	0	NaN
1994	0	0	NaN	0	NaN
1995	0	0	NaN	0	NaN
1996	0	0	NaN	0	NaN
1997	0	0	NaN	0	NaN
1998	0	0	NaN	0	NaN
1999	0	0	NaN	0	NaN
2000	0	0	NaN	0	NaN
2001	0	0	NaN	0	NaN
2002	0	0	NaN	0	NaN
2003	0	0	NaN	0	NaN
2004	0	0	NaN	0	NaN
2005	0	0	NaN	0	NaN
2006	73	0	0.00	7	8.75
2007	83	0	0.00	13	13.54
2008	80	0	0.00	17	17.53
2009	82	0	0.00	21	20.39
2010	85	0	0.00	23	21.30
2011	83	0	0.00	24	22.43
2012	80	1	0.96	23	22.12
2013	85	0	0.00	12	12.37

Economy:ARG					
		Defaults		Others	
Year	Active	#	%	#	%
1992	1	0	0.00	0	0.00
1993	1	0	0.00	0	0.00
1994	23	0	0.00	2	8.00
1995	87	0	0.00	14	13.86
1996	93	0	0.00	25	21.19
1997	84	0	0.00	26	23.64
1998	72	2	1.82	36	32.73
1999	72	1	0.98	29	28.43
2000	66	1	1.11	23	25.56
2001	50	2	2.35	33	38.82
2002	64	9	10.47	13	15.12
2003	68	2	2.38	14	16.67
2004	65	0	0.00	13	16.67
2005	68	0	0.00	5	6.85
2006	70	0	0.00	7	9.09
2007	75	0	0.00	9	10.71
2008	68	0	0.00	16	19.05
2009	67	1	1.30	9	11.69
2010	67	1	1.35	6	8.11
2011	64	0	0.00	9	12.33
2012	64	0	0.00	7	9.86
2013	66	0	0.00	4	5.71

Economy: AUS					
		Defaults		Others	
Year	Active	#	%	#	%
1992	706	1	0.12	109	13.36
1993	808	0	0.00	63	7.23
1994	904	0	0.00	89	8.96
1995	946	1	0.10	82	7.97
1996	991	1	0.09	66	6.24
1997	1,009	3	0.27	99	8.91
1998	1,005	1	0.09	109	9.78
1999	1,041	2	0.18	97	8.51
2000	1,171	7	0.54	108	8.40
2001	1,166	30	2.31	105	8.07
2002	1,182	9	0.70	101	7.82
2003	1,204	9	0.69	96	7.33
2004	1,321	2	0.14	78	5.57
2005	1,437	7	0.46	89	5.81
2006	1,544	5	0.30	115	6.91
2007	1,709	4	0.22	113	6.19
2008	1,691	28	1.50	148	7.93
2009	1,663	30	1.66	111	6.15
2010	1,676	4	0.22	134	7.39
2011	1,685	0	0.00	177	9.51
2012	1,664	3	0.16	170	9.25
2013	1,637	4	0.22	158	8.78

Economy: AUT					
		Defaults		Others	
Year	Active	#	%	#	%
1992	84	0	0.00	3	3.45
1993	101	0	0.00	8	7.34
1994	110	0	0.00	2	1.79
1995	118	0	0.00	2	1.67
1996	116	1	0.82	5	4.10
1997	118	0	0.00	5	4.07
1998	112	0	0.00	14	11.11
1999	108	0	0.00	17	13.60
2000	119	0	0.00	16	11.85
2001	119	1	0.69	24	16.67
2002	110	1	0.78	18	13.95
2003	107	0	0.00	20	15.75
2004	101	0	0.00	25	19.84
2005	101	0	0.00	16	13.68
2006	103	0	0.00	12	10.43
2007	107	0	0.00	11	9.32
2008	105	1	0.85	11	9.40
2009	100	2	1.75	12	10.53
2010	96	1	0.88	17	14.91
2011	86	0	0.00	18	17.31
2012	82	1	1.08	10	10.75
2013	83	0	0.00	15	15.31

(Continued)

Table A.11. *(Continued)*

Economy: BEL

Year	Active	Defaults #	Defaults %	Others #	Others %
1992	136	0	0.00	6	4.23
1993	138	0	0.00	8	5.48
1994	145	0	0.00	11	7.05
1995	149	0	0.00	10	6.29
1996	159	0	0.00	11	6.47
1997	162	0	0.00	18	10.00
1998	174	0	0.00	15	7.94
1999	191	1	0.50	8	4.00
2000	193	1	0.49	10	4.90
2001	186	2	1.00	13	6.47
2002	176	2	1.05	13	6.81
2003	177	2	1.04	14	7.25
2004	170	1	0.54	14	7.57
2005	171	1	0.54	12	6.52
2006	185	3	1.54	7	3.59
2007	221	0	0.00	54	19.64
2008	199	2	0.70	85	29.72
2009	197	2	0.80	52	20.72
2010	195	0	0.00	54	21.69
2011	176	1	0.41	65	26.86
2012	186	1	0.45	37	16.52
2013	169	1	0.42	68	28.57

Economy: BGR

Year	Active	Defaults #	Defaults %	Others #	Others %
1992	0	0	NaN	0	NaN
1993	0	0	NaN	0	NaN
1994	0	0	NaN	0	NaN
1995	0	0	NaN	0	NaN
1996	0	0	NaN	0	NaN
1997	0	0	NaN	0	NaN
1998	0	0	NaN	0	NaN
1999	0	0	NaN	0	NaN
2000	14	0	0.00	10	41.67
2001	21	0	0.00	8	27.59
2002	30	0	0.00	5	14.29
2003	30	0	0.00	11	26.83
2004	36	0	0.00	3	7.69
2005	130	1	0.67	19	12.67
2006	231	0	0.00	36	13.48
2007	241	2	0.64	71	22.61
2008	214	0	0.00	101	32.06
2009	206	0	0.00	82	28.47
2010	186	1	0.36	91	32.73
2011	171	0	0.00	81	32.14
2012	158	0	0.00	71	31.00
2013	163	0	0.00	72	30.64

Economy: BHR

Year	Active	Defaults #	Defaults %	Others #	Others %
1992	0	0	NaN	0	NaN
1993	0	0	NaN	0	NaN
1994	0	0	NaN	0	NaN
1995	0	0	NaN	0	NaN
1996	0	0	NaN	0	NaN
1997	0	0	NaN	0	NaN
1998	0	0	NaN	0	NaN
1999	0	0	NaN	0	NaN
2000	0	0	NaN	0	NaN
2001	0	0	NaN	0	NaN
2002	0	0	NaN	0	NaN
2003	0	0	NaN	0	NaN
2004	29	0	0.00	1	3.33
2005	37	0	0.00	2	5.13
2006	32	0	0.00	8	20.00
2007	36	0	0.00	7	16.28
2008	33	0	0.00	8	19.51
2009	32	0	0.00	14	30.43
2010	29	0	0.00	15	34.09
2011	25	0	0.00	18	41.86
2012	29	0	0.00	19	39.58
2013	29	0	0.00	12	29.27

Economy: BRA

Year	Active	Defaults #	Defaults %	Others #	Others %
1992	0	0	NaN	0	NaN
1993	0	0	NaN	0	NaN
1994	272	0	0.00	8	2.86
1995	278	0	0.00	100	26.46
1996	289	0	0.00	94	24.54
1997	266	0	0.00	135	33.67
1998	286	2	0.45	154	34.84
1999	323	2	0.46	107	24.77
2000	287	1	0.24	127	30.60
2001	275	1	0.24	138	33.33
2002	247	1	0.27	127	33.87
2003	278	3	0.81	89	24.05
2004	272	0	0.00	91	25.07
2005	267	1	0.30	70	20.71
2006	278	0	0.00	61	17.99
2007	351	0	0.00	38	9.77
2008	338	0	0.00	55	13.99
2009	336	0	0.00	39	10.40
2010	328	0	0.00	42	11.35
2011	323	1	0.28	37	10.25
2012	301	3	0.86	43	12.39
2013	290	8	2.40	35	10.51

(Continued)

Table A.11. (*Continued*)

Economy: CAN					
		Defaults		Others	
Year	Active	#	%	#	%
1992	930	1	0.10	111	10.65
1993	1,126	0	0.00	77	6.40
1994	1,316	0	0.00	57	4.15
1995	1,442	0	0.00	76	5.01
1996	1,610	0	0.00	82	4.85
1997	1,773	4	0.21	129	6.77
1998	1,754	9	0.45	253	12.55
1999	1,192	9	0.47	726	37.68
2000	1,112	8	0.61	195	14.83
2001	947	20	1.67	231	19.28
2002	933	4	0.39	79	7.78
2003	929	14	1.36	83	8.09
2004	982	7	0.66	70	6.61
2005	1,041	3	0.27	80	7.12
2006	1,091	3	0.25	108	8.99
2007	1,119	3	0.24	119	9.59
2008	1,110	12	0.97	117	9.44
2009	1,034	12	1.01	141	11.88
2010	1,058	7	0.60	104	8.90
2011	1,079	4	0.33	119	9.90
2012	1,047	9	0.76	135	11.34
2013	1,021	8	0.70	106	9.34

Economy: CHE					
		Defaults		Others	
Year	Active	#	%	#	%
1992	139	0	0.00	32	18.71
1993	172	0	0.00	9	4.97
1994	178	0	0.00	18	9.18
1995	190	0	0.00	15	7.32
1996	209	0	0.00	16	7.11
1997	218	1	0.43	14	6.01
1998	226	0	0.00	13	5.44
1999	248	0	0.00	10	3.88
2000	259	0	0.00	18	6.50
2001	260	1	0.36	14	5.09
2002	252	1	0.37	17	6.30
2003	246	2	0.77	13	4.98
2004	238	1	0.40	13	5.16
2005	246	0	0.00	7	2.77
2006	250	1	0.37	16	5.99
2007	257	0	0.00	9	3.38
2008	253	0	0.00	15	5.60
2009	258	0	0.00	17	6.18
2010	254	0	0.00	17	6.27
2011	247	1	0.37	19	7.12
2012	377	1	0.22	77	16.92
2013	385	0	0.00	155	28.70

Economy: CHL					
		Defaults		Others	
Year	Active	#	%	#	%
1992	0	0	NaN	0	NaN
1993	0	0	NaN	0	NaN
1994	141	0	0.00	5	3.42
1995	166	0	0.00	24	12.63
1996	173	0	0.00	44	20.28
1997	185	0	0.00	37	16.67
1998	173	0	0.00	56	24.45
1999	179	0	0.00	44	19.73
2000	169	0	0.00	41	19.52
2001	167	1	0.47	43	20.38
2002	160	1	0.47	50	23.70
2003	158	0	0.00	58	26.85
2004	164	0	0.00	37	18.41
2005	170	0	0.00	34	16.67
2006	169	0	0.00	44	20.66
2007	189	0	0.00	29	13.30
2008	149	0	0.00	51	25.50
2009	162	0	0.00	29	15.18
2010	164	0	0.00	36	18.00
2011	163	0	0.00	41	20.10
2012	167	0	0.00	49	22.69
2013	163	0	0.00	41	20.10

Economy: CHN					
		Defaults		Others	
Year	Active	#	%	#	%
1992	41	0	0.00	2	4.65
1993	148	0	0.00	0	0.00
1994	281	1	0.35	1	0.35
1995	313	6	1.88	0	0.00
1996	496	7	1.39	1	0.20
1997	718	17	2.31	2	0.27
1998	834	29	3.35	2	0.23
1999	928	27	2.82	1	0.10
2000	1,050	28	2.59	1	0.09
2001	1,150	46	3.82	7	0.58
2002	1,201	49	3.86	21	1.65
2003	1,257	46	3.47	24	1.81
2004	1,343	111	7.51	25	1.69
2005	1,360	97	6.58	17	1.15
2006	1,365	77	5.12	62	4.12
2007	1,443	60	3.75	98	6.12
2008	1,574	49	2.91	62	3.68
2009	1,657	52	2.99	28	1.61
2010	1,959	39	1.91	45	2.20
2011	2,256	22	0.94	61	2.61
2012	2,424	17	0.68	55	2.20
2013	2,396	13	0.51	147	5.75

(*Continued*)

Table A.11. *(Continued)*

Economy: COL

Year	Active	Defaults #	Defaults %	Others #	Others %
1992	0	0	NaN	0	NaN
1993	0	0	NaN	0	NaN
1994	1	0	0.00	0	0.00
1995	46	0	0.00	27	36.99
1996	54	0	0.00	36	40.00
1997	51	0	0.00	44	46.32
1998	60	0	0.00	62	50.82
1999	52	0	0.00	62	54.39
2000	45	0	0.00	39	46.43
2001	53	0	0.00	20	27.40
2002	52	0	0.00	25	32.47
2003	54	0	0.00	15	21.74
2004	53	0	0.00	14	20.90
2005	62	0	0.00	10	13.89
2006	47	0	0.00	25	34.72
2007	48	0	0.00	14	22.58
2008	37	0	0.00	24	39.34
2009	44	0	0.00	10	18.52
2010	42	0	0.00	15	26.32
2011	41	0	0.00	11	21.15
2012	38	1	2.04	10	20.41
2013	41	0	0.00	13	24.07

Economy: CYP

Year	Active	Defaults #	Defaults %	Others #	Others %
1992	0	0	NaN	0	NaN
1993	0	0	NaN	0	NaN
1994	0	0	NaN	0	NaN
1995	0	0	NaN	0	NaN
1996	35	0	0.00	2	5.41
1997	40	0	0.00	1	2.44
1998	46	0	0.00	2	4.17
1999	52	0	0.00	2	3.70
2000	112	0	0.00	4	3.45
2001	137	0	0.00	6	4.20
2002	143	0	0.00	8	5.30
2003	137	0	0.00	19	12.18
2004	132	0	0.00	31	19.02
2005	138	0	0.00	23	14.29
2006	136	0	0.00	12	8.11
2007	137	0	0.00	8	5.52
2008	133	0	0.00	19	12.50
2009	113	0	0.00	34	23.13
2010	118	0	0.00	20	14.49
2011	86	0	0.00	54	38.57
2012	78	0	0.00	58	42.65
2013	55	2	1.69	61	51.69

Economy: CZE

Year	Active	Defaults #	Defaults %	Others #	Others %
1992	0	0	NaN	0	NaN
1993	0	0	NaN	0	NaN
1994	1	0	0.00	0	0.00
1995	52	0	0.00	1	1.89
1996	53	0	0.00	8	13.11
1997	271	0	0.00	361	57.12
1998	240	1	0.35	41	14.54
1999	144	4	1.55	110	42.64
2000	110	6	3.43	59	33.71
2001	84	2	1.24	75	46.58
2002	44	1	0.93	62	57.94
2003	35	0	0.00	38	52.05
2004	43	0	0.00	26	37.68
2005	24	0	0.00	25	51.02
2006	17	0	0.00	19	52.78
2007	13	0	0.00	12	48.00
2008	16	0	0.00	7	30.43
2009	13	0	0.00	9	40.91
2010	17	0	0.00	2	10.53
2011	18	1	4.35	4	17.39
2012	16	0	0.00	5	23.81
2013	13	0	0.00	7	35.00

Economy: DEU

Year	Active	Defaults #	Defaults %	Others #	Others %
1992	396	0	0.00	37	8.55
1993	416	0	0.00	32	7.14
1994	571	0	0.00	58	9.22
1995	595	0	0.00	64	9.71
1996	624	4	0.58	62	8.99
1997	625	1	0.14	78	11.08
1998	720	2	0.26	52	6.72
1999	903	2	0.21	50	5.24
2000	1,030	2	0.18	60	5.49
2001	1,035	21	1.89	53	4.78
2002	959	39	3.57	94	8.61
2003	896	19	1.91	79	7.95
2004	885	7	0.74	50	5.31
2005	905	5	0.53	40	4.21
2006	1,053	4	0.37	34	3.12
2007	1,201	4	0.32	62	4.89
2008	1,282	18	1.29	99	7.08
2009	1,251	10	0.70	177	12.31
2010	1,294	1	0.07	146	10.13
2011	1,324	3	0.18	331	19.96
2012	1,170	11	0.75	294	19.93
2013	915	12	0.97	304	24.70

(Continued)

Table A.11. *(Continued)*

Economy: DNK						Economy: EGY					
		Defaults		Others				Defaults		Others	
Year	Active	#	%	#	%	Year	Active	#	%	#	%
1992	155	0	0.00	19	10.92	1992	0	0	NaN	0	NaN
1993	170	0	0.00	14	7.61	1993	0	0	NaN	0	NaN
1994	173	0	0.00	23	11.73	1994	0	0	NaN	0	NaN
1995	198	1	0.46	17	7.87	1995	0	0	NaN	0	NaN
1996	216	0	0.00	11	4.85	1996	0	0	NaN	0	NaN
1997	211	0	0.00	19	8.26	1997	0	0	NaN	0	NaN
1998	209	0	0.00	28	11.81	1998	0	0	NaN	0	NaN
1999	209	0	0.00	25	10.68	1999	0	0	NaN	0	NaN
2000	208	1	0.44	20	8.73	2000	0	0	NaN	0	NaN
2001	192	5	2.19	31	13.60	2001	0	0	NaN	0	NaN
2002	175	3	1.44	31	14.83	2002	0	0	NaN	0	NaN
2003	172	1	0.52	19	9.90	2003	0	0	NaN	0	NaN
2004	170	1	0.54	15	8.06	2004	0	0	NaN	0	NaN
2005	167	0	0.00	9	5.11	2005	0	0	NaN	0	NaN
2006	183	0	0.00	6	3.17	2006	168	0	0.00	71	29.71
2007	214	1	0.46	4	1.83	2007	200	0	0.00	123	38.08
2008	216	0	0.00	11	4.85	2008	356	0	0.00	40	10.10
2009	209	4	1.78	12	5.33	2009	219	0	0.00	182	45.39
2010	200	0	0.00	15	6.98	2010	201	0	0.00	70	25.83
2011	187	2	0.99	13	6.44	2011	236	0	0.00	15	5.98
2012	176	2	1.05	12	6.32	2012	212	0	0.00	52	19.70
2013	166	4	2.22	10	5.56	2013	240	0	0.00	6	2.44
Economy: ESP						**Economy: EST**					
		Defaults		Others				Defaults		Others	
Year	Active	#	%	#	%	Year	Active	#	%	#	%
1992	144	0	0.00	38	20.88	1992	0	0	NaN	0	NaN
1993	113	0	0.00	98	46.45	1993	0	0	NaN	0	NaN
1994	244	0	0.00	8	3.17	1994	0	0	NaN	0	NaN
1995	247	0	0.00	90	26.71	1995	0	0	NaN	0	NaN
1996	268	0	0.00	73	21.41	1996	0	0	NaN	0	NaN
1997	279	0	0.00	60	17.70	1997	17	0	0.00	0	0.00
1998	240	0	0.00	99	29.20	1998	19	0	0.00	1	5.00
1999	217	0	0.00	86	28.38	1999	19	0	0.00	1	5.00
2000	216	0	0.00	51	19.10	2000	16	0	0.00	3	15.79
2001	189	0	0.00	83	30.51	2001	14	0	0.00	3	17.65
2002	209	2	0.74	61	22.43	2002	11	0	0.00	3	21.43
2003	189	0	0.00	67	26.17	2003	11	0	0.00	0	0.00
2004	158	0	0.00	57	26.51	2004	11	0	0.00	0	0.00
2005	162	0	0.00	44	21.36	2005	12	0	0.00	1	7.69
2006	160	0	0.00	43	21.18	2006	14	0	0.00	1	6.67
2007	151	1	0.51	46	23.23	2007	16	0	0.00	1	5.88
2008	153	2	1.14	20	11.43	2008	17	0	0.00	0	0.00
2009	143	0	0.00	29	16.86	2009	15	0	0.00	2	11.76
2010	141	1	0.62	19	11.80	2010	15	0	0.00	1	6.25
2011	143	0	0.00	14	8.92	2011	15	0	0.00	0	0.00
2012	134	2	1.28	20	12.82	2012	16	0	0.00	0	0.00
2013	132	6	3.82	19	12.10	2013	16	0	0.00	0	0.00

(Continued)

Table A.11. *(Continued)*

Economy: FIN

Year	Active	Defaults #	Defaults %	Others #	Others %
1992	91	0	0.00	0	0.00
1993	93	0	0.00	2	2.11
1994	96	0	0.00	6	5.88
1995	103	0	0.00	4	3.74
1996	110	0	0.00	4	3.51
1997	122	0	0.00	1	0.81
1998	126	1	0.76	5	3.79
1999	145	0	0.00	9	5.84
2000	152	0	0.00	11	6.75
2001	152	0	0.00	11	6.75
2002	144	2	1.28	10	6.41
2003	138	1	0.66	12	7.95
2004	132	0	0.00	10	7.04
2005	132	0	0.00	7	5.04
2006	132	0	0.00	8	5.71
2007	130	0	0.00	4	2.99
2008	127	1	0.76	4	3.03
2009	125	1	0.78	2	1.56
2010	123	0	0.00	4	3.15
2011	121	1	0.81	1	0.81
2012	121	0	0.00	3	2.42
2013	122	1	0.79	3	2.38

Economy: FRA

Year	Active	Defaults #	Defaults %	Others #	Others %
1992	620	0	0.00	61	8.96
1993	635	0	0.00	81	11.31
1994	688	0	0.00	96	12.24
1995	710	0	0.00	125	14.97
1996	758	0	0.00	113	12.97
1997	811	1	0.11	131	13.89
1998	844	0	0.00	164	16.27
1999	849	0	0.00	138	13.98
2000	912	2	0.20	92	9.15
2001	918	8	0.79	93	9.13
2002	875	5	0.50	111	11.20
2003	857	4	0.41	110	11.33
2004	839	3	0.32	103	10.90
2005	847	4	0.42	91	9.66
2006	904	7	0.71	79	7.98
2007	950	7	0.66	98	9.29
2008	904	11	1.04	144	13.60
2009	898	7	0.67	143	13.65
2010	847	2	0.20	174	17.01
2011	805	2	0.21	151	15.76
2012	770	0	0.00	158	17.03
2013	741	2	0.22	155	17.26

Economy: GBR

Year	Active	Defaults #	Defaults %	Others #	Others %
1992	1,075	1	0.09	87	7.48
1993	1,181	0	0.00	46	3.75
1994	1,277	0	0.00	45	3.40
1995	1,405	0	0.00	62	4.23
1996	1,604	0	0.00	66	3.95
1997	1,706	0	0.00	107	5.90
1998	1,690	0	0.00	195	10.34
1999	1,550	1	0.05	289	15.71
2000	1,665	3	0.16	216	11.46
2001	1,685	10	0.54	147	7.98
2002	1,640	15	0.82	169	9.27
2003	1,576	6	0.34	193	10.87
2004	1,747	2	0.11	149	7.85
2005	1,994	2	0.09	202	9.19
2006	2,169	0	0.00	235	9.78
2007	2,226	1	0.04	261	10.49
2008	2,051	27	1.11	353	14.52
2009	1,841	35	1.59	321	14.61
2010	1,767	3	0.15	260	12.81
2011	1,691	10	0.51	260	13.26
2012	1,578	20	1.09	241	13.10
2013	1,553	10	0.57	197	11.19

Economy: GRC

Year	Active	Defaults #	Defaults %	Others #	Others %
1992	89	0	0.00	0	0.00
1993	94	0	0.00	0	0.00
1994	152	0	0.00	2	1.30
1995	179	0	0.00	2	1.10
1996	193	0	0.00	5	2.53
1997	207	0	0.00	5	2.36
1998	226	0	0.00	4	1.74
1999	254	0	0.00	7	2.68
2000	307	0	0.00	8	2.54
2001	312	0	0.00	12	3.70
2002	313	0	0.00	17	5.15
2003	316	0	0.00	10	3.07
2004	317	0	0.00	9	2.76
2005	301	0	0.00	21	6.52
2006	288	0	0.00	17	5.57
2007	281	0	0.00	14	4.75
2008	277	0	0.00	16	5.46
2009	271	0	0.00	21	7.19
2010	274	0	0.00	20	6.80
2011	234	0	0.00	49	17.31
2012	220	0	0.00	42	16.03
2013	199	0	0.00	41	17.08

(Continued)

Table A.11. (*Continued*)

Economy: HKG					
		Defaults		Others	
Year	Active	#	%	#	%
1992	352	0	0.00	11	3.03
1993	418	0	0.00	6	1.42
1994	459	0	0.00	13	2.75
1995	489	0	0.00	7	1.41
1996	518	0	0.00	18	3.36
1997	593	0	0.00	23	3.73
1998	621	2	0.31	27	4.15
1999	654	5	0.73	22	3.23
2000	734	5	0.66	20	2.64
2001	796	9	1.08	28	3.36
2002	905	4	0.42	36	3.81
2003	954	4	0.40	50	4.96
2004	990	0	0.00	56	5.35
2005	1,016	1	0.09	69	6.35
2006	1,061	4	0.36	40	3.62
2007	1,157	2	0.17	30	2.52
2008	1,174	6	0.49	33	2.72
2009	1,219	5	0.40	23	1.84
2010	1,300	1	0.08	26	1.96
2011	1,353	1	0.07	27	1.96
2012	1,403	2	0.14	44	3.04
2013	1,475	5	0.33	27	1.79

Economy: HRV					
		Defaults		Others	
Year	Active	#	%	#	%
1992	0	0	NaN	0	NaN
1993	0	0	NaN	0	NaN
1994	0	0	NaN	0	NaN
1995	0	0	NaN	0	NaN
1996	0	0	NaN	0	NaN
1997	0	0	NaN	0	NaN
1998	0	0	NaN	0	NaN
1999	0	0	NaN	0	NaN
2000	0	0	NaN	0	NaN
2001	0	0	NaN	0	NaN
2002	29	0	0.00	3	9.38
2003	37	0	0.00	6	13.95
2004	48	0	0.00	11	18.64
2005	53	0	0.00	9	14.52
2006	210	0	0.00	16	7.08
2007	243	0	0.00	54	18.18
2008	168	0	0.00	121	41.87
2009	158	0	0.00	80	33.61
2010	151	1	0.51	46	23.23
2011	134	0	0.00	67	33.33
2012	127	1	0.56	49	27.68
2013	117	0	0.00	54	31.58

Economy: HUN					
		Defaults		Others	
Year	Active	#	%	#	%
1992	0	0	NaN	0	NaN
1993	0	0	NaN	0	NaN
1994	0	0	NaN	0	NaN
1995	36	0	0.00	0	0.00
1996	37	0	0.00	9	19.57
1997	38	0	0.00	9	19.15
1998	43	0	0.00	5	10.42
1999	54	0	0.00	6	10.00
2000	50	1	1.72	7	12.07
2001	48	0	0.00	8	14.29
2002	39	0	0.00	12	23.53
2003	42	0	0.00	4	8.70
2004	38	0	0.00	8	17.39
2005	35	0	0.00	7	16.67
2006	38	0	0.00	4	9.52
2007	34	0	0.00	5	12.82
2008	37	0	0.00	1	2.63
2009	39	0	0.00	0	0.00
2010	43	0	0.00	1	2.27
2011	44	0	0.00	6	12.00
2012	46	0	0.00	4	8.00
2013	47	1	1.92	4	7.69

Economy: IDN					
		Defaults		Others	
Year	Active	#	%	#	%
1992	124	0	0.00	27	17.88
1993	152	0	0.00	27	15.08
1994	174	0	0.00	46	20.91
1995	207	0	0.00	40	16.19
1996	230	1	0.38	30	11.49
1997	251	2	0.71	29	10.28
1998	240	19	6.23	46	15.08
1999	254	19	6.53	18	6.19
2000	256	14	4.62	33	10.89
2001	270	14	4.28	43	13.15
2002	265	6	1.80	62	18.62
2003	298	2	0.63	19	5.96
2004	290	5	1.40	62	17.37
2005	273	2	0.57	77	21.88
2006	302	0	0.00	56	15.64
2007	322	2	0.51	65	16.71
2008	291	0	0.00	92	24.02
2009	324	3	0.78	59	15.28
2010	361	2	0.49	46	11.25
2011	381	1	0.24	43	10.12
2012	411	1	0.22	40	8.85
2013	440	1	0.21	37	7.74

(*Continued*)

Table A.11. *(Continued)*

Economy: IND

Year	Active	Defaults #	Defaults %	Others #	Others %
1992	1,484	1	0.06	145	8.90
1993	1,832	0	0.00	193	9.53
1994	2,728	0	0.00	262	8.76
1995	4,024	2	0.05	338	7.75
1996	4,077	3	0.06	1,038	20.28
1997	3,021	11	0.22	1,911	38.66
1998	2,619	9	0.22	1,519	36.63
1999	2,916	13	0.32	1,125	27.75
2000	2,558	11	0.29	1,289	33.41
2001	2,285	6	0.18	1,111	32.66
2002	2,644	6	0.18	752	22.10
2003	2,618	14	0.35	1,363	34.12
2004	2,553	7	0.20	874	25.45
2005	2,509	7	0.22	682	21.33
2006	2,854	10	0.32	307	9.68
2007	2,982	15	0.45	302	9.15
2008	3,048	25	0.69	537	14.88
2009	3,127	38	1.10	288	8.34
2010	3,604	9	0.20	936	20.58
2011	3,372	9	0.21	881	20.67
2012	3,550	26	0.65	425	10.62
2013	3,461	29	0.72	530	13.18

Economy: IRL

Year	Active	Defaults #	Defaults %	Others #	Others %
1992	30	0	0.00	4	11.76
1993	37	0	0.00	4	9.76
1994	38	0	0.00	4	9.52
1995	36	0	0.00	2	5.26
1996	43	0	0.00	0	0.00
1997	49	0	0.00	3	5.77
1998	50	0	0.00	5	9.09
1999	51	0	0.00	5	8.93
2000	58	0	0.00	6	9.38
2001	55	0	0.00	5	8.33
2002	48	0	0.00	7	12.73
2003	43	0	0.00	5	10.42
2004	42	0	0.00	3	6.67
2005	42	0	0.00	2	4.55
2006	47	0	0.00	2	4.08
2007	51	0	0.00	2	3.77
2008	49	0	0.00	3	5.77
2009	44	1	2.04	4	8.16
2010	40	0	0.00	5	11.11
2011	38	0	0.00	2	5.00
2012	33	0	0.00	5	13.16
2013	33	1	2.78	2	5.56

Economy: ISL

Year	Active	Defaults #	Defaults %	Others #	Others %
1992	0	0	NaN	0	NaN
1993	0	0	NaN	0	NaN
1994	0	0	NaN	0	NaN
1995	0	0	NaN	0	NaN
1996	26	0	0.00	0	0.00
1997	33	0	0.00	3	8.33
1998	44	0	0.00	2	4.35
1999	60	0	0.00	8	11.76
2000	59	0	0.00	18	23.38
2001	64	0	0.00	13	16.88
2002	54	0	0.00	15	21.74
2003	42	0	0.00	22	34.38
2004	32	0	0.00	13	28.89
2005	26	0	0.00	12	31.58
2006	24	0	0.00	6	20.00
2007	26	0	0.00	4	13.33
2008	13	4	13.33	13	43.33
2009	10	1	5.88	6	35.29
2010	8	0	0.00	3	27.27
2011	7	0	0.00	5	41.67
2012	11	0	0.00	1	8.33
2013	14	0	0.00	3	17.65

Economy: ISR

Year	Active	Defaults #	Defaults %	Others #	Others %
1992	0	0	NaN	0	NaN
1993	0	0	NaN	0	NaN
1994	9	0	0.00	0	0.00
1995	82	0	0.00	2	2.38
1996	626	0	0.00	6	0.95
1997	632	0	0.00	20	3.07
1998	611	0	0.00	42	6.43
1999	610	0	0.00	54	8.13
2000	596	0	0.00	74	11.04
2001	548	0	0.00	175	24.20
2002	540	2	0.28	169	23.77
2003	530	0	0.00	165	23.74
2004	512	2	0.34	83	13.90
2005	517	0	0.00	53	9.30
2006	543	0	0.00	40	6.86
2007	594	0	0.00	25	4.04
2008	566	0	0.00	45	7.36
2009	566	0	0.00	26	4.39
2010	550	1	0.17	50	8.32
2011	544	1	0.17	43	7.31
2012	488	0	0.00	82	14.39
2013	475	2	0.39	36	7.02

(Continued)

Table A.11. (*Continued*)

Economy: ITA

Year	Active	Defaults #	Defaults %	Others #	Others %
1992	185	0	0.00	4	2.12
1993	181	0	0.00	9	4.74
1994	196	0	0.00	12	5.77
1995	207	0	0.00	15	6.76
1996	213	1	0.44	15	6.55
1997	220	0	0.00	23	9.47
1998	226	0	0.00	17	7.00
1999	253	0	0.00	7	2.69
2000	274	0	0.00	24	8.05
2001	281	0	0.00	17	5.70
2002	276	1	0.34	14	4.81
2003	262	5	1.72	23	7.93
2004	257	3	1.11	10	3.70
2005	264	0	0.00	12	4.35
2006	274	0	0.00	16	5.52
2007	296	0	0.00	15	4.82
2008	287	1	0.32	21	6.80
2009	277	3	1.00	21	6.98
2010	278	1	0.34	16	5.42
2011	280	0	0.00	22	7.28
2012	276	2	0.65	29	9.45
2013	274	2	0.67	22	7.38

Economy: JOR

Year	Active	Defaults #	Defaults %	Others #	Others %
1992	0	0	NaN	0	NaN
1993	0	0	NaN	0	NaN
1994	0	0	NaN	0	NaN
1995	0	0	NaN	0	NaN
1996	65	0	0.00	13	16.67
1997	89	0	0.00	16	15.24
1998	109	0	0.00	30	21.58
1999	105	0	0.00	49	31.82
2000	110	0	0.00	50	31.25
2001	117	0	0.00	40	25.48
2002	114	0	0.00	33	22.45
2003	133	0	0.00	21	13.64
2004	137	0	0.00	16	10.46
2005	154	0	0.00	14	8.33
2006	191	0	0.00	12	5.91
2007	202	0	0.00	20	9.01
2008	220	0	0.00	14	5.98
2009	219	0	0.00	32	12.75
2010	218	0	0.00	23	9.54
2011	211	0	0.00	36	14.57
2012	209	0	0.00	31	12.92
2013	194	0	0.00	37	16.02

Economy: JPN

Year	Active	Defaults #	Defaults %	Others #	Others %
1992	2,531	2	0.08	21	0.82
1993	2,609	3	0.11	25	0.95
1994	2,748	0	0.00	17	0.61
1995	2,928	1	0.03	18	0.61
1996	3,077	4	0.13	22	0.71
1997	3,207	5	0.15	28	0.86
1998	3,264	12	0.36	36	1.09
1999	3,318	6	0.18	47	1.39
2000	3,449	12	0.34	60	1.70
2001	3,557	14	0.39	62	1.71
2002	3,593	33	0.89	92	2.47
2003	3,613	18	0.48	103	2.76
2004	3,726	13	0.34	77	2.02
2005	3,798	9	0.23	93	2.38
2006	3,925	2	0.05	89	2.22
2007	3,978	6	0.15	100	2.45
2008	3,902	32	0.79	110	2.72
2009	3,784	31	0.79	131	3.32
2010	3,686	8	0.21	130	3.40
2011	3,626	6	0.16	99	2.65
2012	3,576	6	0.16	102	2.77
2013	3,565	3	0.08	85	2.33

Economy: KAZ

Year	Active	Defaults #	Defaults %	Others #	Others %
1992	0	0	NaN	0	NaN
1993	0	0	NaN	0	NaN
1994	0	0	NaN	0	NaN
1995	0	0	NaN	0	NaN
1996	0	0	NaN	0	NaN
1997	0	0	NaN	0	NaN
1998	0	0	NaN	0	NaN
1999	0	0	NaN	0	NaN
2000	0	0	NaN	0	NaN
2001	0	0	NaN	0	NaN
2002	7	0	0.00	5	41.67
2003	8	0	0.00	5	38.46
2004	14	0	0.00	11	44.00
2005	3	0	0.00	15	83.33
2006	3	0	0.00	3	50.00
2007	22	0	0.00	13	37.14
2008	23	0	0.00	11	32.35
2009	19	4	9.09	21	47.73
2010	10	0	0.00	21	67.74
2011	14	0	0.00	9	39.13
2012	15	0	0.00	10	40.00
2013	13	0	0.00	12	48.00

(*Continued*)

Table A.11. *(Continued)*

Economy: KOR					
		Defaults		Others	
Year	Active	#	%	#	%
1992	634	0	0.00	1	0.16
1993	643	0	0.00	0	0.00
1994	670	0	0.00	0	0.00
1995	698	0	0.00	1	0.14
1996	740	6	0.80	3	0.40
1997	1,015	36	3.38	15	1.41
1998	902	92	8.36	106	9.64
1999	957	19	1.86	44	4.31
2000	1,150	12	1.00	40	3.33
2001	1,274	20	1.51	30	2.27
2002	1,441	15	1.01	32	2.15
2003	1,491	11	0.72	30	1.96
2004	1,503	9	0.58	52	3.32
2005	1,545	8	0.50	57	3.54
2006	1,625	2	0.12	12	0.73
2007	1,699	2	0.12	14	0.82
2008	1,735	5	0.28	35	1.97
2009	1,721	8	0.44	83	4.58
2010	1,736	10	0.54	98	5.31
2011	1,749	3	0.16	84	4.58
2012	1,728	8	0.44	77	4.25
2013	1,736	11	0.61	66	3.64

Economy: KWT					
		Defaults		Others	
Year	Active	#	%	#	%
1992	0	0	NaN	0	NaN
1993	0	0	NaN	0	NaN
1994	0	0	NaN	0	NaN
1995	0	0	NaN	0	NaN
1996	52	0	0.00	1	1.89
1997	66	0	0.00	2	2.94
1998	67	0	0.00	1	1.47
1999	70	0	0.00	6	7.89
2000	69	0	0.00	11	13.75
2001	73	0	0.00	0	0.00
2002	76	0	0.00	6	7.32
2003	94	0	0.00	0	0.00
2004	100	0	0.00	3	2.91
2005	137	0	0.00	4	2.84
2006	159	0	0.00	4	2.45
2007	172	0	0.00	16	8.51
2008	176	0	0.00	14	7.37
2009	181	2	0.93	31	14.49
2010	182	0	0.00	42	18.75
2011	160	1	0.44	65	28.76
2012	183	0	0.00	37	16.82
2013	186	0	0.00	25	11.85

Economy: LKA					
		Defaults		Others	
Year	Active	#	%	#	%
1992	0	0	NaN	0	NaN
1993	1	0	0.00	0	0.00
1994	1	0	0.00	0	0.00
1995	122	0	0.00	1	0.81
1996	137	0	0.00	38	21.71
1997	137	0	0.00	34	19.88
1998	153	0	0.00	30	16.39
1999	151	0	0.00	35	18.82
2000	147	0	0.00	38	20.54
2001	166	0	0.00	22	11.70
2002	175	0	0.00	25	12.50
2003	177	0	0.00	28	13.66
2004	189	0	0.00	12	5.97
2005	205	0	0.00	10	4.65
2006	209	0	0.00	13	5.86
2007	218	0	0.00	8	3.54
2008	214	0	0.00	14	6.14
2009	221	0	0.00	9	3.91
2010	238	0	0.00	2	0.83
2011	259	0	0.00	9	3.36
2012	275	0	0.00	4	1.43
2013	276	0	0.00	2	0.72

Economy: LTU					
		Defaults		Others	
Year	Active	#	%	#	%
1992	0	0	NaN	0	NaN
1993	0	0	NaN	0	NaN
1994	0	0	NaN	0	NaN
1995	0	0	NaN	0	NaN
1996	0	0	NaN	0	NaN
1997	0	0	NaN	0	NaN
1998	0	0	NaN	0	NaN
1999	0	0	NaN	0	NaN
2000	33	0	0.00	5	13.16
2001	33	0	0.00	11	25.00
2002	41	0	0.00	3	6.82
2003	39	0	0.00	9	18.75
2004	40	0	0.00	1	2.44
2005	40	0	0.00	0	0.00
2006	39	0	0.00	2	4.88
2007	37	0	0.00	3	7.50
2008	38	0	0.00	0	0.00
2009	38	0	0.00	1	2.56
2010	38	0	0.00	2	5.00
2011	33	1	2.50	6	15.00
2012	32	0	0.00	1	3.03
2013	31	1	2.94	2	5.88

(Continued)

Table A.11. *(Continued)*

Economy: LUX

Year	Active	Defaults #	Defaults %	Others #	Others %
1992	2	0	0.00	1	33.33
1993	2	0	0.00	1	33.33
1994	2	0	0.00	0	0.00
1995	32	0	0.00	9	21.95
1996	30	0	0.00	16	34.78
1997	38	0	0.00	10	20.83
1998	32	0	0.00	14	30.43
1999	34	0	0.00	12	26.09
2000	31	0	0.00	14	31.11
2001	28	0	0.00	14	33.33
2002	28	0	0.00	9	24.32
2003	27	0	0.00	11	28.95
2004	35	0	0.00	7	16.67
2005	38	0	0.00	6	13.64
2006	37	0	0.00	15	28.85
2007	35	0	0.00	10	22.22
2008	27	0	0.00	14	34.15
2009	23	0	0.00	9	28.13
2010	20	1	3.45	8	27.59
2011	14	0	0.00	10	41.67
2012	14	0	0.00	5	26.32
2013	19	0	0.00	2	9.52

Economy: LVA

Year	Active	Defaults #	Defaults %	Others #	Others %
1992	0	0	NaN	0	NaN
1993	0	0	NaN	0	NaN
1994	0	0	NaN	0	NaN
1995	0	0	NaN	0	NaN
1996	0	0	NaN	0	NaN
1997	0	0	NaN	0	NaN
1998	0	0	NaN	0	NaN
1999	0	0	NaN	0	NaN
2000	16	0	0.00	1	5.88
2001	34	0	0.00	9	20.93
2002	35	0	0.00	4	10.26
2003	33	0	0.00	4	10.81
2004	27	0	0.00	10	27.03
2005	32	0	0.00	3	8.57
2006	31	0	0.00	4	11.43
2007	32	0	0.00	6	15.79
2008	27	0	0.00	8	22.86
2009	28	0	0.00	9	24.32
2010	32	0	0.00	4	11.11
2011	27	1	2.78	8	22.22
2012	29	0	0.00	5	14.71
2013	29	0	0.00	8	21.62

Economy: MAR

Year	Active	Defaults #	Defaults %	Others #	Others %
1992	0	0	NaN	0	NaN
1993	0	0	NaN	0	NaN
1994	0	0	NaN	0	NaN
1995	0	0	NaN	0	NaN
1996	16	0	0.00	0	0.00
1997	40	0	0.00	3	6.98
1998	48	0	0.00	1	2.04
1999	47	0	0.00	5	9.62
2000	51	0	0.00	2	3.77
2001	52	0	0.00	7	11.86
2002	51	0	0.00	7	12.07
2003	50	0	0.00	7	12.28
2004	48	0	0.00	7	12.73
2005	54	0	0.00	2	3.57
2006	56	0	0.00	6	9.68
2007	69	0	0.00	3	4.17
2008	77	0	0.00	1	1.28
2009	75	0	0.00	2	2.60
2010	73	0	0.00	4	5.19
2011	74	0	0.00	1	1.33
2012	76	0	0.00	1	1.30
2013	73	0	0.00	4	5.19

Economy: MEX

Year	Active	Defaults #	Defaults %	Others #	Others %
1992	0	0	NaN	0	NaN
1993	0	0	NaN	0	NaN
1994	99	0	0.00	25	20.16
1995	98	0	0.00	32	24.62
1996	105	0	0.00	20	16.00
1997	116	0	0.00	23	16.55
1998	113	0	0.00	19	14.39
1999	110	1	0.73	26	18.98
2000	106	1	0.81	17	13.71
2001	106	1	0.79	19	15.08
2002	97	0	0.00	28	22.40
2003	103	3	2.44	17	13.82
2004	109	0	0.00	10	8.40
2005	100	0	0.00	24	19.35
2006	105	0	0.00	10	8.70
2007	103	0	0.00	17	14.17
2008	93	2	1.68	24	20.17
2009	101	2	1.75	11	9.65
2010	106	2	1.65	13	10.74
2011	106	1	0.78	22	17.05
2012	105	0	0.00	12	10.26
2013	112	6	4.84	6	4.84

(Continued)

Table A.11. *(Continued)*

Economy: MKD					
		Defaults		Others	
Year	Active	#	%	#	%
1992	0	0	NaN	0	NaN
1993	0	0	NaN	0	NaN
1994	0	0	NaN	0	NaN
1995	0	0	NaN	0	NaN
1996	0	0	NaN	0	NaN
1997	0	0	NaN	0	NaN
1998	0	0	NaN	0	NaN
1999	0	0	NaN	0	NaN
2000	0	0	NaN	0	NaN
2001	0	0	NaN	0	NaN
2002	0	0	NaN	0	NaN
2003	0	0	NaN	0	NaN
2004	0	0	NaN	0	NaN
2005	61	0	0.00	61	50.00
2006	84	0	0.00	71	45.81
2007	94	0	0.00	73	43.71
2008	71	0	0.00	78	52.35
2009	68	0	0.00	68	50.00
2010	64	0	0.00	58	47.54
2011	59	0	0.00	69	53.91
2012	52	1	0.86	63	54.31
2013	42	0	0.00	76	64.41

Economy: MLT					
		Defaults		Others	
Year	Active	#	%	#	%
1992	0	0	NaN	0	NaN
1993	0	0	NaN	0	NaN
1994	0	0	NaN	0	NaN
1995	0	0	NaN	0	NaN
1996	5	0	0.00	0	0.00
1997	6	0	0.00	0	0.00
1998	7	0	0.00	0	0.00
1999	7	0	0.00	1	12.50
2000	9	0	0.00	0	0.00
2001	9	0	0.00	2	18.18
2002	9	0	0.00	2	18.18
2003	10	0	0.00	3	23.08
2004	11	0	0.00	2	15.38
2005	11	0	0.00	2	15.38
2006	13	0	0.00	0	0.00
2007	14	0	0.00	3	17.65
2008	14	0	0.00	6	30.00
2009	12	0	0.00	4	25.00
2010	12	0	0.00	2	14.29
2011	14	0	0.00	2	12.50
2012	19	0	0.00	1	5.00
2013	20	0	0.00	2	9.09

Economy: MYS					
		Defaults		Others	
Year	Active	#	%	#	%
1992	351	0	0.00	8	2.23
1993	399	0	0.00	2	0.50
1994	457	0	0.00	7	1.51
1995	517	0	0.00	2	0.39
1996	602	0	0.00	0	0.00
1997	692	0	0.00	2	0.29
1998	697	14	1.92	20	2.74
1999	703	8	1.11	12	1.66
2000	735	8	1.06	15	1.98
2001	737	9	1.18	18	2.36
2002	767	8	1.00	27	3.37
2003	821	3	0.36	21	2.49
2004	901	3	0.33	18	1.95
2005	981	1	0.10	27	2.68
2006	997	5	0.48	29	2.81
2007	967	6	0.58	70	6.71
2008	934	14	1.39	61	6.05
2009	920	14	1.43	48	4.89
2010	926	18	1.84	32	3.28
2011	927	5	0.52	33	3.42
2012	909	6	0.63	40	4.19
2013	898	5	0.54	30	3.22

Economy: NGA					
		Defaults		Others	
Year	Active	#	%	#	%
1992	0	0	NaN	0	NaN
1993	0	0	NaN	0	NaN
1994	0	0	NaN	0	NaN
1995	0	0	NaN	0	NaN
1996	0	0	NaN	0	NaN
1997	0	0	NaN	0	NaN
1998	0	0	NaN	0	NaN
1999	0	0	NaN	0	NaN
2000	0	0	NaN	0	NaN
2001	0	0	NaN	0	NaN
2002	123	0	0.00	22	15.17
2003	75	0	0.00	66	46.81
2004	113	0	0.00	41	26.62
2005	131	0	0.00	24	15.48
2006	136	0	0.00	33	19.53
2007	166	0	0.00	26	13.54
2008	179	0	0.00	44	19.73
2009	188	0	0.00	25	11.74
2010	179	0	0.00	24	11.82
2011	159	0	0.00	35	18.04
2012	161	0	0.00	19	10.56
2013	177	0	0.00	20	10.15

(Continued)

Table A.11. *(Continued)*

Economy: NLD					
		Defaults		Others	
Year	Active	#	%	#	%
1992	158	0	0.00	6	3.66
1993	167	0	0.00	4	2.34
1994	174	0	0.00	6	3.33
1995	187	0	0.00	4	2.09
1996	193	1	0.50	5	2.51
1997	201	0	0.00	14	6.51
1998	211	0	0.00	10	4.52
1999	215	0	0.00	20	8.51
2000	204	1	0.44	20	8.89
2001	181	5	2.39	23	11.00
2002	161	11	5.82	17	8.99
2003	153	1	0.59	16	9.41
2004	145	0	0.00	10	6.45
2005	140	0	0.00	9	6.04
2006	137	1	0.69	7	4.83
2007	136	0	0.00	8	5.56
2008	128	1	0.71	11	7.86
2009	123	3	2.29	5	3.82
2010	120	0	0.00	6	4.76
2011	116	0	0.00	8	6.45
2012	111	0	0.00	10	8.26
2013	105	1	0.88	7	6.19

Economy: NOR					
		Defaults		Others	
Year	Active	#	%	#	%
1992	78	0	0.00	9	10.34
1993	95	0	0.00	2	2.06
1994	113	0	0.00	3	2.59
1995	134	0	0.00	2	1.47
1996	158	0	0.00	4	2.47
1997	195	0	0.00	10	4.88
1998	217	0	0.00	18	7.66
1999	201	0	0.00	30	12.99
2000	194	1	0.44	32	14.10
2001	216	2	0.80	31	12.45
2002	201	5	2.07	36	14.88
2003	186	3	1.31	40	17.47
2004	196	0	0.00	22	10.09
2005	235	0	0.00	14	5.62
2006	252	0	0.00	45	15.15
2007	270	0	0.00	42	13.46
2008	246	4	1.37	42	14.38
2009	229	6	2.19	39	14.23
2010	219	1	0.40	29	11.65
2011	220	1	0.43	12	5.15
2012	214	0	0.00	15	6.55
2013	200	2	0.90	21	9.42

Economy: NZL					
		Defaults		Others	
Year	Active	#	%	#	%
1992	29	0	0.00	1	3.33
1993	31	0	0.00	0	0.00
1994	40	0	0.00	0	0.00
1995	43	0	0.00	1	2.27
1996	45	0	0.00	3	6.25
1997	48	0	0.00	0	0.00
1998	50	0	0.00	1	1.96
1999	56	0	0.00	0	0.00
2000	61	0	0.00	1	1.61
2001	70	0	0.00	0	0.00
2002	75	0	0.00	0	0.00
2003	87	0	0.00	0	0.00
2004	102	0	0.00	1	0.97
2005	108	0	0.00	0	0.00
2006	113	0	0.00	0	0.00
2007	122	0	0.00	1	0.81
2008	115	0	0.00	13	10.16
2009	122	0	0.00	9	6.87
2010	123	0	0.00	14	10.22
2011	122	1	0.74	12	8.89
2012	120	0	0.00	19	13.67
2013	123	2	1.47	11	8.09

Economy: PAK					
		Defaults		Others	
Year	Active	#	%	#	%
1992	0	0	NaN	0	NaN
1993	0	0	NaN	0	NaN
1994	0	0	NaN	0	NaN
1995	0	0	NaN	0	NaN
1996	0	0	NaN	0	NaN
1997	0	0	NaN	0	NaN
1998	243	0	0.00	119	32.87
1999	338	0	0.00	123	26.68
2000	368	0	0.00	155	29.64
2001	317	0	0.00	178	35.96
2002	429	0	0.00	96	18.29
2003	456	0	0.00	68	12.98
2004	500	0	0.00	41	7.58
2005	493	0	0.00	85	14.71
2006	469	0	0.00	99	17.43
2007	480	0	0.00	83	14.74
2008	240	0	0.00	300	55.56
2009	514	0	0.00	67	11.53
2010	492	0	0.00	52	9.56
2011	505	0	0.00	102	16.80
2012	457	0	0.00	88	16.15
2013	462	0	0.00	21	4.35

(Continued)

Table A.11. *(Continued)*

Economy: PER

Year	Active	Defaults #	Defaults %	Others #	Others %
1992	1	0	0.00	0	0.00
1993	1	0	0.00	0	0.00
1994	25	0	0.00	0	0.00
1995	99	0	0.00	20	16.81
1996	95	0	0.00	46	32.62
1997	123	0	0.00	35	22.15
1998	109	0	0.00	62	36.26
1999	93	0	0.00	69	42.59
2000	86	0	0.00	65	43.05
2001	64	0	0.00	63	49.61
2002	75	0	0.00	49	39.52
2003	68	0	0.00	47	40.87
2004	77	0	0.00	41	34.75
2005	78	0	0.00	43	35.54
2006	76	0	0.00	39	33.91
2007	93	0	0.00	25	21.19
2008	81	0	0.00	50	38.17
2009	89	0	0.00	35	28.23
2010	90	0	0.00	32	26.23
2011	81	0	0.00	37	31.36
2012	80	0	0.00	38	32.20
2013	65	0	0.00	46	41.44

Economy: PHL

Year	Active	Defaults #	Defaults %	Others #	Others %
1992	83	0	0.00	21	20.19
1993	110	1	0.78	18	13.95
1994	126	0	0.00	28	18.18
1995	156	0	0.00	16	9.30
1996	177	0	0.00	14	7.33
1997	186	0	0.00	20	9.71
1998	176	1	0.49	29	14.08
1999	186	3	1.49	12	5.97
2000	169	2	0.97	36	17.39
2001	163	3	1.46	40	19.42
2002	161	5	2.35	47	22.07
2003	174	5	2.33	36	16.74
2004	176	7	3.00	50	21.46
2005	181	3	1.36	36	16.36
2006	189	2	0.91	28	12.79
2007	191	2	0.90	30	13.45
2008	185	1	0.47	29	13.49
2009	203	2	0.88	23	10.09
2010	207	0	0.00	17	7.59
2011	218	0	0.00	14	6.03
2012	222	0	0.00	15	6.33
2013	224	0	0.00	15	6.28

Economy: POL

Year	Active	Defaults #	Defaults %	Others #	Others %
1992	0	0	NaN	0	NaN
1993	0	0	NaN	0	NaN
1994	26	0	0.00	19	42.22
1995	58	0	0.00	0	0.00
1996	77	0	0.00	0	0.00
1997	129	0	0.00	2	1.53
1998	186	0	0.00	3	1.59
1999	211	0	0.00	2	0.94
2000	217	1	0.44	8	3.54
2001	221	1	0.44	4	1.77
2002	205	2	0.88	21	9.21
2003	190	3	1.44	15	7.21
2004	207	0	0.00	8	3.72
2005	235	1	0.41	7	2.88
2006	248	0	0.00	12	4.62
2007	316	0	0.00	10	3.07
2008	418	0	0.00	3	0.71
2009	452	0	0.00	11	2.38
2010	536	0	0.00	7	1.29
2011	711	0	0.00	17	2.34
2012	807	7	0.83	28	3.33
2013	837	5	0.56	43	4.86

Economy: PRT

Year	Active	Defaults #	Defaults %	Others #	Others %
1992	1	0	0.00	0	0.00
1993	69	0	0.00	12	14.81
1994	81	0	0.00	11	11.96
1995	91	0	0.00	18	16.51
1996	92	0	0.00	23	20.00
1997	94	0	0.00	26	21.67
1998	87	0	0.00	33	27.50
1999	88	0	0.00	25	22.12
2000	86	0	0.00	17	16.50
2001	70	0	0.00	21	23.08
2002	62	0	0.00	20	24.39
2003	63	0	0.00	7	10.00
2004	68	0	0.00	6	8.11
2005	65	0	0.00	6	8.45
2006	62	0	0.00	13	17.33
2007	58	0	0.00	9	13.43
2008	57	0	0.00	8	12.31
2009	56	0	0.00	9	13.85
2010	57	0	0.00	5	8.06
2011	55	2	3.13	7	10.94
2012	55	0	0.00	4	6.78
2013	51	0	0.00	9	15.00

(Continued)

Table A.11. (*Continued*)

Economy: ROM					
		Defaults		Others	
Year	Active	#	%	#	%
1992	0	0	NaN	0	NaN
1993	0	0	NaN	0	NaN
1994	0	0	NaN	0	NaN
1995	0	0	NaN	0	NaN
1996	0	0	NaN	0	NaN
1997	0	0	NaN	0	NaN
1998	78	0	0.00	1	1.27
1999	341	0	0.00	28	7.59
2000	362	0	0.00	89	19.73
2001	338	0	0.00	175	34.11
2002	288	0	0.00	193	40.12
2003	280	0	0.00	172	38.05
2004	299	0	0.00	119	28.47
2005	324	1	0.20	179	35.52
2006	514	0	0.00	159	23.63
2007	717	0	0.00	704	49.54
2008	596	0	0.00	411	40.81
2009	466	0	0.00	456	49.46
2010	526	0	0.00	315	37.46
2011	451	1	0.11	479	51.45
2012	361	0	0.00	371	50.68
2013	360	2	0.28	344	48.73

Economy: RUS					
		Defaults		Others	
Year	Active	#	%	#	%
1992	0	0	NaN	0	NaN
1993	0	0	NaN	0	NaN
1994	0	0	NaN	0	NaN
1995	0	0	NaN	0	NaN
1996	0	0	NaN	0	NaN
1997	77	0	0.00	22	22.22
1998	26	2	1.59	98	77.78
1999	34	0	0.00	45	56.96
2000	66	0	0.00	55	45.45
2001	71	0	0.00	77	52.03
2002	52	0	0.00	105	66.88
2003	77	0	0.00	65	45.77
2004	101	3	1.76	66	38.82
2005	171	1	0.41	74	30.08
2006	218	1	0.25	174	44.27
2007	308	0	0.00	180	36.89
2008	260	0	0.00	257	49.71
2009	301	9	2.19	101	24.57
2010	320	1	0.22	124	27.87
2011	281	2	0.42	196	40.92
2012	262	1	0.24	161	37.97
2013	188	1	0.18	365	65.88

Economy: SAU					
		Defaults		Others	
Year	Active	#	%	#	%
1992	0	0	NaN	0	NaN
1993	0	0	NaN	0	NaN
1994	0	0	NaN	0	NaN
1995	0	0	NaN	0	NaN
1996	0	0	NaN	0	NaN
1997	0	0	NaN	0	NaN
1998	0	0	NaN	0	NaN
1999	0	0	NaN	0	NaN
2000	60	0	0.00	4	6.25
2001	63	0	0.00	4	5.97
2002	65	0	0.00	3	4.41
2003	68	0	0.00	2	2.86
2004	71	0	0.00	0	0.00
2005	76	0	0.00	0	0.00
2006	84	0	0.00	0	0.00
2007	105	0	0.00	2	1.87
2008	126	0	0.00	1	0.79
2009	133	0	0.00	1	0.75
2010	145	0	0.00	0	0.00
2011	147	0	0.00	1	0.68
2012	155	0	0.00	1	0.64
2013	158	1	0.62	2	1.24

Economy: SGP					
		Defaults		Others	
Year	Active	#	%	#	%
1992	177	0	0.00	11	5.85
1993	198	0	0.00	4	1.98
1994	232	0	0.00	3	1.28
1995	249	1	0.39	6	2.34
1996	269	1	0.36	9	3.23
1997	295	1	0.32	18	5.73
1998	318	4	1.19	13	3.88
1999	354	4	1.07	15	4.02
2000	424	0	0.00	18	4.07
2001	435	2	0.43	31	6.62
2002	444	2	0.42	32	6.69
2003	498	1	0.19	15	2.92
2004	571	1	0.17	12	2.05
2005	622	4	0.62	15	2.34
2006	664	2	0.29	24	3.48
2007	708	0	0.00	20	2.75
2008	705	3	0.40	41	5.47
2009	714	15	1.97	31	4.08
2010	724	0	0.00	34	4.49
2011	704	1	0.13	54	7.11
2012	703	0	0.00	38	5.13
2013	707	0	0.00	31	4.20

(*Continued*)

Table A.11. (*Continued*)

Economy: SVK

Year	Active	Defaults #	Defaults %	Others #	Others %
1992	0	0	NaN	0	NaN
1993	0	0	NaN	0	NaN
1994	0	0	NaN	0	NaN
1995	0	0	NaN	0	NaN
1996	0	0	NaN	0	NaN
1997	0	0	NaN	0	NaN
1998	12	0	0.00	7	36.84
1999	12	0	0.00	26	68.42
2000	12	0	0.00	13	52.00
2001	13	0	0.00	15	53.57
2002	19	0	0.00	16	45.71
2003	42	0	0.00	22	34.38
2004	41	0	0.00	34	45.33
2005	43	0	0.00	25	36.76
2006	51	0	0.00	37	42.05
2007	23	0	0.00	52	69.33
2008	36	0	0.00	26	41.94
2009	31	0	0.00	31	50.00
2010	50	0	0.00	17	25.37
2011	49	0	0.00	47	48.96
2012	48	0	0.00	30	38.46
2013	45	0	0.00	20	30.77

Economy: SVN

Year	Active	Defaults #	Defaults %	Others #	Others %
1992	0	0	NaN	0	NaN
1993	0	0	NaN	0	NaN
1994	0	0	NaN	0	NaN
1995	0	0	NaN	0	NaN
1996	0	0	NaN	0	NaN
1997	0	0	NaN	0	NaN
1998	71	0	0.00	7	8.97
1999	95	0	0.00	7	6.86
2000	109	0	0.00	21	16.15
2001	118	0	0.00	36	23.38
2002	100	0	0.00	44	30.56
2003	103	0	0.00	19	15.57
2004	111	0	0.00	20	15.27
2005	87	0	0.00	36	29.27
2006	75	0	0.00	28	27.18
2007	62	0	0.00	23	27.06
2008	66	0	0.00	15	18.52
2009	56	1	1.22	25	30.49
2010	71	1	1.23	9	11.11
2011	60	0	0.00	17	22.08
2012	56	2	3.28	3	4.92
2013	49	2	3.45	7	12.07

Economy: SWE

Year	Active	Defaults #	Defaults %	Others #	Others %
1992	116	0	0.00	3	2.52
1993	141	0	0.00	2	1.40
1994	170	0	0.00	2	1.16
1995	184	0	0.00	0	0.00
1996	220	0	0.00	15	6.38
1997	263	0	0.00	26	9.00
1998	296	0	0.00	21	6.62
1999	338	1	0.28	19	5.31
2000	372	2	0.49	38	9.22
2001	364	4	1.00	33	8.23
2002	348	7	1.82	30	7.79
2003	337	3	0.82	27	7.36
2004	349	1	0.27	23	6.17
2005	374	2	0.52	12	3.09
2006	422	0	0.00	19	4.31
2007	499	1	0.19	13	2.53
2008	509	2	0.37	30	5.55
2009	498	4	0.75	33	6.17
2010	502	2	0.38	29	5.44
2011	496	2	0.38	34	6.39
2012	478	1	0.19	46	8.76
2013	479	3	0.60	22	4.37

Economy: THA

Year	Active	Defaults #	Defaults %	Others #	Others %
1992	277	0	0.00	1	0.36
1993	328	0	0.00	2	0.61
1994	371	0	0.00	1	0.27
1995	400	1	0.24	9	2.20
1996	420	7	1.57	20	4.47
1997	371	19	4.18	65	14.29
1998	343	18	4.35	53	12.80
1999	327	13	3.50	31	8.36
2000	309	19	5.31	30	8.38
2001	312	9	2.65	19	5.59
2002	335	3	0.85	14	3.98
2003	363	4	1.06	12	3.17
2004	403	2	0.47	22	5.15
2005	428	3	0.66	24	5.27
2006	464	0	0.00	12	2.52
2007	466	2	0.41	16	3.31
2008	464	1	0.20	26	5.30
2009	474	8	1.62	11	2.23
2010	478	5	1.02	7	1.43
2011	480	2	0.40	12	2.43
2012	494	1	0.20	7	1.39
2013	521	1	0.19	6	1.14

(*Continued*)

Table A.11. *(Continued)*

Economy: TUR

Year	Active	Defaults #	Defaults %	Others #	Others %
1992	8	0	0.00	0	0.00
1993	15	0	0.00	0	0.00
1994	29	0	0.00	0	0.00
1995	197	0	0.00	4	1.99
1996	222	0	0.00	1	0.45
1997	247	0	0.00	10	3.89
1998	275	0	0.00	3	1.08
1999	271	0	0.00	10	3.56
2000	296	2	0.63	18	5.70
2001	284	0	0.00	17	5.65
2002	286	0	0.00	8	2.72
2003	284	0	0.00	6	2.07
2004	296	0	0.00	0	0.00
2005	302	0	0.00	3	0.98
2006	315	0	0.00	4	1.25
2007	318	0	0.00	7	2.15
2008	315	0	0.00	5	1.56
2009	315	0	0.00	3	0.94
2010	336	0	0.00	1	0.30
2011	360	0	0.00	3	0.83
2012	393	0	0.00	8	2.00
2013	411	0	0.00	7	1.67

Economy: TWN

Year	Active	Defaults #	Defaults %	Others #	Others %
1992	232	0	0.00	2	0.85
1993	255	0	0.00	1	0.39
1994	289	0	0.00	1	0.34
1995	363	0	0.00	0	0.00
1996	428	0	0.00	1	0.23
1997	489	0	0.00	3	0.61
1998	551	4	0.71	11	1.94
1999	680	7	1.01	8	1.15
2000	785	8	0.99	17	2.10
2001	880	7	0.77	19	2.10
2002	981	9	0.88	36	3.51
2003	1,071	2	0.18	28	2.54
2004	1,333	5	0.37	25	1.83
2005	1,354	9	0.63	66	4.62
2006	1,384	3	0.21	38	2.67
2007	1,444	3	0.20	35	2.36
2008	1,448	6	0.40	48	3.20
2009	1,492	7	0.46	28	1.83
2010	1,589	1	0.06	24	1.49
2011	1,659	2	0.12	36	2.12
2012	1,701	2	0.11	46	2.63
2013	1,746	2	0.11	42	2.35

Economy: UKR

Year	Active	Defaults #	Defaults %	Others #	Others %
1992	0	0	NaN	0	NaN
1993	0	0	NaN	0	NaN
1994	0	0	NaN	0	NaN
1995	0	0	NaN	0	NaN
1996	0	0	NaN	0	NaN
1997	0	0	NaN	0	NaN
1998	26	0	0.00	22	45.83
1999	36	0	0.00	41	53.25
2000	62	0	0.00	29	31.87
2001	25	0	0.00	75	75.00
2002	11	0	0.00	39	78.00
2003	18	0	0.00	18	50.00
2004	30	0	0.00	25	45.45
2005	59	0	0.00	23	28.05
2006	102	0	0.00	50	32.89
2007	160	0	0.00	70	30.43
2008	114	0	0.00	117	50.65
2009	83	1	0.45	138	62.16
2010	57	0	0.00	80	58.39
2011	55	0	0.00	39	41.49
2012	61	0	0.00	38	38.38
2013	70	0	0.00	65	48.15

Economy: USA

Year	Active	Defaults #	Defaults %	Others #	Others %
1992	5,270	14	0.26	107	1.98
1993	5,896	27	0.44	161	2.65
1994	6,645	21	0.30	256	3.70
1995	6,981	16	0.22	381	5.16
1996	7,537	21	0.26	418	5.24
1997	7,764	53	0.63	531	6.36
1998	7,442	80	0.95	859	10.25
1999	7,080	91	1.12	936	11.55
2000	6,846	123	1.59	778	10.04
2001	6,093	200	2.84	756	10.72
2002	5,643	148	2.35	507	8.05
2003	5,272	90	1.54	472	8.09
2004	5,241	37	0.65	374	6.62
2005	5,218	36	0.64	379	6.73
2006	5,184	26	0.47	372	6.66
2007	5,108	25	0.45	465	8.31
2008	4,856	71	1.34	366	6.91
2009	4,579	106	2.12	315	6.30
2010	4,491	33	0.68	307	6.35
2011	4,341	34	0.72	333	7.07
2012	4,268	37	0.81	264	5.78
2013	4,323	13	0.29	212	4.66

(Continued)

Table A.11. *(Continued)*

Economy: VEN					
		Defaults		Others	
Year	Active	#	%	#	%
1992	0	0	NaN	0	NaN
1993	0	0	NaN	0	NaN
1994	13	0	0.00	0	0.00
1995	15	0	0.00	4	21.05
1996	14	0	0.00	2	12.50
1997	48	0	0.00	16	25.00
1998	45	0	0.00	21	31.82
1999	39	0	0.00	22	36.07
2000	38	0	0.00	12	24.00
2001	29	1	2.38	12	28.57
2002	20	0	0.00	20	50.00
2003	25	0	0.00	10	28.57
2004	28	0	0.00	8	22.22
2005	28	0	0.00	8	22.22
2006	27	0	0.00	7	20.59
2007	23	0	0.00	7	23.33
2008	25	0	0.00	30	54.55
2009	26	0	0.00	24	48.00
2010	20	0	0.00	13	39.39
2011	29	0	0.00	17	36.96
2012	15	0	0.00	18	54.55
2013	15	0	0.00	10	40.00

Economy: VNM					
		Defaults		Others	
Year	Active	#	%	#	%
1992	0	0	NaN	0	NaN
1993	0	0	NaN	0	NaN
1994	0	0	NaN	0	NaN
1995	0	0	NaN	0	NaN
1996	0	0	NaN	0	NaN
1997	0	0	NaN	0	NaN
1998	0	0	NaN	0	NaN
1999	0	0	NaN	0	NaN
2000	4	0	0.00	0	0.00
2001	8	0	0.00	0	0.00
2002	19	0	0.00	0	0.00
2003	22	0	0.00	0	0.00
2004	24	0	0.00	0	0.00
2005	29	0	0.00	0	0.00
2006	49	0	0.00	0	0.00
2007	205	0	0.00	1	0.49
2008	290	0	0.00	4	1.36
2009	367	0	0.00	27	6.85
2010	661	0	0.00	22	3.22
2011	740	1	0.13	50	6.32
2012	735	0	0.00	87	10.58
2013	732	0	0.00	109	12.96

Economy: ZAF					
		Defaults		Others	
Year	Active	#	%	#	%
1992	0	0	NaN	0	NaN
1993	389	0	0.00	39	9.11
1994	418	0	0.00	19	4.35
1995	463	0	0.00	28	5.70
1996	491	0	0.00	11	2.19
1997	533	0	0.00	21	3.79
1998	572	2	0.32	56	8.89
1999	594	3	0.46	52	8.01
2000	543	6	0.98	61	10.00
2001	466	9	1.56	101	17.53
2002	352	8	1.69	112	23.73
2003	329	1	0.26	54	14.06
2004	292	2	0.59	44	13.02
2005	296	2	0.60	37	11.04
2006	305	0	0.00	27	8.13
2007	332	0	0.00	39	10.51
2008	340	0	0.00	24	6.59
2009	320	1	0.28	34	9.58
2010	314	1	0.30	20	5.97
2011	314	2	0.60	19	5.67
2012	295	5	1.54	24	7.41
2013	292	2	0.62	30	9.26

APPENDIX B: PERFORMANCE ANALYSIS

Table B.1. Accuracy Ratios (AR) and Area Under Receiver Operating Characteristic (AUROC) for different economies.

	AR				AUROC			
Economy	**1 mth**	**1 yr**	**2 yr**	**5 yr**	**1 mth**	**1 yr**	**2 yr**	**5 yr**
AUS	0.812	0.644	0.521	0.367	0.906	0.822	0.762	0.688
CHN	0.593	0.524	0.449	0.317	0.797	0.765	0.731	0.677
HKG	0.696	0.431	0.322	0.204	0.848	0.716	0.662	0.605
IND	0.725	0.648	0.561	0.464	0.862	0.824	0.781	0.734
IDN	0.698	0.640	0.534	0.355	0.849	0.822	0.770	0.689
JPN	0.913	0.827	0.769	0.637	0.956	0.913	0.885	0.820
MYS	0.839	0.741	0.654	0.419	0.919	0.871	0.828	0.715
PHL	0.677	0.604	0.566	0.461	0.838	0.803	0.785	0.737
SGP	0.775	0.635	0.449	0.277	0.887	0.818	0.726	0.642
KOR	0.882	0.723	0.648	0.614	0.941	0.862	0.826	0.812
TWN	0.865	0.738	0.670	0.507	0.932	0.869	0.836	0.756
THA	0.837	0.754	0.702	0.571	0.918	0.878	0.853	0.793
USA	0.938	0.816	0.705	0.517	0.969	0.909	0.854	0.764
CAN	0.928	0.794	0.660	0.484	0.964	0.897	0.831	0.746
DNK	0.889	0.806	0.647	0.481	0.944	0.903	0.825	0.744
FRA	0.869	0.684	0.620	0.529	0.934	0.842	0.810	0.766
DEU	0.884	0.724	0.609	0.501	0.942	0.863	0.806	0.756
NLD	0.809	0.754	0.650	0.548	0.904	0.878	0.827	0.778
NOR	0.961	0.807	0.617	0.337	0.981	0.904	0.810	0.672
GBR	0.900	0.726	0.577	0.394	0.950	0.864	0.790	0.700
AsiaDev	0.860	0.724	0.644	0.535	0.930	0.862	0.823	0.771
EMR	0.822	0.737	0.664	0.508	0.911	0.869	0.833	0.758
EU	0.878	0.724	0.597	0.429	0.939	0.862	0.799	0.717

Note: The calibration groups, Developed Asia, Emerging Markets and Europe, are indicated by AsiaDev, EMR and EU. Only economies with more than 20 defaults are listed.

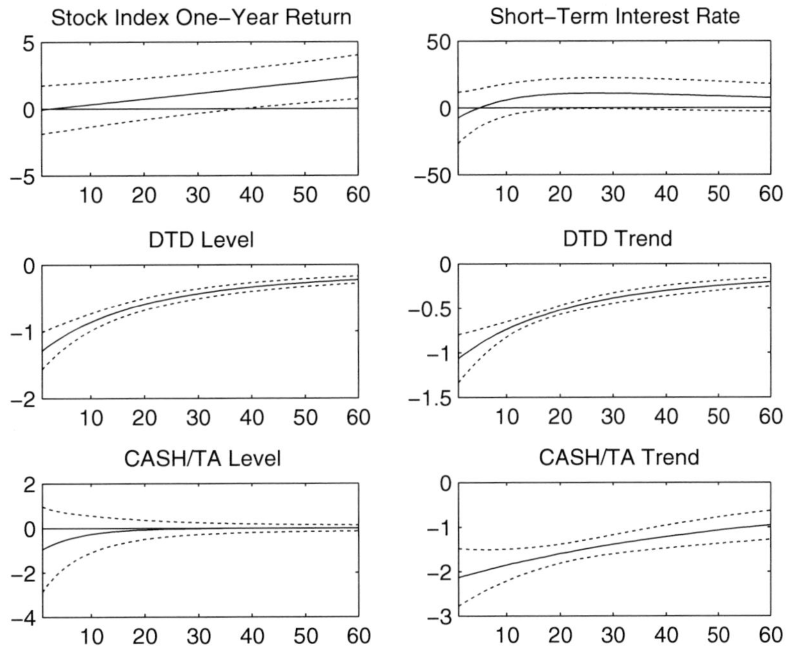

Figure B.1. Plots of US default parameters across all horizons for the Stock index one-year return, Short-term interest rate, DTD Level, DTD Trend, CASH/TA Level and CASH/TA Trend. Solid lines are the parameter estimates and dashed lines are the 90% confidence level. Horizontal axis is the horizon in months.

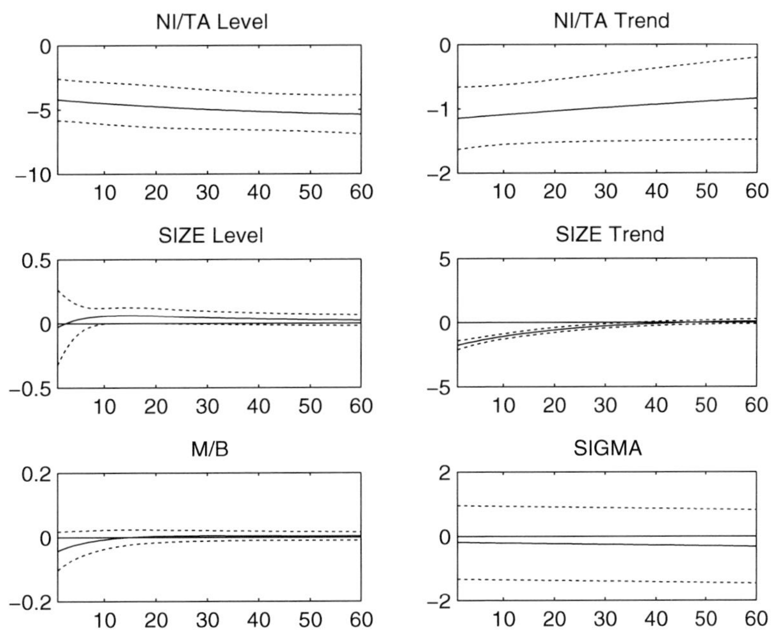

Figure B.2. Plots of US default parameters across all horizons for the NI/TA Level, NI/TA Trend, SIZE Level, SIZE Trend, M/B and SIGMA. Solid lines are the parameter estimates and dashed lines are the 90% confidence level. Horizontal axis is the horizon in months.

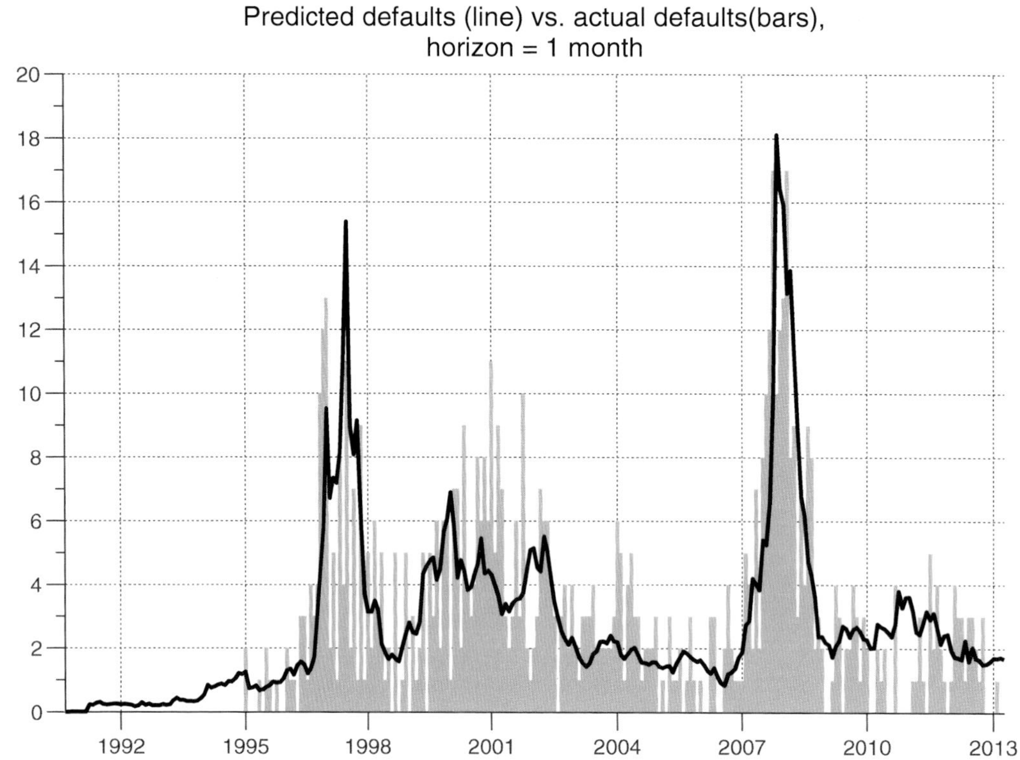

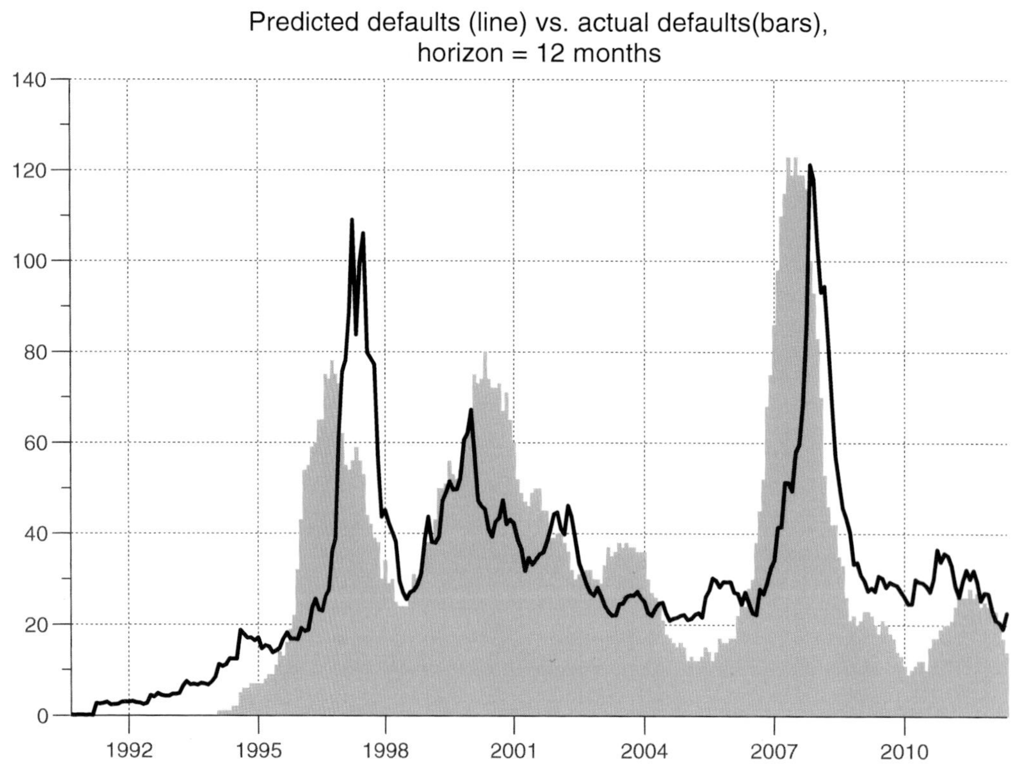

Figure B.3. Performance test for the Developed Asia, in sample.

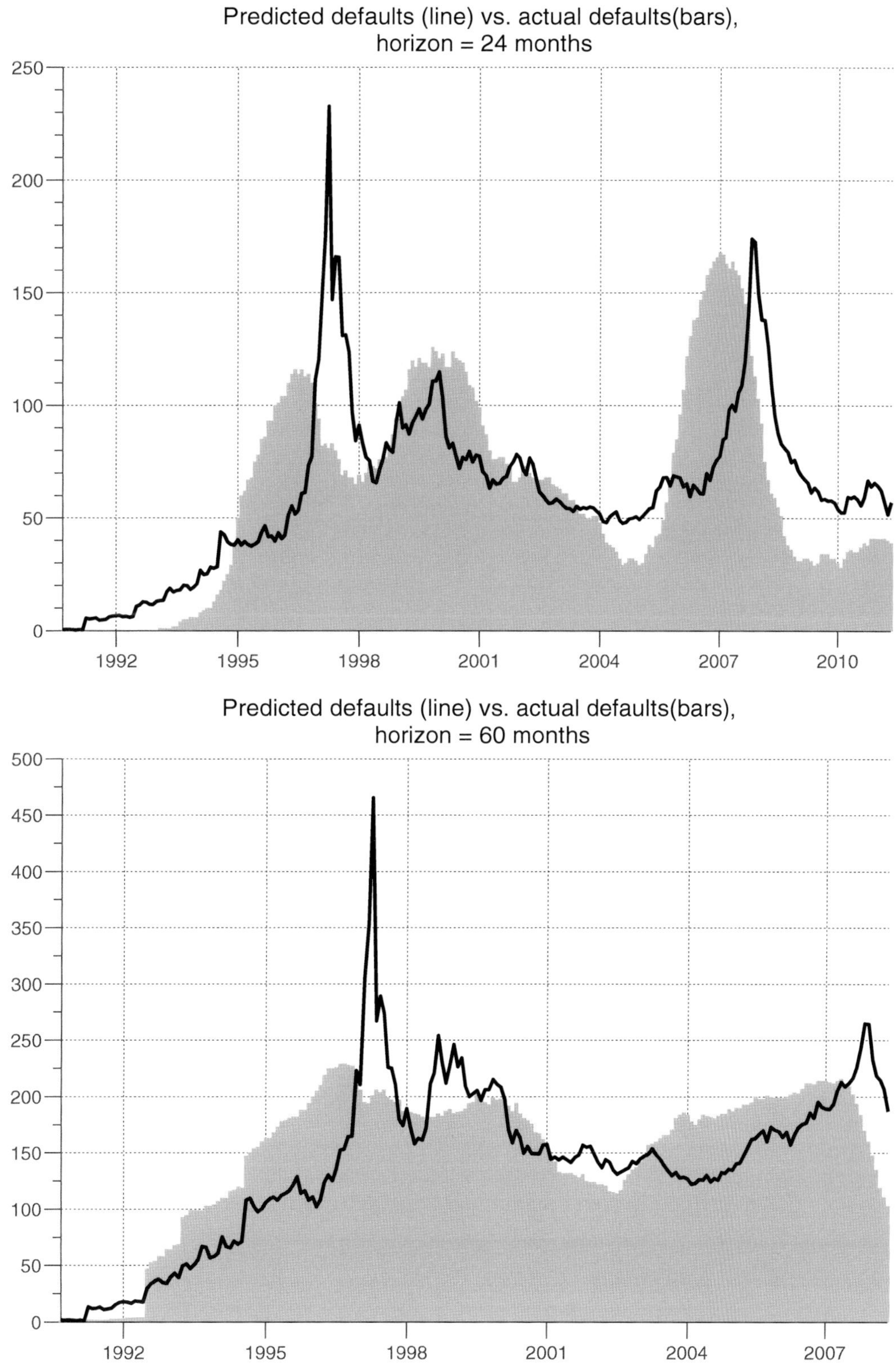

Figure B.3. *(Continued)*

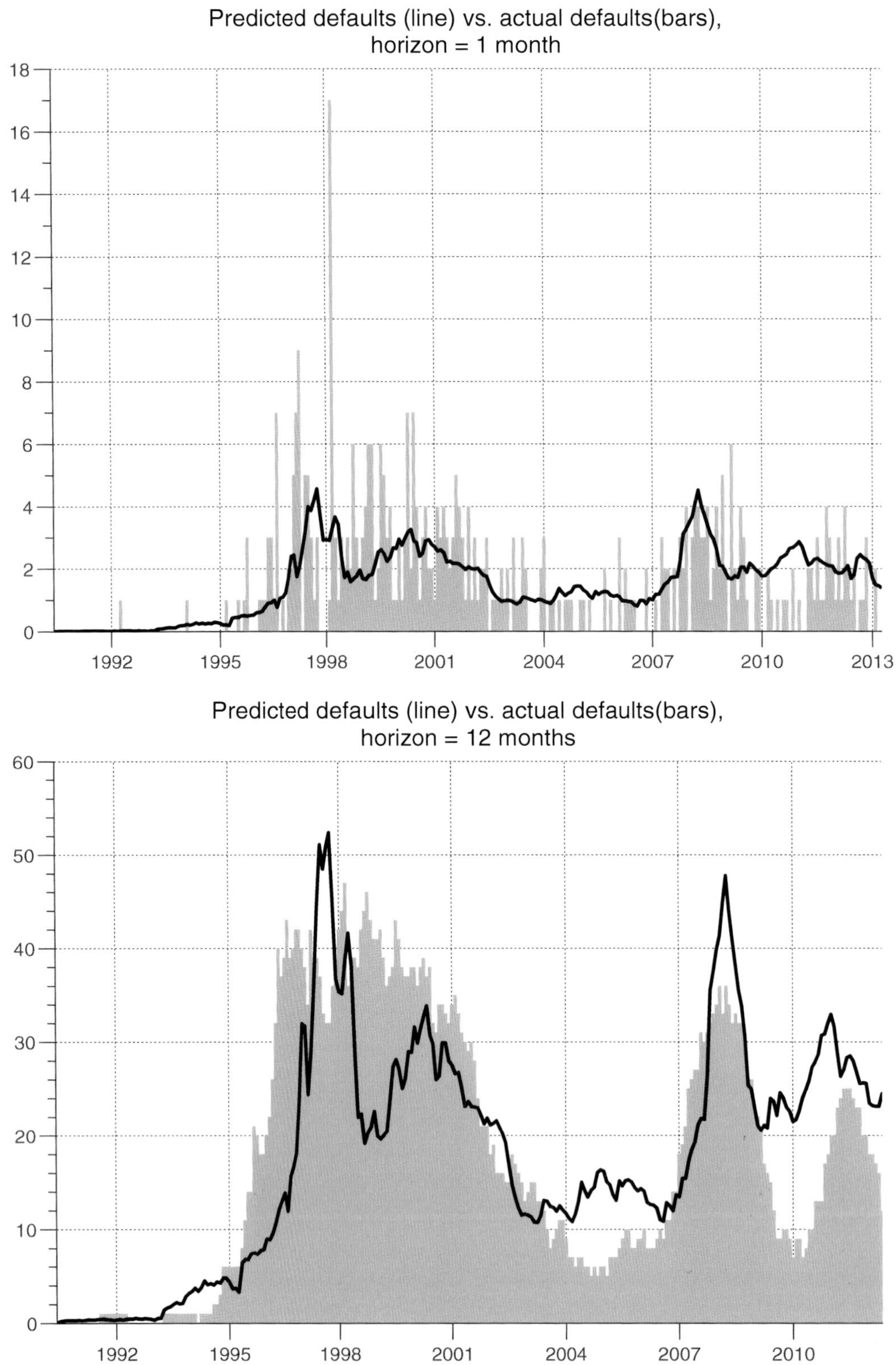

Figure B.4. Performance test for the Emerging Market, in sample.

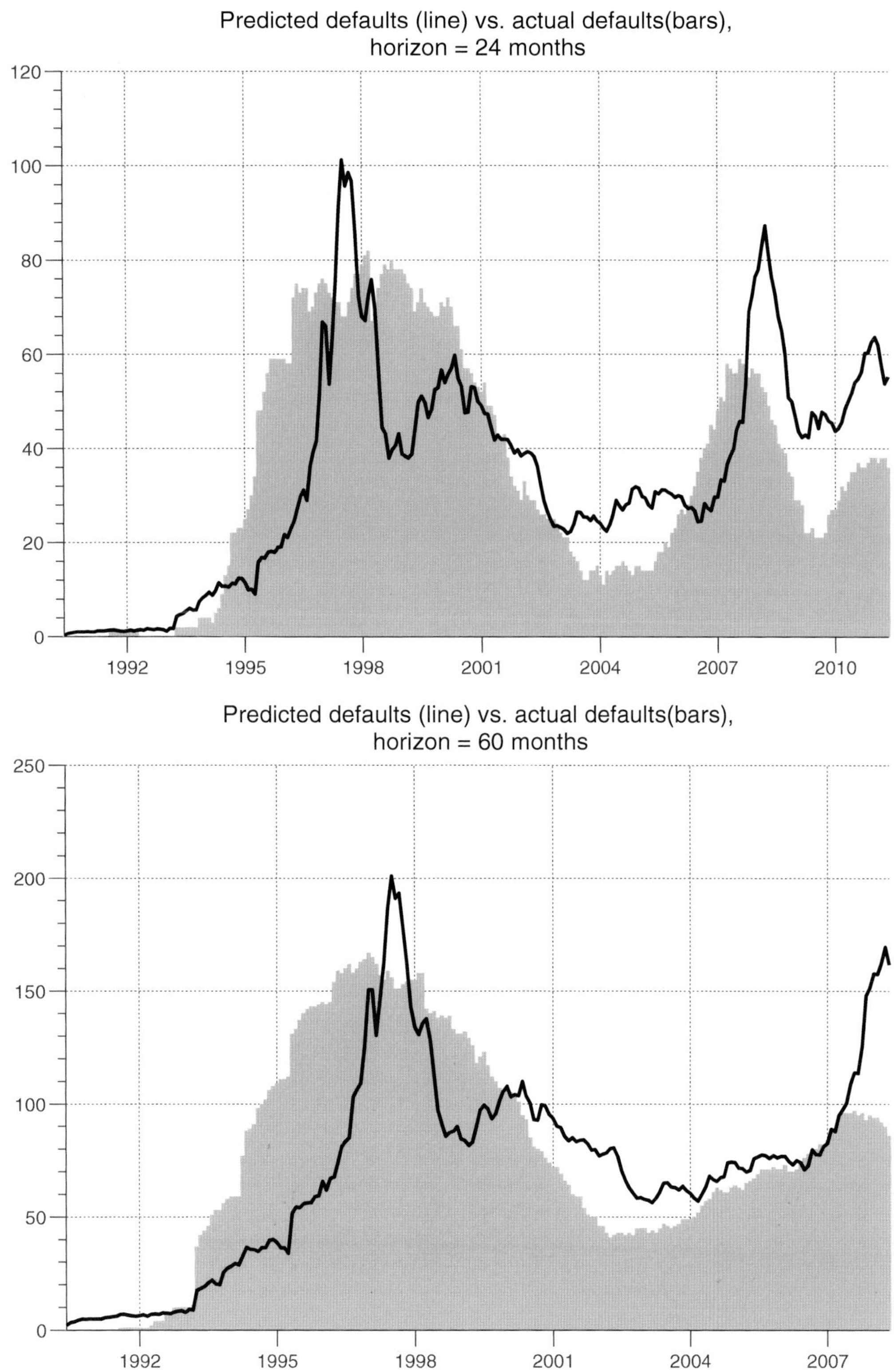

Figure B.4. *(Continued)*

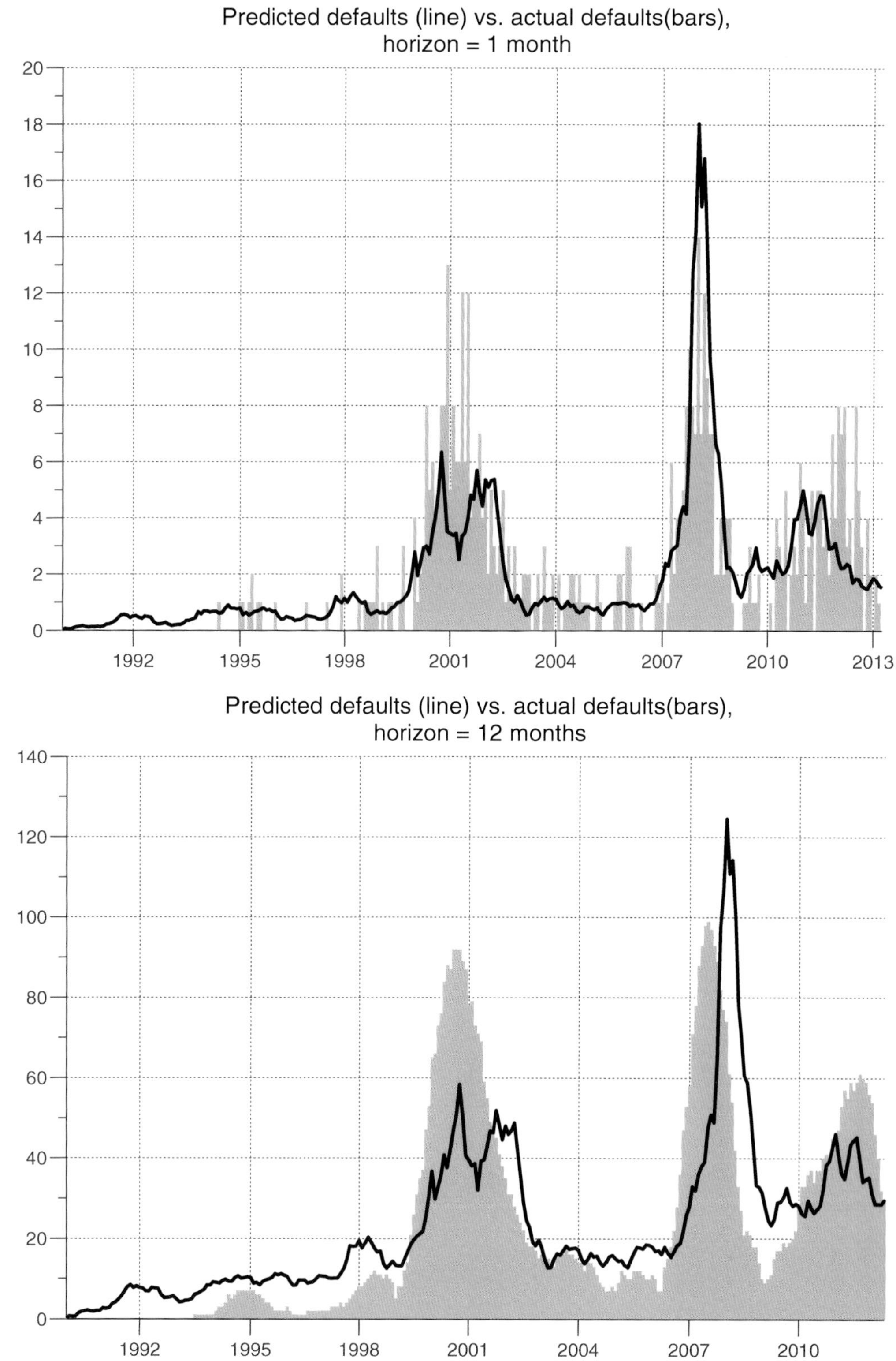

Figure B.5. Performance test for the Europe group, in sample.

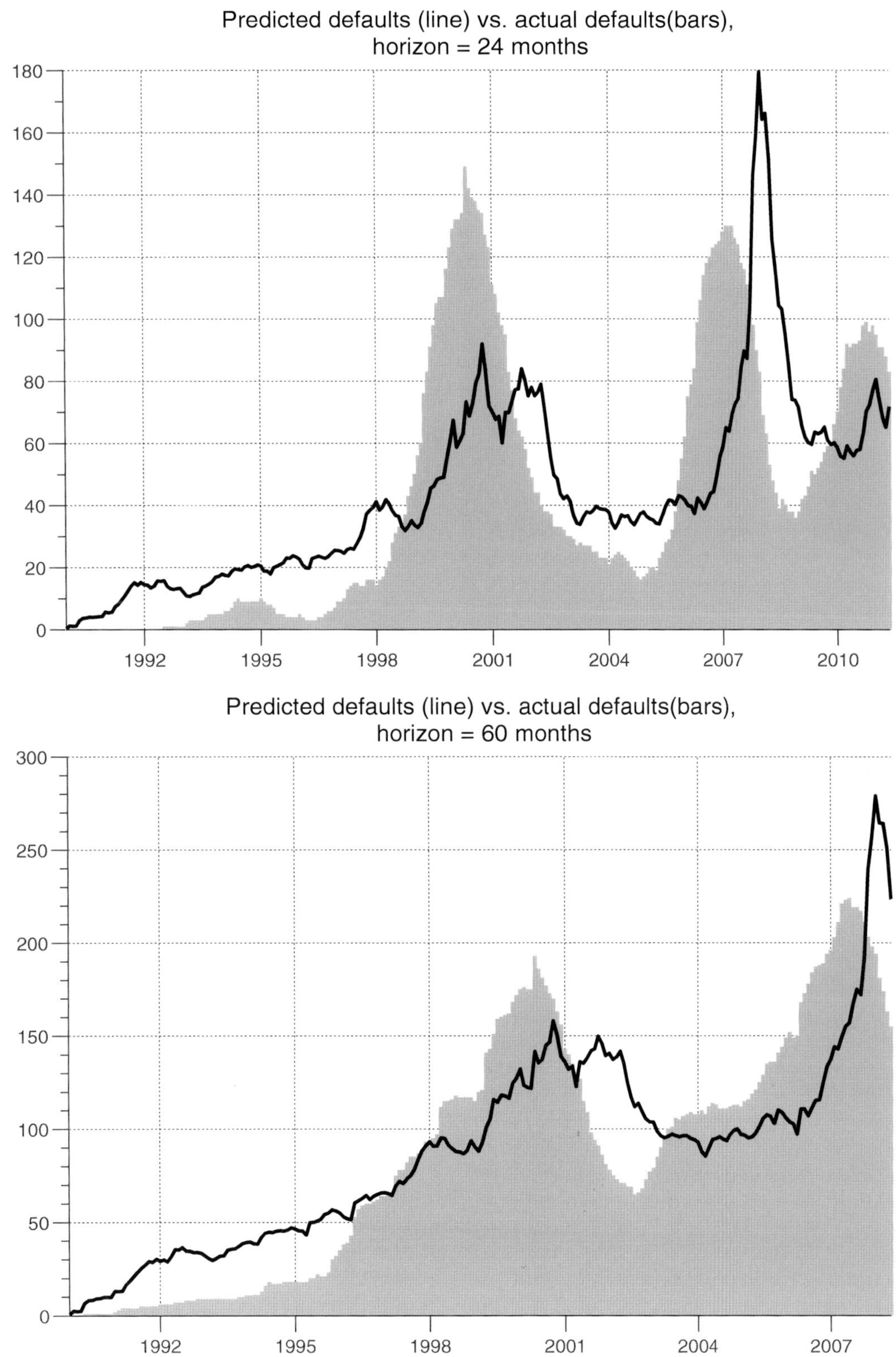

Figure B.5. *(Continued)*

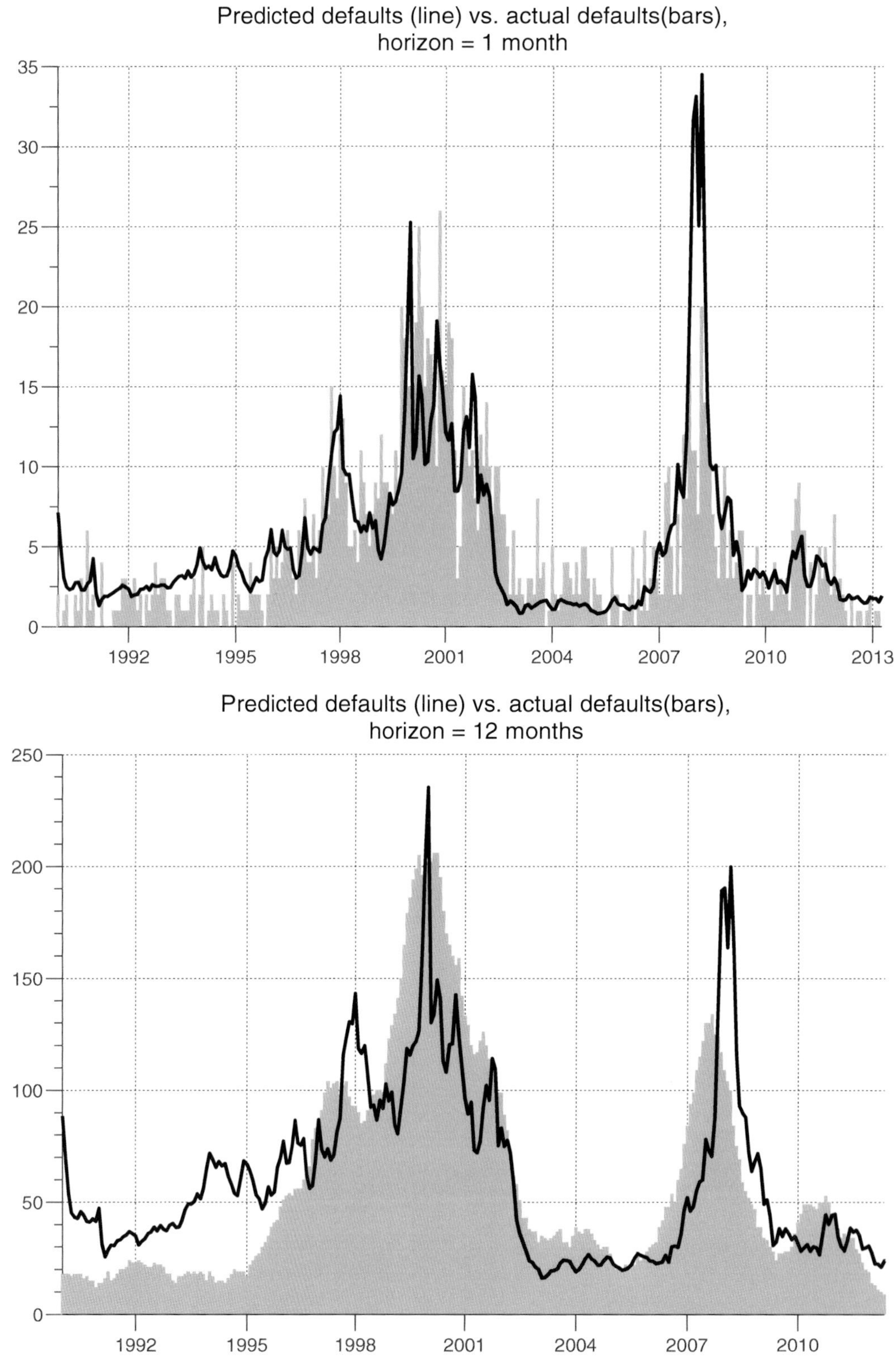

Figure B.6. Performance test for North America group, in sample.

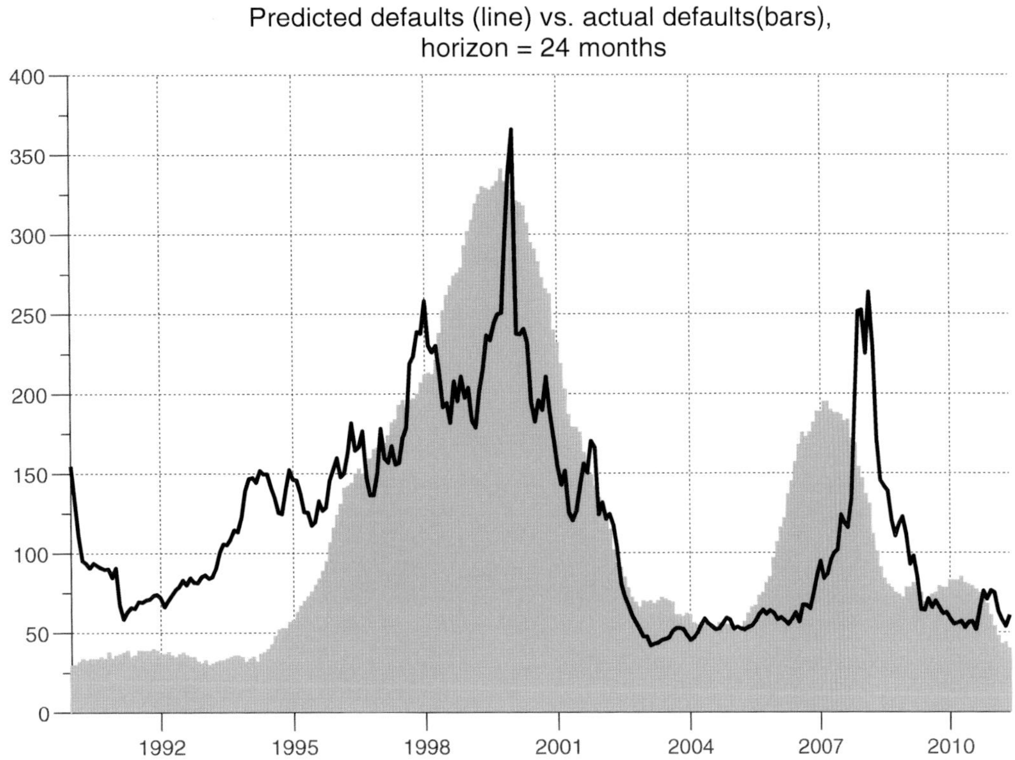

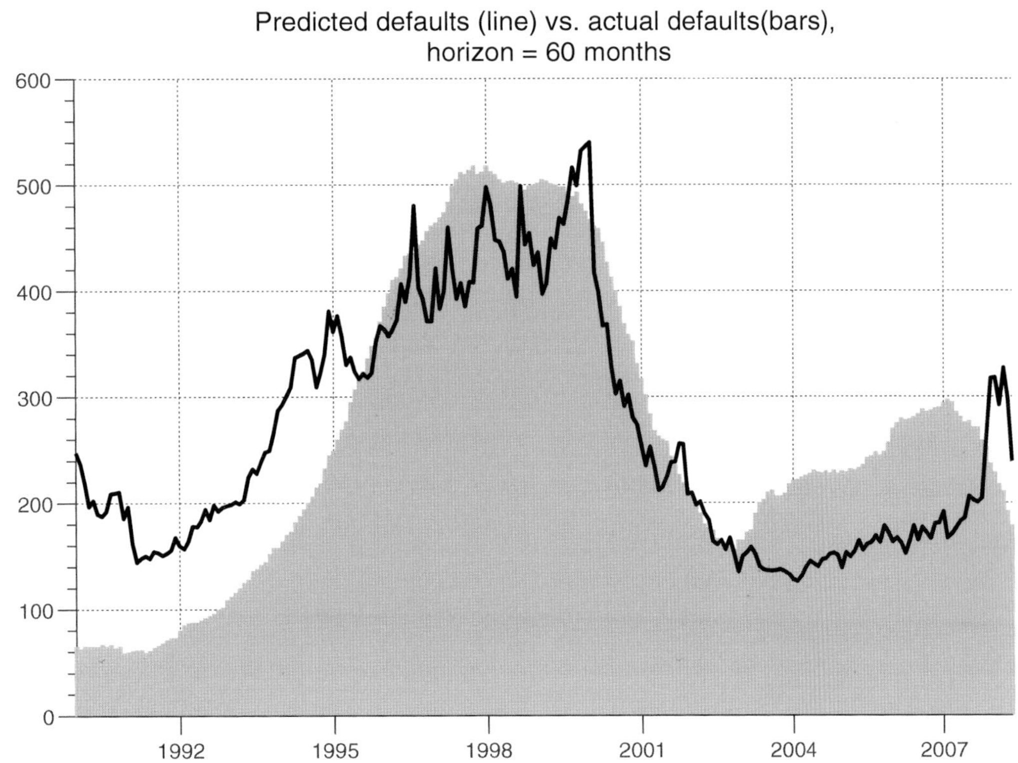

Figure B.6. (*Continued*)

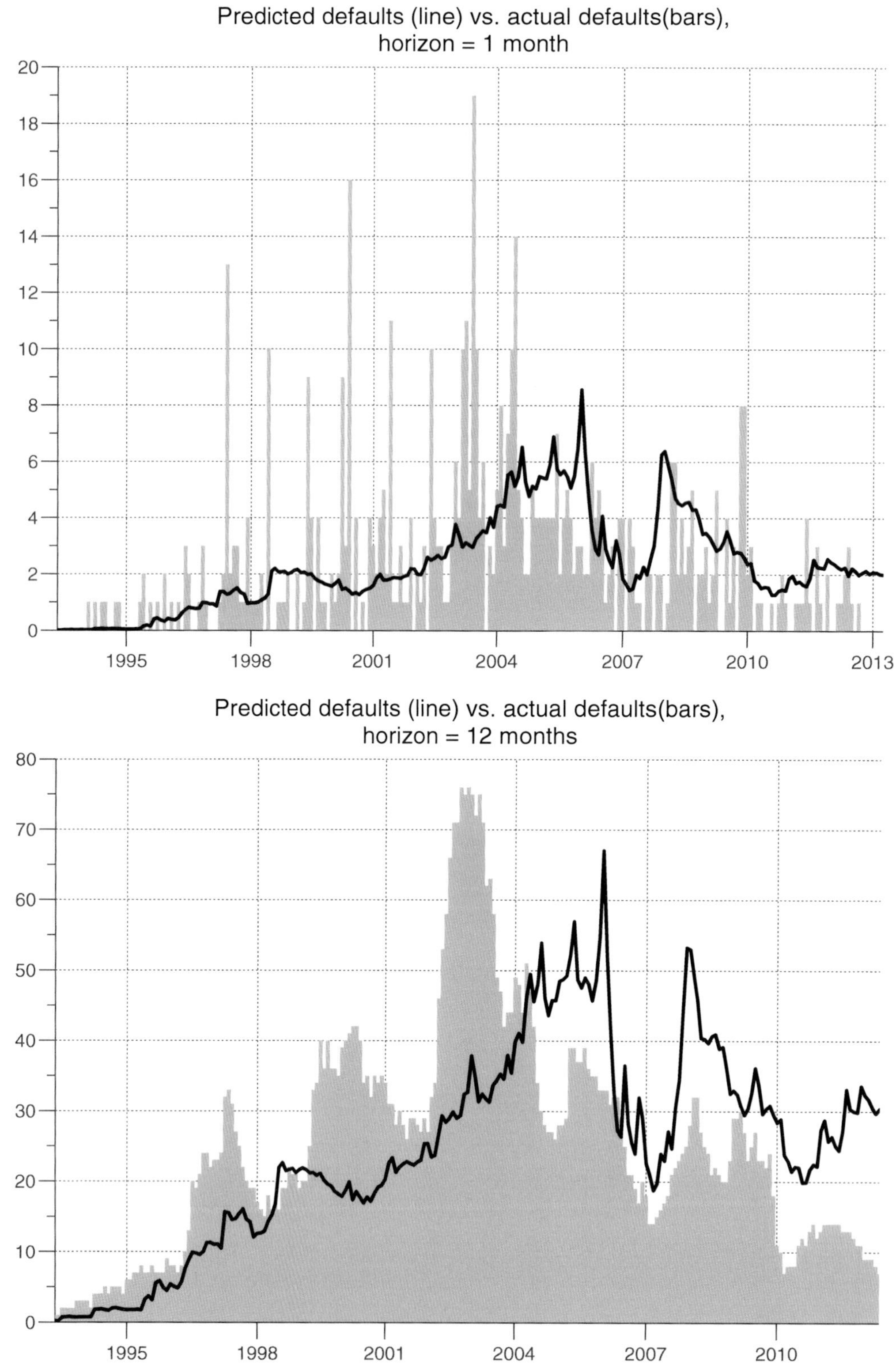

Figure B.7. Performance test for China, in sample.

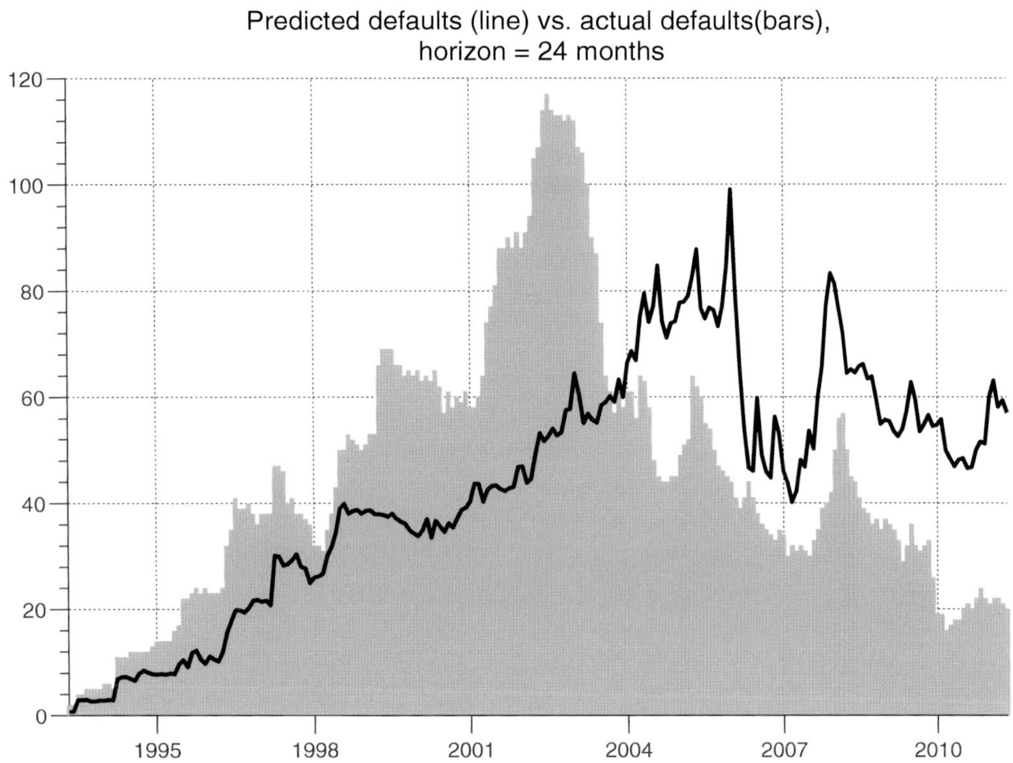

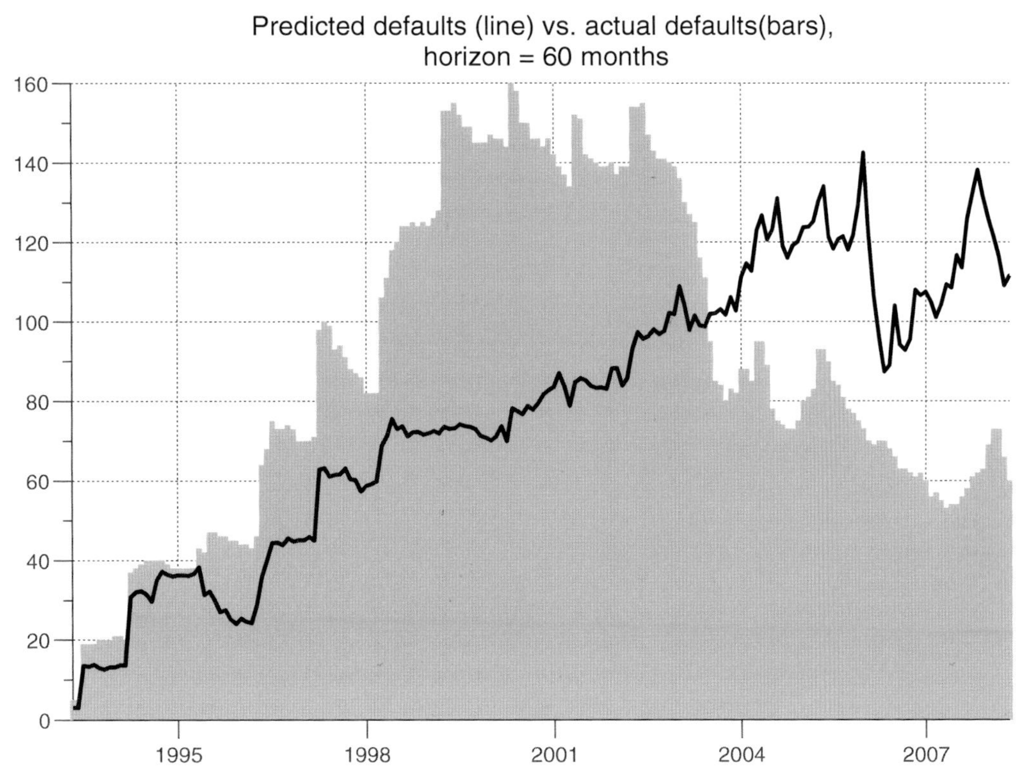

Figure B.7. (*Continued*)

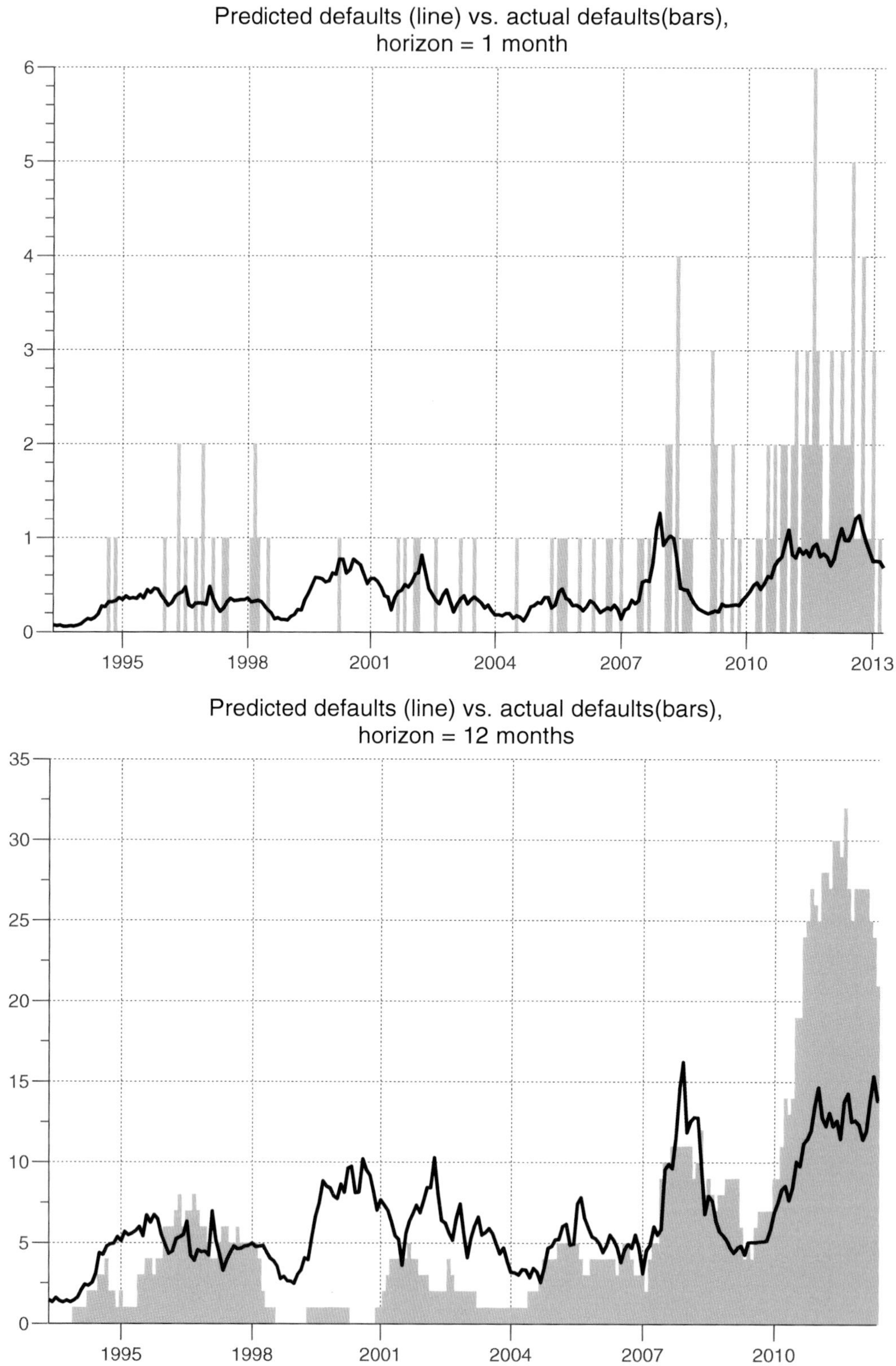

Figure B.8. Performance test for India, in sample.

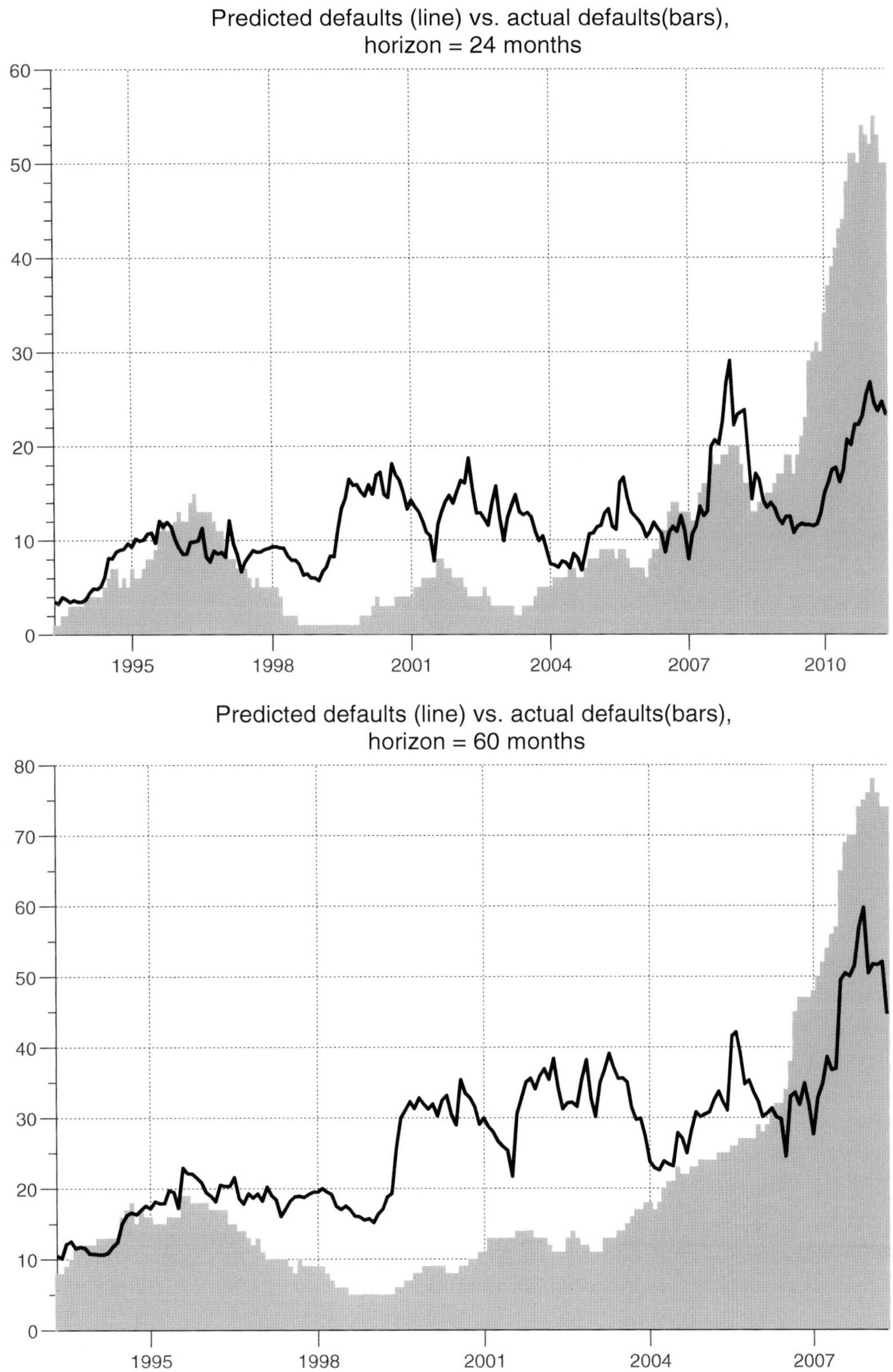

Figure B.8. (*Continued*)

REFERENCES

Anderson, L., J. Sidenius and S. Basu (2003), All Your Hedges in One Basket. *Risk*, pp. 67–72.

Chopin, N. (2012), A Sequential Particle Filter Method for Static Models. *Biometrika*, 89, pp. 539–551.

Crosbie, P. and J. Bohn (2003), Modeling Default Risk. Moody's KMV Technical Document.

Del Moral, P., A. Doucet and A. Jasra (2006), Sequential Monte Carlo Samplers. *Journal of Royal Statistical Society B*, 68, pp. 411–436.

Duan, J.-C. (1994), Maximum Likelihood Estimation Using Price Data of the Derivative Contract. *Mathematical Finance*, 4, pp. 155–167.

Duan, J.-C. (2000), Correction: Maximum Likelihood Estimation Using Price Data of the Derivative Contract. *Mathematical Finance*, 10, pp. 461–462.

Duan, J.-C. (2010), Clustered Defaults. National University of Singapore Working Paper.

Duan, J.-C. and K. Shrestha (2011), Statistical Credit Rating Methods. *Global Credit Review*, pp. 43–64.

Duan, J.-C. and E. Van Laere (2012), A Public Good Approach to Credit Ratings From Concept to Reality. *Journal of Banking & Finance*, 36, pp. 3239–3247.

Duan, J.-C. and T. Wang (2012), Measuring Distance-to-Default for Financial and Non-Financial Firms, *Global Credit Review*, 02, pp. 95–108.

Duan, J.-C., J. Sun and T. Wang (2012), Multiperiod Corporate Default Prediction — A Forward Intensity Approach. *Journal of Econometrics*, 170, 191–209.

Duan, J. C. and A. Fulop (2013), Multiperiod Corporate Default Prediction with the Partially-Conditioned Forward Intensity. National University of Singapore Working Paper.

Duffie, D., L. Saita and K. Wang (2007), Multi-Period Corporate Default Prediction with Stochastic Covariates. *Journal of Financial Economics*, 83, pp. 635–665.

Duffie, D., A. Eckner, G. Horel and L. Saita (2009), Frailty Correlated Default. *Journal of Finance*, pp. 2089–2123.

Kiefer, N. M., T. J. Vogelsang and H. Bunzel (2000), Simple Robust Testing of Regression Hypotheses. *Econometrica*, 68, pp. 695–714.

Merton, R. C. (1974), On the Pricing of Corporate Debt: The Risk Structure of Interest Rates. *Journal of Finance*, 29, pp. 449–470.

Nelson, C. R. and A. F. Siegel (1987), Parsimonious Modeling of Yield Curves. *Journal of Business*, 60, pp. 473–489.

RMI (2012), NUS-RMI Credit Research Initiative Technical Report. *Global Credit Review*, 2, pp. 109–167.

Shao, X. (2010), A Self-Normalized Approach to Confidence Interval Construction in Time Series. *Journal of the Royal Statistical Society: Series B*, 72, pp. 343–366.

Shumway, T. (2001), Forecasting Bankruptcy More Accurately: A Simple Hazard Model. *Journal of Business*, 74, pp. 101–124.